Regulating Charities

In this volume, charity commissioners and leading charity policy reformers from across the world reflect on the aims and objectives of charity regulation and what it has achieved. *Regulating Charities: The Inside Story* represents an insider's review of the last quarter century of charity law policy and an insight for its future development.

Charity Commissioners and nonprofit regulatory agency heads chart the nature of charity law reforms that they have implemented with a "warts and all" analysis. Influential sector reformers who assess the outcomes of their policy agitation joined them. All reflect on the current state of charities in a fiscally restrained environment, often with conservative governments, and offer their views on productive regulatory paths available for the future.

This topical collection brings together major charity regulation actors and will be of great interest to anyone concerned with contemporary third-sector policy making, public administration, and civil society.

Myles McGregor-Lowndes is a Professor and the founding Director of the Australian Centre for Philanthropy and Nonprofit Studies at the QUT Business School, Australia.

Bob Wyatt is Executive Director of the Muttart Foundation, a private Canadian foundation that has engaged in issues of charity regulation for more than two decades.

Routledge Studies in the Management of Voluntary and Non-Profit Organizations

Series Editor:
Stephen P. Osborne,
University of Edinburgh, UK

For a full list of titles in this series, please visit www.routledge.com

This series presents innovative work grounded in new realities, addressing issues crucial to an understanding of the contemporary world. This is the world of organised societies, where boundaries between formal and informal, public and private, local and global organizations have been displaced or have vanished, along with other nineteenth-century dichotomies and oppositions. Management, apart from becoming a specialized profession for a growing number of people, is an everyday activity for most members of modern societies.

Similarly, at the level of enquiry, culture and technology, and literature and economics, can no longer be conceived as isolated intellectual fields; conventional canons and established mainstreams are contested. Management, Organization and Society addresses these contemporary dynamics of transformation in a manner that transcends disciplinary boundaries, with books that will appeal to researchers, student and practitioners alike.

Also available from Routledge:

The Management of Nongovernmental Development Organizations
An Introduction
David Lewis

Financial Management in the Voluntary Sector
New Challenges
Paul Palmer and Adrian Randall

Strategic Management for Nonprofit Organizations
Roger Courtney

Regulating Charities
The Inside Story
Edited by Myles McGregor-Lowndes and Bob Wyatt

Regulating Charities
The Inside Story

**Edited by
Myles McGregor-Lowndes and
Bob Wyatt**

Routledge
Taylor & Francis Group

LONDON AND NEW YORK

First published 2017
by Routledge

2 Park Square, Milton Park, Abingdon, Oxfordshire OX14 4RN
52 Vanderbilt Avenue, New York, NY 10017

Routledge is an imprint of the Taylor & Francis Group, an informa business

First issued in paperback 2019

Copyright © 2017 Taylor & Francis

Library of Congress Cataloging-in-Publication Data
A catalog record for this book has been requested.

ISBN: 978-1-138-68054-8 (hbk)
ISBN: 978-0-367-24291-6 (pbk)

Typeset in Sabon
by Apex CoVantage, LLC

Contents

Foreword

In 1991, I was asked to serve as a legal adviser in the Czechoslovak Parliament. My first task was to help develop the country's nonprofit laws. With Vaclav Havel as president, creating space for civil society was a top priority. To jumpstart the process, we looked for a book that analysed the nonprofit laws of different jurisdictions, but our search was unsuccessful. Comparative nonprofit law was an emerging field. No law school taught comparative nonprofit law, few researchers wrote about the subject, and human rights activists dubbed the international freedom of association "the neglected right."

That was 25 years ago. Since then, comparative nonprofit law has grown from a nascent, niche issue to a topic of global interest. For example, UN Secretary-General Ban Ki-moon, President Obama, Archbishop Tutu, and Aung San Suu Kyi have each provided a welcome via video at the International Center for Not-for-Profit Law's Global Forum on Civil Society Law. Of even greater significance, thousands of people are now working on initiatives affecting the legal and regulatory framework for nonprofits around the world. As a result, the number of requests for comparative information has increased exponentially. A quick Internet search reveals a significant amount of information. Researchers have compiled the nonprofit laws of 200 countries and territories, but it is virtually impossible to find a book that provides comparative information on the regulation of charities and other nonprofit organizations. This book helps fill this information gap. Focused on five common law jurisdictions, it shares comparative perspectives on cornerstone issues, including the following:

- the role of regulators (compliance, advice, promoting the "charity brand," etc.);
- the division of regulatory responsibilities in federal jurisdictions;
- the benefits and disadvantages of a tax-based regulatory system versus a Charity Commission model;
- the relationship between government regulation and sectoral self-regulation;

- ways to promote both the independence and accountability of regulators;
- staffing and resource challenges confronting regulators;
- the regulation of advocacy and "political" activities;
- the impact of counterterrorism measures on the regulation of charities; and
- the regulatory response to new entrants, including social enterprises.

The authors are an all-star cast. They have played leading roles as charity regulators and sector leaders, and they provide "behind-the-scenes" perspectives that help explain recent developments in charity regulation. The authors share their stories in a clear and compelling fashion, providing insights that can help inform regulatory reform around the world. This book is an important contribution to the field, and it is certain to become a go-to reference for colleagues interested in charity regulation.

Douglas Rutzen
President and CEO
International Center for Not-for-Profit Law

Acknowledgments

This book owes much to the effort of others.

Our thanks go to the contributors, who graciously accepted our editorial suggestions and met deadlines in a way that made our task much easier. Their enthusiasm for the project was infectious and, each could have written a book on his or her experiences of charity regulation. Some travelled long distances to Canada in order to participate in a review and critique of the first chapter drafts and did so with good humour. At the Canadian contributors' meeting, Peter Faid and Yvonne Smith ably facilitated the proceedings, keeping the participants on time, on message, and on their toes to generate new insights into their contributions. Laird Hunter, Susan Manwaring, Peter Broder, and Gordon Floyd acted as fearless critical friends at the contributors' meeting to leave no stone unturned or dark corner unexplored. The Muttart Foundation was generous in facilitating that meeting, consistent with the part it has played for decades in seeking to improve the regulatory environment for charities and build the capacity for sound charity regulation.

Anne Overell and Francis Hannah at the Queensland University of Technology provided research and editorial assistance above and beyond the call of duty. Thanks also to Susan Phillips and Matthew Turnour for reading the manuscript. We both also acknowledge the patience of our employers in allowing us to devote time to this project.

Finally, thanks to our partners Jenny and Kathryn for their forbearance.

Contributors

Sue Barker is the director of Sue Barker Charities Law, a boutique law firm based in Wellington, New Zealand, specialising in charities law and public tax law. In 2015, the firm was voted Boutique Charities Law Firm of the Year—New Zealand, at the Corporate LiveWire Legal Awards. Sue is a director of the Charity Law Association of Australia and New Zealand, and a co-author of the text *The Law and Practice of Charities in New Zealand*. In 2016, Sue was made an honorary national life member of the National Council of Women of New Zealand Incorporated for her work assisting the Council to regain their charitable registration.

Elizabeth T. Boris, Ph.D., holds the Waldemar A. Nielsen chair of philanthropy at the McCourt School of Public Policy at Georgetown University and is an Urban Institute fellow. She was the founding director of the Center on Nonprofits and Philanthropy at the Urban Institute, which she led from 1996 to 2016, and the Nonprofit Sector Research Fund at the Aspen Institute, which she led from 1991 to 1996. She is co-editor with C. Eugene Steuerle of *Nonprofits and Government: Collaboration and Conflict*, now in its third edition. She is a co-author of *State Regulation and Enforcement in the Charitable Sector*, a study of charity offices across the United States. Elizabeth is the author of many other research studies on topics ranging from government contracting with nonprofits to performance management and family foundations. She serves as an adviser and board member for many nonprofit groups, and in 2006, she received the Distinguished Achievement and Leadership Award from the Association for Research on Nonprofits and Voluntary Action.

Lindsay Driscoll has been working in the field of charity law and governance for over 35 years. She is currently a consultant with Bates Wells and Braithwaite, a governance consultant, and is a guest lecturer at Cass Business School. She also works internationally on charity and civil society law and regulation. Lindsay read jurisprudence at Oxford University and as a solicitor specialized in trusts and tax. She then spent five years as assistant registrar general in Kenya and lecturer at the Kenya School of Law. On returning to the United Kingdom, she worked for the National

Council for Voluntary Organisations, becoming head of law and governance before joining Sinclair Taylor and Martin as a partner specializing in charity law. She left the firm to serve as a legal commissioner with the Charity Commission for England and Wales for five years. Lindsay has written and spoken extensively on charity law and regulation, both in the United Kingdom and internationally. She was a member of the executive committee of the Charity Law Association for many years and the chair of the steering group for the Code of Governance for the Voluntary and Community Sector. She has served on the boards of many UK charities, was the chair of the board of the International Center for Not-for-Profit Law, and is on the supervisory board of the European Center for not-for-profit law and the board of the Pemsel Case Foundation.

Sir Stuart Etherington has been involved in the leadership of voluntary organizations and policies surrounding them throughout his career, and as such, he has become a leading commentator, both through his writing and his media profile. He was appointed chief executive of the National Council of Voluntary Organisations in 1994, having previously been chief executive of the Royal National Institute for Deaf People, a major UK charity. Among his many current and former roles, Stuart is a member of the Economic and Social Committee of the European Union and the chair of London United. He is chair of trustees of the Patron's Fund and chaired a cross-party review looking at the structure of the regulation of fundraising. He is also an IES honorary fellow. He has been a trustee of Business in the Community; the chair of the BBC Appeals Advisory Committee; a member of the Community and Social Affairs Committee of Barclays Bank; former chair of Guidestar UK, Treasurer of CIVICUS, a global civil society organization; chair of CIVICUS Europe; council member of the Institute of Employment Studies; and an advisory group member for the Policy Centre at the British Academy and for the Lord Mayor's Trust Initiative. Among his government appointments, he has served on the Cabinet Office Performance and Innovation Unit's Advisory Board on the Voluntary Sector and HM Treasury's Cross Cutting Review on the role of the Voluntary Sector. Sir Stuart was knighted in 2010 for services to the voluntary sector.

Richard Fries was chief commissioner of the Charity Commission from 1992 to 1999. As head of the Commission, he was responsible for leading the programme of modernization, which was initiated when he was under secretary in the Home Office, the government department responsible for charity and voluntary sector matters. He held that post from 1987 to 1991, having joined the Home Office as a career civil servant in 1965. After retiring in 1999, Richard Fries was chair of the board of the International Center for Not-for-profit Law (from 1999 to 2005) and a visiting fellow in the Centre for Civil Society at the London School of Economics (2000 to 2006). During this period, he was involved in initiatives to reform charity and not-for-profit law and regulation in Britain, Europe, and the wider world. Now fully retired, he is a trustee of a number of charities including the Open Society Foundation London, the Webb Memorial Trust, NMC Recordings, and the Pimlico Chess Club. Richard has always lived in London and is married with three adult children and six grandchildren.

Trevor Garrett was chief executive of the New Zealand Charities Commission from its establishment in 2005 until its functions were merged into the Department of Internal Affairs in 2012. Prior to that appointment, he was for 13 years chief executive of the Casino Control Authority in New Zealand. Trevor's public service career has included a mixture of being a regulator and being a manager of community funding schemes and advisory services, including as the chief executive officer for the Ministry of Recreation and Sport. He has worked closely with international regulators and was a member of a United Nations expert working group on preventing terrorist financing abuse of the nonprofit sector. He was chairman of the International Association of Gaming Regulators, has lectured internationally on gaming regulation, and was a member of the advisory committee for the International Gaming Institute at the University of Nevada. Trevor's academic qualifications include a master of science (Hons), Indiana University, and master of public policy, Victoria University. He participated in the Senior Managers in Government Program at Harvard University, and he has held academic posts in recreation planning and social policy. Trevor's community involvement has included chairing education and sports organizations; he is the patron of Physical Education New Zealand; he has been inducted onto the Wall of Fame at Otago University's School of Physical Education, he was awarded a Distinguished International Alumni Award from the School of Public Health at Indiana University. He received the 1990 Commemoration Medal for services to New Zealand.

Cindy M. Lott serves as program director and teaches in nonprofit management programs at Columbia University's School of Professional Studies. Previously, she served as executive director and senior counsel to the National State Attorneys General Program at Columbia Law School, and within that program, she was the developer and lead counsel to the Charities Regulation and Oversight Project from 2006 to 2015. Currently, Cindy M. Lott is also a senior fellow at the Center on Nonprofits and Philanthropy at the Urban Institute, working in conjunction with the Institute's Tax Policy and Charities project, and is a member of the IRS Advisory Committee on Tax Exempt and Government Entities (2015–18). She develops and moderates a series of national convenings on state and federal regulation of the charitable sector, is engaged in research regarding regulatory capacity and enforcement at the state level, and is a frequent speaker at national conferences in the areas of philanthropic and nonprofit state regulation, compliance, management, and governance. Cindy M. Lott is a graduate of Yale Law School (1993) and clerked for the US Court of Appeals, First Circuit. She is admitted to practice in the District of Columbia, Indiana, and Massachusetts. She served as chief counsel (2004) and deputy counsel (2000) to the Democratic National Convention, has worked in private practice, and served as chief counsel for advisory services in the Indiana Attorney General's office, as well as section chief for administrative and regulatory litigation in that office.

Terry de March is an independent consultant assisting charitable organizations in areas such as governance, strategic planning, and evaluation. From 2009 to 2013, Terry was honorary visiting professor, Cass Business School, City University London. From 2007 to 2009, he was the director general of the Charities Directorate, Canada Revenue Agency, where he was responsible for the overall management and administration of the federal regulation of registered charities under the Income Tax Act. Immediately prior to this, and from 2003, he held the position of director of policy, planning, and legislation, where he brought forward some of the most important administrative/common law policies for the regulation of charities. Terry sat as a member of both the initial Government/Voluntary Sector Roundtable for Regulatory Reform leading to the Working Together report to government, and the Joint Roundtable on Regulatory Reform whose work culminated in the most significant changes to the regulatory regime for Canadian charities in over 20 years. Prior to his term with Canada Revenue Agency, Terry worked for the Department of Justice where he directed a number of granting programs providing social justice–related funding to the charitable and not-for-profit sectors. Terry also has many years of experience in the policy and regulatory world of government, working for the most part in the ongoing development of the Canada Pension Plan and Old Age Security Pension programs.

Myles McGregor-Lowndes OAM is a professor at the QUT Business School, Queensland University of Technology. He was the founding director of the Australian Centre for Philanthropy and Nonprofit Studies from 2001 to 2014. As a lawyer, he has acted for many nonprofit organizations and served on a variety of nonprofit boards. He has written extensively about nonprofit tax and regulation. Myles was a contributing member of the 2010 Productivity Commission Inquiry into the Contribution of the Not-for-Profit Sector in Australia, which recommended the establishment of the Australian Charities and Not-for-profits Commission (ACNC). He is a founding member of the Australian Taxation Office's Charities Consultative Committee and the ACNC's Advisory Board, an honorary member of Fundraising Institute Australia, and founding director of Australian and New Zealand Third Sector Research and the Charity Law Association of Australia and New Zealand.

Marcus Owens is an attorney practising with the law firm of Loeb & Loeb, LLP, in their Washington, DC, office, where he advises charities and other tax-exempt organizations with regard to federal tax and state charity law matters. Prior to entering private practice in 2000, Marcus spent 25 years with the US Internal Revenue Service in the agency's Exempt Organizations Division, which is responsible for administering the federal tax rules that apply to charities and other nonprofit organizations. From 1990 until 2000, Marcus was the director of the division. He is a member of the bar of the District of Columbia and of Florida, and he is a director of the Pemsel Case Foundation—a Canadian foundation focused on the law of charities. Marcus is also an adjunct lecturer in the nonprofit management program at Columbia University's School of Professional Studies.

Susan Pascoe AM is the inaugural commissioner for the Australian Charities and Not-for-profits Commission, Australia's first national, independent regulator of charities. Prior to this appointment, Ms Pascoe was commissioner of the State Services Authority in Victoria. In this role, she chaired or co-chaired reviews into the regulation of the not-for-profit sector (2007–08), the design and governance of regulatory bodies in the state of Victoria (2008–09), and Victoria's Indigenous Employment Strategy (2008–09). In 2009, she was appointed as one of three commissioners for the Royal Commission into Victoria's Black Saturday Bushfires. Ms Pascoe's earlier career was in education. She participated in state, national, and international efforts to improve the quality and equity of school education, served as president of the Australian College of Educators, CEO of the Victorian Curriculum, and Assessment Authority and chief executive of the Catholic Education Commission of Victoria. Other appointments have included chair of the Australian National Commission for UNESCO, patron for the Melbourne Parliament for the World's Religions, and chair or member on a number of education, health, and government boards. Susan's significant achievements and leadership were acknowledged in 2007 when she was appointed member of the Order of Australia for service to education and the community through a range of executive roles, development and implementation of curriculum policy, and contribution to international initiatives and resources for educators in the Pacific region.

Ursula Stephens is a former Australian Senator (2002 to 2014), now providing advisory services in leadership training, enterprise development, social entrepreneurship, community education capacity building, and social change campaigns. As a national legislator, Ursula's roles included that of Parliamentary Secretary for Social Inclusion and the Voluntary Sector (2007 to 2010). She was involved in developing policy and programs to strengthen support for Australia's most vulnerable people, and developing a social inclusion agenda that promoted a national approach to child protection, early intervention services for families at risk, people living with disability and mental illness. She has been a strong advocate for the not-for-profit sector in Australia.

Bob Wyatt has been executive director of the Muttart Foundation since 1989. A private foundation approaching its sixty-fifth anniversary, Muttart has been involved for several decades in trying to improve the regulatory environment within which charities in Canada work. Bob co-chaired the Joint Regulatory Table of the Voluntary Sector Initiative, a joint exercise between the federal government and the voluntary sector, which examined some of the legislation governing charities. He has served on the boards of a number of charities, including that of Imagine Canada, the national peak body.

1   Introduction

Myles McGregor-Lowndes and Bob Wyatt

English charity law and its regulation have undergone more change in the last 25 years than during the previous century. The Charity Commission for England and Wales (CCEW), regarded as the mother of charity regulators, has created an accessible public register of charity information, embraced digital technologies, implemented a statutory definition of charity, rattled the cage of religious and educational institutions by insisting that they prove their public benefit, tackled regulating political purposes, and responded to a collapse in public trust in charities precipitated by tax and fundraising abuses. The Commission has also modernised its work practices and governance, and together with the sector has faced challenges to their independence from government. Business-charity hybrid organisations have also arisen to complicate charity regulation.

Significant change was also afoot in the English Antipodes, New Zealand, and Australia. They adopted English charity law from colonisation, but not a central regulator such as the Charity Commission. Recently, both countries have replaced low-key, self-regulatory regimes with Commission-style agencies,[1] enacted a statutory definition of charity, and adopted full financial and activity reporting on modern digital public registries. An interesting feature is that policy developments in these countries appear not to have been a staged incremental process, a political reaction to a public scandal, or party political or ideologically driven reform. Instead, they have resulted from laborious, decade-long campaigns by the sector, although perhaps after some initial suspicion. More changes have ensued in both jurisdictions, with incoming conservative governments intent on disestablishing the newly established commissions—a plan that succeeded in New Zealand, where the Charities Commission ceased in 2012. The dearth of charity case precedents for decades in both countries was also broken with a series of significant superior courts cases, including decisions that departed from the restrictive English precedent about political purposes.[2]

Canada and the United States have had relatively stable legislative regimes and formal administrative infrastructure for charities over the last quarter of a century, but change has occurred and more is afoot. Long ago, they each adopted English charity law in varying degrees, with charity regulation constitutionally in the hands of their states and provinces. National charity regulation was located in their national tax agencies. Both countries have faced serious challenges to their administrative independence from political masters, creating internal and external controversies for regulators. The Canada Revenue Agency (CRA) has moved closer to the charitable sector in conversing about legislative and administrative reforms over the period. In Canada, federal governments of all persuasions have attempted to constrain charities that seek to be players in the political sphere, but none has been as divisive as the recent Harper conservative government. It specifically funded CRA to audit charities with a public policy bent, which has been interpreted by some as payback for environmental charities objecting to government-encouraged oil pipeline development. However, CRA has also had to face abuse of the tax system on an industrial scale by promoters of tax avoidance schemes for charitable gift deductions. CRA has been hampered with limited effective regulatory tools, legacy issues with a partially digitised public charity register, and little assistance from provincial charity regulators.

The US Internal Revenue Service (IRS), as a regulator of charities with slim resources, has always faced a challenging environment. The United States has a significant population of diverse, hybridising, and sector-hopping organisations that are responsible for the delivery of critical public goods of education and health, as well as complex legislative provisions, uncompromising professional advisers, and fundraisers with a high-risk appetite. Political parties from both sides have sought to influence administration of charities involved in political activities and fundraising. Recently, there have been murmurs about the IRS having lost the confidence of both sides of Congress to regulate charities. The core worth of charity oversight is being questioned, with excessive government interference and serious proposals to roll back generous gift deductions. Unlike the Canadian provinces, the US states are seeking to move into this growing regulatory vacuum with innovative plans to provide a more effective regulatory presence within constrained budgets.

The working lives of this book's editors have also coincided with this era of charity law and regulation. Both are active sector participants as well as periodically being co-opted into charity regulatory agencies or government and occasionally have been involved with those in foreign jurisdictions. We have appreciated becoming acquainted with charity regulators in such capacities, often continuing the relationship through sector forums long after their terms have concluded. An idea was incubated at an international forum in late 2014 to compile the reflections of charity regulators, to capture an insider's review of charity regulation and policy during the last quarter of the century, and to draw on insights for its future development. Those at the forum were enthusiastic about the project, and that enthusiasm carried into their first drafts, which were nearly three times the specified word limit. To balance their contributions, invitations were extended to influential sector reformers in each jurisdiction to interject their reflections about charity law and regulation. These are people with exceptional insights, gleaned from being on the front line of regulatory action and reform processes over the whole quarter century.

The orthodox plan for a comparative law and policy project is to prepare an issues template and have each jurisdictional commentator describe the functional legal or policy problem and then the jurisdiction's response.[3] This facilitates comparison, analysis, and synthesis of issues in the editors' final chapter, but such a functional approach may neglect the wider cultural context.[4] Further, the chosen template may reflect the editors' immediate experience, which can taint, constrain, and even pre-determine the contributions. We decided to take a slightly different methodological tack, releasing contributors from a given template and allowing them to concentrate instead on their reflections or narrative—the inside story.

Those who are part of the charitable sector are good storytellers—a characteristic which may emanate from the sector's religious roots, or from a grounding in social work, or successful fundraising where the story is an essential art form. As leaders tell their stories, they build narrative accounts for their organisations, helping them understand what they think organises their experiences and controls and predicts events. Charity law itself can be viewed as a story. It is found in the tales told to professional advisers by charity officials and recounted by lawyers to regulators and courts. Judges tell the parties' stories in case decisions, and politicians respond to stories of injustice amplified by the press; and then there is the story embodied in legislation.[5]

We encouraged regulators to provide a narrative expressed in their lived and told stories. How do they make sense of their regulatory agency, its actions, and its relationships with others? Sense-making has been used to provide insights into factors that surface as organisations address either uncertain or ambiguous situations.[6] It occurs as a social activity in that plausible stories are preserved, retained, or shared, becoming a reality that emerges from efforts to create order and make sense, retrospectively, of what has occurred. Often chronological time is replaced with kairotic time, time punctuated by meaningful events or dramas, in the retelling of sagas.[7] Readers should not be surprised if apparently conflicting accounts appear in different contributors' narratives, or if they depart from authorised histories or accepted views.

Initially, contributors were invited to share headline issues that they intended to cover; these were then collated and shared with all. Draft chapters were prepared and circulated before an in-person meeting of nearly all contributors. The Muttart Foundation graciously facilitated the meeting and allowed a little over a day's review and comment by contributors, who were joined by some long-time sector commentators. Contributors then set about revising their drafts and editing to meet the word limits.

We acknowledge that the selection of jurisdictions (England and Wales, the United States of America, Canada, Australia, and New Zealand) is Anglo-Saxon, common law centric, and incomplete. There are no civil law regulators, which might have resulted in a richer analysis and the new regulators of Scotland and Ireland are missing. Our publisher has page limits and bringing together the reflections of a selection of common law charity regulators is enough of a logistical challenge. We hope others may build on our work in the future. Having jurisdictions with a common heritage and shared experience does have advantages for an initial foray into this topic.

All the chosen jurisdictions have been swept during the last quarter century by the megatrends of new digital technologies, innovative social media, globalisation of trade, and capital and social discourse, as well as experiencing the challenges of financial crises, austerity budgeting, and terrorism. At the beginning of our period, Prime Minister Thatcher's application of private-sector management ideas to the public sector and policy processes led to citizens being viewed as customers and market force accountabilities affected not only the shape of English charity regulation but also quickly spread to Australia, New Zealand, and North America. The application of what soon became known as New Public Management (NPM) affected all charity regulators. It has also affected charities that are recipients of government funding in providing community services and other public goods.

Two developments have been apparent in all jurisdictions under consideration. Both are contributions originating from the academy, but have practical significance for charities and those who oversee them. The first is the new knowledge created by the "invention of the nonprofit sector" and its investigation by scholars.[8] Although far from complete in its coverage, it provides new theoretical and empirical insights about charities and their behaviours, which were previously unavailable. The second is the emergence of responsive regulation in the emerging field of regulatory studies.[9] Regulators are now provided with a range of practical tools, derived from sophisticated theories, which have broken free from merely invoking the free market, or classic command and control government strategies. Regulators now use the regulatory pyramid, risk compliance continuums, stick-and-carrot incentives, and co-option of third parties to do some regulatory heavy lifting—all encouraged by times of fiscal restraint.

A short note is warranted on the terms used, as it is usual for editors to settle on uniform meanings. Words such as charity, nonprofit, not-for-profit, third-sector organisation, and nongovernment organisation have technical meanings, but are often used casually and interchangeably even in one jurisdiction. There are also the complexities of translations across jurisdictions to be considered. However, in telling their narratives, the authors have been left to use the language that comes naturally to them so as not to detract from their discourse. This means that readers will need to be vigilant as to different meanings used by authors. We turn now to introducing and locating the contributors in the last quarter century and in their jurisdiction.

England and Wales

The first set of reflections focuses on the Charity Commission for England and Wales over the last 25 years. Two former Charity Commissioners and the head of the umbrella association for charities, who were central actors during this period, wrote these chapters, and their insights are revealing. The origins of the modern Charity Commission may be traced to the Charitable Trusts Act 1853, but our examination begins with the commissioner, Richard Fries, charged with the modernisation of the Charity Commission during the decade of the 1990s. The Woodfield Report was the first major review of English charities law and its regulation since the passing of the Charities Act 1960.[10] Richard was a career civil servant in the British Home Office, and before his appointment as charity commissioner, he was the under secretary responsible for overseeing the implementation of the Woodfield Report. During the 1990s, Richard drove a modernisation agenda for the Charity Commission. He reflects on the journey of nudging the Commission from a quasi-judicial facilitative body to one with supervisory and investigative capacity. This meant a closer engagement with charities, as the Commission experimented with influencing behaviour through education, training, and guidance documents. Early sceptics of this approach were being heard then, and their rhetoric would grow in the coming decades. The establishment of a functioning charity register was a mark of this period made possible by deft manoeuvring to garner resources for an ever hungry information technology programme. The advent of a register open to public scrutiny also required greater clarity of the registration criteria. This process pushed the charitable object boundaries wider, bringing them closer to contemporary public sentiment. This work later informed the agenda for statutory guidance in 2006. By the turn of the century, this definitional work allowed the commencement of a formal review of the register to ensure that the public could have confidence in its accuracy.

Lindsay Driscoll then takes up the English narrative. From 2003 to 2008, Lindsay was a legal commissioner at the Charity Commission. Her background was as a specialist charity lawyer in private practice, and before that, she was with the National Council for Voluntary Organisations (NCVO), where she rose to head the Legal and Governance Department. During this period, she was involved in leading the charity sector's response to the Charities Bill 1992. While at the Commission, she was at the centre of the introduction of the statutory definition of charity, the creation of the charity tribunal, and other significant reforms contained in the Charities Act 2006. Rarely has the definition of English charity seen such reform activity, but her view is that the reforms mostly confirmed the practices of the Commission developed since the 1990s. She reflects on the controversial guidance on public benefit and revised commission guidelines on political activities that occupied so much of the sector agenda during this period. The Commission was, at the same time, developing its internal governance and regulatory approach, dealing with issues of its own independence as well as protecting the sector's independence and being confronted with the terrorism agenda. The role of the Commission was again being pushed and pulled between that of police officer and friend of the sector, and the issue of its independence was raised by sector umbrella bodies, public service, politicians, and views of a succession of Charity Commission chairs. Lindsay also offers her insights on the developments after the slashing of Commission's funding in 2012 and future challenges for the sector and its regulation.

Sir Stuart Etherington concludes this section with his reflections on English charity regulation from a sector perspective. His length of tenure at the charity umbrella association and appointments to reform inquiries by successive governments place him in a unique position to consider charity regulation and the Commission. He was appointed chief executive of NCVO in 1994, having previous experience as a CEO of a major charity. The NCVO is a membership organisation that represents the interests of over 11,000 charities and voluntary bodies. Sir Stuart's government appointments gave him an added vantage point. These include the Prime Minister's Delivery Unit, the Cabinet Office Performance and Innovation Unit's Advisory Board on the Voluntary Sector, HM Treasury's Cross Cutting Review on the Role of the Voluntary Sector and recently as chair of the Cabinet Office's Review of self-regulation of fundraising. The theme of Sir Stuart's reflections is the pressure applied to a rapidly growing and diverse sector which requires public trust and confidence to be able to operate effectively. He points to charities being buffeted by increasing public expectations about the acceptable levels of accountability, transparency, and scrutiny driven by an inquisitive and antagonist popular press magnified by social media. Added to this is the increasing muddying of boundaries between government, business, and charity sectors. Government bodies are morphing into charities, charities are hybridising with business, and a good number inhabit a twilight zone between sectors, thus adding to the public confusion. Sir Stuart couches the role of the regulatory framework as being to "protect and promote charity," but he concludes that charities have to control their destiny through self-regulation and individual relationships with their supporters. He proceeds to this position after reviewing NCVO's role in the Charities Act 2006, litigation over public benefit status, charity CEO remuneration, the failure of fundraising self-regulation, and its reconstruction in the face of unprecedented popular press attention. The chapter also includes critical examination of the Commission's governance and its independence.

United States

Just about everything to do with philanthropy, charity, and nonprofit organisations in the United States is conducted on a grand scale, and it has been thus for a considerable period. Its regulation sometimes amazes those involved, just as much as it does those observing from foreign shores. Marcus Owens spent 25 years with the IRS, including as director of the Exempt Organizations Division from 1990 until 2000. In that capacity, he was the chief decision maker regarding design and implementation of federal tax rulings and enforcement programs for exempt organisations, political organisations, and tax-exempt bonds. He also served as the IRS's primary liaison with other federal agencies, Congress, and state regulators on issues involving exempt organisations. Since that time, he has been in professional legal practice specialising in federal tax issues relating to tax-exempt organisations, including charities and issue advocacy groups. He is also co-chair of the Subcommittee on Audits and Appeals of the Exempt Organizations Committee of the American Bar Association Tax Section. This expertise as a specialist lawyer is acknowledged in several legal service-ranking publications.

The reflections of Marcus Owens about the current state of US charity regulation are sobering. The culprits for this situation are underfunding, difficulty with attracting suitable talent, poorly drafted legislation, inadequate regulatory tools, inability to coordinate with state regulators, and Congress's hostility from both sides. Marcus details his view of the basis of charity regulation and how this influenced the beginning of the modern era of charity regulation in the mid-1970s, before examining the contributing factors for its current demise. A joint state-federal regulatory commission, funded by the charitable sector, is a possible way forward, but it is the first step in a major re-evaluation of the relationship between government and charities. Until the federal political landscape alters, charity options for functional reform are limited.

Elizabeth T. Boris was the founding director, from 1991 to 1996, of the Aspen Institute's Nonprofit Sector Research Fund, the first grant-making program devoted to supporting research on the nonprofit sector and philanthropy. Before her tenure at the Aspen Institute, Elizabeth was vice-president for research at the Council on Foundations, where she developed the research program and directed it for 12 years. More recently, Elizabeth was the founding director of the Center on Nonprofits and Philanthropy at the Urban Institute in Washington, DC, where she conducted research on, and evaluations of, nonprofit organisations and the policy issues that affect them.

Cindy M. Lott is a co-author with Elizabeth. Her background is as a private legal practitioner who has served as chief counsel in the Indiana attorney general's office. Cindy is currently the executive director and senior counsel to the National State Attorneys General Program at Columbia Law School. The centre works closely with Attorneys General in the development and dissemination of relevant legal information and includes a Charities Regulation and Oversight Project, and as lead counsel for this program, Cindy has convened a series of national conferences on state regulation of the charitable sector. She served on the Independent Sector Policy Committee for 2015, and she is a member of the BBB's Wise Giving Alliance board.

Elizabeth T. Boris and Cindy M. Lott offer a perspective of US charities informed by their experience as sector leaders and researchers. Their observations of US charity regulation begin with an assessment of the charity sector and its challenges. They point out that not only are charities growing in their economic and social significance in the United States but also their global reach is expanding both on the ground and through the Internet. At the same time, the traditional boundaries are expanding, with new philanthropic strategies, hybrid legal structures, charity financing, digital fundraising innovations, increased political functions of charities, and government outsourcing of community services. Government support for charity regulation at both state and federal levels is in decline, and there is actually a rollback of charity tax concessions, with debate about further reductions. Gaps in the regulatory fabric are now quite apparent and growing. They cite as an example the regulatory gap between state-based solicitation laws and fundraising with its social media applications. The gap is set to widen, as state regulators are unable to secure the technological resources to meet the challenge, and the IRS cannot share records and intelligence with state regulators. However, there are some green shoots of innovative digital solutions in the form of shared state registries. Until governments give regulators the mandate and resources to play a meaningful regulatory role, the public will have to rely on their own devices to access reliable information, and charities will have to consider self-regulation.

Peering into their crystal ball to the future of US charity regulation, the authors see factors such as technological innovation that will both drive new charitable activities and mischiefs, as well as regulatory tools. Charity globalisation and the resultant jurisdictional frictions for charities and regulators will increasingly be a source of frustration. Finally, whether states can fill the regulatory void left by the retreat of IRS regulation and the future of leadership at the IRS are critical issues. For the immediate future, major federal legislative reform is unlikely, and there are indications that some states may step up their supervision of charities.

Canada

Canada, like the United States, has a national tax agency as de facto charity regulator; the provinces have the constitutional jurisdiction to oversee charities. The major difference is that Canada follows the English common law more closely in form and substance. Over the last 25 years, some regulatory reform initiatives have involved substantial consultations with the charitable sector but have delivered meagre reforms. Recently, gift deduction fraud was perpetrated on a grand scale, and some parts of the charitable sector felt aggrieved at specially funded CRA audits concerning advocacy activities. Our contributor who reflects on these issues is Terry de March, a former regulator and career Canadian civil servant, who rose in 2007 to be appointed director general of the Charities Directorate at CRA. Previously, Terry had spent five years with the Federal Department of Justice where he was director of Innovation, Analysis and Integration. In that role, Terry sat as a member of two government/voluntary sector roundtables on regulatory reform which culminated in the most significant changes to the regulatory regime for charities in over 20 years. Terry joined CRA in 2003, first as director of Policy, Planning and Legislation where he brought forward some of the most important administrative, common law policies for the regulation of charities and later as director general of the Charities Directorate. Currently, he serves as special adviser to its Legislative Policy and Legislative Affairs Branch.

Terry opens his reflections by stating clearly that the Canadian Charities Directorate aims to reduce the risk of harm to charities, the public, and the tax system. From the government's and the bureaucracy's perspective, any relaxation of regulatory control means an increased risk of harm. So while there has been coordinated sector agitation for reforms and an independent regulatory agency, the government has delivered small incremental changes. In his view, the sector's hankering for an English-style charity commission with objects of capacity building will not be fulfilled unless the public calls for such reform in reaction to some major issue, or governments decide on it for their own reasons. Terry analyses the reforms that have been achieved and then turns his attention to a possible agenda for future reforms, including regulator independence.

Bob Wyatt shares his insights into the last 25 years of Canadian charity regulation from a sector perspective. Bob joined the Muttart Foundation in 1989, and under his direction, it has taken a leading role in helping to increase the charitable sector's capacity. Bob's skill in facilitating government, the sector, and professional advisers to "play nicely in a meaningful open discussion sandpit," combined with the foundation's work in making capacity-building grants to the charity sector over this period and its national consultations on regulatory reform give his reflections special insight. He has led ongoing consultations between government and the sector on issues of regulatory reform including as co-chair of the Joint Table on Regulatory Reform created during the Voluntary Sector Initiative.

Bob uses a roller-coaster metaphor to introduce the reader to the highs, lows, and wobbles of charity reform developments. The 1990s opened with dissatisfaction with CRA's delays and narrow views, adverse judicial decisions, government funding cuts, and many looking towards the CCEW as it evolved into a progressive and supportive regulator. Later that decade, the progressive government began to move towards a closer relationship with the charity sector, and a sector-commissioned report made recommendations for a statutory definition of charity, an independent regulator in the form of a commission, and reform of the charity advocacy rules. This led to a formal government consultation known as the Joint Regulatory Table (JRT), with Bob as co-chair. A new conservative government tightened funding and introduced measures to deal with charity financing of terrorism. This was followed by a private member's bill to cap the salaries of charity CEOs; abusive charity tax scams propelled the introduction of conditions for holding office in a charity, without sector consultation; and the finance markets suffered meltdown. Bob identifies a running sore during the whole period in the involvement of charities in public policy issues. Bitter discourse between the conservative federal government and charities about their involvement in the policy process was sparked by a proposed oil pipeline, but soon spread to charities accepting foreign donations and concerns about terrorism financing. The government used the budget to resource CRA to conduct a political activities audit program that was not well received by the sector. Some relief came to the charitable sector in 2015 with the election of a new progressive government. The post-election agenda is still being developed, but Bob's view is that once again the independence of CRA is back on the agenda, together with an enhanced system of judicial review.

New Zealand

New Zealand transformed its charity regulation from a minimal level to establishing a Charities Commission in one step—although this followed 16 years of reform discussions. The Commission was then dis-established by the government only six years later, despite charity sector protests. Trevor Garrett was chief executive of the New Zealand Charities Commission from its establishment in 2005 until its functions were merged into the Department of Internal Affairs in 2012. He reflects on his experience of being the first and last CEO of the Commission. As a career public servant, his appointments included chief executive officer for the Ministry of Recreation and Sport before being appointed chief executive of the Casino Control Authority, responsible for the licensing and regulation of casinos in New Zealand. He was also chairman of the International Association of Gaming Regulators and a member of the advisory committee for the International Gaming Institute at the University of Nevada, Las Vegas.

As the first NZ Charities Commissioner, Trevor gives us an insight into the practical matters for a green fields charity regulator faced with an unknown number of potential charity registrations. He recounts how the Commission "muddled through," creating an appropriate organisational culture, coping with initial processing loads, educating the sector, and creating a digital register and registration process that were fit for purpose. Later came the decision-making process for charity registration and its evolution. The definition of charity and its interpretation by the Commission has been an area of contest with the sector in New Zealand, and Trevor examines the definitional boundaries of sport and advocacy in detail. He concludes by making some incisive comments on the dis-establishment of the Commission concerning its transition costs and independence, and on emerging issues about appealing judicial decisions and commercial operations of charities.

Sue Barker is a lawyer who founded the first boutique charity law firm in New Zealand, and she shares her reflections on recent charity law reforms in that country. Sue began her career at the Inland Revenue Department (IRD), but after qualifying as a lawyer progressed to the Crown Law Office, acting as counsel for the Commissioner of Inland Revenue and the attorney general. She later commenced private practice with commercial law firms before founding her own. Her work with charities has included assisting with submissions on the Charities Bill as it progressed through New Zealand's legislative process and undertaking charity litigation including the application by the National Council of Women of New Zealand Incorporated to regain its registered charitable status following its controversial deregistration by the Commission in 2010.[11] Her chapter gives a critical-sector perspective on the development of charity regulation from before the Commission's advent to the present day. Sue examines the consequences of some serious deficiencies in the final process to develop the form of the Charities Act 2005 and then moves to assess how the Commission has performed in a range of areas such as its regulatory approach and administrative interpretation of the definition of charity. Clearly, she is disappointed in many respects. A number of structural barriers, such as the rights to appeal and independence of the Commission, are considered before concluding with a shopping list of items for future reform.

Australia

The last jurisdiction addressed is Australia. It has the newest charity regulator, the Australian Charities and Not-for-profits Commission (ACNC), which was established in 2012. Over 15.5 million words in six national inquiries over two decades preceded the establishment of the Commission. Again, there was no scandal, public mischief, or political ideology driving the ACNC's establishment, but rather sector initiatives. It too faced the prospect of early extinction, but after languishing for three years in a bureaucratic void, it was reprieved.

Susan Pascoe is the inaugural commissioner of the ACNC, and shares her views on the Commission's regulatory journey. Susan's earlier professional background was in education, serving as chief executive of the Catholic Education Commission of Victoria (currently one of Australia's largest charities). She also had significant charity-sector experience, serving on a number of boards. From 2006, Susan moved to the public sector where she served until 2011 as a commissioner at the State Services Authority in Victoria, focusing on regulatory reform. In this role, she chaired a review of the regulation of the Victorian nonprofit sector in 2007–08, before being appointed to lead the taskforce preparing administrative infrastructure for the proposed ACNC.

Susan sets the scene for charity reform in Australia by noting that six national inquiries over a 15-year period recommended some form of charity regulation independent of the Australian Tax Office, the national regulator by default. At first, some charities were suspicious, but many altered their views in later years. Conservative governments were reluctant to implement such recommendations on policy and philosophical grounds, but the progressive side of politics was persuaded otherwise. For them, the decades-long microeconomic reform of the government and business sectors had bypassed the charities sector, and the sector argued that a regulator was required to promote trust and confidence. As head of the taskforce to establish the ACNC, Susan gives an eyewitness account of the preparations and the policy debates around the legislative arrangements. She describes how the ACNC's senior staff crafted an internal culture to provide services in sector education, advice, research, and red tape reduction with a digital-by-default business process and public register. The legislative objective of red tape reduction sets the ACNC apart from other charity regulators and has been challenging, as their only tool is persuasion of other federal agencies and often recalcitrant state governments. She provides interesting reflections on managing the ACNC during those early years when a hostile government was actively seeking to dismantle it and a succession of ministers were put in charge, and as a consequence, other state and federal agencies were reluctant to cooperate with it, frustrating one of its legislated mandates. We will return in the final chapter to make some comparisons between what happened in Australia and New Zealand.

Dr Ursula Stephens contributes another side of the story of Australian charity regulation as a former federal politician with a background in the community sector. Ursula served for 12 years in the Australian Senate, concluding in 2014 shortly after the election of a conservative government. She was a strong advocate for the charity sector, assisting to put charity reform on the Labor party platform and negotiating the National Compact between the Australian federal government and the charities sector. She was part of the Senate Inquiry into the disclosure regime of Australian charities; she also served as parliamentary secretary to the Prime Minister and parliamentary secretary for Social Inclusion, and acted as special adviser to the assistant treasurer on the establishment of the ACNC.

Ursula's overview of the Australian charitable sector focuses on the emergence of NPM in government administration, leading to significant disruptions for charities delivering community services and exacerbating fractured relationships between sector representational bodies and governments at all levels. The chapter then moves on to her account of how the Labor federal government developed and then implemented its agenda for charity reform over several years, culminating in the creation of the ACNC. This process involved a complex web of intra-government committees, with sector champions, sector consultation forums, and arduous national forums with state and territory governments. The politicians' encouragement for a unified representative sector voice is an underlying theme that has not been realized in Australia, where there has never been more than a loose and shifting coalition of sector personalities. The coming to power of a conservative government with a bag of election promises to wind back charity reform, as well as plans to cut welfare funding and introduce market forces into community services, galvanised vocal parts of the sector to advocate for the retention of the ACNC and charity reforms. Cabinet reshuffles, leadership change, and continued sector lobbying finally had the government effectively reverse the policy before the recent election. Ursula concludes that only part of the reform agenda has been implemented to date, and the sector will require tenacity to complete the task in the future.

Conclusion

This compilation brings together reflections of regulators and prominent leaders in the charity sector, from England and Wales, the United States, Canada, New Zealand, and Australia on the last 25 years of change in their jurisdictions. It is an insider's review of charity regulation and charity law reform, with some prognostications about what the future may hold. All contributors reflect on the current state of charities in a fiscally restrained environment and offer their views on productive regulatory paths available for the future. We have encouraged them to tell their stories as they understand them, and this may not be how others make sense of, or interpret the same events. The result is a rich tapestry of insights across jurisdictions dealing with fundamentally similar legal and regulatory issues, but with situational variance.

The final chapter offers the editors' own perspective on the contributions. We gather and explain converging and diverging themes in regulatory policy; regulatory policy transfers, drifts, or inertia at both the level of law makers and regulators; the impact of new regulatory philosophies and tools such as nudging, soft law, and self-regulation; and strategies for regulating in the climate of austerity budgets, scandals, and impugned political neutrality—an ambitious task more suited to several doctoral studies. With two jurisdictions creating new regulatory agencies, there might be clues in the narratives as to whether it is preferable to have an independent regulatory structure for the charitable sector, to embed their regulation in a central tax agency, or to have regulation diffused among states or ministries. Finally, we did not resist reflecting on the contributors' sense of the future for charity regulation, nor the urge to polish our own crystal ball to see what promise lies in the future for charity reform.

Notes

1 In New Zealand, the Charities Commission was established in July 2005; in Australia, the Australian Charities and Not-for-profits Commission commenced in December 2012.
2 *AID/WATCH Incorporated v Commissioner of Taxation* [2010] HCA 42; (2010) 241 CLR 539; *Re Greenpeace of New Zealand Incorporated* [2011] 2 NZLR 815.
3 Konrad Zweigert and Hein Kötz, *Introduction to Comparative Law* (Oxford: Oxford University Press, 3rd ed., 1998).
4 Anthony Infanti, "Spontaneous Tax Coordination: On Adopting a Comparative Approach to Reforming the US International Tax Regime," *Vanderbilt Journal of Transnational Law* 35 (2002): 1105.
5 Leon Wolff, "Let's Talk about Lex: Narrative Analysis as Both Research Method and Teaching Technique in Law," *Adelaide Law Review* 35 (2014): 3.

6 K. E. Weick, *Sensemaking in Organisations* (Thousand Oaks, CA: Sage, 1995).
7 B. Czarniawska, "On Time, Space and Action Nets," *Organization* 11 (2004): 777.
8 P. D. Hall, "A Historical Overview of Philanthropy, Voluntary Associations and Nonprofit Organizations in the United States, 1600–2000," in *The Nonprofit Sector: A Research Handbook*, eds. W. W. Powell and R. Steinberg (New Haven: Yale University Press, 2006), 32.
9 I. Ayres and J. Braithwaite, *Responsive Regulation: Transcending the Deregulation Debate* (New York: Oxford University Press, 1992).
10 House of Commons, Parliamentary Panel on Charity Law, *Charities: A Framework for the Future*, Cm. 694, (London: Her Majesty's Stationery Office, 1989).
11 *National Council of Women of New Zealand Incorporated v Charities Registration Board* [2014] NZHC 3200, [2015] 3 NZLR 72.

England and Wales

2 Towards Regulation

Modernizing the Original Charity Commission

Richard Fries[1]

Charity and the Charity Commission in the 1980s

The Charity Commission is the regulator of charity for England and Wales. Since the passing of the Charities Act 2006, this title has had a statutory basis. However, the Charity Commission has not been designed as a regulator. The 2006 Act (now consolidated into the Charities Act 2011), set out the Commission's role at length but, while giving a self-contained legal and constitutional base, the provisions of the Act are in fact the culmination (so far!) of a long process of reform and modernization, a piecemeal process which did not start out with the conscious intention of converting the Commission into a regulatory body. To understand the Commission, it is necessary to start with its origins and, in particular, its status—and state—in the 1980s. The legal and constitutional basis for charity is essential to this understanding.

This chapter deals with the initial phase of the modernization of the Commission at the end of the twentieth century. By that time, there was general agreement that the Commission had sunk to a low ebb after years of neglect. The chapter focuses on the programme set up to reform the Commission and its implementation. As outlined in this chapter, the programme was based on a systematic review of the powers of the Commission and the way they were being used. It was not a piecemeal reform, but neither was it a fundamental rethinking of the rationale for the Commission in the modern world, let alone of the suitability of charity as a legal framework for voluntary action in the late twentieth century. The chapter explains that the basis for modernization did not involve notions of regulation, far less an aim of turning the Commission into the "regulator of charities," as it has subsequently become designated. The aim of the modernization programme was rather on the one hand to enable the Commission to support the effectiveness of charities with advice and guidance and, where necessary, intervention (on carefully limited criteria) and on the other hand to make charities properly and publicly accountable. The chapter then describes the steps taken to realize this aim, and the way in which the Commission's thinking about its proper role and the appropriate form of accountability for charities informed the modernization programme and its implementation. It describes particular initiatives, such as the development, in consultation with the charitable sector and parliamentarians, of new, more flexible guidelines for the basis on which charities might undertake political activities, and the first steps towards the modernization of charitable status itself through the Review of the Register of Charities.

However, before embarking on the account of the modernization process, it is important to note that the chapter covers charity regulation in England and Wales, not the United Kingdom as a whole. In the context of a volume dealing with the different experiences of different common law jurisdictions, the reason for this is significant. The simple explanation is that the common law basis for charity in England is the Preamble to the Charitable Uses Act of 1601 (commonly referred to as the Statute of Elizabeth I), predating the creation of the United Kingdom. The Preamble continues to be the foundation of the common law of charity in England and Wales (which constitute a single legal jurisdiction) but has never applied to Scotland or Ireland. They constitute separate charity law jurisdictions (Northern Ireland and the Republic of Ireland being, of course, two separate jurisdictions though deriving from common roots).

The 1601 Act could be described as being concerned with charity regulation in that it envisaged the appointment of commissioners to check compliance with the terms of (English and Welsh) charitable trusts. The origins of the Charity Commission lie in this tradition and explain why the jurisdiction of the first standing commission, though established in 1853, long after the creation of the United Kingdom, is confined to England and Wales. At the same time, tax issues came to play an important role in charity. Like other common law jurisdictions, responsibility for tax issues is led at the "federal" level—i.e. UK-wide. In consequence, the tax authorities have an interest in charities and the tax relief they enjoy across the United Kingdom. The courts determined that for this purpose, the charity law of England and Wales should be applied to all parts of the United Kingdom. As tax relief became increasingly important, Inland Revenue (then the UK tax authority) became involved in charity matters throughout the United Kingdom. In the absence of charity commissions in Scotland and Northern Ireland, Inland Revenue became in effect their charity regulator—applying English charity law there! This unsatisfactory situation has been rectified in recent years by the creation of the equivalent of charity commissions in Scotland (the Office of the Scottish Charity Regulator under the Charities and Trustee Investment Act 2005) and Northern Ireland (The Charity Commission for Northern Ireland under the Charities Act (Northern Ireland) 2008), applying their own charity law.

The most important point which emerges from this simplified account of the origins of charity regulation in the United Kingdom is that oversight of charities is charity, not tax, led. This is not to say that the tax authorities have no role in the supervision of charities. Inland Revenue naturally dealt with claims for tax relief, and, given the importance to tax collection of the Charity Commission's responsibility for determining charitable status, the Inland Revenue had a legitimate interest in its decisions. The Charity Commission, therefore, gave Inland Revenue an opportunity to comment on novel registration applications.

While independent public regulatory bodies have a long history in Britain, the growth in the 1980s of the policy of privatizing functions hitherto undertaken by public bodies established a more general need for regulatory bodies, in particular to supervise privatized utilities. The need to modernize the Charity Commission also became recognized in the 1980s; it was not, however, consciously influenced by the notion of regulation—a term applied to charity only later. There are two fundamental reasons for this—reasons which have influenced the modernizing process right to the present day. First, the Commission was established in the nineteenth century as a quasi-judicial body exercising the powers of the Chancery Court. Its core function was to help charities to operate effectively under the legal framework applying to them. This was primarily a support, not a regulatory function. And, second, the nature of charity—"private action, public benefit" as the government report of 2001 neatly entitled it—is an essentially independent activity of private individuals, rather than a public or governmental function. This makes regulation by a governmental body (as the Commission was and remains) inappropriate. The question arises as to whether regulation of charity is proper at all.

It may seem a quibble to emphasize the necessity for charities to be accountable but to demur at their being regulated. There is, however, an important—and all too often neglected—distinction in forms of accountability. Regulation makes the bodies concerned liable to enforceable intervention by the regulator—one may call this "enforceable accountability." Equally important is accountability which consists of openness about the body's activities, finances, governance, and so on, but which does not involve the body in being subject to intervention by a regulator substituting its judgment for that of the body concerned—one may call this "explanatory accountability." This distinction highlights the importance of the ultimate independence which charities must retain. Of course, this independence must be exercised within the law, and to that extent, charities are necessarily subject to intervention, but, as discussed in the body of this chapter, the criteria for intervention must be strictly limited. The independence of charities is paramount.

The Commission was reconstituted by the Charities Act 1960, itself a modernizing piece of legislation designed to transform an essentially Dickensian legal institution into an effective administrative agency responsible for maintaining a public register of charities. The Commission also had powers inherited from the courts to remedy abuse by charities. These were exercised administratively in parallel with court powers and subject to court oversight. By the 1980s, it was clear that further reform was needed. Public and parliamentary concerns led the Home secretary, then the sponsoring Minister for the Commission, to set up a review of its operation. A distinguished retired civil servant, Sir Philip Woodfield, led the review in the form of a new government mechanism, the "efficiency scrutiny review," which was a mechanism designed to find savings in public expenditure based on a critical examination of the purpose of the functions under review. This suited the agenda for Commission reform ideally, with the added advantage that the Treasury could not but welcome the use of this cost-cutting mechanism! The resulting Woodfield Report of 1987 set out the blueprint for reform. It was entitled the *Scrutiny of the Supervision of Charities*,[2] but this use of the label "supervision" was as near as the review got to the idea of regulating charity, with regulation being a concept which did not feature in the report. It proposed a substantial redirection of the Commission, underpinned by strengthened powers. (By a sleight of hand, the report pronounced its reforms cost neutral to disarm a sceptical Treasury!)

The implementation of the Woodfield Report, given effect through administrative reform of the Commission and new charities legislation in 1992 (which was consolidated with remaining provisions of the 1960 Act to become the Charities Act 1993), laid the basis for the progressive modernization of the Charity Commission up to the present day. (Indeed, the Charities Act 2011 is the consolidating legislation incorporating provisions of the 1993 Act.) To understand charity regulation under the 1993 Act (and indeed subsequent reforms), it is therefore necessary to understand the Woodfield proposals and the nature of the Commission which the Woodfield Report was designed to modernize.

Principles of Reform

The reform process was based on two fundamental principles. The first was that the legal basis for charity, as a form of organization, was left untouched by statute. Neither the Charities Act 1960 nor the reforms of the 1993 Act addressed the question of what constituted charity, with this being left to the common law. (The extent to which this principle was overturned by the Charities Act 2006/2011 is for a later chapter, but it is important to the pre-2006 role of the Commission that it had to operate on the basis of the common law of charity.) The second fundamental principle was that, in the words of the 1960 Act carried through the subsequent legislation, including, in principle, the 2011 Act, the Commission (or, more properly in the pre-2006 language, "the Commissioners") might not "act in the administration" of a charity.

The fundamental independence of charities, the absolute responsibility of their trustees, was thus enshrined in statute. It is the essence of charity and its place in society. Strengthening the supervision (or regulation) of charities must start from that premise. The essence of the legal concept of charity is that it provides a secure legal and organizational basis through which private citizens, individually or collectively, can seek to tackle social problems or to benefit society on their initiative and according to their own views of what is needed. It is the antithesis of central planning. People must be free to experiment, and they deserve encouragement, for example, by the tax benefits charities enjoy. Given the benefits of charitable status, charities must be accountable, but the nature of their accountability must reflect their independence. Charities must be open: the public must know how they use their resources and how their governance and management operate. However, accountability should not extend to interference from an external regulatory agency. The test for intervention must be illegality or impropriety.

These principles reflect the role of the courts in relation to charities. Determining whether a trust was charitable, upholding compliance with the terms of the trust, and amending the terms if they became inoperable required application to the Chancery Court, which was notoriously slow and expensive. Concern in the nineteenth century that charitable resources were being misused or neglected by corrupt or lazy trustees prompted the creation of the Charity Commission to exercise the courts' powers more cheaply, efficiently, and speedily. Tackling neglect and abuse does not seem to have had the prominence in the Commission's agenda accorded to exercising the powers of amending inoperable trust terms (making "schemes," such as administrative and cy près schemes). Even by the 1980s, many charities had the form of limited companies (limited by guarantee). The fact that this organizational form gave trustees the protection of limited liability was an essential safeguard for charities. Trust form, carrying unlimited liability for trustees, was unsuitable for entrepreneurial charities, but charity law remained based on trust law, even though the "mem and arts" form of charitable companies was very different from trust form.

The Charities Act 1960 gave the Commission increased administrative functions. In status, it became (and remains) a "non-ministerial department" funded entirely out of public funds, but, though part of government, it exercises its functions wholly independent of ministers. Its accountability is to Parliament, through ministers, rather than to ministers. The Commissioners were appointed by the Home Secretary. As part of the reform process, appointments were made on the basis of public advertisement and interview by an appointments panel, which included a nongovernmental member. While government appointment might seem to encroach on the Commission's independence, it can fairly be asserted that, certainly up to the turn of the millennium, government scrupulously respected the independence of the Commission. Similarly, while the Commission's dependence on public funding opened the possibility of government control through financial restrictions and influence by the Treasury and the Home Office, in practice, it can confidently be asserted that, once government accepted the modernization programme initiated by the Woodfield Report, the necessary funding to implement it was allocated to the Commission. By the 1980s, concerns similar to those giving rise to the nineteenth-century reforms became significant. In the words of the Woodfield Report, "lethargic and neglectful trustees" were putting charitable resources at risk, and the powers of the Commissioners, ineffectually operated, were inadequate for their responsibilities.

There were wider issues over the adequacy of the legal basis for charity for the modern world. The governmental reform agenda addressed by the Woodfield review left these unaddressed. And public confidence in charities depended on their effectiveness as much as "mismanagement and abuse" (the trigger for Commission intervention under the 1960 Act). Reflecting the principle that, subject to these triggers, how a charity sought to fulfil its purposes was for the trustees alone, the 1960 Act did give the Commission the general function of "promoting the effective use of charitable resources," but this function was to be fulfilled by encouraging the development of better methods of administration, providing charity trustees with information and advice, and investigating and checking abuses. Whether the outcomes of charitable activities were worthwhile was for the trustees, not the Commission, to determine, provided their charity was administered properly.

In practice, by the 1980s, the register of charities was not being maintained properly, requirements in the 1960 Act for the return of accounts were not being enforced, and capacity of the Commission to play an active, as distinct from a reactive, role in promoting even the limited functions of the 1960 Act was negligible. Under-resourcing, particularly over introducing modern computerized systems, was a significant factor, if not accepted by the Treasury. The chief commissioner at that time was committed to reform and sought to engage with the charitable sector. There was a clear and urgent need for a thoroughgoing review of the Commission's rationale and operations.

The Woodfield Report

The form of the reforms proposed by Woodfield was, in the report's words, "directed towards fostering a greater realisation of the responsibilities of trustees." Partly in principle, partly to make savings to fund a "realignment of the balance of the Commission's activities," Woodfield proposed that Commission "hand-holding" functions, such as requiring charities to obtain Commission consent for such things as property transactions and the facility by which charities' investments were held by the official custodian, a statutory officer of the Commission, should be drastically scaled back or abolished altogether. (Aware that funding might be an issue, the report did recommend that provision should be made for the Commission to charge for registration and for some other functions. Despite the Treasury's concern over the cost of the reforms, this recommendation was not pursued.) The savings realized should be redeployed to modernization and computerization of the register of charities, systematization of the return of annual accounts by charities, and increased capacity to investigate and remedy maladministration and abuse, supported by strengthened powers, in particular a power to appoint a "receiver and manager" to exercise some or all of the responsibilities of the trustees of charities where gross failures had been found. Though the review did not make recommendations for modernizing the constitution of the Commission, it did emphasize the need for the Commission to make its general advice to trustees more accessible (and accessibly written). To encourage greater understanding of the nature of charities and their activities in the modern world, the report recommended strengthening the board by the appointment of two additional Commissioners with wider experience, particularly of the charitable sector.

The Scrutiny Report was submitted (and published) in 1987. Its recommendations were accepted (in the face of resistance by the Treasury, sceptical of the value of the Commission and of the resource-neutral claim). Implementation had to be spread out over the next decade, first while primary legislation was prepared and then while the framework for exercising the Commission's new powers was developed and obsolete functions shed. Equally important was the need for Commission staff to be given time to adjust to the new roles involved. As anticipated by Woodfield, the funding of new functions, in parallel with the necessarily drawn-out process of winding down functions forgone, involved significant additional funding. What was not envisaged by the report, but feared by the Treasury, the long-term result was a substantial permanent increase in Commission resourcing—a doubling of staff (to 700, at least during the transition period), and an extensive IT programme, funded by a fourfold increase in the Treasury grant. On the retirement of the chief commissioner (a career civil servant) who had started the reform process, a new head of the Commission and the two additional commissioners proposed by Woodfield were recruited from the charitable and business sectors to lead the implementation of the report.

While the necessary legislation was developed, administrative reforms were started immediately. The focus on supervision was met by the creation of a new strengthened "Monitoring and Investigation Division" in the Commission, reinforced by the recruitment of qualified accountants and led by an experienced investigator recruited from government. The newly established executive director post oversaw the whole programme. In parallel, an IT unit was set up to develop a comprehensive computerization programme for the Commission's operations and for the register of charities. The process of reforming the annual accounting requirements for charities was also started in advance of the legislation needed to underpin it. One of the new Commissioners was specifically chosen with accounting qualifications to lead the process, with the Commission's new accountants and an external committee of charity finance directors and accountants. Meanwhile, the process of scaling down consents work, and investment holding was set in train.

The modernization programme involved a fundamental change of culture for the Commission. Hitherto, much of the work was led by the legal staff. Given that only 22 of the 330 staff were lawyers at the time of the

Woodfield Report, it was inevitable that more responsibility would have to be placed on administrative staff, many newly recruited, mainly from other government departments. One sign of the cultural change was the incredulity of Commission staff when the IT programme was first unveiled at the idea that work would be computer based, contrasted with their impatience only a couple of years later at the slowness of the first desktops. The modernization process was overseen by a management committee of senior staff chaired by the executive director, reporting to the Commission's board, which included, alongside the five commissioners, senior members of staff. Behind the organizational changes lay a conscious change of ethos. From a spirit of legal compliance, the Commission moved to the aim of maintaining public confidence in charity, supported by an ethos of seeking to apply the law and other requirements in ways which helped charities achieve their objectives so far as possible. The way in which guidance was made available to charities was reformed first to express it as intelligibly as possible for trustees without legal knowledge and then to make it available on the website established under the computerization programme. (The computerized register of charities became the vehicle of two-way communication between the Commission and charities to an extent unimaginable when Woodfield was setting out the reforms.)

The strategy for the Commission which emerged through the process of modernization transformed the Commission's relationship to the sector from one of largely piecemeal reaction to an active continuous relationship. From being essentially a vehicle of public information (and inadequate at that) registration became the entry point, or "Gateway," as the Commission called it, into a continuous relationship of support and supervision. It also, of course, made a reality of the accountability of registered charities by their online accessibility, to the Commission and the public at large, through the submission of an annual report and accounts in standard (proportionate) form. Individual and general supportive guidance was developed. The use of investigation and remedial action, enhanced under the new legislation and reforms, remained a backstop, but was used actively when problems were identified, albeit usually informally rather than explicitly invoking legal power.

Modernizing the Commission

In setting the modernization programme off, the Commission set its aim as maintaining public confidence in charity. What determined public confidence needed to be spelt out—legal and financial integrity, of course—but how far did that require the Commission to address questions of the credibility of charitable status and charity law? And in so far as public expectations of the value of charitable activity determined public confidence in charity, how far could the Commission's supervision extend to questions of the efficiency and effectiveness of charities? How far did the status of being a charity registered with the Charity Commission entitle donors and the interested public in general to expect standards of efficiency, let alone valuable results? Even if the public expected this, how far did the Commission have the competence to pronounce on such matters? In addressing these issues, the Commission had to take account of the changing nature of the charitable sector and, in particular, its relationship with the public sector. The frequently expressed concerns about the charitable sector's growing dependence on public funding, which significantly affects the way the charitable sector is viewed today, were beginning to be aired in the 1980s. In particular, there were fears that many charities were becoming dependent on funding contracts from central and local government, thus becoming over-influenced by government policies. Increasing the effectiveness of Commission supervision had to ensure that it strengthened, rather than undermined, the independence of charities. The Commission's approach was summarized under the headline of support and supervision—providing advice and guidance on matters within the Commission's remit and competence, backed up by powers to intervene to remedy mismanagement and abuse. At the outset, this combination provoked controversy within the charitable sector: how could the Commission combine the roles of support and policing?

To provide a framework for the implementation of the Woodfield reform programme, the Commission needed to articulate its strategy. Strategic planning was a novel concept for Commission staff (and indeed new to government departments and agencies in general). Starting from its initial simplistic slogan, "It's for charity," Commission planning focused on the Commission's role of "giving the public confidence in the integrity of charity." This formula was settled on—after some considerable debate, especially over the need to focus on integrity rather than aspiring to a wider role for promoting charity effectiveness—in the strategy enunciated in the "Statement of Departmental Aims and Objectives" finally set in 1997.[3] The aim was to be realized through three objectives:

- to deliver an effective legal, accounting, and governance framework for charities and the charitable sector;
- to improve the governance, accountability, efficiency, and effectiveness of charities; and
- to identify and deal with abuse and poor practice.

The Commission's answer to the "support/enforcement" challenge was in effect to develop a three-part programme:

- seeking to articulate and enforce the legal requirements of charitable status;
- providing a framework of accountability through which charities were properly open and accountable to the public at large; and
- developing expertise to promote good governance and administration.

The Commission was clear that the advice-investigation dichotomy was oversimplified. As the second strand of this three-part programme makes clear, making charities transparent and accountable was an important strand in its own right, neither "advice" nor "policing." The dilemma—and the debate with the sector—was especially how to develop and demarcate this third strand. In part, this drew on the lessons of the Commission's new active engagement with charities through investigations, but equally through support contact, partly by developing partnership with the sector. The chief commissioner's introduction to the Commission's Annual Report for 1994 argued that the Commission "must do everything we can to support the sector in meeting the challenge of increasing its efficiency and effectiveness and of improving its standards of administration and financial management." It was noted that "increasing the effectiveness of the charitable sector has, since 1960, been the Charity Commission's fundamental duty," stemming from the 1960 Act's provision that the Commission's general function was "promoting the effective use of charitable resources."[4]

The presumption that the Commission's essential responsibility is law enforcement is too narrow and misleading. Clearly, the integrity of charities depends on their complying with the requirements of charity law, and the Commission's responsibility is to enforce that. It is also obvious that charities must not act beyond their powers: they must seek to fulfil the purposes that entitle them to charitable status and its benefits, and not go beyond them, limiting and legalistic though that may sometimes seem. However, the integrity of charities cannot be defined solely by specific legal prescriptions. The fundamental basis for charitable action is to do what is in the best interests of the charity and, negatively, to avoid doing what may damage it. Thus good governance and financial management are central to the integrity of charities. There are principles on which guidance and good practice can be enunciated, but enforceable requirements would be inappropriate. The Commission must therefore go wider than a law enforcement role. However, in going beyond that role, it was essential to develop an active partnership with the charitable sector. The legitimacy of the Commission's engagement with the governance and management of charities derives from the expertise it develops in its day-to-day work with charities. However, it has neither the authority nor the expertise to override the judgment of charities' trustees. Promoting good standards requires active cooperation with the sector bodies committed to raising standards.

The 1997 framework may be regarded as the origin of the statutory statement of objectives, functions, and duties set out in the Charities Act 2006. An explicit statement of duties is conspicuously absent from the 1997 statement. However, one of the statement's principal purposes was to support internal Commission management in bringing the practice of Commission staff into line with the reformed role of the Commission. For internal purposes, as required by developing civil service practice, performance targets were set for Commission functions (Key Performance Indicators, or KPIs, in the language of the day). This was an essential task of modernization since one of the most frequently expressed criticisms of the Commission was the inordinate time taken in making decisions, for example, in dealing with registration applications. As required by a government-wide initiative, the Commission set service standards for the fulfilment of its functions. For registration, the commitment was to deal with 90 per cent of applications within 15 working days. A measure of the Commission's progress was that, while performance initially fell well below that, by 1998, the level achieved was 93 per cent.

As already noted, a fundamental element in the modernization involved giving administrative staff greater responsibility for making decisions, focusing the use of scarce (and expensive) legal staff on difficult and novel issues in support of the administrative staff. Updating guidance materials for staff was, therefore, a priority, particularly as one cause of concern among the charitable sector was inconsistent decisions given by different offices of the Commission. In order to lead this process, a policy unit was set up—a novel concept for the Commission at that stage.

Underlying the internal modernization process was the need to inculcate a new ethos—that the aim of the Commission should be to help charities to operate effectively within the framework of charity law. Decisions should be informed by a spirit of how the requirements of charity law could be applied to facilitate the aims of charities in seeking to achieve public benefit within their charitable purposes. A key feature of the pre-reform Commission was its lack of real engagement with the charitable sector: while prepared to advise, on the law especially, it was not reaching out to understand what trustees and staff were seeking to achieve. The then chief commissioner had started bridging this gap in the 1980s and it became a fundamental aim of new initiatives. These included a programme of secondments of Commission staff to charities and outreach meetings where Commission staff could discuss their work with charities and learn more directly about issues of most concern to the charities.

One particular focus was on producing guidance materials for charity trustees on their role and responsibilities. As noted earlier, a key concern identified by the Woodfield review was "lethargic and neglectful" trustees. A study carried out jointly by the Commission and the National Council for Voluntary Organisations (NCVO) demonstrated, admittedly on the basis of a small sample, an alarming degree of ignorance about the key place trustees had in the governance of charities. Far too many trustees regarded their role as merely supportive or even honorific; many were not even aware that they were trustees in law, with all the responsibilities attached to the role. This presented the Commission with something of a dilemma: how to educate trustees about their responsibilities without frightening people from taking on this essential public service. The Commission developed a range of ways of informing and reassuring people about trusteeship, including a video starring the comedian Sir Lenny Henry (as he now is). As the Commission's ability to communicate with charities and their trustees improved, particularly with the computerization of the charities' register (which became in effect the Commission's address book), new guidance material was produced and disseminated to charities. In particular, *The Essential Trustee: What You Need to Know*, set out in clear (non-legal) and encouraging language the essence of the trustee's role and responsibilities and the role of the Commission as a source of advice and guidance.[5] A regular newsletter on developments sent to all charities supported this. To develop the trusteeship programme, supported by an advisory committee of people from the sector, the Commission set up a charity services unit as a focal point of information about trusteeship. Its role was explicitly to work with the sector, in particular working closely with NCVO's Trustee Services Unit, set up to take forward their part of the programme. This was a prime example of the Commission's programme of working in partnership with the charitable sector and its representative bodies.

Supervision

The other immediate priority was to put in place arrangements for the "supervision" of (registered) charities, giving effect to the spirit of the Woodfield Report. Establishing a properly resourced unit in the Commission could be done immediately (drawing on additional "transitional" funding which the Treasury, with ill humour, allocated to the Commission in response to the report). However, full implementation inevitably took some years, since, quite apart from the need to develop staff to what was in effect a new role, it depended on the new powers and reporting framework established by the new legislation. In particular, it naturally took some time to establish standardized but proportionate reporting and accounting requirements, which would be the basis for Commission monitoring.

In 1996, the new statutory framework requiring charities to prepare and submit an annual report and accounts, and an annual return, according to the legislated financial thresholds, was brought into operation after consultation with the charitable sector. A new *Statement of Recommended Practice for Accounting by Charities* (SORP)[6] set out the substance of the reporting requirements. A committee of charity finance professionals led by the Commission and endorsed by the accountancy authorities after public consultation prepared the statement. That the accountancy world entrusted this process to the Commission was a mark of the Commission's progress in developing credible expertise, as was the conference the Commission staged to launch the SORP and the programme of presentations the Commission's accountants gave to promote it. As its name makes clear, the SORP does not set out mandatory legal requirements for reporting, but neither is it a set of "take it or leave it" suggestions for charity reporting. Charities are expected to follow the guidance set out in the SORP to demonstrate that their accounts should show "a true and fair view," and if they deviate from it, they are expected to show justification. This is to ensure that charities' reports and accounts are based on common definitions of principles so that their financial performance and standards can be compared, thereby giving effect to the need for charities to be genuinely accountable. The SORP has in effect three fundamental purposes: to make charities publicly accountable, to provide the Commission with the annual returns it needs to supervise charities, and, equally important, to be a basis for good management by charities. Thus it was designed to be useful to charities as well as being a vehicle for accountability and monitoring.

Once the new statutory returns started to come in, the Commission established a monitoring unit in the Liverpool office to ensure compliance with the requirements of the regulations. In fact, ensuring submission of the required returns from all charities was, and still remains, a challenging task. The unit's task was also, more substantively, to identify issues which called for follow-up action. Some might be issues of legal propriety, such as payment to trustees; more commonly it might be issues of governance and finances which appeared to risk the charity's viability. For the latter, the unit started an initiative of identifying factors which put charities at risk.

Right from its establishment, the ethos of the Commission's investigation division was to seek to identify charities at risk or in need of help and advice. As the *Annual Report 1993* put it, the aim was "to provide support and, where necessary, take investigative action; and, ultimately, to provide assurance to the charity sector and to the public as to the general good health of charities."[7] The balance was strongly on the side of supportive interventions wherever possible. For example, governance and administrative weaknesses which were identified through monitoring could normally be dealt with by informal discussions with the charity concerned, followed up by further monitoring if necessary, rather than by investigatory intervention. This reflects the fact that the powers of the Commission are "remedial," to put charities on a sound footing, not impose sanctions on trustees. It also reflects the fact that the cause of difficulties was generally not wilful misconduct and far less deliberate abuse. Typical management issues identified were lack of clarity over the responsibilities of trustees and management, for example, a dominant founder or director, inadequate oversight of finance and administration, and problems arising from the interaction between charities and non-charitable subsidiaries. The development of the Commission's supportive outreach work seemed the right way to respond. This led to the Commission establishing a systematic programme of visits to charities in this spirit.

Even where investigatory intervention was needed, the issues were principally of maladministration, covering a grey area from negligence to deliberate misconduct rather than fraudulent abuse. (Misuse of charities in pursuit of terrorism hardly surfaced in the 1990s, in stark contrast to the post-9/11 concerns.) The Commission did, however, demonstrate its ability to use its strengthened powers as soon as the new legislation came into force, in particular the power to appoint a receiver and manager to take over the responsibilities of trustees in serious cases, which supported the Commission's ethos of aiming to remedy problems rather than seeking sanctions. A good example of the early use of this new power concerned a charity providing residential care to people with mental disabilities. The charity had encountered administrative problems which put it at risk. The appointment of a receiver and manager made it possible to restructure the charity's management and financial systems.

Fundraising

Though not reaching the salience it has currently, fundraising became an increasing matter of concern to the Commission. The Charities Act 1992 had included provisions on fundraising but these did not affect the Commission directly (and therefore were not consolidated into the 1993 Act). The Commission became "increasingly concerned about fundraising carried out by organisations which are not charities, but which give the public reason to think that they are."[8] The Commission took the view, endorsed by the courts, that its powers of investigation could be used in such cases. The 1998 report cites the case of a commercial company which used teams of rose sellers to tour pubs, clubs, and restaurants encouraging people to purchase flowers and give donations to charity. Working with the police, convictions were obtained for theft.

Guidance

The development of guidance material was an essential complement to the monitoring process, and the Commission initiated a programme of guidance booklets tackling issues which were giving rise to problems. A good example, which bears out the relationship between fundamental legal requirements and good practice, was the guidance produced, after consultation with the charitable sector, on reserves. Lack of reserves could obviously endanger the financial security of a charity; on the other hand, accumulating reserves beyond the charity's needs was misuse of charitable funds, but charity law merely dictates that charity trustees have a duty to use their resources for their charitable purposes. Guidance on prudent financial management could not—should not—prescribe specific amounts to be held as reserves. The Commission's aim was to develop sufficient awareness and a judicious balance between prudence and risk taking among trustees in whom responsibility for financial management, and answerability, ultimately lies. The Commission did suggest guidelines that charities should normally aim to have reserves equivalent to between two years and three months expenditure, though even that would be subject to judicious exceptions. However, in consultation, the general view of the sector was that even that was too prescriptive, so the Commission focused on the need for charities to have an explicit policy on reserves which the trustees should be able to justify.

Schemes and Orders

The traditional work of the Charity Commission, giving consents and making schemes, continued on a reduced basis following the implementation of the legislation to give effect to the Woodfield reform programme. A significant change was the emphasis on supporting charities to meet the changing circumstances of the modern world (the Commission's aim of delivering a framework fit for current needs). Issues such as facilitating mergers between charities which could address complementary aims better as a single entity became a more significant part of the Commission's programme, supported by greater flexibility over modifying charitable objectives. This applied also to modernizing the constitutions and even the purposes of charities.

The need for an active approach is well illustrated by the case of the Huntingdon Commons and Lammas Rights charities. By the 1990s, the small number of freemen of Huntingdon qualifying for benefit under these ancient charities were each receiving over £30,000 a year, which was a situation the Commission pronounced, with masterly understatement, "to be inconsistent with the application of charitable funds"! A scheme was made to widen the purposes of the charities for the general charitable benefit of Huntingdon.[9] The old common law principle of cy près, by which old trusts which became unrealizable might be amended to the most similar realizable purpose, had been somewhat relaxed by the 1992 legislation (a process taken much further in 2006). As a result, the Commission could support charities frustrated by anachronistic purposes in providing an objective more suited to modern-day needs, without having to incur the expense of court application. A striking example was the modernization of the Bridge House Trust, the ancient City of London charity which maintained bridges to the City. The Commission was able to provide the Trust with a wider set of purposes making it a major grant giver for charitable purposes throughout London.

Campaigning

While political campaigning in breach of charity law gave rise to few investigations numerically, it was a source of great controversy. The right of the voluntary sector to engage in public debate over issues of concern to them is rightly regarded as vitally important. Charity law appeared to be very restrictive. The Commission's guidance, based on court judgments, in particular—unusually recent in charity law practice!—in the Amnesty case of 1981,[10] virtually prohibited engagement by charities in the political process. A quote from the guidance the Commission issued after the Amnesty judgement exemplifies the point: "Charities, whether they operate in this country or overseas, must avoid seeking to influence or remedy those causes of poverty which lie in the social, economic and political structures of countries and communities." This was derived from the clear conclusion of the courts that charities could not be political—fair enough, if that meant party political, but the courts defined political as concerning the law and government policy. Given the increasing focus of NGOs seeking to tackle poverty on tackling causes and not just alleviating consequences, this was a significant threat to policies of aid charities. A complaint arising from political controversy over the role NGOs played in Third World issues led to a Commission investigation which found Oxfam to have breached the constraints of the law by taking a critical position towards policies and practices of certain governments in countries where it had anti-poverty programmes. While the outcome of the Commission's formal investigation was no more than a warning, the inhibiting effect, and unwelcome publicity, were very damaging.

In response, NCVO set up a working group representing charities to seek reforms. The Commission engaged with the NCVO review and with the Parliamentary All-Party Group on Charity seeking a way to interpret the law which allowed proper scope for the sector's role of contributing to, and influencing, public policy and government practice. This proved a demanding challenge, solved by distinguishing between the charitable purposes of charities, which could not be political, and the activities charities undertook to achieve their purposes. The activities must not be party political but, provided they were directed at achieving the charitable purpose, they could be political in the wide sense of charity law. Charities could thus contribute to discussions of public policy and the law, and could engage confidently in campaigning against government policies where they thought them damaging to the charitable aims they were pursuing.

Both the sector and politicians welcomed the interpretation promulgated in Commission guidance. It still forms the basis for the balance struck between the need for charities to keep the confidence of the public by avoiding identification with political parties and the importance of their being able to engage vigorously and without fear of "regulatory" restraint in public affairs. Indeed, the cautious formulation of the balance in the Commission's initial guidance came to seem unduly restrictive, but the issue remains one of lively dispute. It is a notable example of the Commission's role in actively developing the legal framework and not simply confining itself to passive interpretation of the legal inheritance.

Review of the Register

Perhaps the most radical initiative which emerged from the modernization programme was the Review of the Register. Certainly, it provoked a good deal of controversy, at least among charity lawyers. Concern over the concept of charity, and the ancient common law basis for determining it, had been expressed on and off for many years. However, equally, there were anxieties, particularly at the political level, about stirring up controversial issues, notably charitable status for elite public schools. (This concern was shown to be fully vindicated by the controversies which even the limited attempt to tackle the issue as undertaken in the 2006 Act provoked.) The consensus among charity lawyers was that the common law system was, in principle, well able to meet the needs of the modern world. This was based on the contention that the courts had the power to apply modern thinking to the framework inherited from, and developed out of, the Preamble of the 1601 Charitable Uses Act. In practice, few cases came to court, but at the time that the Woodfield Report was set up, there was no effective lobby for legislative reform. So the 1993 Act remained silent on the issue.

This presented the Commission with a dilemma. Difficulty over getting charitable status for bodies tackling issues which did not fit directly into the inherited framework was a matter of concern in the voluntary sector. Moreover, the Commission's professed aim of providing a framework which encouraged charitable activity for the modern world challenged it to use its registration responsibilities constructively. The Commission had done this on a piecemeal basis before the modernization programme started. A notable example was accepting that bodies seeking to promote racial and community harmony, manifestly in the public interest in twentieth-century Britain, ought to be able to benefit from charitable status. The process of reforming the Register prompted more systematic thought about the need for an effective modernizing mechanism and the part the Commission should play in exercising its registration function.

The dilemma continued to arise in the day-to-day registration work of the Commission alongside the modernization programme. Some significant decisions revealed the approach the Commission evolved, rooted in the charity law process of basing the determination of charitable status on the inheritance of court decisions developed from the Preamble to the 1601 Act, but recognizing it had to acknowledge changing needs and circumstances. Key decisions included accepting the public interest benefit in having organizations promote ethical standards in business and corporate responsibility, including giving support to whistleblowers. Another example accepted the growing importance of fair trade in aid policy, through such initiatives as the "fair trade" mark. The corollary of accepting new issues was the question of issues no longer relevant to the public interest in the modern world. The key decision in this respect concerned gun clubs, charitable on the old view that they supported the country's defence capacity. The Commission decided that this principle was no longer sustainable in the modern world.

These decisions, particularly the Commission's use of its power to remove bodies from the Register of Charities, prompted concern among charity lawyers. The Commission recognized the need to set out a principled rationale for its approach rather than leaving it to case-by-case statements, especially as the computerization programme gave it a unique opportunity, and indeed obligation, to review the Register as a whole. Wider public interest in what constituted charity was also relevant. This was encapsulated in the recommendation of the wide-ranging review of the state of charity undertaken by the Deakin Commission, set up by NCVO. Its report published in 1996 recommended that the law on charitable status should be modernized and simplified on the basis of what, in modern-day circumstances, constituted public benefit.[11] While the new (Labour) government was notably support-ive of the voluntary sector and embraced recommendations of the Deakin Report, such as the development of a "compact" between the public and charitable sectors, it was reluctant to tackle the controversial issue of chari-table status head on. Clearly, the Commission could not reform the law as such, but it could develop the agenda for reform by demonstrating what could, and could not, be achieved under the law as it stood. Accordingly, in April 1999, after a lengthy consultation period, the Commission launched a systematic programme of reviewing charitable status and the existing mechanism for determining it.[12] Given the modernization and computeriza-tion of the Register, there was a generally accepted need for some form of process to ensure that the renewed Register was accurate. By contrast, how this process should be conducted, and in particular just what approach the Commission should adopt, was contested.

The Commission started from the premise that the credibility of the Reg-ister was vital for public confidence in charity and its role in the modern world. This reflected the fact that the decisions of the Commission to accept the charitable status of voluntary organizations and include them on the Register constituted in law authoritative confirmation that the body was a charity. The Commission affirmed that, in exercising this function "within the law," it exercised the powers of the courts. As noted at the outset of this chapter, this was in fact the original rationale for creating the Commis-sion. However, this reaffirmation at the end of the twentieth century proved controversial among charity lawyers. That the Commission should follow court judgments was accepted on all sides (though this meant that some of its decisions, for example, in relation to charitable status for amateur sports bodies, were very cautious). However, what proved contentious was the approach the Commission should adopt where court judgments were lack-ing, or old, and therefore arguably superseded (as some did indeed argue in relation to sports). The Commission was clear that public confidence in the arrangements for determining charitable status depended on its ability to keep pace with changing needs. In a (legally) ideal world, it might well have been preferable for the courts to be engaged regularly to determine new issues. The fact was, however, that there were few new court judgments, largely because the Commission dealt with the determination of charitable status through applications for registration. Even if applicants who were refused registration wanted to appeal to the courts, the cost was usually too great a deterrent. The proposal that a "suitors' fund" should be estab-lished to finance appeals to determine significant cases out of public funds was unsurprisingly rejected out of hand by government. (The more practical solution of a review mechanism was finally adopted with the establishment of the Charity Tribunal under the 2006 Act.)

Accordingly, it seemed both right and desirable that the Commission should apply the principles laid down by the courts for applying changing circumstances in interpreting the inheritance of court judgments to new issues. Lord Wilberforce had summarized the principle, saying court decisions "have to keep the law as to charities moving as new ideas arise or old ones become obsolete or satisfied."[13] This approach was applied in a series of "thematic" reviews, which proved a very powerful mechanism for addressing issues not satisfactorily covered explicitly in previous court judgments. A high point was the Commission's acceptance of human rights, previously regarded as political, as a proper charitable purpose in 2003. (It might be noted that the very notion of setting out principles for determining applications by subject was itself regarded by some as an improper deviation from the legal "case-by-case" principle.)

The role of public opinion was another source of controversy. Determining charitable status by an opinion poll of "Joe Public," as a leading charity law commentator disparaged the Commission's approach, was improper. Not that this was the Commission's approach, but the need to balance public acceptance of the legal framework for charity with principles of public interest and benefit, extending to minority and unpopular issues, was, and remains, an important issue in charity registration and regulation at large. Alongside addressing the substance of what purposes were charitable in the modern world, the review included a statement of "the essential characteristics of charity," focusing on public benefit, independence, and being non-political. A spin-off of this was the development of a statement of the hallmarks of a well-run charity, in effect guidance on good governance for trustees to apply and for the Commission to use as a check for its monitoring role.[14] This document became a key statement of what the Commission looked for in reviewing charities' governance arrangements.

Conclusion

By the turn of the millennium, the modernization process had been going on for a dozen years, but it could not be regarded as complete. That the Commission had undergone a fundamental change was undeniable, and the commitment of the Commission's staff to the upheavals involved was greatly to their credit. To a greater or lesser extent, the transformation was welcomed. In particular, the interactive relationship between the Commission and charities, aided by the computerization programme, was very beneficial. Inevitably, there were critical voices, reflecting a scepticism towards the ethos the Commission had adopted, in particular, the contention that it should be primarily an enforcement body. This view of the Commission is, for reasons set out in the body of this chapter, a fundamental misconception of its role, and labelling it "the regulator of charities" encourages this misconception. The intention in giving this account of the first dozen years of the Commission's modernization has been to correct that misconception.

Notes

1 I am grateful for the comments of Lindsay Driscoll and other friends and colleagues from my time at the Charity Commission.
2 Philip Woodfield et al., *Efficiency Scrutiny of the Supervision of Charities* (London: Charity Commission, 1987).
3 Charity Commission, *Annual Report of the Charity Commissioners for England and Wales 1997* (London: HMSO, 1998), Annex A.
4 Charity Commission, *Annual Report of the Charity Commissioners for England and Wales 1993* (London: HMSO, 1994), Introduction.
5 Charity Commission, *The Essential Trustee: What You Need to Know*, Detailed Guidance No. CC3 (London: Charity Commission, 1997).
6 Charity Commission, *Statement of Recommended Practice for Accounting by Charities* (London: Charity Commission, 1997).
7 Charity Commission, *Annual Report 1993*.
8 Charity Commission, *Annual Report of the Charity Commissioners for England and Wales 1998* (London: HMSO, 1999), 23.
9 Charity Commission, *Annual Report 1993*, paras 103ff.
10 *McGovern v Attorney-General* [1982] Ch 321.
11 National Council on Voluntary Organisations, *Meeting the Challenge of Change: Voluntary Action into the 21st Century, Report of the Commission on the Future of the Voluntary Sector* (London: NCVO, 1996).
12 Charity Commission, *The Review of the Register of Charities* (London: Charity Commission, 1999).
13 *Scottish Burial Reform and Cremation Society v Glasgow City Corporation* [1968] AC 138, 154.
14 Charity Commission, *The Hallmarks of a Well-Run Charity*, Detailed Guidance No. CC60 (London: Charity Commission, 1999).

3 The Reforming Regulator

Lindsay Driscoll

Introduction

The period following 2000 saw a continuation and expansion of the reforms to the Charity Commission introduced by the 1993 Charities Act but with a change in language as the Commission was now universally referred to as the regulator of charities. The primary objective of the Commission to increase public trust and confidence in charities remained the same, but debate continued as to how this could best be achieved and the proper role or roles of the Commission.

The period from 2000 to 2016 saw significant changes, and this chapter examines important issues including whether it was possible for the Commission to be both friend and policeman, to be both adviser and regulator. If all were possible and appropriate, what should be the balance between them and how did this fit in with self-regulation and the role of umbrella bodies, and was co-regulation the answer? What was the Commission's role with regard to the effectiveness of charities? For most of this period, a broad approach to regulation prevailed, with equal weight placed on the strands of support and effectiveness, compliance and accountability. Support and advice services grew with increased engagement with the sector, whilst the approach to compliance cases was reassessed with a decrease in the number of statutory inquiries. Since 2012, there has been a change in the balance, with the emphasis now firmly on compliance, influenced by a substantial cut in resources; criticism from several sources, particularly parliamentary committees, that the Commission was insufficiently robust; and external factors such as the counter-terrorism agenda.

Independence from government—of both charities, particularly as they took on more public services, and the Commission, as concerned its legal status and governance—remained an important theme. The Commission's independence from the sector was also an issue: how far should its role to champion the sector extend, and did the increased emphasis on support and engagement and closer links with charities compromise its independence? The governance of the Commission, linked to its own transparency and accountability, came to the fore, again mirroring greater awareness of these issues in charities.

The major event was the passing of the Charities Act 2006 (the Act), which it has been said was subject to more consultation and parliamentary scrutiny than any other piece of legislation in the United Kingdom. This Act made changes to the structure of the Commission, modernised aspects of charity law, established a tribunal for appeals against Commission decisions, introduced a new legal structure for charities, and, for the first time, established a statutory definition of charity. However, all this was overshadowed by the debate on the public benefit requirement, particularly as it applied to independent schools. Political activities of charities continued to be a hot topic, with calls from the sector for a change in the law and the publication of new guidance by the Commission in 2008. And a new factor influencing the stance of regulation was government concerns about charities' links to funding terrorism.

Since 2000, there have been four different chief charity commissioners (later, chairs) with very different backgrounds: John Stoker, a career civil servant; Geraldine Peacock, a former charity leader; Dame Suzi Leather, with a background of numerous public appointments; and William Shawcross, a writer. Changes in chief commissioners brought with them changes in style at the Commission. Under Geraldine Peacock, there was a major rebranding exercise with the crown replaced by a T-shirt[1] indicative of a new closer relationship with the sector and the communities they served, summed up in the new vision of "Charity working at the heart of society." Under William Shawcross, the stance of the Commission has been that of a robust regulator.

The Role of the Commission

After the reforms of the 1990s, the beginning of the noughties saw a high mark in the breadth of the Commission's role made possible by the freeing up of resources under the previous reforms. New thinking on the role of the Commission was explained in the publication in 2003 of *The Charity Commission and Regulation*,[2] which set out a broad approach to regulation covering compliance, accountability, and effectiveness, all considered essential for maintaining and increasing public trust and confidence.

> Our approach is to regulate so as to promote compliance with charity law and to equip charities to work better. Our work should enable charities to maximise their potential and enhance their accountability to donors and those who benefit. . . . The end result should be increased public trust and confidence.[3]

The three strands carried equal weight, and regulation was given a broad meaning and seen as a continuum, with advice and support as a proactive means of promoting compliance on one end of the spectrum and formal inquiries with use of statutory powers on the other end. This approach was followed in the Commission's Strategic Review of 2005, which set out the four heads of mission as follows: enabling charities to maximise their impact, ensuring compliance with legal obligations, encouraging innovation and effectiveness, and championing the public interest in charity. A presentation of the time refers to the twin approaches of "steel and empathy." Underpinning the review was the concept of proportionate, risk-based regulation. Action should be proportionate to the issues and risk involved and take account of the capacity of the organisation to comply. Changes made to introduce proportionality included minimising regulation for smaller charities by increasing thresholds for both registration and reporting and audit requirements. The Commission was reorganised to achieve this with the introduction of a small charities unit using a light-touch approach for charities with an income under £10,000, a large charities unit pursuing more active engagement with charities having an income over £10 million, and fast-track self-certification for straightforward consents.

Long consultations leading up to the Act continued the debate on the reconciliation of the advice and compliance roles. The National Council for Voluntary Organisations (NCVO) in particular argued that the primary function of the Commission should be compliance, leaving the major part of the support role to umbrella bodies. The Strategy Unit Report published in 2001[4] recommended that the Commission should have clear strategic objectives in statute. Following this, the Act set out five objectives:

- to increase public trust and confidence in charities;
- to promote awareness of the operation of the public benefit requirement;
- to promote compliance by charity trustees with their legal obligations in exercising control and management of the administration of their charities;
- to promote the effective use of charitable resources; and
- to enhance the accountability of charities to the donors, beneficiaries, and general public.

Later, these broad objectives were criticised by the Public Administration Select Committee (PASC)[5] as being "far too vague and aspirational in character. . . . The 2006 Act represented an ambition which the Commission could never fulfil even before budget cuts were initiated."[6] The Commission's functions and powers were also drafted very broadly in the Act. The Strategy Unit Report recommended that the advisory role should be defined in statute to give a clearer focus on regulatory issues, but the Act failed to include any specific reference to advice, instead relying on a wide function to encourage and facilitate better administration of charities.

Advice Work

Advice work was expanded through a number of different methods and media. Casework was continued for detailed ongoing advice to individual charities. A new call centre approach, Charity Commission Direct, was introduced for one-off telephone advice, and the website was enhanced to include more guidance. The number and scope of publications were expanded, and the design and style changed in line with the rebranding to be more user-friendly. All new publications were translated into plain English, and many included cheerful photographs of people in the community. New publications included not only regulatory guidance such as that on political activities but also publications setting out good practice and more general advice on such topics as insurance and mergers. This gave rise to criticism, particularly by charity lawyers, on the long-standing issue that, in its publications, the Commission failed to make a clear enough distinction between the musts and the shoulds—the regulatory requirements and good practice.

The support and advice role was enhanced by the engagement and partnership initiatives assisted by the new eagerness of Commission staff and commissioners to get out and meet charity trustees. Up to 600 review visits were carried out each year when Commission staff sat down with trustees and senior staff of charities to discuss governance and other issues; an engagement programme was introduced, which saw commissioners and directors go into large and high-profile charities to meet the chair and chief executive; and the Commission took part in conferences, workshops, and clinics round the country. All these initiatives were very much a two-way process and increased the knowledge and understanding of the Commission as much as that of the charity trustees.

Accountability Role

A new method of increasing accountability was the introduction in 2005 of the Summary Information Return (SIR) for larger charities, with the returns posted on the Register of Charities. This had been recommended in the Strategy Unit Report, with the aim to focus on impact and enable comparisons to be made between similar organisations. When the draft form was first introduced, it was presented as an opportunity for charities to "tell their story" and explain in simple language what they were set up to do, how they were doing it, and what their impact was. This was not met with much enthusiasm from the charities, who often failed to see it as an opportunity to communicate to the public but rather as another bureaucratic form. In light of these reactions, the SIR was revised and relaunched in an attempt to increase acceptance of it. It was later abolished in 2013 and more focused information was obtained through additional questions in the Annual Return. The 2015 Annual Return included new questions on how much funding charities had received from government grants and contracts, their pay policy, and financial controls.

Another part of each year's Annual Return requires charities to confirm that any serious incidents which took place in the previous year have been reported. Serious incident reporting has become an important regulatory tool for the Commission. The definition of a serious incident set out in guidance is very wide and includes serious harm to beneficiaries, significant financial loss to the charity, serious criminality, and other significant non-compliance and breaches of trust or abuse which could impact significantly on public trust and confidence in charity.[7] As a matter of good practice, the Commission requires any serious incidents to be reported to them immediately, and in September 2014, the Commission issued an alert stating that failure to report a serious incident may be considered mismanagement and lead to regulatory action.

Another accountability initiative "Accounts aren't optional," the first major campaign to get more charities to file accounts on time, was launched in October 2003 when the Commission targeted lawyers, accountants, local authorities, and grant givers, as well as charity trustees.[8] The need to file accounts on time has remained a major theme for over a decade. The approach was later toughened up, first by naming and shaming defaulters in red on the register of charities, and more recently by the opening of statutory inquiries into "Double Defaulters." The different initiatives have met with some success: in 2015–16, 87 per cent of accounts were filed on time, up from 75 per cent in 2007–08. The work on accounting standards for charities continued with the publication of the revised edition of the Charity Statement of Recommended Practice by Charities (SORP) in 2005.

Compliance Work

Compliance remained an essential strand of the Commission's work, but the approach changed with the decision to open formal statutory inquiries only when legal powers and sanctions, such as those to freeze bank accounts or to remove or suspend charity trustees, were required. This led to a decrease in the number of inquiries opened and use of legal powers. Other compliance cases were conducted outside the inquiry framework.

The Commission's role in investigating charities' links to terrorism became increasingly important. One of the first investigations was that of the North London Central Park Mosque involving Abu Hamza,[9] and cases increased after the attacks of September 2001 in the United States. The first operational guidance on charities and terrorism was published in 2003, reaffirming the central position of the Commission in investigating links to terrorism and enforcing law and policy in this area. A landmark case was that of Interpal in 2003, when the Commission asserted its position as an independent, evidence-based regulator by refusing to follow the United States' lead and take action against Interpal without clear evidence.

The temperature rose in 2007. The year before, the government had announced a review into the financing of terrorism by charities, and to pre-empt this, NCVO published their own report.[10] This argued that existing regulation was sufficient to deal with the threat and the Commission's independence from government must be protected to shore up confidence in its ability to take a proportionate and impartial response. A consultation document published in May 2007[11] made a number of recommendations on how the Commission could be more proactive in its work involving charity links to terrorists. These included working more closely with other agencies and enhancing its investigative function. The document drew attention to the Commission's ad hoc relationships with other agencies involved in counterterrorism, the desk-based approach, and the fact that investigators were generalists, with experience in charity law rather than terrorist financing. The Commission's response in August 2007 stressed that actual instances of terrorist involvement and abuse of charities were extremely low in number, but when they did occur, the Commission was uniquely placed to deal with them. The response concluded with a robust defence of the Commission's independence and approach to regulation: "The Commission will continue to . . . take a balanced approach which is evidence and risk-based, targeted and proportionate . . . and maintain its strategic and operational independence in line with its statutory remit."[12]

The Commission went on to publish its counterterrorism strategy in December 2007; it took a four-pronged approach, focusing on raising awareness, oversight, and supervision of charities in high-risk areas, cooperation with law enforcement agencies and other government regulators, and intervention to disrupt the use of charities for terrorist purposes. In his book on the effect of counterterrorism policy and law in civil society,[13] Mark Sidel praises the central role of the Commission in this area and points to the value of having an organisation with detailed knowledge of the sector which works with other agencies where appropriate and also works constructively with the sector to improve governance arrangements and financial and administrative controls.

A by-product of the work on charities' links to financing of terrorism was the Commission's International Programme. This was a response to the recommendations of the Financial Action Task Force on the regulation of NGOs.[14] The Programme worked with regulators in countries identified as high risk to strengthen their regulation of NGOs. The work was based on the Commission's own regulatory stance, and the model used, known as the Regulatory Bridge, drew on the interrelationship of the building blocks of an effective regulatory system: the sector, self-accountability, government, and public and funders.

Regulation, Self-Regulation, and Co-regulation

The last fifteen years have seen an increase in self-regulation initiatives on the part of umbrella and intermediary bodies and increased partnership working between these bodies and the Commission. The Strategy Unit Report had a short and rather dismissive section on self-regulation, stating,

> Whilst there have been some promising attempts at self regulation
> (including fundraising, accreditation and quality standards) very often

these have failed to win sufficient sector-wide support or impetus. An understandable reluctance to adopt imperfect initiatives has on occasion led not to their subsequent development and introduction but to resistance to change and maintenance of the status quo.[15]

Earlier, failed attempts at forming generalist accreditation bodies were replaced by a quality standards approach, and here NCVO led the way by setting up the Quality Standards Task Force in 1997. In time, this resulted in many umbrella bodies adopting quality standards for their member bodies. An example of the partnership working between the Commission and sector bodies was the Commission's programme of endorsing quality assessment systems.[16] It produced criteria for endorsement including requirements that the systems should be consistent with their own guidance on good practice, *The Hallmarks of an Effective Charity*,[17] and should cover all legal requirements for a charity.

A key part of any quality standards framework is governance, which is also a major focus of the Commission in line with the primary legal responsibility of charity trustees under charity law. Over the years, a significant proportion of cases of misconduct or mismanagement investigated by the Commission have included weak or defective governance as one of the causes. In 2004, the Commission updated its key guidance on the legal responsibilities of trustees,[18] which remains core regulatory guidance. To complement this guidance and cover good practice, a consortium of umbrella bodies from the sector came together in 2005 to produce the Code of Governance for the Voluntary and Community Sector[19] conceived as being "by the sector, for the sector." This received the support of the Commission, and it has continued as a good example of regulation and self-regulation working side by side.

It is the area of fundraising which has been the most problematic. The Commission has never played a major role in the regulation of fundraising, only getting involved when there is misconduct or mismanagement on the part of charity trustees. Concerns about poor practices in fundraising by charities were addressed in the Strategy Unit Report by a recommendation that the government should support a new fundraising body to develop self-regulation. This would be based on a new voluntary code of practice with a power for the minister to introduce statutory regulation if self-regulation failed. The Fundraising Standards Body was set up in 2006 to take on the self-regulation role, with membership on a voluntary basis. Its success was evaluated in Lord Hodgson's Review of the Charities Act in 2012,[20] which made a number of recommendations for improvement but concluded that membership should not be compulsory and self-regulation should continue, subject to a further review in five years' time. In fact, a review came sooner when, in summer 2015, cases of malpractice in fundraising led to a crisis in public trust and confidence. The government speedily commissioned a review of the regulation of fundraising by charities, and the resulting report[21] made far-reaching recommendations, including the setting up of a single new regulator, covering all types of fundraising and working with other regulators, including the Commission, in a co-regulatory approach.[22]

Co-regulation had been introduced by the Act for some exempt charities such as universities, where a principal regulator has primary responsibility for regulation, with some aspects carried out jointly with the Commission. Lord Hodgson's Review[23] recommended that other groups of charities would benefit from a flexible form of co-regulation with another existing regulator or umbrella body and possibilities could range from signposting to full delegation. However, many umbrella bodies rejected the idea of delegated powers of regulation, as they believed it would lead to potential conflicts of interest and role confusion.

The Status of the Commission

It has often been said that an important strength of the Commission is its independence, both from the government and the sector. The 2005 mission statement of the Commission stressed its status as an independent regulator. However, independence is as much a matter of perception as reality, and during the passage of the Charities Bill, there was heated discussion on how independence from government could be strengthened, both in terms of legal status and governance. Some argued that independence was not consistent with its current status as a non-ministerial government department. During the debates in the House of Lords, the Minister Baroness Scotland stated, "Under the Bill [the Commission] will remain an independent regulator completely free from government control."[24] The response to this from Lord Phillips was that "the public will not believe that if the Charity Commission has non-ministerial departmental status it is completely free of influence from or behind the arras of government or indeed senior opposition politicians."[25] Other models were considered, but after considerable debate, no change was made to the Commission's status. As a compromise, the question of independence was partially addressed by the introduction of a provision that "in the exercise of its functions the Commission shall not be subject to the direction or control of any Minister of the Crown or other government department."[26]

The NCVO Discussion Paper on Charity Commission Independence[27] published in 2015 looked again at alternative structures for the Commission, but concluded that although alternatives had considerable advantages, none of the structures would be entirely appropriate, and there was not a strong enough case to warrant constitutional change. Although the formal legal status of the Commission was unchanged by the Act, the structure was changed by recreating it as a body corporate rather than a body of individual commissioners. The Act provided for an enlarged board of up to nine members, including the chair, all appointed by the Minister as before. The board had to include two lawyers and have, between its members, experience in charity law, charity accounts, operation and regulation of charities of different sizes, and descriptions and conditions in Wales. The appointment of the chair and members of the Commission has remained an important factor in the question of independence from government. Until 2012, all appointments were made by the Minister following a process of open competition. When William Shawcross was appointed as chair in 2012, the public appointments procedure had been changed with the introduction of an additional process of a pre-appointment hearing to examine the preferred candidate before the PASC. The Committee members voted on party lines, giving rise to concerns as to the politicisation of the appointment. This was not a fresh issue, as similar allegations had been made against Dame Suzi Leather's appointment. The potential politicisation of chair appointments was addressed in the NCVO Report of 2015, with the recommendation that there should be greater parliamentary involvement in the process to secure increased transparency and better accountability.

Following recommendations in the Strategy Unit Report, the governance of the Commission was changed from a unitary to a non-executive board. The role of the chief charity commissioner was split between the new chair and chief executive of the Commission, and the executive directors now attended board meetings in an advisory capacity. A governance review was carried out to consider the practical effect of these changes, leading to the Charity Commission Governance Framework in 2007. This set out in some detail the respective roles of the chair and chief executive and the relationship between the board and the executive. At the time, the boundaries were observed rigorously, but the issue was reopened in a National Audit Office (NAO) Report of 2015,[28] which raised concerns that the board had become too involved in the Commission's operations.

To increase the transparency and accountability of the Commission, an annual public meeting and bimonthly open board meetings were introduced. The governance framework included a commitment that all major decisions on the interpretation of charity law, Commission policy and practice, and other substantive issues would be made in public, only reserving confidential items for a closed session. Considerable time was taken in planning for the introduction of the open meetings with visits to similar meetings held by other public bodies. To encourage attendance, meetings were scheduled around the country and advertised directly to charities and on the website. However, despite these efforts, attendance was low, and they were later discontinued and replaced by quarterly public meetings in different parts of the country for presentations by the Commission and questions from the public.

The Charities Act 2006 Definition of Charity

The initiative for charity law reform came from the voluntary sector itself with the Deakin Report,[29] followed by the report of the Charity Law Reform Advisory Group in 2001.[30] The same year, Tony Blair commissioned a much wider review of the law and regulation of charities by the Performance and Innovation Unit (later renamed the Strategy Unit). This was part of the third-way agenda of partnership with the voluntary sector and included objectives to modernise the legal framework for charities, decrease red tape, and, again, increase public confidence.

The Charity Law Reform Advisory Group Report examined the case for a new definition of charity but rejected both a wide definition and a statutory codification in favour of application of the same strong public benefit test across all four heads of charity. The main objection to a new definition was stated to be that measures "to simplify the law, for example, by codifying it would inevitably reduce the flexibility inherent in the current system and this would be too great a price to pay."[31] This argument was not accepted by the Strategy Unit Report published in September 2002, which was concerned with both flexibility and clarity and recommended a statutory definition with an expanded list of purposes which would "make the overall framework much clearer both for charities and the public."[32] Their list included nine specific purposes and one catch-all, extending the list to 12 purposes in the final version of the Act. The Strategy Unit also recommended introducing a single public benefit test for all charities, reforms of the Commission, a Charity Appeals Tribunal, and a new incorporated legal structure for charities. The government's response, published a year later,[33] accepted most of the recommendations. The resulting draft bill was published in 2004 and went through yet another period of scrutiny by a joint committee of both Houses, with further opportunity for written and oral submissions. The Act finally received royal assent in November 2006.

The definition in the Act was essentially a restatement of the existing common law position with some clarifications, rewordings, and minor extensions. Several purposes already accepted by the Commission, both under the Review of the Register and in individual registration cases, were included in the list, such as the promotion of religious or racial harmony, or equality and diversity, and the advancement of human rights and conflict resolution. A twofold test for a purpose to be charitable was set out:[34] it must be both within the listed descriptions of purposes and for the public benefit. To retain flexibility, the list included a catch-all provision to include any purpose recognised as charitable under existing charity law and a stepping-stone approach to include any purpose which may reasonably be regarded as analogous to or within the spirit of any such purpose.[35]

The introduction of the statutory definition has not seen a significant number of new particular purposes accepted by the Commission for registration. The extension of the advancement of amateur sports to include those involving mental skill or exertion has seen bridge and chess clubs accepted. The wide wording of some new heads such as the "advancement of citizenship and community development"[36] and "the advancement of the arts, culture, heritage or sciences"[37] suggested an extension, but so far, there has been little development. One reason for this has been that the

Commission has taken the view that the Act includes a list of "descriptions" of purposes, not all of which are charitable purposes in their own right.

Public Benefit

The thorny issue of public benefit was the greatest challenge to the Commission board throughout this period, and at times, it appeared to be all consuming. Substantial resources in terms of staff and board time were expended in addressing a complex, controversial, and, at times, political issue without the necessary statutory underpinning. When the matter was considered by the PASC post-legislative scrutiny in 2013, they concluded,

> In our view it is for Parliament to resolve the issues of criteria for charitable status and public benefit and not the Charity Commission which is a branch of the executive. In this respect the Charities Act 2006 has been an administrative and financial disaster for the Charity Commission and for the charities involved, absorbing vast amounts of energy and commitment as well as money.[38]

Changes to the public benefit test were first proposed in the NCVO consultation document[39] and then taken up in the Strategy Unit Report, which recommended that the Commission should identify charities likely to charge high fees and undertake a rolling programme to check that provision was made for wider access.[40] The example given was that independent schools charging high fees would need to make significant provision for those who could not afford the school fees. Straight away, the focus moved to the charity status, and particularly tax breaks, of independent schools, for long a political touchstone of the left. From then on, throughout the consultations and during the passage of the Bill, all the public focus was on independent schools. This led to extensive coverage in the press on what was often referred to as the Schools Bill and protracted debate in parliament.

The first stage of the public benefit debate turned on the question of whether there should be any definition on the face of the Bill. The Commission's position was that the removal of the presumption of public benefit would not make a substantial difference, and any duty to review the public benefit of charities should be clearly defined in legislation with clear criteria. The matter came to a head in August 2004 when the Commission was called to give evidence before the Scrutiny Committee. The disagreement between the Home Office and the Commission then became public in what the chair of the Committee referred to as "a dog's breakfast."[41] He also spoke of the Home Office "twisting arms."[42] The matter was resolved by the so-called concordat setting out agreed principles from the Privy Council case of *Re Resch's Will Trusts*,[43] which, together with the abolition of the presumption, would be the basis of strengthening the public benefit requirement. At the heart of all the discussion was the true meaning of the judgment in Resch's case, which concerned the charitable status of a fee-charging hospital. It was studied and re-studied, and some lawyers even claimed to have a copy by their bedside in the hope of inspiration, but as Lord Phillips said in the House of Lords Debate, "Re Resch is a blancmange—it is a foundation for nothing but a sinking feeling."[44] Discussion continued in the parliamentary debate as to the need for a full or partial definition of public benefit, similar to that in the Scottish legislation. An amendment to that effect failed, but, in an attempt to shore up the public benefit requirement, a new statutory objective for the Commission was added to promote awareness and understanding of the operation of the public benefit requirement, and a duty was placed on charity trustees to have regard for the Commission's public benefit guidance. In addition, trustees were required by SORP to use the Trustees Annual Report to confirm compliance with their new duty and explain how their activities provided public benefit.

Once the Act had been passed, work started on the high-level and sub-sector guidance on the public benefit requirement. Lacking a statutory definition, the Commission set out its approach to

> interpret [the] case law in the context of modern circumstances, taking into consideration the new framework for charitable status set out in the Act, the existing case law, and the fact that the presumption of public benefit for some types of charities [had] been removed . . . [and] also . . . the impact of the Human Rights Act.[45]

Another sometimes conflicting strand was the concern that public benefit should chime with wider public understanding of the term, again raising questions of the role of Joe Public in the development of charity law. Initiatives to explore and test the concept of public benefit in the modern setting were tried including the convening of a Citizens Forum where a representative sample of 50 members of the public met for a day and were taken through the main issues and voted on them. Meetings were also held with faith-based charities to explore the practical application of public benefit principles to religion. The high-level guidance was finally published in January 2008 and the sub-sector guidance at the end of that year. A rolling programme of public benefit assessments followed. Predictably, within five years, there were three cases on public benefit in the Tribunal in the three most controversial areas: independent schools, benevolent funds with a restricted beneficial class, and churches with limited access.

The first case on the Commission's Public Benefit Guidance was brought in 2010, both as a reference from the Attorney General and an application for judicial review by the Independent Schools Council, with the NCVO and an ad hoc Education Review Group as interveners.[46] The result could be said to be a draw: whilst the Upper Tribunal quashed parts of the guidance as being obscure or wrong in law, they also concluded that there should always be more than de minimis or token benefit for the poor. However, it was for the trustees of charitable schools and not the Commission to decide what was appropriate in their own circumstances. The guidance was extensively rewritten, and the new shorter version was published in 2013.[47] The case on benevolent funds was another reference from the Attorney General and concerned poverty charities where beneficiaries had a common nexus.[48] The Upper Tribunal held that such charities remained charitable after the implementation of the Act and did not need to satisfy the public benefit test as regards a sufficient section of the public. The third case, brought by the Plymouth Brethren in 2012 against a Commission decision to refuse registration, was withdrawn and agreement reached on the changes to the governing document required to meet the public benefit test. The Commission's stance had provoked a barrage of criticism from MPs about a perceived anti-Christian bias at the Commission.

Was the PASC right in its assessment that the Commission's work on public benefit was a waste of resources? Although any change in the law may have been minimal, and full compliance with the public benefit reporting requirements is patchy, there is more emphasis on public benefit in the registration process, and it has certainly led some charity trustees to focus more on the benefits they provide and the public they serve. Interestingly, it is probably in independent schools where there has been the most change in practice, with increased bursaries and partnerships with state schools.

The Charity Tribunal

The scarcity of High Court decisions on charitable status led to a call for a Charity Tribunal to provide a cheaper, faster, simpler process to appeal against decisions of the Commission. The objectives were twofold: to provide greater accountability of the Commission and to provide a forum for the development of new case law for charities. The Act provided for a tribunal and included a schedule setting out the Commission decisions where an appeal would lie and the standing of the applicant required in each case. The Tribunal was established in 2008, and a year later under the reorganisation of the Tribunals Service it became the First Tier Tribunal (Charity).

Has the Charity Tribunal been a success? It was established on the basis that there would be about 50 cases a year but began very slowly with only 15 applications in the first two-and-a-half years. Since 2013, there has been an increase in applications, which now number about 19 a year—many fewer cases than anticipated, but substantially more than previous appeals to the High Court. The hope that it would be a cheaper option is also only now being realised. At first, counsel was usually instructed, but now the number of self-represented applicants is growing. A number of cases are still struck out for lack of standing or because they are outside the jurisdiction. In his Review, Lord Hodgson recommended that the schedule should be abolished and access to the Tribunal simplified.

In terms of its objectives, the Tribunal has, to some extent, increased the accountability of the Commission by causing it to tighten up on procedures. One example of this comes from the successful appeal in 2009 of Nagendram Seevaratnam against the Commission's removal of him as a trustee on the grounds of links to the proscribed Tamil Tigers.[49] The Tribunal criticised the Commission for its conduct of the case, particularly in gathering evidence, including a failure to have important documents translated. Under the second objective, apart from the three public benefit cases, the number of cases on definition has been quite small and in his Review, Lord Hodgson reminded the Tribunal of the important role it has to reflect emerging social mores. Two significant cases are the *Human Dignity Trust* case,[50] on the boundaries of the purpose of promoting human rights, and a 2015 case concerning regulation of the press,[51] where objects to promote high standards of ethical content and best practice in journalism were accepted as charitable, being analogous to trusts tending to promote the ethical and moral improvement of the community.

Political Activities

The period from 2002 to 2008 saw calls for a liberalisation of the rules on political activities by charities through a change in the law or the Commission's guidance. The Strategy Unit report recommended that the Commission's guidance on political activities should be revised to have a less cautionary tone and greater emphasis on permitted activities, but that the legal position should remain the same. The resulting 2004 guidance was more positive in tone but placed the issue of political activities firmly in the context of the risk-management duties of trustees. This did not allay concerns that the lack of clarity on the extent of permissible activities led to self-censorship by trustees.

A catalyst for further change came from an advisory group on campaigning, chaired by Baroness Helena Kennedy QC, set up in 2007 to look at constraints on campaigning and advocacy imposed by the law. The report[52] recommended a change in the law to remove the dominant and ancillary rule, and permit charity trustees to engage exclusively in political campaigning in furtherance of their charitable purposes, so long as they did not support political parties. In response to the Kennedy Report, the Commission carried out a major revision of their guidance. The new version[53] started by stressing the important campaigning role of charities. It removed the express references to the problematic concept of ancillary activities and in its place stated that a charity may choose to focus most or all of its resources on political activity for a period, provided that the activity does not become the reason for the charity's existence. In practice, the question of political activities is mainly one raised at registration and is only a factor in a small number of operational compliance cases (a total of 13 in 2014–15).[54] For charities, compliance with the Lobbying Act[55] has caused more concerns, as have proposals for restricting the use of government funds for campaigning.

Independence of Charities

The substantial increase in public service delivery by charities in this period raised a number of questions about their independence from government. In 2011, the Independence Panel, a watchdog of senior charity experts, was set up to monitor the independence of the sector over a five-year period. Their reports have drawn attention to several issues arising from public service delivery, including contractual gagging clauses, and commissioning that does not support the sector's independence and diversity. They have also raised concerns about the impact of the Lobbying Act and truncated government consultations. A specific legal issue facing the Commission on public service delivery was how far charities could go in using their own funds to provide services where a public authority was under a legal duty to provide them and, more generally, what degree of independence from the authority was required. In 2004, the commissioners allowed an appeal against the refusal to register two organisations set up to take over leisure services from the local authority. In their decision, they went on to set out general principles concerning the independence of charities in connection with the provision of public services.[56]

Changes at the Commission Since 2012

The period since 2012 has seen substantial changes at the Commission in terms of their regulatory stance, priorities, and services. There are a number of reasons for this. The initial reason was a slashing in the funding of the Commission. The revenue funding has been cut by half in real terms from £31.7 million in 2007–08 to £21.2 million in 2015–16, with staff numbers reduced from 600 to 285. The Coalition government accelerated cuts from 2010, but the Commission did at least escape the "Bonfire of the Quangos," which saw such bodies as the Commission for the Compact and the Office for Civil Society Advisory Body abolished. The cuts required the Commission to re-examine its regulatory focus, and in 2011, following consultation, they published a new Strategic Plan for 2012–2015. This set out two clear priorities: developing the compliance and accountability of the sector and developing the sector's self-reliance. The support and advice work would be met primarily by web-based advice to promote good governance.

In the Plan, the vision became "Charities you can support with confidence" and the mission was based on a threefold concept: charities know what they have to do; the public knows what charities do, and charities are held to account. The Plan included a commitment to be more proactive in compliance work and to work more closely with other regulators and law enforcement agencies. In delivering the priorities, the Commission would focus on its new risk framework, greater use of technology so that all transactions with charities and the public would be fully digitized, and organizational effectiveness. Alongside the Strategic Plan, a document on the application of the Commission's risk framework[57] set out the priority compliance areas, including serious financial loss, criminality and misuse for terrorist purposes, and serious harm to vulnerable beneficiaries.

The theme of increasing self-reliance of charities involved more signposting to sector bodies so that the Commission would not be the first port of call for tailored advice, and unnecessary contact with the Commission would be kept to a minimum. Economic necessity was turned to advantage, as trustees were encouraged to take full responsibility for running their charities. This theme was repeated in Lord Hodgson's Report, which had a key objective to create conditions in which people in charities were encouraged to use their own judgment.

The other major factor in the Commission's change in stance was highly critical reports from the NAO, the Public Accounts Committee (PAC), and the PASC. This scrutiny of the Commission was triggered by the high-profile tax avoidance case of the Cup Trust in 2013,[58] which received substantial press coverage and brought the chair and chief executive before the PAC to explain their actions. The resulting NAO report in 2013[59] found that the Commission was not taking tough enough action against charities involved in mismanagement and misconduct, and called for a greater use of its legal powers. This was followed two months later by an even more damning report by the PAC,[60] which found that the Commission was still performing badly, had no coherent strategy, and was not fit for purpose. The Commission's response has seen a substantial increase in the number of inquiries opened and use of its legal powers. In 2015–16, there were 53 inquiries opened and 1,073 instances of use of legal powers, up from 12 inquiries and 188 uses of legal powers in 2011–12.[61] The tougher approach to tackling abuse and mismanagement has been implemented in a number of ways, and the opening of every inquiry is now usually announced in a press release, as is the Inquiry Report, with lessons learned for all charity trustees. Another key development is the Charities (Protection and Social Investment) Act 2016, which not only closes loopholes but also gives additional powers and sanctions to the Commission, including a wide discretionary power to disqualify trustees and a power to issue statutory warnings. The tone of pronouncements and guidance has also changed: the *Essential Trustee*[62] has been revised again and this guidance has been broadened out to include good practice and also toughened up by stressing the consequences of non-compliance. The new robust approach has met with approval from the NAO[63] and PAC.[64] The response from the sector has been more mixed and has reawakened the debate on the proper role of the Commission and the best way to maintain public trust and confidence. Whilst some would agree that it is in the interest of the sector that the bad apples be exposed, others bemoan the change from an enabling to an enforcement regulator.[65]

In 2015, the debate moved on, with very extensive negative press coverage, not only of cases of predatory fundraising targeting the vulnerable but also the failure of a high-profile charity, Kids Company, raising concerns about the government's funding of this charity and, more generally, poor governance and administration in charities. This has led to calls from the press and parliamentarians for tougher regulation of charities. A 2015 matter, which went to the heart of both the Commission's role and the public trust and confidence objective, involved the funding by charities of an advocacy group, CAGE, which appeared to defend terrorists and caused outrage in the press. The Commission put "intense regulatory pressure" on two foundations to confirm that they would never fund the group in the future. CAGE brought an application for judicial review, challenging the Commission's action on several grounds including that it was acting outside its powers. In the event, the application was withdrawn when all parties agreed on a statement that the Commission had no power to require trustees to fetter their discretion under their general power to give advice and guidance.

Friend or Policeman?

The increased emphasis on compliance has been part of a wider, ongoing debate as to whether the Commission can be both friend and policeman, and the need to retain independence from the sector as much as from the government. In the 2005 Strategic Plan, the fourth head of mission was stated as championing the public interest in charity. This came out of discussion on the boundaries of the role of the Commission as advocate for the sector. Was advocating the cause of charities to government and the public consistent with the role of regulator, or did it compromise its independence? Recognising concerns about the risk of regulatory capture, the wording of the mission was limited to championing the public interest in charities, but support remained an important role. The Commission's advice role itself gave rise to criticism by the PASC in 2013 on the grounds that it compromised its independence: ". . . by seeking to be an advice service the Commission also risks a conflict of interest: it cannot simultaneously maintain public confidence in the charitable sector whilst also acting as champion of charities and the charity sector."[66] The risk of becoming too close to the sector was raised by a Commission representative in 2015:

> Everyone within the Commission is painfully aware of the balance between "enforcement and enabling," [the Commission's director of policy and communications] stresses. "It got out of kilter in the past. The question we have to ask ourselves is not, 'Does everybody like us?' As a regulator, if the answer to that is yes then you're almost certainly not doing a decent job."[67]

Part of the shift from the sector's friend to the sector's policeman is the Commission's increased emphasis on the donors to charity rather than the charities themselves. This is encapsulated by the change in vision from "Charity working at the heart of society" to "Charities you can support with confidence." In a speech in November 2015, William Shawcross confirmed this when he stressed that the Commission's main responsibility is to the public, and robust regulation is needed to ensure that they trust charities, as the public favours robustness.[68]

Future Challenges

How far has the Commission achieved its underpinning statutory objective to increase public trust and confidence in charities, and has one approach been more successful than another? It is difficult to say. Surveys are carried out biennially for the Commission to test this, and over the years, the scores have been fairly consistent around 6.7 out of 10. However, the latest survey in 2016[69] showed a clear decrease to 5.8. The major reasons for the drop were cited as general media stories about charities and media coverage on how charities spend donations. To restore public trust, steps are being taken by the sector to address public concerns, particularly about fundraising, and to increase transparency, improve governance, and promote the positive impact of charities. However, as with other institutions, the fall from grace is unlikely to be reversed fully in the short or medium term, so the challenge ahead for the Commission will be to work to maintain high levels of trust in charities in the face of increased scrutiny, both of the sector and of itself.

Another key challenge is resourcing of the Commission. The sharp decrease in funding has been followed by freezing of the budget for five years from 2015. In response, the Commission has said that this is not sustainable and some form of charging is inevitable.[70] The power to charge for prescribed functions was included in the 1992 Act; however; the power was never used, not least because, under the Act, all fees raised are payable to the Consolidated Fund. The proposal to introduce charging would require new legislation and is controversial: according to a survey carried out by the Commission, two-thirds of charities oppose it, whereas three-quarters of the public support it.[71] Some believe that it is the taxpayer rather than the donor who should bear the cost, and, again, issues of independence are raised on both sides, but all agree that in order to provide effective regulation in an era when the role for charity is increasing, additional funds must be provided from some source.

Notes

1 The crown was reintroduced as the logo in 2016.
2 Charity Commission for England and Wales, *The Charity Commission and Regulation* (London: Charity Commission, 2003).
3 Charity Commission, *Charity Commission and Regulation*.
4 Prime Minister's Strategy Unit, *Private Action, Public Benefit: A Review of Charities and the Wider Not-for-Profit Sector* (London: Home Office, 2002), accessed

August 9, 2016, http://webarchive.nationalarchives.gov.uk/+/http:/www.cabinet
office.gov.uk/media/cabinetoffice/strategy/assets/strat%20data.pdf.

5 House of Commons, Public Administration Select Committee, *The Role of the Charity Commission and "Public Benefit": Post-Legislative Scrutiny of the Charities Act 2006*, Third Report of Session 2013–14, HC 76 (London: The Stationery Office, 2013), accessed August 8, 2016, http://www.publications.parliament.uk/pa/cm201314/cmselect/cmpubadm/76/76.pdf.
6 HC Public Administration Select Committee, *Role of the Charity Commission*, 12.
7 "Reporting Serious Incidents; Guidance for Trustees," *Charity Commission* http;//www.gov.uk/government/uploads/system/uploads/attachment_data/file/375979/Reporting_Serious_Incidents_lowink.pdf.
8 Patrick McCurry, "Commission Tightens Grip on Late Accounts," *Third Sector*, November 26, 2003, accessed August 30, 2016, http://www.thirdsector.co.uk/commission-tightens-grip-late-accounts/article/616105.
9 Charity Commission for England and Wales, *Inquiry Report: North London Central Mosque Trust* (2003).
10 Nolan Quigley and Belinda Pratten, *Security and Civil Society: The Impact of Counter-Terrorism Measures on Civil Society Organisations* (London: National Council for Voluntary Organisations, 2007).
11 Home Office and HM Treasury, *Safeguards to Protect the Charitable Sector from Terrorist Abuse (England and Wales): Consultation Paper* (2007).
12 Quoted by Mark Sidel, *Regulation of the Voluntary Sector: Freedom and Security in an Era of Uncertainty* (New York: Routledge, 2010), 48–49.
13 Sidel, *Regulation of the Voluntary Sector*.
14 Financial Action Task Force, *Combating the Abuse of Non-Profit Organisations: International Best Practices* (Paris: FATF, 2002), accessed August 15, 2016, http://www.fatf-gafi.org/media/fatf/documents/recommendations/11%20FATF%20SRIX%20BPP%20SRVIII%20October%202003%20-%20COVER%202012.pdf.
15 Strategy Unit, *Private Action, Public Benefit*, 90.
16 This was ended in 2016.
17 Charity Commission for England and Wales, *The Hallmarks of an Effective Charity*, Guidance No. CC10 (London: The Commission, 2008), accessed August 8, 2016, https://www.gov.uk/government/publications/the-hallmarks-of-an-effective-charity-cc10.
18 The current edition is Charity Commission for England and Wales, *The Essential Trustee: What You Need to Know*, Guidance No. CC3 (London: The Commission, 2015), accessed August 8, 2016, https://www.gov.uk/government/publications/the-essential-trustee-what-you-need-to-know-cc3.
19 "Good Governance: A Code for the Voluntary and Community Sector," accessed August 8, 2016, www.governancecode.org. Founding members are Association of Chief Executives of Voluntary Organisations; Small Charities Coalition; ICSA: The Governance Institute; NCVO; and Wales Council for Voluntary Action.
20 Lord Hodgson, *Trusted and Independent: Giving Charity Back to Charities. Review of the Charities Act 2006* (London: The Stationery Office, 2012).
21 National Council for Voluntary Organisations, *Regulating Fundraising for the Future: Trust in Charities, Confidence in Fundraising Regulation* (London: NCVO, 2015).
22 The Fundraising Regulator was launched in July 2016.
23 Hodgson, *Trusted and Independent*.
24 House of Lords Debates, "Official Report of the Grand Committee on the Charities Bill," vol. 669, col. 886 (January 20, 2005).
25 House of Lords Debates, "Official Report of the Grand Committee on the Charities Bill," vol. 669, col. 126GC (February 10, 2005).
26 Charities Act 2006, s. 6(1).

27 National Council for Voluntary Organisations, *Charity Commission Independence: NCVO Discussion Paper* (London: NCVO, 2015).

28 National Audit Office, *Follow-Up on the Charity Commission: Report by the Comptroller and Auditor General*, HC 908, Session 2014–15 (London: NAO, 2015).

29 National Council for Voluntary Organisations, *Meeting the Challenge of Change: Voluntary Action into the 21st Century, Report of the Commission on the Future of the Voluntary Sector* (London: NCVO, 1996).

30 National Council for Voluntary Organisations, Charity Law Reform Advisory Group, *For the Public Benefit: A Consultation Document on Charity Law Reform* (London: NCVO, 2001).

31 NCVO Charity Law Reform Advisory Group, *For the Public Benefit*, 29.

32 Strategy Unit, *Private Action, Public Benefit*, 38.

33 Home Office, *Charities and Not for Profits: A Modern Legal Framework: The Government's Response to "Private Action, Public Benefit"* (London: Home Office, 2003).

34 Charities Act 2006 s 2(1); see now, Charities Act 2011, s. 2(1).

35 Charities Act 2006 s. 2(2)(m), 2(4); see now Charities Act 2011, s. 3(1)(m).

36 Charities Act 2011, s. 3(1)(e).

37 Charities Act 2011, s. 3(1)(f).

38 HC Public Administration Select Committee, *Role of the Charity Commission*, 30, 55.

39 NCVO, *For the Public Benefit*.

40 Strategy Unit, *Private Action, Public Benefit*, 41, para 4.28.

41 Joe Gill, "Charities Bill News: Mactaggart: I'll Resolve the Disagreement," *Third Sector*, (July 28, 2004), 4.

42 Gill, "Charities Bill News."

43 *Re Resch's Will Trusts; Le Cras and the Perpetual Trustee Company Ltd and Ors* [1969] 1 AC 514.

44 House of Lords Debates, "Official Report," vol. 669, col. 120GC (February 9, 2005).

45 Charity Commission for England and Wales, *Analysis of the Law Underpinning the Advancement of Education for the Public Benefit* (London: Charity Commission, 2008), 2, accessed August 15, 2016, https://www.gov.uk/government/uploads/system/uploads/attachment_data/file/358532/lawedu1208.pdf

46 *Independent Schools Council v Charity Commission for England and Wales* [2011] UKUT 421 (Upper Tribunal, Tax and Chancery Chamber, 13 October 2011); [2012] 1 All ER 127.

47 Charity Commission for England and Wales, *Public Benefit: The Public Benefit Requirement*, Guidance PB1 (London: Charity Commission, 2013), accessed August 15, 2016, https://www.gov.uk/government/publications/public-benefit-the-public-benefit-requirement-pb1.

48 *Attorney General v The Charity Commission for England and Wales and Ors* (Determination of reference) [2012] UKUT 420 (Upper Tribunal, Tax and Chancery Chamber, 20 February 2012).

49 *Seevaratnam v The Charity Commission for England and Wales, and Her Majesty's Attorney General* [2009] UKFTT 378 (First Tier Tribunal (Charity) General Regulatory Chamber, 13 October 2009).

50 *Human Dignity Trust v The Charity Commission for England and Wales* [2014] UKFTT (First Tier Tribunal (Charity) General Regulatory Chamber, 9 July 2014).

51 *Vernor-Miles and Ors v The Charity Commission for England and Wales* (First Tier Tribunal (Charity) General Regulatory Chamber, 15 June 2015).

52 Advisory Group on Campaigning in the Voluntary Sector, *[Report]* (London: Bates Wells and Braithwaite Solicitors, 2007).

53 Charity Commission for England and Wales, *Speaking Out: Guidance on Campaigning and Political Activities by Charities*, Guidance No. CC9 (London: Charity Commission, 2008).

54 Charity Commission for England and Wales, *Tackling Abuse and Mismanagement. Report of Investigations and Compliance Case Work 2014–15* (London: Charity Commission, 2015).

55 Transparency of Lobbying, Non-party Campaigning and Trade Union Administration Act 2014 c. 4.

56 *Applications for Registration of (i) Trafford Community Leisure Trust and (ii) Wigan Leisure and Community Trust* (Decisions of the Charity Commissioners for England and Wales, 21 April 2004), accessed August 16, 2016, https://www.gov.uk/government/publications/trafford-community-leisure-trust-and-wigan-leisure-and-culture-trust.

57 Charity Commission for England and Wales, *Application of the Charity Commission's Risk Framework* (London: Charity Commission, 2012). The current edition is 2016.

58 David Ainsworth, "Analysis: The Cup Trust and the Charity Commission," *Third Sector*, February 19, 2013, accessed August 15, 2016, http://www.thirdsector.co.uk/analysis-cup-trust-charity-commission/governance/article/1171166.

59 National Audit Office, *The Regulatory Effectiveness of the Charity Commission: Report by the Comptroller and Auditor General*, HC 813, Session 2013–14 (London: NAO, 2013), accessed August 15, 2016, https://www.nao.org.uk/wp-content/uploads/2013/11/10297-001-Charity-Commission-Book.pdf.

60 House of Commons Committee of Public Accounts, *The Charity Commission*, 42nd report of Session 2013–14, HC 792, (London: The Stationery Office, 2014).

61 Charity Commission, *Annual Report and Accounts 2015 to 2016*.

62 Charity Commission, *The Essential Trustee*, 2015.

63 National Audit Office, *Follow-Up on the Charity Commission*.

64 National Audit Office, *Follow-Up on the Charity Commission*. House of Commons Committee of Public Accounts, *Inquiries: Parliament 2010*, accessed August 16, 2016, http://www.parliament.uk/business/committees/committees-a-z/commons-select/public-accounts-committee/inquiries/parliament-2010/follow-up-on-charity-commission/.

65 Tim Smedley, "Charity Commission and the Voluntary Sector: What Has Gone Wrong?" *The Guardian*, February 12, 2015.

66 HC Public Administration Select Committee, "Conclusions and Recommendations," *Role of the Charity Commission*, 52, accessed August 15, 2016, http://www.publications.parliament.uk/pa/cm201314/cmselect/cmpubadm/76/76.pdf

67 Smedley, "Charity Commission and the Voluntary Sector."

68 Emily Corfe, "Charity Commission's Main Responsibility Is to the Public, Says Shawcross," *Civil Society News*, November 20, 2015, http://www.civilsociety.co.uk/governance/news/content/20801/public_is_charity_commissions_main_responsibility_says_shawcross.

69 Populous, *Public Trust and Confidence in Charities, 2016* (London: Charity Commission, 2016), accessed August 15, 2016, https://www.gov.uk/government/publications/public-trust-and-confidence-in-charities-2016.

70 Rebecca Cooney, "Charging Charities for Regulation Is 'Inevitable', says Shawcross," *Third Sector*, September 17, 2015, accessed August 30, 2016, http://www.thirdsector.co.uk/charging-charities-regulation-inevitable-says-shwacross/governance/article/1364451.

71 Populous, *Trust and Confidence in the Charity Commission, 2015* (London: Charity Commission, 2015) accessed August 30, 2016 https://www.gov.uk/government/uploads/system/uploads/attachment/data/file/438017/Trust_and_Confidence_in_the_Charity_Commission_2015_pdf.

4 Reflections on Modernizing and Reforming Regulation

Sir Stuart Etherington[1]

Introduction

This chapter provides an overview of recent developments in law and regulation for charities in England from the perspective of the National Council for Voluntary Organisations (NCVO), an umbrella body providing support to charities and representing their interests to the government and other external bodies. From government reviews of the whole legislative framework, to good practice developed by the sector itself on topical issues such as high pay and fundraising, the past ten years have brought fundamental change to how charities are regulated.

The NCVO is the largest representative body for charities and voluntary organizations in England. It works alongside its sister councils in Scotland, Northern Ireland, and Wales, with whom it collaborates on UK-wide issues. Established in 1919, NCVO now has over 11,000 members and is in contact with many more organizations through its advice, information, and policy work. Members include the largest and most renowned charities in England, as well as many of the smallest organizations working at a local community level. Nationally, NCVO campaigns on generic issues affecting the whole of the voluntary and community sector in England and provides briefings and advice on current and future trends and their likely impact on the sector. It is also at the leading edge of research into, and analysis of, the voluntary sector. It works with its members and others to develop policies that meet their needs as well as to influence policies and initiatives developed by external bodies, including the government, which impact on them. An example of this is NCVO's work on charity law reform.

Background and Context

Charities rely on public support, both directly, in terms of giving their time and money, and indirectly, in terms of public goodwill towards the sector as a whole. However, there is increasing evidence suggesting that the "charity brand" is at risk. According to a report published by the Charity Commission in the spring of 2016, public trust and confidence in charities has fallen to the lowest recorded level since monitoring began in 2005. The report finds the fall in trust and confidence can be attributed to critical media coverage of charity practices, distrust about how charities spend donations, and a lack of knowledge among the public about where their donations go. Perceptions of aggressive fundraising tactics have also contributed to the decline in trust.

This has happened within an operating environment for charities which over the last 20 years has changed considerably, demanding that organizations adapt to a number of fundamental shifts in their role and in their relationship with government and society more broadly. In particular, it is becoming increasingly apparent that charities need to engage with a public and media more ready to question and challenge their actions and motives than in the past. Furthermore, the charity sector has grown exponentially over the past couple of decades and now undertakes a huge range of activities. This has also meant that the characteristic diversity of the sector has become even more apparent. In the United Kingdom, the charity sector includes many different types of charities. They range from village halls, playgroups, and hospital radios run largely, and often exclusively, by volunteers through to household names such as national medical research charities, international development charities, museums, and art galleries, as well as hospitals, religious organizations, and independent schools charities. The nature of what they do and the breadth of their operations inevitably determines how they are regulated and organized. However, these factors also determine how the public views and understands charities. Therefore, regulation—and most importantly how it can enhance accountability and improve transparency—is a key issue for the sector. Indeed, in no other area have changes been more evident than in the regulatory one pertaining to charities' accountability to the public.

The Size and Scope of the UK Charity Sector

There is a long history of charitable activity in the United Kingdom, the latest research from NCVO showing that there were just over 160,000 charities operating in 2012–13.[2] Voluntary organizations vary in size, from very large household name charities to small organizations. Although the sector is perhaps best known by the work of larger organizations, operating at national or international levels, such as Cancer UK or Oxfam, the majority of charities are very small and often local in character. On the other hand, the larger organizations are small in number but large in terms of economic activity: between them the largest 5,000 organizations (those with income greater than £1 million) account for 78 per cent of the sector's total income. The 577 charities with income greater than £10 million account for nearly half of the sector's income and spending.

Government is one of the two key sources of income for the voluntary sector, alongside income from individuals. Income from government comes in two main types: grants and contracts. While organizations of all sizes receive income from all levels of government, from both grants and contracts, it is predominantly the larger organizations that receive these funds: government income makes up 38 per cent of funding for major organizations (incomes above £10 million) and 32 per cent of income for large organizations (income between £1 million and £10 million). By contrast, only 16 per cent of small and micro-organizations (those with income below £100,000) receive funding from government sources. In 2012–13, the sector as a whole received £13.3 billion from government bodies, of which 83 per cent was earned through contracts or fees. The majority of the sector's income from government comes from relationships with local government, amounting to £6.8 billion. Central government and the NHS accounted for £5.8 billion, while the remaining £696 million came from the European Union, international governments, and international agencies such as the United Nations.

Until 2009–10, government-sourced income grew and was a key factor in the growth of the sector over that period. In 2001–02, the sector received £10.2 billion from government, and by 2009–10, this had grown to £15.2 billion. However, this income has fallen every year following the pattern of declining general government spending over the same period. In real terms, the sector's income from government in 2012–13 was £1.9 billion less than the peak in 2009–10. The biggest decline (£1.2 billion) occurred between 2010 and 2011, and 2011 and 2012 (the first full year after the government's spending review), followed by a drop of around £500 million between 2011 and 2012, and 2012 and 2013. Another trend of the last decade has been a switch from grants to contracts, although this ratio has stabilized since income from government has started falling. In 2003–04, grants peaked at £6 billion, with over half of all income from the government. Since then, contracts have grown in importance, as grants have fallen. In 2012–13, grants made up just 17 per cent of income from the government (£2.2 billion).

The other key source of income comes from individuals: this comprises both voluntary income (such as donations and legacies) and earned income (coming, for example, from sales of merchandise and fees for events or services). In 2012–13, individuals contributed £18.8 billion, representing 46 per cent of the sector's income. Once again, there is a difference between large and small organizations: larger organizations have the smallest share of income from individuals (44 per cent), whilst small and micro-organizations have the largest share (56 per cent). However, the figures show that public support for charities remains strong. Voluntary organizations received £9 billion from individual donations and legacies. In 2012–13, donations from individuals generated almost £7 billion, accounting for 37 per cent of all individual income and 17 per cent of total income.

Given both the value of the sector's contribution to society and the public's willingness to support charitable activity, it is essential that there is a robust legal and regulatory framework in place to protect and promote charity. This is necessary to ensure that only those organizations with charitable purposes receive the benefits of charitable status and that these organizations are accountable for the work that they do. In this way, charity law plays an important role in upholding public trust and confidence in the concept of charity as well as in individual charities.

Charity Law Reform and the Charities Act 2006

As highlighted in previous chapters, the role and functions of the Charity Commission have been reviewed and updated a number of times during its existence, mainly in response to government-led modernization programmes and through statutory intervention. However, it was the charity sector that first acknowledged that charity law needed to be updated in order to meet the needs of charities and the public in the twenty-first century. The first detailed proposals for reform of charity law came from within the charity sector, specifically from a working group set up by NCVO (the Tumin Committee)[3] to look at the role and relevance of UK charity law in modern times.

One of the findings of the report emphasized the significance of charitable status for charities, pointing out that the main benefit of charitable status is not tax relief but the public credibility that it lends to the organization, encouraging the giving of time and money. This public credibility is based on the knowledge that registered charities are regulated by a public body which has powers to monitor organizations and investigate if it suspects that something is amiss. The badge of credibility is important not only to the public but also to institutional funders and grant-making charitable trusts. The working group concluded that the law protected and promoted charitable activity but highlighted a growing gap between public perceptions of what was, or should be, charitable and what was actually charitable in law. There was a real concern that unless it was addressed, the disparity would, in time, undermine public support for and confidence in charity. It therefore recommended that the law be reformed to emphasize the principle of public benefit as the main justification for the advantageous tax treatment and other benefits that charities receive. The government's Strategy Unit drew a similar conclusion in its review of the legal and regulatory framework for charities and the wider not-for-profit sector.[4] Although this had a much wider remit than NCVO's, it too identified a need to update the legal definition of charity to make it more relevant to the twenty-first century and recommended that public benefit should be at the heart of this. This was one of a number of recommendations to modernize the law and to create a better working environment for charities, which had wide support from both within the sector and beyond, and formed the basis of the Charities Act 2006.

Charity, Charitable Purposes, and Public Benefit

The Charities Act 2006 sought to update the law so that a lay audience would more easily understand it, and it would reflect more accurately the range of organizations which are, or should be, charitable in modern society. It did this by expanding the existing four heads of charity to create a new list of 13 purposes that are charitable in law. The Act did not create new purposes or exclude existing ones, but rather the system of classification was updated to resemble public perceptions more closely and to make the legal definition of charity more readily understandable for a lay audience. Importantly, the courts are still able to consider whether new purposes not listed are, in fact, charitable. This flexibility means that the law can continue to evolve and develop in response to needs not yet identified without recourse to further legislation.

The 2006 Act also purported to remove the presumption of public benefit previously given to certain categories of charity. The effect of this was that all charities would have to demonstrate that they benefit the public in some way. This requirement affects both existing charities as well as those applying for charitable status for the first time. The aim was to put "public benefit at the heart of charity" and to bring "legal" charity closer to the general public perception of what is charitable. By applying the public benefit test to all charities, the law makes it clear to the public that charities are organizations that benefit the public and therefore are deserving of their support. However, the Charities Act does not define public benefit. This is mainly because it would be difficult to come up with a clear legal definition encompassing the diversity of charitable purposes that exists today, let alone what may be considered charitable in future, or one that is able to take account of changing public perceptions and attitudes as to what constitutes public benefit. Instead, it was decided that it should be the Charity Commission, the main regulator of charities in England and Wales, to assess on a case-by-case basis whether public benefit is provided. This would be done by using the test it previously applied to charities falling under the fourth head of charity—that is, other purposes beneficial to the community.

Public Benefit and Charging Fees

Following the coming into force of the Charities Act 2006, the Charity Commission produced new guidance outlining its approach to public benefit. This new guidance had three central planks:[5]

- first, that there is no presumption that any charitable purpose is for the public benefit, and therefore public benefit must now be proved in every case;
- second, that assessing public benefit involves scrutinizing a charity's activities; and
- third, that any institution that excludes the poor cannot be charitable.

The revised guidance in particular stated,

> Where a charity charges high fees that many people could not afford, the trustees must ensure that the benefits are not unreasonably restricted

by a person's ability to pay and the people in poverty are not excluded from the opportunity to benefit.[6]

The change in the Commission's treatment of public benefit became a prominent point of contention among lawyers, academics, and the charity sector on account of its perceived impact on charities that charge fees (notably, but not exclusively, independent schools) and on religious charities. It was therefore no surprise that, not long after this new regime came into force, a challenge was made to the Charity Commission and its guidance on public benefit. Once again, action came from the charity sector itself and specifically from the Independent Schools Council (ISC), the representative body for independent schools. The ISC sought a judicial review of the Commission's guidance when two schools were told they had to make changes in order to maintain their status as charities. The ISC's claim was that certain guidance of the Commission should be quashed on the basis that the guidance included errors of law in respect to the public benefit requirement, particularly as applied to fee-charging independent schools. The ISC especially disliked the Charity Commission's emphasis on bursaries.

The judicial review was heard by the Upper Tribunal, alongside a separate reference made by the Attorney General, who asked the court to review the interpretation of the law in relation to public benefit and fee-charging charities more generally.[7] From the outset, the case was seen as a potential landmark in charity law, since the Tribunal found itself responsible for interpreting the most contentious area of charity law, the question of public benefit, and how the much-debated term should be applied in practice. It was hoped that the decision would bring some long awaited clarity for the benefit of the charity sector as a whole. NCVO was an intervening party to the judicial review proceedings in order to ensure that the issues raised were approached from a principled point of view. The view was that the Tribunal's ruling would have implications for all charities, not only charitable schools, because the issues were closely related to the challenges faced by other fee-charging charities such as private hospitals, care homes, arts organizations, and amateur sports clubs. In particular, some of the key issues that arose from the proceedings were the following:

- To what extent must charitable benefit be offered to those who cannot afford to pay any relevant fees?
- To what extent must such benefits, when offered to those who cannot afford the fees, be the same as or similar to those for which the fees are paid?
- To what extent should such benefits, when offered to those who cannot afford the fees, consist of fee remission?

Therefore, it was important for the interests of the wider sector to be represented.

The Upper Tribunal ruled clearly in support of the view that determining public benefit must lie with the trustees. Its decision confirmed that the Charity Commission's approach to the public benefit requirement was too restrictive in terms of its application to fee-charging charities, such as public schools and hospitals. The decision also suggested that the presumption removed by section 4(2) never really had the force of a "true" legal presumption and operated more as a simple "predisposition" for judges considering the public benefit of potentially charitable trusts. The Upper Tribunal held that fee-charging independent schools had to give more than a token benefit to the poor in order to fulfil the public benefit test, but that once such a low threshold had been reached, what the trustees decided to do in running the school was a matter for their discretion. The approach to be applied when assessing whether the public benefit requirement has been satisfied was to look at what a trustee, acting in the interests of the community as whole, would do in all the circumstances of the particular school and to ask what provision should be made once the threshold of benefit going beyond the de minimis level had been met. The Tribunal ruled that each case depended on its own facts. It was not possible to be prescriptive about the nature of the benefits which a school had to provide to the poor, nor the extent of them. It was for the trustees of the school concerned to assess and address how their obligations might best be fulfilled in the context of their own particular circumstances. There was no reason why the provision of scholarships or bursaries to students who could pay some, but not all, of the fees should not be seen as for the public benefit. Provided that the operation of the school was seen overall as being for the public benefit, with an appropriate level of benefit for the poor, a subsidy for the not-so-well off was to be taken into account. There would be one or more minimum benefit below which no reasonable trustees would go, but subject to that, the level of its provision was properly a matter for trustees' discretion and not for the Charity Commission or the courts. In particular, it was not for the Commission or the courts to impose on trustees of a school their own idea of what was, and what was not, reasonable.

The Upper Tribunal expressly limited its decision to educational charities. However, it was immediately clear that the principles set out in the decision would be of direct relevance to other fee-charging charities. In particular, by upholding the ISC's argument that the Commission had taken too active a role in deciding whether fee-charging schools were doing enough to provide a public benefit, the decision was seen as giving trustees more freedom to make their own decisions, without worrying about the involvement of the regulator.

Campaigning and Political Activity by Charities

Another area that was identified by the charity sector as inadequate and in need of reform was the law on campaigning and the rules affecting how charities could support citizen advocacy. An advisory group, led by some of the leading representatives working in the field of charity campaigning, analysed the legal restrictions on campaigning and concluded that the existing position was "a minefield of confusion, obstruction and outdated interpretations of the law."[8] In particular, the advisory group examined how charity law might be causing constraints to charities' engagement with the political process. The main criticism was that the legal restrictions on campaigning by charities rested on twentieth-century case law, which established that charities may not have political objects. Political activity was defined as not only furthering the interests of a political party but also campaigning to secure or oppose any change in the law or policies of national and local government at home or overseas.[9] Existing case law was also seen as restrictive, since it permitted political activities by charities only if they remained ancillary and did not become the long-term dominant means of carrying out charitable purposes. While the Charity Commission's guidance on campaigning and political activities at the time[10] reflected this legal position, it was seen as excessively cautious and unclear. In particular, concerns over what would constitute "ancillary" and "dominant" in practice meant that charities were frequently inhibited in how freely they campaigned, and the definition of "dominant" in the Charity Commission's guidance was not satisfactory:

> What is dominant is a question of scope and degree upon which trustees must make a judgment. In making this judgment trustees should take into account factors such as the amount of resources applied and the period involved, the purposes of the charity and the nature of the activity.

The "dominant and ancillary rule" was considered particularly difficult to sustain in the context of several purposes codified by the Charities Act 2006 as being charitable despite being inherently political, such as the prevention of poverty, the advancement of human rights, citizenship, and animal welfare. The separation of charities from politics, which had always been problematic, developed into something artificial and in many cases unsustainable.

The advisory group made a number of recommendations to improve the regulatory framework of campaigning in a way that would enable charities to engage better in political campaigning in furtherance of their charitable purposes without going against the fundamental principle that charities must never support or oppose a political party, or throwing open the door to abuse. Most importantly, the advisory group advocated for a change in the interpretation of the law to remove the dominant and ancillary rule where the organization's purposes are otherwise charitable. The aim was to put an end to charities having to police themselves to ensure political activities do not predominate and would mean that an unduly restrictive legal framework would no longer inhibit the campaigning impulses of charities. The recommendations received wide support in recognition of charities' long tradition of engaging in campaigning activities and their unique place to advocate for legislative or policy change and give expression to the voices of diverse (and often under-represented) groups in society. Moreover, there was a growing acknowledgement that charities have an increasingly important role in advocating change and carrying out political campaigning work. The issue was also seen in light of the well documented disengagement of the public from political parties and traditional methods of participation, compared to a growing membership of single-issue campaigning organizations.

The Charity Commission agreed to revise its guidance on campaigning and political activities, scrapping the distinction of dominant and ancillary for a much more practical distinction between general campaigning and political activities. The revised guidance also sought to address criticism that it is too risk averse by providing a much more positive endorsement of charitable campaigning as a central part of how modern charities achieve their aims and recognizing that trustees have the discretion to decide when and how much to campaign. For example, issues such as promotion of human rights are more likely to suggest a need for political campaigning, but it is a matter of weighing benefits against risks in pursuing the charity's purposes.[11]

Chief Executive Pay

The debate about the pay of senior staff in charities has re-surfaced periodically over the years. This was not viewed as an issue within the regulatory remit of the Charity Commission, and the Commission had traditionally refrained from engaging in these debates on the basis that the levels of pay are a matter for trustees' discretion. However, in the summer of 2013, a national newspaper published research[12] showing that 30 senior executives at 14 foreign aid charities were paid more than £100,000 a year, triggering a strong reaction from some members of the public, including donors. The article opened a wider discussion on the pay of charity chief executives and put the issue of transparency among charities under the spotlight. The chair of the Charity Commission, William Shawcross, also intervened in the debate, claiming that disproportionately high salaries risked bringing organizations and the whole charity sector into disrepute. Although there is no strong evidence of such a debate influencing the long-term behaviour of the majority of donors or levels of public trust in charity, some surveys have shown a high level of concern about charity executives' salaries potentially affecting donors' giving,[13] and the debate revealed once again a mismatch between the public's perception of charities and the realities of the sector. This was made worse by the fact that most charities were poorly equipped to explain to the public what they do and how they spend their money.

The sector's response, led by NCVO, was to set up an independent inquiry into senior executive pay[14] in order to develop recommendations that would assist charity trustees in exercising their responsibility for setting the pay of their senior executives. This would be done by

- exploring the arguments about what are appropriate levels of pay for charity senior executives and how these levels should be arrived at;
- exploring the relationship between salary levels and public trust and confidence in the sector as a whole; and
- producing definitive guidelines for charity trustees to take into account when setting salaries, informed by a broad debate on the issues involved.

It also became clear that the inquiry needed to extend its remit to include making good practice recommendations about the process charity trustees should follow in setting pay in today's context and how they should explain these decisions to their supporters and the wider public.

One of the key challenges for the inquiry was to address the broader misconceptions about charities, which continue to be widely held among the public, including donors. Research suggests that the public's understanding of the term "charity" is far narrower than the legal definition.[15] While the legal definition includes many institutions such as schools, the arts, and medical research institutions, all of which require specialist staff, the public perception remains that charities are largely run on a voluntary basis and do not require full-time professional and technical staff to manage and deliver their aims. In particular, it was found that a large part of the public makes no distinction between a small local voluntary organization with which they are familiar and a major medical research or disaster relief charity, simply because both are charities. The view is that neither should pay for their staff, because they are in essence voluntary organizations. In reality, while charities of all sizes share an ethos of existing to better the lives of others, one size does not fit all. The voluntary sector is hugely diverse: there are many different types of charities contributing to society in a wide variety of ways. They are faced with different challenges of organization and service delivery, particularly as they grow. Moreover, in the last two decades, many overlaps have developed between the public, private, and voluntary sectors. On the other hand, it is a given in the charity sector that any judgement of pay levels should take into account the values and purpose of each particular charity. Donors expect this, and the inquiry felt it was important to remind trustees that this should be at the forefront of their minds as they decide pay levels. The inquiry therefore needed to balance quite divergent views, ranging from those who think that charities should be entirely led and run by volunteers to those who believe the pay of senior staff in charities needs to be consistent with their peers in other sectors in order to attract and retain professional expertise to deliver the charity's aims.

The view was that this challenge would be best addressed by moving down the twin tracks of guidance and transparency: detailed guidance for trustees, who have the clear responsibility for pay policy, and a much higher level of transparency to easily and speedily inform those existing and would-be donors for whom pay levels are a major factor in their giving. The inquiry made a number of recommendations, but no doubt the most important was that independently audited charities (those with income over £500,000) should publish the names and salaries of their senior executives in a prominent place on their websites, accompanied by an explanation of pay policy and how it advances their charitable objectives.[16] Given donors' legitimate concerns about where their money is going and wider concerns about pay policies and costs, charities should not shy away from more open communication about senior staff pay levels and pay polices. The inquiry found very few examples of this open communication in charities' annual reports or on their websites.[17] In fact, charities having income over £500,000 must disclose in their accounts the number of staff whose remuneration is £60,000 or more, or explain why they do not.[18] Once again, the key issue was to address the changes in the public's expectations and to respond to calls for greater transparency and disclosure. In the United Kingdom, such calls have already led to requirements for both listed companies and public bodies to publish more information about how they reward their senior staff.[19] For charities, which are funded wholly or partly by public money in the form of donations and tax reliefs, the additional pressure to tell the public how their money is spent has clear implications for how they explain their pay decisions to donors, beneficiaries, and the public.

Self-Regulation of Fundraising

Various forms of self-regulation mostly cover fundraising in the United Kingdom. In particular, the Charities Act 2006 does not specifically regulate fundraising. Rather, the sector was given an opportunity to develop a self-regulatory system, with the government retaining a residual power to legislate if this failed. The initial set up for the self-regulatory system included three main bodies: the Fundraising Standards Board (FRSB) as the main adjudicator, the Institute of Fundraising (IoF) as the professional association, and the Public Fundraising Association (PFRA) as the body responsible for face-to-face fundraising. This arrangement for the regulation of charitable fundraising was included in Lord Hodgson's review of the Charities Act 2006.[20] Although supporting the view that self-regulation of fundraising is preferable to statutory regulation (self-regulation is more flexible, responsive, and cost effective), the Hodgson Review saw a need for clarification of the roles, responsibilities, and powers of the different bodies involved in the self-regulatory landscape. It strongly recommended a simplification of the system as a necessary step forward to realize a simple, donor-focused, self-regulatory scheme.

Despite Lord Hodgson's recommendations, the structure and operation of self-regulation remained unchanged, and the complexity of the system was not addressed. Indeed the related weaknesses—such as the low public awareness of a means of complaining and widespread confusion about the roles and responsibilities of each body—escalated into major problems. This became apparent in the spring of 2015 when a number of negative media stories revealed malpractices in the fundraising activities of some of the largest charities in the country, adding to a considerable amount of public discontent about charities' fundraising practices.

The death of England's oldest poppy seller, Olive Cooke, was a watershed moment for charity fundraising amid claims that the tragedy had been precipitated by an excessive amount of fundraising requests by charities.[21] Although it was later clarified by the family that charities were not to blame, questions about the tactics used by charities in their fundraising had been raised and needed to be addressed. The FRSB, having acknowledged that overwhelming fundraising requests were thought to have been one of the factors involved in her death, launched an investigation into the allegations. In an interim investigation report, the FRSB found that the public wants more control over the way in which charities communicate with them and particularly in how many times people are asked to give to charity.[22] Separately, however, an undercover media investigation revealed further fundraising malpractices involving charities.[23] This once again put into question the behaviour of charities in this area and in turn the effectiveness of the self-regulatory framework of fundraising.

An independent sector-led review[24] was therefore tasked with assessing the self-regulatory system and making recommendations on changes that might be needed to ensure better protection of the public's interests and to address the public concern over intrusive or aggressive fundraising methods. In particular, the review was asked to consider whether sufficient checks and balances are in place, either in charities themselves or in the self-regulatory system, to retain public trust in organizations that fundraise. One of the key challenges for the review was to address the calls for direct government intervention and for self-regulation to be replaced by statutory rules. Ultimately, however, it was charities' duty to bring about change.

What was apparent from the start of the review and throughout its process was that charities understood the need for change and the need to take responsibility for a better relationship with their donors and the wider public. The sector was clear that fundraising is a critical, necessary way for charities to support those in need. The work of charities and voluntary organizations is too important not to use fundraising, but charities were equally clear that it must be undertaken in a responsible, respectful manner that views donors as long-term partners and strengthens public trust and confidence in charities. The review's main recommendation, therefore, was to preserve self-regulation, as it remains the most appropriate mechanism for the charity sector to show its commitment to high ethical standards, which safeguard public trust and confidence. However, self-regulation would be strengthened by being provided with a statutory "backstop." This is what is known as co-regulation, and it should reflect a "three lines of defence" model:

- Trustees would act as the first line of defence because they are accountable for the charity's fundraising activities and have the responsibility to ensure fundraising is carried out in compliance with the law and to high ethical standards.
- A specialized fundraising regulator would provide the second line of defence if malpractice occurred and its intervention was necessary to protect the public interest.
- The relevant statutory regulator would be the last line of defence, acting as the backstop in cases that raised regulatory concerns on issues falling within its remit and powers.

With regard to charity fundraising in England and Wales, the principle should be that the Charity Commission would have a role when the Fundraising Regulator has evidence of fundraising practices that, in addition to being in breach of the rules, raise concerns about breach of trustees' duties, including the duty to safeguard the reputation of the charity. The Charity Commission's interest would be based on the fact that serious or persistent failures in fundraising may represent a wider governance failure.

The review also recommended a number of changes to the existing regulatory framework, with the key ones being

- to abolish the FRSB and establish a new Fundraising Regulator, with a universal remit to adjudicate all fundraising complaints and stronger sanctions for noncompliance;
- to fund the new Fundraising Regulator via payment of an automatic levy, based on fundraising expenditure;
- to move administration of the Code of Fundraising Practice to the new Fundraising Regulator;
- to merge the IoF and the PFRA into a single professional organization; and
- to transfer the regulatory aspects of the PFRA's work to the Fundraising Regulator.

The Fundraising Regulator commenced operation on July 7, 2016.[25] Ultimately, however, the key change that is required is one of culture: self-regulation can only be successful if those it is intended to regulate want it to be. Previously, there had been a disconnect between the ethos and values of some charities and their fundraising practices. Now charities need to aspire to view and conduct their fundraising not simply as a way to raise money, but most importantly as a conduit between their donors and the causes they wish to support. This is not only a matter of public interest but also key to the long-term sustainability of charities because it depends on a relationship with the public based on confidence and respect.

It is in this spirit that NCVO set up a working group tasked with developing good practice recommendations on how charities should communicate with their donors for fundraising purposes.[26] The working group considered one aspect of how donors can take more control of their giving—specifically, how they give consent to the fundraising relationships with the charities that they support. The recommendations aim to create a stronger and more coherent framework that protects the interests of donors and potential donors, and re-establishes a basis of trust and confidence in charity fundraising practices. The ultimate result should be to meet the public's increased expectations about how charities conduct themselves and will therefore be a way in which charities can demonstrate to their donors and the wider public their commitment to good fundraising practice, and to maintaining public trust and confidence.

The Charity Commission's Governance and Independence

Independence from both government and party politics is vital for the Charity Commission, particularly as the regulator of a sector that is characterized by its party political neutrality. Independence is necessary for its effective functioning and for its credibility in the eyes of the general public and the charities it regulates. A charity regulator perceived to be political risks undermining perceptions of charities more generally. Perceived independence—being seen to be independent—is just as important as actual independence. However, over the years, the Charity Commission has been subject to criticisms that it allows itself to be used as a political football by the government of the day and is drawn into political agendas. Most criticism has been directed at whoever is the chair at the time—a ministerial appointee. During her tenure, the previous chair Dame Suzi Leather was accused of politicking when the Commission challenged the charitable status of private schools. More recently, the current chair, Mr Shawcross, has been accused of steering the Commission towards a clampdown on charity campaigning. At the time of Mr Shawcross's appointment in 2012, opposition members of the Public Administration Select Committee raised concerns about his support for the Conservative Party and voted against his appointment.

It is not necessary to accept that the accusations of political bias levelled against both current and previous Commission boards have any merit in order to see that they can be damaging. In the case of the Charity Commission, the issue is that the organization must be manifestly independent and seen as free from improper interference by any government. Charities cannot afford their regulator to be anything other than beyond all suspicion. It was with these concerns in mind that NCVO announced its intention in autumn 2014 to look at the legal status and governance of the Charity Commission. By that time, it was eight years since the Commission had been restructured under the Charities Act 2006, and while that legislation did much to improve charity law, its reforms to the Commission's governance have created some new problems.

The revised structure replaced a small board of commissioners comprised of lawyers and civil servants with a more diverse board. In doing so, the law opened up the pool of potential commissioners for the government to select from, with the intention that the Commission would become more responsive. But further problems stem from the Charity Commission's status as a non-ministerial department. This legal structure has been found wanting with regard to both its independence from the executive and its accountability to Parliament.[27] The case for a review of the Charity Commission's governance was made even more compelling by the recent report by the National Audit Office, which highlighted a blurring of the executive and oversight functions.[28] While acknowledging that the board's involvement in executive functions from late 2013 to mid-2014 could be justified by the need to address the under-performance issues highlighted in the first National Audit Office report,[29] concerns are raised about the risk that the board's continuing involvement in executive matters for an extended period could limit its independence and ability to hold the executive to account effectively. The aim of the review was to find alternative legal structures and models of governance that would enable the regulator to put questions about its political neutrality to rest for good, and free it from further accusations of political bias in its work.

The new Charities (Protection and Social Investment) Act 2016,[30] under which the Commission has been granted a range of additional powers, presents further reason for a review. As tools to enable the Commission to tackle abuse more swiftly and effectively, most of these powers seem reasonable. However, during the pre-legislative scrutiny carried out by the Joint Committee on the Protection of Charities Bill, a number of concerns were raised about how the powers could be used.[31] This reinforces how important it is for the Commission to be seen to be acting independently and free from the pressures of any political agenda.

The review started by exploring some alternative legal structures for the Charity Commission. However, while some of the alternatives examined would offer considerable advantages, the review concluded that none of them would be entirely appropriate for the Charity Commission, and there was not a strong enough case to warrant such considerable constitutional change.[32] It therefore focused on the governance of the Commission and how the current model could be strengthened. The discussion paper argued that the current appointment process could be improved by distancing the role of chair of the Charity Commission from executive control, thereby addressing the issue of perceived independence. It is not suggested that ministerial involvement should be removed from the process entirely, but evidence about how the appointment process has worked for the National Audit Office, the Electoral Commission, the Parliamentary and Health Service Ombudsman, and the Office for Budget Responsibility indicates that greater parliamentary involvement is a benefit by securing increased transparency in the process and better accountability of the position. Drawing lessons from these models, the review concluded by suggesting a number of ways in which the appointment process for the chair of the Charity Commission could be improved, such as

- giving formal control of the appointment to the House of Commons;
- widening the membership of the parliamentary committee responsible for the pre-appointment hearing so it includes representatives of both houses;
- giving Parliament an effective power of veto at the pre-appointment hearing;
- making the term non-renewable and fixed;
- requiring, in the event of keeping the possibility of reappointment, that this follows a parliamentary hearing similar to the pre-appointment hearing; and
- requiring a unanimous vote for appointment.

Role of the Press

The UK media has played an important role in raising many of these issues, which has required reaction and reform from the sector. This is most evident with regard to the debate about executive salaries, which has been a major theme of recent years. However, concerns about charities' campaigning roles are also not uncommon. And, of course, fundraising methods adopted by charities have been a major area of interest for the UK press in the past year. What has emerged in recent years is a press that is increasingly willing to scrutinize and question charities. As charities have taken on greater scale, profile, and influence, it is unsurprising that the media have taken a growing interest in their work. The concerns of the media frequently reflect a narrative that sees large professional charities as detached from their roots, increasingly self-interested and part of the establishment. In many ways, this reflects a reality for many charities, whose scale and influence have increased. However, the disparity between public notions of what a charity "should" look like—run by volunteers on a shoestring—and the professional way in which many larger charities actually operate, has proved fertile ground for media stories. While journalists rely on and value charities as much as ever for stories and comment on their areas of expertise, there is clearly growing willingness to treat charities, as institutions themselves, with scepticism. This is part of a broader decline of public confidence in institutions made more visible in the case of charities by their increasing visibility and changed role in society.

Conclusion

In recent years, there has been an upsurge of interest in the accountability and legitimacy of charities, both in England and abroad. In part, this may be linked to the relatively higher profile of the charity sector arising from their increasing role in providing public services and the prominence of charity-led campaigns, but debates about the sector's accountability are also taking place against a backdrop of declining public trust and confidence in all social institutions, public, private, and voluntary. This decline is linked to the fact that today people are less deferential and have higher expectations than in the past, but it has also been linked to the issue of accountability and to a perceived lack of transparency in the way charities function. This perception is of greatest concern to charities: people's willingness to participate in voluntary action and support charities is based on the belief that they can be trusted to make a difference. A more cynical and less trusting public is likely to demand more evidence of this before agreeing to support a cause. This is in a context where the boundaries between the public, private, and voluntary sectors are continuously blurring: bits of the state are turning into charities and mutuals, social enterprises blend business and social purposes, and individuals might not need charities to achieve their goals. In such a world, charities need not only prove why they are different and distinctive, but they also need to be clear that their values accord with those who do want to "do good" and that their practices reflect such values.

Improving the regulatory framework in which they operate, reforming the law to reflect what it means to be a modern charity, and adhering to high standards in all their activities are some of the steps that many charities have already taken. However, the ongoing challenge for charities is to engage with the public in ways that will maintain and enhance people's trust and confidence. As other sectors have learned at their cost, once public trust and confidence have been lost, it is very difficult to regain. Charities, therefore, need to show their supporters that they exist to make a difference, and they can be trusted to do so. This is not something that can be achieved simply by increasing the level of regulation. The onus must be on charities themselves to become more transparent, being clearer about what they do, how they do it, and how well they do it.

Notes

1 Sir Stuart Etherington would like to express his gratitude to Elizabeth Chamberlain, head of policy at NCVO, for her assistance and support in writing this chapter.
2 "UK Civil Society Almanac 2015," National Council for Voluntary Organisations, http://data.ncvo.org.uk/a/almanac15/big-picture/, published June 6, 2015.
3 The work of the Tumin Committee was prompted by the need to examine in detail the recommendations for reform of charity law and the regulatory regime proposed by the Deakin Commission: National Council for Voluntary

Organisations, *Meeting the Challenge of Change: Voluntary Action into the 21st Century, Report of the Commission on the Future of the Voluntary Sector* (London: NCVO, 1996).

4 Prime Minister's Strategy Unit, *Private Action, Public Benefit: A Review of Charities and the Wider Not-for-Profit Sector* (London: Home Office, 2002), accessed August 9, 2016, http://webarchive.nationalarchives.gov.uk/+/http:/www.cabinet office.gov.uk/media/cabinetoffice/strategy/assets/strat%20data.pdf.

5 Charity Commission for England and Wales, *Charities and Public Benefit: The Charity Commission's General Guidance on Public Benefit* (London: Charity Commission, 2008). NOTE: this edition of the Guidance has been quashed and replaced by the 2013 edition.

6 Charity Commission for England and Wales, *Charities and Public Benefit* (2008), section F10.

7 *Independent Schools Council v Charity Commission* [2011] UKUT 421 (UK Upper Tribunal, Tax and Chancery Chamber, 13 October 2011). The Attorney General's Reference consisted of a series of specific questions about the operation of charity law in relation to a hypothetical independent school.

8 Advisory Group on Campaigning and the Voluntary Sector, *[Report]* (London: Bates Wells and Braithwaite Solicitors, 2007) (Baroness Helena Kennedy QC, chair), p.2.

9 Charity Commission for England and Wales, *Speaking Out: Guidance on Campaigning and Political Activity by Charities*, Guidance No. CC9 (London: Charity Commission, 2008), 5. See also *McGovern v Attorney-General* [1982] Ch 321.

10 This edition of the Guidance was withdrawn and replaced by the 2008 edition.

11 Charity Commission, *Speaking Out*, 8, 9.

12 Christopher Hope, "30 Charity Chiefs Paid More than £100,000," *Daily Telegraph*, August 6, 2013, accessed October 14, 2016, http://www.telegraph.co.uk/news/politics/10224104/30-charity-chiefs-paid-more-than-100000.html.

13 See Sue Wixley and James Noble, *Mind the Gap: What the Public Thinks about Charities*, (London: New Philanthropy Capital, 2014), accessed August 23, 2016, http://www.thinknpc.org/publications/mind-the-gap/; Ipsos Mori, Social Research Institute, *Public Perceptions of Charity: A Report for the Charities Act 2006 Review* (London: Ipsos MORI, 2012), accessed August 23, 2016, https://www.gov.uk/government/uploads/system/uploads/attachment_data/file/79276/Charities-Act-Review-2006-Public-Perceptions-of-charity.pdf.

14 National Council for Voluntary Organisations, "Executive Pay Inquiry Announced," *Press Release*, October 11, 2013, accessed October 14, 2016, https://www.ncvo.org.uk/about-us/media-centre/press-releases/470-executive-pay-inquiry-announced.

15 Ipsos Mori Social Research Institute, *Public Perceptions of Charity*, accessed October 23, 2016, https://www.gov.uk/government/uploads/system/uploads/attachment_data/file/79276/Charities-Act-Review-2006-Public-Perceptions-of-charity.pdf.

16 National Council for Voluntary Organisations, *Report of the Inquiry into Charity Senior Executive Pay and Guidance for Trustees on Setting Remuneration* (London: NCVO, 2014), accessed October 14, 2016, https://www.ncvo.org.uk/images/news/Executive-Pay-Report.pdf.

17 National Council for Voluntary Organisations, *Report of the Inquiry into Charity Senior Executive Pay*, 27.

18 Charity Commission for England and Wales, *Accounting and Reporting by Charities: Statement of Recommended Practice 2005* (London: Charity Commission, 2005).

19 For example, see Localism Act 2011, s. 38 (local authorities' pay policy statement); Companies Act 2006 c. 46, chap 6 (quoted companies' directors' remuneration reports).

20 Lord Hodgson, *Trusted and Independent: Giving Charity Back to Charity: Review of the Charities Act 2006* (London: The Stationery Office, 2012), accessed August 23, 2016, https://www.gov.uk/government/uploads/system/uploads/attachment_data/file/79275/Charities-Act-Review-2006-report-Hodgson.pdf.

21 Paul Bentley, Lucy Osbourne, and Katherine Faulkner, "Shame of Charities that Prey on the Kind-hearted and Drove Olive Cooke to Death: Organisations Who Exploited Pensioner's Kind Heart Admit to Sending Begging Letters," *Daily Mail*, May 16, 2015, accessed May 20, 2015 http://www.dailymail.co.uk/news/article-3083859/Shame-charities-drove-Olive-death-Organisations-exploited-pensioner-s-kind-heart-admit-sending-begging-letters.html.

22 Fundraising Standards Board, *Investigation into Charity Fundraising Practices: Interim Report* (London: FRSB, 2015), accessed August 23, 2016, http://www.frsb.org.uk/wp-content/uploads/2015/06/FRSB-Interim-investigation-report_Published-9June2015.pdf.

23 Daily Mail Investigations Unit, "New Shame of Charities: Widower's Details Were Passed on 200 Times Leading Him to Lose £35,000 and Get 731 Demands for Cash," *Daily Mail*, September 1, 2015, accessed September 2, 2015 http://www.dailymail.co.uk/news/article-3217506/New-shame-charities-Widower-s-details-passed-200-times-leading-lose-35-000-getting-731-demands-cash.html.

24 National Council for Voluntary Organisations, *Regulating Fundraising for the Future: Trust in Charities, Confidence in Fundraising Regulation* (London: NCVO, 2015) (chaired by the author), accessed August 20, 2016, https://www.ncvo.org.uk/images/documents/policy_and_research/giving_and_philanthropy/fundraising-review-report-2015.pdf.

25 See https://www.fundraisingregulator.org.uk/.

26 National Council for Voluntary Organisations, *Charities' Relationships with Donors: A Vision for a Better Future* (London: NCVO, 2016), accessed October 14, 2016, https://www.ncvo.org.uk/images/images/about_us/media-centre/NCVO_-_Charities_relationships_with_donors.pdf.

27 Jill Rutter, *The Strange Case of Non-Ministerial Departments* (London: Institute for Government, 2013), accessed August 23, 2016, http://www.instituteforgovernment.org.uk/publications/strange-case-non-ministerial-departments.

28 National Audit Office, *Follow-Up on the Charity Commission: Report by the Comptroller and Auditor General*, HC 908, Session 2014–15 (London: NAO, 2015).

29 National Audit Office, *The Regulatory Effectiveness of the Charity Commission: Report by the Comptroller and Auditor General*, HC 813, Session 2013–14 (London: NAO, 2013), accessed August 23, 2016, www.nao.org.uk/wp-content/uploads/2013/11/10297-001-Charity-Commission-Book.pdf.

30 Enacted as the Charities (Protection and Social Investment) Act 2016, c. 4 (royal assent March 22, 2016).

31 House of Lords and House of Commons Joint Committee on the Draft Protection of Charities Bill, *Draft Protection of Charities Bill: Report*, HL Paper 108, HC 813 (London: The Stationery Office, 2015), accessed August 20, 2016, www.publications.parliament.uk/pa/jt201415/jtselect/jtcharity/108/108.pdf.

32 For the full analysis, see National Council for Voluntary Organisations, *Charity Commission Independence: Discussion Paper* (London: NCVO, 2015), accessed August 21, 2016, https://www.ncvo.org.uk/images/documents/policy_and_research/independence_and_values/charity-commission-independence-ncvo-discussion-paper-april-2015.pdf.

United States of America

5 Challenged Regulators

Marcus Owens

Introduction

This chapter will review the trajectory of charity regulation in the United States from the standpoint of a former federal government regulator. The review will begin with an overview of the tax-based system of charity regulation in the United States and its linkage to English common law concepts of charity. The historic basis for US charity regulation will be traced through to the birth of the current modern system of regulation in 1969, during a period characterized by a general recognition of the need for proactive government regulation of charities. The review will continue through recent changes triggered more by political pressure than any notions of more effective and better-structured regulation. In addition to the shifts in regulatory structure and philosophy, the review will analyse the difficulties that the current US tax-based structure has in performing its role, including adapting to developments that occur outside the structure of federal tax law, such as the development of hybrid legal structures that purport to meld elements of charity with notions of private enterprise.

Structural Overview

It has been nearly 50 years since the modern charity oversight system in the United States was formed. During that time, the oversight regime, administered by the Internal Revenue Service (IRS), has gone from a relatively focused and coordinated system—albeit one struggling with the challenges of underfunding, understaffing, and poorly drafted legislation—to a system that seems to be racing to dismantle itself. What has changed in recent years has been the orientation of IRS management to the task of charity oversight and the emergence of an extraordinary level of hostility in Congress to the very idea of nonprofit oversight, including charity oversight. The day-to-day challenges faced by the IRS in administering the federal charity laws have essentially remained the same since the modern structure was created in 1974.[1]

The stunning changes in recent years can be attributed to changes in leadership, both within the agency and in Congress, rather than in the performance of the rank-and-file employees carrying out the oversight task. Indeed, as recounted by the Commission on Private Philanthropy and Public Needs in an extensive review of the charitable sector in the United States during the 1970s, the expert view in that era was that placing the charity oversight function in the IRS would ensure stable funding and staffing. Moreover, the agency's apolitical nature (only the two highest employees are political appointees: the commissioner and the chief counsel) would protect the charity oversight function from politically charged interference from both the executive and legislative branches of government. Because the nation had just weathered Watergate and the revelations of the notorious Nixon administration's "enemies list," administrative stability and insulation from political winds were paramount.

Since 2013, the United States has undergone a prolonged period of unplanned re-evaluation and restructuring of its system of charity regulation at the federal level, driven by partisan political pressure from Congress. In order to evaluate the developments since 2013 and the United States' experience with charity regulation more generally, particularly in comparison to charity regulation in other countries, it is important to understand how the US system evolved and the complex and uncoordinated nature of the legal regime applicable to charity operations. The regulation of charities in the United States is a function of the common law heritage of the US legal system and the division of responsibility between the federal and state governments. As already noted earlier, oversight of charities at the federal level is principally the responsibility of the IRS, a subsidiary agency of the Treasury Department. Although Congress and the Treasury Department have responsibility for tax policy—Congress enacting the Internal Revenue Code and Treasury issuing regulations under the Code—enforcement of tax law is assigned to the IRS. Making the IRS responsible for oversight of charities reflects the fact that the standards for charity behavior are set forth in federal tax law. The implications of assigning what is essentially a regulatory function to the government's main revenue-raising agency will be discussed later in this chapter. Suffice it to say that the overarching mission of the IRS is the collection of tax revenue, and, as a result, the regulatory mission of charity oversight is fundamentally different from, indeed out of step with, the prevailing agency dynamic. The inevitable tension between the IRS's role as tax collector and its role as charity regulator has presented a huge challenge for those charged with undertaking the regulation of charities. From the perspective of those within the IRS and Treasury, rational decision making would favor the allocation of tax enforcement resources to those functions that will generate the most revenue for the fisc, to the detriment of those functions that do not, and charities regulation is not a significant revenue raiser.

Given that the charity rules are embedded in the Internal Revenue Code, the standards for behavior are generally defined as an exception from the otherwise generally applicable rules of taxation of financial transactions, coupled with the circumstances under which that exception would be compromised. Even though the statutory language setting forth the structure of IRS oversight and the class of organizations qualifying as charities is a function of a comparatively modern statute—the predecessor of the current Internal Revenue Code of 1986 dates from 1913—the terminology used by Congress in delineating the boundaries of the class tracks the more historical language of the common law when identifying charitable purposes. That class of organizations now plays a major role in the delivery of education, health care, and social services generally in the United States.

The extent of the authority of the IRS is defined and limited by the specific terms of the Internal Revenue Code, thus the IRS does not have general equity powers to address charity misbehavior by restoring the charity to appropriate operations. The closest that the tax law comes to equity is with regard to financial diversions for the benefit of those in positions of control or significant influence over the charity. In such a scenario, the tax rules mandate correction, for example, making the charity whole so that the transgressing individual may avoid a punitive excise tax. If the tax rules are abused more generally, the default regulatory mechanism is to punish the charity by levying a tax on it, even if that step curtails the ability of the organization to carry out its charitable mission or perhaps even drives the entity to bankruptcy.

Although the IRS is the principal charity overseer, other federal agencies have limited roles based on particular statutes that authorize agency action, often within the larger sphere of mission-related activities of the agency. For example, the US Postal Service administers rules governing fundraising through the mail. Despite the clear congressionally mandated division of responsibility for charity oversight reflected in the division of regulatory activity between the IRS and other federal agencies, Congress also enacted a strict privacy rule as part of the Internal Revenue Code that effectively prevents the IRS from coordinating enforcement efforts among the various agencies or with state Attorneys General, which have the primary responsibility for oversight at the state level.[2] Thus, despite a commonality of mission between federal and state agencies, the IRS is compelled to operate behind a screen that effectively prohibits, indeed criminalizes, the sharing of information and other resources between similarly tasked regulators. Ironically, the same privacy rule contains an exception that authorizes the IRS to share taxpayer information with state revenue offices (but not with state agencies with a charity oversight role), thus enabling the agency to fully coordinate tax enforcement regarding taxable enterprises and persons at both the federal and state level, ensuring a level of uniformity in tax administration that is simply unattainable with regard to charity oversight. Efforts to correct this apparent mistake in legislative drafting have had little success, with the result that charities avoid the sort of coordinated federal-state tax enforcement that applies to all other taxpayers in the United States. In light of the criminal penalties that apply to any IRS employee who violates the privacy rule, the specter of the rule also inhibits coordination with well-intentioned outside groups that want to assist with complex tasks for which the IRS may have inadequate expertise and resources, for example, with the development of software and procedures for electronic filing of charity documents—a task that requires access to information that is only found behind the privacy firewall.

In contrast, at the state level, as noted earlier, oversight responsibility rests primarily with the state Attorney General, not the state tax collector, although other state agencies may have specialized roles. Apart from Louisiana, whose legal heritage is based on the Napoleonic Code, each state Attorney General's authority over charities is drawn, in the first instance, from common law. The common law jurisdiction is then subject to an overlay of statutory law, which varies from state to state. The authority of other state agencies is based in state statutory law, analogous to the interaction that federal agencies other than the IRS have with charities. For example, the general licensing of organizations to conduct business within a given state is usually the responsibility of the secretary of state or a consumer protection agency, particularly with regard to fundraising regulation, and state departments of education will typically have a role in overseeing the educational standards of private schools.

The common law heritage of both federal and state charity laws results in a base of similar legal principles upon which Congress and the various state legislatures have enacted modifications, often in response to specific matters in front of the relevant legislative body at the time. The result is an imperfect congruence of definitions in the otherwise common terminology. That is, organizations may be deemed charities for purposes of state law but not federal law, and vice versa, and restrictions on charity behavior may well differ between the federal government and the states, and between the states. The difference in definitions can be a source of confusion, particularly among charities that operate with volunteers or others who do not have particular expertise in charity regulation; the confusion is exacerbated when charities operate in more than one state, as is likely to happen with fundraising appeals. Charities, therefore, must adapt their internal control systems to respond to differing behavioral standards and reporting requirements to avoid missteps that could have a significant disruptive effect, such as a suspension of fundraising or other operations until matters are brought into compliance. One commentator even observes, "The taxing statutes rarely track with precision the notion of what is charitable for purposes of rendering a [charitable] disposition valid."[3] Even within the boundaries of the Internal Revenue Code, the definition of "charitable" varies. For example, section 2055(a)(2) specifically provides that a bequest to an organization for the "encouragement of art" qualifies as a charitable bequest for the purposes of the estate tax, while section 501(c)(3), defining the class of organizations entitled to income tax exemption as charities, contains no such specific reference. The net result of the variations and nuances of the legal terminology coupled with overlapping federal tax rules and state law is a fine stew, seemingly guaranteed to ensure that voluntary compliance and efficient, consistent regulation will be a significant administrative challenge.

The Early United States Experience

Before the appearance of a federal income tax, and the consequent need for a definition of those organizations that are not subject to tax, questions concerning charities arose at the state, rather than the national level, and then in the context of litigation rather than direct regulation. The context for charity litigation typically involved the application of common law notions such as the possible impact of the rule against perpetuities, or uncertainty regarding the purpose or object of a charitable devise, and judicial analysis often made reference to English court decisions and treatises.[4] The incorporation of English precedents into decisions in US state courts has resulted in the grounding of US charity law in early English law, but this incorporation has not been without some turbulence. In the immediate wake of independence from England, a number of states followed the lead of Virginia and summarily revoked all English statutes and Acts of Parliament which had been applicable in the state as a former colony, including the Statute of Charitable Uses. Some states simply purged their laws of all references to the role of the Crown,[5] while others followed the lead of Massachusetts, where the state constitution specifically provided for the incorporation of English common law and statutes.

It was not until 1844 that the uncertainties in the relationship of English common law and statutory law in US charity jurisprudence were resolved by the Supreme Court in the case of *Vidal v. Girard's Executors*.[6] In *Vidal*, the Supreme Court considered the case of a wealthy Philadelphia resident who left nearly $7,000,000, a considerable sum in 1831, the year of Vidal's death, to a variety of beneficiaries, including various relatives, the city of New Orleans, several charities, and the city of Philadelphia in trust to establish a school for poor white male orphans. Vidal's heirs challenged the devise to the city of Philadelphia on the grounds that the Statute of Charitable Uses was not in effect in Pennsylvania, hence no charitable trust could be created. The Supreme Court disagreed, finding that charitable uses existed at common law prior to the Statute of Charitable Uses, which merely affirmed the existence of such uses and provided for their enforcement. The Supreme Court went on to uphold the ability of the city of Philadelphia to accept and administer a charitable trust.

With the emergence of federal rules based in tax law, beginning in 1913, federal courts were faced with the need to define the boundary between tax-exempt status for charities and taxable status for other financial enterprises. Congress provided little direction or definition with regard to the boundary—a situation that has endured to this day—so federal courts looked to state court interpretations of the same concept for guidance. The result has been the incorporation of English common law and statutory-law notions of charity into Supreme Court and federal court decisions interpreting the Internal Revenue Code via the reliance on state court decisions that referenced English legal principles. Nevertheless, the general absence of clear statutory definitions for key terminology in federal tax law has had a beneficial aspect—namely, that the notions of charitable purpose are sufficiently flexible that they can evolve to reflect societal change. However, it has also had a negative aspect in that the same ambiguity that provides adaptability injects uncertainty into the calculus and a potential for inconsistent interpretation, sometimes simultaneously, by the IRS, the courts, and the general public.

A seminal event in US charity law, and a good illustration of the relationship of English common law and English statutory law to both state charity law and federal tax law in this country, can be found in the 1983 US Supreme Court decision in *Bob Jones University v. United States*.[7] In that case, the Court addressed the issue of whether an educational charity, a private university, must serve a public purpose and not be contrary to established public policy. The fact that Bob Jones University offered a program of instruction to a body of regularly enrolled students and conferred degrees upon the completion of a course of study was not questioned by the IRS or the Court, but by the University's racially discriminatory policies with regard to student behavior, such as its prohibition on interracial dating, were a concern to both. The *Bob Jones University* case also provides an example of how the IRS has been required to confront sensitive questions of public policy that Congress has avoided addressing. Racial discrimination in education had been found by federal courts to be a clear violation of the US Constitution since a series of Supreme Court decisions in the mid-1950s, yet Congress had not provided any guidance to either the Treasury or the IRS as to how that concept should be reflected in tax law enforcement. It thus fell to the Exempt Organizations Division of the IRS to address one of the important public policy crises of the twentieth century—namely, the "Massive Resistance" campaign by conservative groups using racially discriminatory private schools to circumvent the Supreme Court's orders in the two *Brown v. Board of Education* cases, which found racial discrimination in education to be in violation of the Constitution and subsequent public school desegregation orders. The IRS and its Exempt Organizations Division proceeded, facing the dual challenges of enforcing a federal court order mandating that the agency deny or revoke the tax-exempt status of racially discriminatory schools in Mississippi, a focal point of the Massive Resistance campaign, and dealing with Congress, which enacted restrictions on IRS funding to prevent the agency from issuing public rules to enable compliance with court ordered racial desegregation.

The IRS found its tools to deal with the issue of racial discrimination in education in the link between the concept of charity in the federal tax rules and norms of charitable behavior drawn from English common law.

The relevant section of the Internal Revenue Code providing for tax-exempt status for private universities is section 501(c)(3), which provides for tax-exempt status for organizations "organized and operated exclusively for religious, charitable, scientific, testing for public safety, literary or educational purposes." The statute is silent with regard to matters of illegality and public policy, while the relevant Treasury regulations[8] note that the term "charitable" as it appears in the statute is used in its "generally accepted legal sense," but otherwise does not add a specific gloss regarding public policy. The IRS revoked the tax-exempt status of Bob Jones University on the grounds that the institution violated fundamental public policy and the university appealed the loss of status to the federal courts. The IRS action was thus one of the first, if not the first, clear applications of the notion that charities engaged in activities that violate law and public policy are not entitled to tax-exempt status. In due course, the challenge to the IRS action reached the Supreme Court, but by that time, then president Ronald Reagan refused to allow the Department of Justice to argue the case before the Court. However, he did permit the department to appoint a private litigator, William T. Coleman, to present the case on behalf of the IRS, thus neatly underscoring the sensitivity of charity oversight, particularly where common law principles have been judicially grafted onto the body of codified tax law, and then intersect with sensitive public policy issues, such as racial discrimination.

Given the statutory context for the IRS action, the Court reached back to earlier Supreme Court decisions for guidance, including its 1877 decision in *Ould v. Washington Hospital for Foundlings*,[9] which dealt with whether a foundling hospital is a charity. In the course of its analysis in *Ould*, the Court was required to examine "the early English statutes and the early decisions of the courts of law and equity," finding 46 "specifications of pious and charitable uses recognized as within the protection of the law, in which were embraced all that were enumerated in the statute of Elizabeth." The Court further noted, "A charitable use, where neither law nor public policy forbids, may be applied to almost anything that tends to promote the well-doing and the well-being of social man." The English precedents thus enabled the Court to find that the formation of a hospital for abandoned children was, indeed, charitable, even though no further definition of the charitable class to be served was provided for in the hospital's charter.

Over a century later, the Court in *Bob Jones* again reached back through *Ould* to English law for precedent and quoted *Commissioners for the Special Purposes of Income Tax v. Pemsel*[10] to find that "trusts for the advancement of education" and "for other purposes beneficial to the community" qualified as charities within the meaning of section 501(c)(3) of the Internal Revenue Code of 1954. In doing so, the Court dispensed with an argument advanced by Bob Jones University that the specific and separate enumeration of educational purposes in the flush language of section 501(c)(3) precluded the application of historic notions and limitations of charitable, as distinct from educational purposes drawn from the common law. The Court then noted that an examination of the legislative history of the statute reveals "unmistakable evidence" that Congress intended that charities seeking tax-exempt status "must serve a public purpose and not be contrary to established public policy." The Court also observed that tax-exempt status for certain institutions that are deemed "beneficial to the social order of the country as a whole, or to a particular community, are deeply rooted in our history, as that of England." Bob Jones University was held to be in violation of a clearly defined public policy against racial discrimination in education and thus not entitled to federal tax exemption under section 501(c)(3).

In *Bob Jones*, the Supreme Court demonstrated that even though federal tax law applying to charities is embedded in the Internal Revenue Code, a statutory creation of Congress, gaps and ambiguities should be interpreted in the context of its heritage in English common law. In this, it was following a clear judicial practice that has been firmly established in both state and federal courts in matters involving charities. In addition, the IRS gained experience in dealing with high-profile public policy issues and scenarios.

Emergence of Federal Regulation of Charities

As originally drafted, the US Constitution authorized Congress to "lay and collect" taxes only if the taxes were "apportioned among the several States which may be included in this Union, according to their respective number," or the tax was in proportion to the census. The Supreme Court interpreted the restrictions as precluding a tax based on income, leaving tariffs and excise taxes as the principal sources of revenue for the government. The limitations and economic dislocations that accompanied the use of tariffs on trade as a source of revenue, particularly as government became larger and its financial needs greater, moved Congress to propose an amendment to the Constitution to permit the enactment of an income tax. By 1913, a sufficient number of states had ratified the amendment to make it the Sixteenth Amendment to the US Constitution, thereby permitting taxes to be enacted, in addition to those based on census data and customs duties. Congress then passed the Revenue Act of 1913, which, among other matters, levied income taxes on both individuals and corporations.

The Revenue Act also provided for exemptions from income tax for certain types of organizations, including charities, using language that is substantially similar to that in the current Internal Revenue Code. As the United States lacked a Charity Commission or similar specialized regulatory body, the Bureau of Internal Revenue, as the administrator of the income tax was then known, also became the federal charity regulator by virtue of the need to distinguish between taxable and non-taxable economic activity. For nearly 30 years, however, the level of charity oversight by the Bureau was minimal, with no formal process or requirement by tax-exempt organizations to report on their existence and financial activities. Charitable tax-exempt status was a matter of self-declaration by the charity, with the Bureau's regulatory role essentially limited to denying donors a federal tax deduction for a charitable contribution in those situations where the agency believed that a charity did not qualify for that status, or attempting to collect income tax from organizations that came to the Bureau's attention in some manner, typically because of the public nature of their "transparently profit-making activities."[11] With the advent of the Second World War, and an increasing governmental need for revenue, the absence of information about the charities became a concern to the Treasury Department. In 1941, the Treasury promulgated a regulation requiring an annual information reporting form for charities, the Form 990,[12] and shortly afterward, Congress incorporated the regulatory filing requirement into a statutory requirement.

The Development of Modern Federal Charity Oversight

During the 1940s, Congress and the Treasury became increasingly concerned with the extent of commercial activity occurring within tax-exempt organizations—that is, outside the tax system—and with the lack of transparency in the operation of charities. Matters quickly came to a head after the C. F. Mueller Company, the largest producer of pasta in the United States, was restructured as a charitable corporation with the profits, and eventually the ownership, of the corporation to be donated to the New York University School of Law. The Company endeavored to use its relationship to the university's tax-exempt status to shelter the Company's profits from taxation. The IRS attempted to assess income tax against the Company, and was successful in Tax Court, however, in *C. F. Mueller Co. v. Commissioner of Internal Revenue*,[13] the Court of Appeals reversed the Tax Court and held that the Company was entitled to charity status based on the fact that it devoted all its income to the law school. New York University was not alone, however, as Union College purchased Allied Stores Corporation, one of the largest department stores in the United States. Adolph J. Sabath, then a member of the House of Representatives from Illinois, announced that "Universities own haberdasheries, citrus groves, movies, cattle ranches, the Encyclopedia Britannica (owned by the University of Chicago), and a large variety of other enterprises."[14]

Congressional hearings ensued, and eventually Congress enacted the Revenue Act of 1950, which set the stage for the modern era of charity oversight, characterized by operational and financial reporting to the IRS and thereby to the general public through the public release of the annual federal tax reporting form, known as the Form 990, and a series of specific limitations and constraints on charity behavior through excise taxes and income tax exposure for certain types of charity income that is generated from business activity that is unrelated to the tax-exempt purpose of the organization. The Form 990, of which there are several versions corresponding to the financial size of the filing organization, is required to be filed annually by virtually every tax-exempt organization, with limited exceptions for certain organizations, such as churches and similar houses of worship. A special version of the form, the Form 990-PF must be filed by a category of tax-exempt organizations known as private foundations. Private foundations are distinguished from other types of charities by the pattern of their income, essentially derived from a single or small group of donors, or from investments, as would be the case with an endowment. In addition to the annual information return, Congress has mandated that the application for tax-exempt status is also a public record, once approved, and is available from the IRS upon request and from the charity itself.

Structure of Modern Federal Charity Oversight

The legal structure of charity oversight, as embedded in the Internal Revenue Code, has evolved since the Revenue Act of 1950. Even though Congress has periodically adjusted the relevant provisions, the applicable tax rules continue to fall into two categories: 1) a series of classification sections, coordinated with income tax rules, listing purposes deemed charitable, and dividing organizations with charitable purposes into two categories, public charities and private foundations, based on income patterns and activities and 2) a series of regulatory sections using excise taxes applicable to certain specified behavior by charities or those individuals that manage them, effectively restricting or prohibiting certain behavior deemed inappropriate. In the wake of the Tax Reform Act of 1969, which enacted complex tax rules, and the subsequent Employee Retirement Income Security Act of 1974, Congress put in place the key legal and administrative structures specifically designed to ensure consistent and effective administration of the tax laws. That structure endured until the IRS Restructuring Act of 1998, which was the first step in returning the IRS oversight capabilities essentially to a pre-1969 structure—that is, one that reflected a point in time in which there were far fewer charities and a far less complex tax-based regulatory structure.

The IRS faces a number of significant challenges in meeting its oversight responsibilities for tax-exempt organizations. In many respects, the challenges have remained essentially unchanged in the 40 years since the general framework was put in place in 1974, in a manifestation of Congressional concern with the level of attention and amount of resources devoted by the IRS to the regulatory functions of charity oversight. While the level of funding by Congress and the executive branch is, perhaps, the most common concern expressed by commentators, other factors also have a negative impact on the IRS's oversight of tax-exempt organizations. The current antagonistic attitude of Congress towards the agency has exacerbated the long-standing challenges and added a new element: managerial disruption triggered by dramatic personnel changes. This has resulted in the replacement of all executive and managerial personnel from the commissioner down to mid-level management within the Exempt Organizations Division, the very function charged with oversight of charities.[15] In addition, in order to expedite the processing of applications for tax-exempt status from newly formed organizations, the IRS has promulgated a radically shortened application known as the Form 1023-EZ. This abandons the "long-form" application's detailed list of financial and operational questions and documentation submission, replacing it with a self-certified checklist of yes/no questions, effectively converting the application process into a registration process.

Whether the new application process will trade short application processing times for significant post-application enforcement challenges remains to be seen. Whether or not any enforcement concerns emerge from the organizational changes wrought by the new IRS management team, the IRS will continue to face challenges arising from embedding charity oversight into tax law and assigning administration to the tax collection agency. The key concerns identified here relate to inadequate funding, civil service and institutional constraints, and the inefficiencies inherent in using tax law as a regulatory tool.

Inadequate Funding

The number of tax-exempt organizations continues to grow and there is every indication, based on IRS records reflecting a generally steady growth over the last two decades, that the number will continue to increase.[16] IRS staffing and other resources dedicated to oversight of these organizations have fallen or remained stagnant,[17] and there is no evidence that historical levels of oversight have been adequate to ensure that significant abuses can be identified and addressed in a timely manner. Because of the dynamic of the federal budget process, noted as far back as 1977 by the Filer Commission,[18] the original intention that an amount of funds equivalent to revenue collected under the section 4940 tax (an annual excise tax of 2% of the income of private foundations, enacted as part of the Tax Reform Act of 1969) be spent on overseeing tax-exempt organizations has never been realized.[19] Executive branch budget requests and congressional appropriations, to the extent that they identify amounts for oversight of tax-exempt organizations, bear no relationship to the section 4940 tax, and information on resources devoted to the oversight function is not published regularly. This means that no comparisons can be made over time of the amount collected under section 4940 and the resources allocated to oversight. It is quite likely that the section 4940 tax generates amounts of revenue for the federal government that far exceed the amounts spent by the IRS on oversight.

Civil Service Constraints

A separate and more significant challenge, over and above the question of annual budgets, is the larger issue of the ability of the federal government to be competitive in hiring and retaining qualified personnel. Effective tax administration requires highly trained accountants, attorneys, and other professionals to review increasingly complex financial transactions and relationships. The compensation that can be offered by the IRS is set on a government-wide basis, and although adjustments can be made based on geographic differences in the cost of living and through intentional manipulation of job descriptions, those steps are limited in impact and number. Historically, it has been very difficult for the IRS to compete with the private sector for specialized personnel, particularly in large metropolitan areas, and for more senior or experienced positions. For example, in 2015, the maximum base compensation of the Senior Executive Service, the highest-level career employee classification in the federal government was $183,300, approximately the salary of a mid-level associate in a large law firm.

Institutional Constraints

The primary function of the IRS is to ensure that taxpayers, whether individuals or businesses, pay the appropriate amount of federal income tax, and IRS systems and procedures are designed to support that tax collecting role. Historically, IRS internal management information systems have been designed to track tax returns and related matters of for-profit organizations and individuals. In a rational, economic approach to the task, these have been adapted to address some of the management information requirements of the tax-exempt organizations function. Other IRS systems follow this pattern of development as well. For example, despite the unique public nature and function of the Form 990 series returns, electronic filing systems and procedures for them have been a by-product or offshoot of the planning, development, and implementation of electronic filing of the corporate tax return. Even the development of formal guidance in interpreting federal tax law applicable to tax-exempt organizations must compete for institutional attention with revenue-producing matters at top levels within the IRS and the Department of the Treasury.

Inefficiencies in Tax Law as a Regulatory Mechanism

The authority given to the IRS to serve as the sole nationwide regulatory body for tax-exempt organizations is limited by the specific language and scope of the Internal Revenue Code. For example, some of the excise taxes applied to tax-exempt organizations are in the nature of a penalty, intended to discourage egregious behavior, rather than generate tax revenue. Enforcement of these is tied to the system of annually filed tax returns, even though a more timely oversight and reporting mechanism, triggered by a particular act or event, might be far more effective and certainly would help improve public perception of the policing of bad acts. Examples are section 4958, dealing with excess benefit transactions (excessive compensation in the public charity context), section 4941, involving self-dealing (financial transactions between a private foundation and those in charge of the foundation), and section 4944, regarding investment policy (penalizing investments that are so risky as to endanger the ability of a private foundation to carry out its charitable activities). Depending on the date of filing, a return for a year in which a questionable financial transaction or investment is made might be filed as much as 10 months and 15 days after the close of the year in which it occurred (the regular due date plus extensions) and could be nearly two years after the actual event if it took place early in a given tax year. In the case of political campaign intervention, that will typically be after the relevant election is over. It would be far more effective, for example, if reporting of the transgression were required within a relatively short period after the discovery of the event, thus allowing for a quick IRS review of the return and its accuracy and reflection of the underlying events.

Relying on an annual tax return filing as the trigger for regulatory action makes it impossible to address issues of concern in a timely manner. The Internal Revenue Code recognizes the need for quick action only in the case of "flagrant" violations of the prohibition on political campaign expenditures, thus allowing the IRS to determine and assess taxes immediately and to enjoin further political campaign intervention. But timely enforcement of standards upon discovery of a violation should be the rule, not the exception, and is, in fact, the case with state attorney general oversight.

Other provisions drafted for administering taxation of for-profit organizations and individuals have terms that actually hamper efficient and effective administration involving tax-exempt organizations. For example, section 6103 deals with the privacy of taxpayer information and permits close cooperation and information sharing between the IRS and state revenue offices with regard to income tax matters. Because the language of the statute refers to state tax agencies, which typically do not regulate charities, it precludes a similar level of coordination between the IRS and state charity regulators. Given the public nature of charities, charity regulation should not be shackled to these kinds of strict limits on disclosure that are designed to protect private persons' confidential tax information, but instead provide regulatory arbitrage opportunities for organizations seeking to mask their activities from public view or control regulator access to information.

Difficulty Generating Guidance

In the US federal tax system, the Department of the Treasury is responsible for tax law guidance, including, in decreasing importance, regulations, notices, announcements, revenue rulings, and revenue procedures. Regulations provide a more nuanced explanation of statutory language and can have the force and effect of law. Notices and announcements serve a similar purpose, but with less precedential impact. Revenue rulings describe the IRS's view of the application of tax law and regulations to a particular fact pattern, much like a truncated court decision. Revenue procedures describe how taxpayers might comply with particular provisions of tax law, such as the filing of applications for exemption from federal income tax. All guidance involving tax-exempt organizations, including charities, is reviewed by the Office of Tax Policy in the Treasury Department, which traditionally has had a single attorney assigned to that task. While the larger staff in the IRS Office of Chief Counsel assists in the development of guidance, all guidance must cross the desk of the single attorney in the Treasury Department assigned to tax-exempt organizations matters. The guidance staffing constraint thus inhibits the ability of the Treasury and the IRS to address new developments in the charitable sector that do not arise from tax legislation passed by Congress.

As a result, new developments, such as the rise of hybrid legal structures for the conduct of activities traditionally considered to be the province of charities, do not receive official analysis by Treasury and the IRS. Those wishing to use the new structures for appropriate activities are thus without guidance as to how the tax law might apply to them, and anyone focused on using the structures for inappropriate purposes has free rein. Examples of such hybrid legal structures are divided essentially into two groups: 1) those based on the concept of a corporation, including the "benefit corporation" and the "flexible purpose corporation" and 2) those based on the concept of the limited liability company, the only current example of which is the "low-profit limited liability company" or L3C. Some states have enacted legislation providing for a status known as the "B corporation," which is not a separate legal structure, but rather a certification that a corporation (or other form of legal entity) satisfies certain criteria indicative of socially responsible operations.

The distinctions between the various new forms are often subtle. For example, a benefit corporation has an articulated purpose that has a material positive impact on society and the environment and can be required by statute to take into consideration the interests of workers, community, and environment as they may emerge over time. Such entities are also typically required by statute to issue a public annual report on the organization's performance towards meeting social and environmental goals. In contrast, the flexible purpose corporation, as articulated in California state law, permits the entity to take into account purposes that do not involve pure profit making, similar to a benefit corporation, but only to the extent that the alternative purposes are set forth in the entity's articles of incorporation. Neither the benefit corporation nor the flexible purpose corporation statutes purport to have any linkage to the concepts of charity in the Internal Revenue Code.

Hybrid legal structures using the limited liability company form rather than the corporation, of which the L3C is the only current example, are formed in those states that have adopted a modification of their traditional limited liability company rules to authorize the formation of limited liability companies that must be formed and operated for a purpose that is considered charitable under the Internal Revenue Code. Because an L3C has owners that need not be charities, it is not itself a charity, or tax-exempt, and can distribute any profit from its "charity-like" operations to the owners of the L3C. While an L3C is a for-profit corporation from a tax perspective, and contributions to it are not eligible for deduction as charitable contributions by donors, the L3C's charitable purposes make it a potentially useful vehicle for private foundations, and charities more generally, that want to harness profit-motivated investors in a charitable cause, which is an approach being adopted by the Bill and Melinda Gates Foundation according to media reports.[20] Whether any of the new hybrid forms of charitable activity prove to be useful additions to the charitable sector or not, the existence of hybrids and any implications for true charities that engage with them, will need to be addressed by charity regulators at some point. The ability of the Treasury and the IRS to do so from a federal perspective is hobbled by the limitations on the generation of tax law guidance more generally.

A Path Forward

The challenges outlined earlier suggest a system under some strain and potentially near the breaking point in terms of its ability to police the boundary between appropriate and inappropriate charity behavior. Key elements of a new approach would include decoupling charity oversight from the IRS and, indeed, from the federal government itself. The function could perhaps be shifted to a commission jointly overseen by the federal and state agencies concerned with charity behavior, but with funding from the charitable sector rather than governmental sources, thus lessening the constraints imposed by civil service rules and the Internal Revenue Code.[21] A key focus of a new approach should be transparency in administration, including enforcement actions, both to the general public and to other agencies at the federal and state levels. That transparency should include a robust program of formal and informal guidance updated in a timely manner. In particular, barriers to obtaining guidance from the regulator should be reduced to the greatest extent possible to encourage voluntary compliance with the charity rules.

Conclusion

The oversight of charities in the United States is in the midst of significant change resulting in the dismantling of the governmental structure that has been in place for 40 years. The abruptness of the change and its genesis in partisan congressional investigations suggest that careful and systematic consideration of the changes and possible alternatives have not been undertaken. As a result, the historic challenges of situating charity oversight rules in a tax statute and enforcement in a tax collection agency have not been addressed. It is not yet clear whether a new structure will emerge to ensure compliance with federal tax laws or if the change is the first step in a major re-evaluation of the relationship between government and charities in the United States.

Notes

1 The Employee Retirement Income Security Act of 1974 authorized the creation of a separate function within the IRS to administer the federal tax rules applicable to pension plans and tax-exempt organizations, including charities. Before the Act, the provisions had been administered by various offices located in components of the agency devoted to other functions.
2 Section 6103 of the Internal Revenue Code essentially prohibits the disclosure of any taxpayer-specific information to anyone outside the IRS. While there is a limited number of exceptions, the general effect of the provision is to make coordination of enforcement actions essentially impossible.
3 Mark L. Ascher et al., *Scott and Ascher on Trusts* (New York: Aspen Publishers, 5th ed., 2006) §37.1.4, p. 2374.
4 Ascher et al., *Trusts*, §37.1.3, p. 2369.
5 Marion Fremont-Smith, *Foundations and Government—State and Federal Law and Supervision* (New York: Russell Sage Foundation, 1965).
6 2 Howard 127, 11 L. Ed. 205 (1844).
7 *Bob Jones University v. United States*, 461 U.S. 574 (1983).
8 Treasury Reg. §1.501(c)(3)—1(d)(2).
9 93 U.S. 303 (1877).
10 *Commissioners for Special Purposes of the Income Tax v. Pemsel* [1891] AC 531.
11 *Internal Revenue Manual* §7.27.4.1.2 (02–23–1999).
12 Treasury Decision 5125, 1942–1 C.B. 101.
13 *C. F. Mueller Co. v. Commissioner of Internal Revenue*, 190 F.2d 120 (3rd Cir. 1951).
14 Congressional Record, Vol. 96, Part 7, pp. 9273–9274, reprinted in *Internal Revenue Manual* §7.27.4.1.2 (02–23–1999).
15 For an overview of recent changes at the IRS, see Evelyn Brody and Marcus Owens, "Exile to Main Street: The I.R.S.'s Diminished Role in Overseeing Tax-Exempt Organizations," *Chicago-Kent Law Review* 91 (2016): 859. (Symposium on Nonprofit Oversight Under Siege: An International Comparison of Regulatory Models).
16 "SOI Tax Stats: Tax-Exempt Organizations and Nonexempt Charitable Trusts: IRS Data Book Table 25," Internal Revenue Service, last reviewed or updated March 30, 2016, https://www.irs.gov/uac/SOI-Tax-Stats-Tax-Exempt-Organiza tions-and-Nonexempt-Charitable-Trusts-IRS-Data-Book-Table-25.
17 "National Taxpayer Advocate Delivers Annual Report to Congress; Focuses on Taxpayer Bill of Rights and IRS Funding," *IRS News Release*, (IR-2014–3), accessed January 9, 2014, https://www.irs.gov/uac/Newsroom/National-Tax payer-Advocate-Delivers-Annual-Report-to-Congress;-Focuses-on-Taxpayer-Bill-of-Rights-and-IRS-Funding.
18 Commission on Private Philanthropy and Public Needs, *Giving in America: Toward a Stronger Voluntary Sector* (The Commission, 1975), (Chairman, John H. Filer), accessed July 26, 2016, http://hdl.handle.net/2450/889.
19 Joint Committee on Internal Revenue Taxation, *General Explanation of the Tax Reform Act of 1969* (JCS-16–70) (Washington: US Government Printing Office, 1970), 29, accessed July 26, 2016, https://archive.org/details/generalexplanati00jcs1670.
20 Sarah Max, "From the Gates Foundation, Direct Investment, Not Just Grants," *New York Times*, March 12, 2015, accessed July 26, 2016, http://www.nytimes.com/2015/03/13/business/from-the-gates-foundation-direct-investment-not-just-grants.html.
21 A detailed description of one such alternative approach can be found in: Marcus S. Owens, "Charity Oversight: An Alternative Approach," *Columbia University Academic Commons* (2013), accessed July 26, 2016, doi:10.7916/D8154F1D.

6   Reflections on Challenged Regulators

Elizabeth T. Boris and Cindy M. Lott

Introduction

Nonprofit organizations in the United States have a long and complex history of interaction with the major institutions of the state and the market, although for the most part they have operated in relative obscurity. They have enjoyed a fair amount of trust with ordinary citizens who come in contact with them and a relatively loose regulatory regime.[1] As Dennis Young writes, nonprofits are at times in complementary, supplementary, and adversarial relationships with government,[2] and in some respects, they have similar types of relationships with businesses. In this chapter, we focus on the challenges of regulating charities in the context of a growing, changing, and more visible nonprofit sector; a global economic system that is creating unprecedented wealth for some and leaving many behind; and a national political environment that is extremely polarized.[3]

In response to the globalizing economy, many United States charities operate internationally; mirroring society, they are unequal in size and resources, and reflecting political polarization, many are part of, and affected by, the contentious political currents. These trends affect federal and state regulatory agencies in terms of resources, tools, and skills required to oversee and appropriately regulate the nonprofit sector and the charities within it. Our concern is that these agencies are not resourced adequately for the oversight they must exert to ensure public benefit and maintain public trust in this vital growing and changing part of our society. Although there are many oversight challenges, three major issues stand out: information necessary for effective oversight is not freely available; there is no central locus of expertise for federal oversight; the regulations themselves do not provide the level of transparency required for effective oversight. Government agencies and nonprofit watchdog organizations do valiant work, but are hampered in the scope and depth of their analyses by limited public information and access to resources.

There is growing recognition that oversight of charities requires attention in the face of political pressures, inadequate resources, and sheer growth of the sector. Despite this recognition, there is no overarching effort by the sector to document their needs or propose improvements, as occurred in the past through the Commission on Foundations and Private Philanthropy (the Peterson Commission), the Commission on Private Philanthropy and Public Needs (the Filer Commission), and the Independent Sector Panel on the Nonprofit Sector.[4] In each of those examples, there was a focused effort to collect objective information to respond to government investigations of foundations and concerns about the charitable sector. This research was used to recommend policies and advocate for changes in regulations.

The Peterson Commission, funded by John D. Rockefeller III and several foundations, was established to look into and make recommendations concerning foundations in the wake of the investigations by Representative Wright Patman from 1961 to 1972 and the subsequent 1965 Treasury Report on foundations. Following the passage of the 1969 Tax Reform Act, which created a new regulatory framework for foundations and the nonprofit sector, the Commission on Private Philanthropy and Public Needs, referred to as the Filer Commission after its chair John H. Filer, was created to conduct nonpartisan research and make recommendations for changes. The Filer Commission commissioned the first broadscale, systematic research on the charitable sector and made recommendations for improving the sector and softening some elements of the 1969 regulations. Many of those recommendations became law in subsequent years.

The latest sector effort to affect public policy toward the sector came about in October 2004 when Independent Sector, a membership association of foundations and nonprofits, encouraged by the Senate Finance Committee, created a panel of more than 100 experts on the sector including nonprofit and foundation leaders, researchers, accountants, lawyers, academics, regulators, and others to recommend actions to strengthen governance and ethical conduct in the sector. Work groups conducted and commissioned research, held hearings, and issued papers and final reports that provided analyses of issues related to transparency, governance, and accountability, and made recommendations to Congress.[5]

There have not been similar sector-wide efforts to inform and influence policies toward the sector in the intervening years. Advocacy is piecemeal. National associations respond to regulatory and tax change proposals that are made in Congress as they come up, and state associations do the same at the state level. They also advocate for incremental changes that may succeed over time, but the major nonprofit associations do not have a coordinated regulatory reform strategy for the sector. There is perhaps even a fear that such a strategy may create too much visibility and have negative unintended consequences. Advocacy initiatives tend to be on behalf of subgroups (education, health, etc.) and are generally not pursued through coordinated sector-wide efforts. Sector leadership organizations are struggling to make issues affecting the sector visible and to create the will to advocate more forcefully for a regulatory environment that enhances its ability to serve public needs.

Growth and Change

The nonprofit sector in the United States is growing and changing. Historically, this sector of American society was nearly invisible. This has changed. Along with increasing growth and global reach is heightened visibility in the media, online, and inside and outside of government. Although its economic impact is small compared to government and business, recent research by the National Center for Charitable Statistics at the Urban Institute shows that the 1.56 million nonprofit organizations comprising the nonprofit sector in the United States account for an estimated 5.4 per cent of GDP and employ about 10 per cent of the labor force. They hold $5.2 trillion in assets and have expenditures of about $2.1 trillion.[6] Their growth rate outpaces both government and business. Such statistics generate visibility in the broader society. Charities, the focus of this book and this chapter, form the largest part of the US nonprofit sector with about one million organizations; they are affected by their growing visibility and the trends in the larger sector of which they are a part.

Charities are growing faster than other parts of the nonprofit sector, and as of 2013, they accounted for "just over three-quarters of the nonprofit sector's revenue and expenses and more than three-fifths of nonprofit assets."[7] With growth and visibility have come challenges, both internal and external. The diversity of the charitable portion of the sector, comprising a majority of small human services, arts, environmental, and other nonprofits, alongside less than 5 per cent of very large hospitals, universities, and others, results in generalizations and policy proposals that are often problematic when applied across the variety of large and small organizations. Regulatory policies must be crafted and applied carefully to provide appropriate oversight for the diverse segments of the sector and to do so without causing undue burdens.

The sector is also changing in many ways. Charities are more reliant on fee-for-service income (47 per cent) and government grants and contracts (33 per cent) than they are on donations (13 per cent).[8] They are also increasingly exploring social enterprises and impact investing, all of which require professional staff. Many have added websites and social media presence with online fundraising capacity in addition to traditional mail, telephone, and face-to-face methods. Government grants and contracts require sophisticated accounting, transparency, and performance measurement.[9] Competition with other charities and businesses to provide services requires marketing, online presence, and communications. Mergers of nonprofits with other nonprofits and buyouts of hospitals by for-profit companies are occurring,[10] and it is questionable whether the current reporting on Form 990 is adequate to oversee these types of activities.

Philanthropy is also changing and becoming more complex. More people are giving online and through smartphones. Increasing numbers of middle-income earners are creating donor-advised funds (DAFs) organized under the umbrella of financial services companies (Fidelity, Vanguard, and others) as well as in nonprofits and community foundations.[11] High net worth individuals are pledging and giving mega gifts to their private foundations and to favored nonprofits in the United States and globally, and also investing in or creating "for-benefit" corporations and L3C partnerships that are hybrid organizations with characteristics of charities and businesses.[12] Some foundations are engaging in impact investing and social impact bond (SIBS) deals in collaboration with governments and businesses.[13] These complex activities require appropriate technology and specialized skills for adequate oversight by regulatory agencies, whose job it is to ensure that such funds are dedicated to charitable purposes and do not benefit individuals or businesses inappropriately. Again, there are questions of adequate transparency and reporting to monitor these types of activities.

The political use of nonprofits is another growing phenomenon introducing complex arrangements which require oversight to ensure that they stay within the law. Political figures are creating high-profile charities and foundations to conduct work in their districts, raising their visibility and buffing their images,[14] and wealthy individuals are creating foundations, charities, social welfare organizations (section 501(c)(4)), political action committees (PACs), and DAFs to promote their ideological and political agendas.[15] At the same time, nonprofits interested in affecting public policy are setting up related section 501(c)(4) organizations for lobbying purposes, and some have established PACs.[16] Some nonprofits are raising and spending enormous sums to affect political campaigns, and all of these activities have implications for the oversight activities of federal and state regulatory agencies. They must have access to data, appropriate technology, and trained staff to oversee increasingly complex and diverse organizational activities, some of which appear designed to obscure accountability. Without such resources, they cannot ensure nonprofits are operating lawfully. In the context of a growing and changing nonprofit sector, there is increasing questioning of current definitions of organizations entitled to tax-exemption and charity status, as well as the adequacy of existing mechanisms of oversight and regulation.[17] Observers talk about the blurring of boundaries between nonprofits and businesses, and between nonprofits and government. Policing the lines is becoming more difficult.

Federal and state resources to oversee and regulate nonprofits have not expanded commensurately with the growth and complexity of the sector, and in some respects, they have declined. As Marcus Owens outlines in Chapter 5, resources for IRS activities have declined, and as nonprofit oversight is not part of its primary tax collection mission, those functions do not have a high priority in terms of resource allocation. Even requiring that the annual disclosure documents, IRS Forms 990, be filed electronically and fully accessible online for regulators and the public has not been realized at this point, despite the fact that they are virtually the only disclosure tools in the regulatory arsenal. And, unfortunately, congressional scrutiny of the

IRS has tended to reflect the current political polarization, with budget cuts undermining, rather than building, oversight capacity. At the state level, resources for charity oversight appear to be static despite growth in the nonprofit sector.[18] There is also a serious lack of technological capacity at the state level to take advantage of lower cost options for electronic data mining and online oversight options. With the exception of a handful of states, most state charity officials do not have online access to either their registration forms or the Forms 990 of nonprofits in their states.

Tax Exemption

Questions about which organizations deserve tax exemption seem to be increasing at the federal and state levels. Most nonprofits in the United States are exempt from income tax at the federal level, and many are exempt from state property and sales taxes, although exemption can vary by type of organization and from jurisdiction to jurisdiction. Challenges to tax-exempt status often assert that the nonprofit actually operates as a business or does not provide enough "charitable" benefits to the community. Large universities, hospitals, and foundations, all considered charitable under federal regulations, have robust income streams and significant assets. These have become targets for some policy makers seeking new revenues to close budget gaps without raising taxes on individuals or businesses. In cases involving universities and hospitals, there is sometimes an implicit or explicit challenge to the charitable status of the entity in question, and denying exemptions from property taxes is a way for local policy makers to boost property tax revenues.[19] Challenges to tax-exempt status are occurring across the country, but are particularly prevalent in the older cities of the northeast that have large well-endowed charitable institutions that effectively reduce the amount of property tax the communities might otherwise collect. In these cases, negotiated payments in lieu of taxes (PILOTs) or payments for services (SILOTs) are often made to local community governments on a case-by-case basis. Rationalizations for the payments include the use of community services such as trash collection and police and fire protection. As communities continue to search for revenues to defray local budget deficits, conflicts arising from these ad hoc arrangements are likely to increase and, over time, may rise to the level of a search for more uniform solutions, reduced property tax exemptions, or narrowing of the class of entities entitled to tax-exempt status.

Blurring Lines with Business

Hospitals are a special case. Over the last three decades, for-profit firms have been acquiring nonprofit hospitals—a trend accelerated by the 2010 Affordable Care Act (ACA). The resulting mergers and the shakeout of the healthcare sector have resulted in huge complex conglomerations that look very like their for-profit counterparts, raising questions about the charitable status of these nonprofits. Under the ACA, hospitals must report on their community benefits annually on their IRS Forms 990, adding to the oversight burden. Critics ask the following questions: should these nonprofit hospitals have tax-exempt status? How do they differ from for-profit hospitals?[20] How much community benefit do they, or should they, provide? Is there adequate oversight of the community benefits they provide? Should they have a special status under the tax code? With the sea change in health care in the United States, and the pronounced changes wrought by the ACA, many regulatory questions remain open.

Hybrid Organizations

Another type of for-profit blurring is occurring through the creation of for-benefit organizations. These have missions characteristic of nonprofit organizations embedded in a for-profit enterprise model, and states are increasingly passing legislation to permit such organizations. This issue will be discussed later in the chapter.

Charitable Income Tax Deduction

A related conversation concerns the charitable tax deduction and the appropriateness of providing an incentive for giving. Should the government allow individuals and corporations to make gifts to charities and deduct those gifts from taxes owed? How effective is the incentive? How much incentive for giving is necessary? Who benefits, by how much, and at what cost to the public treasury? Regulatory questions include how much oversight of these deductions occurs and how much is appropriate? Because oversight is limited, is fraud more prevalent, especially for gifts that need to be valued, such as property or other non-cash gifts? With limited resources for audits, one suspects that the system operates mostly on trust. What are the appropriate indicators to identify fraud in the field? These issues concern the substantive workings in the sector, but they also play into larger conversations in the public arena regarding trust in the charitable sector.

Charities view deductibility of donations as an incentive that promotes giving among taxpayers who itemize their tax deductions, so they naturally oppose proposals to reduce the deductibility levels or restrict the organizations eligible for the deduction. Economists argue about the tax efficiency of the deduction, but the consensus of the research is that the charitable tax incentive returns more revenues to charities than the corresponding cost of lost taxes to the government, estimated at about $40 billion.[21] A further analysis suggests that not all of this forgone revenue would be captured by taxes if the charitable deduction were to disappear.[22] Billionaires who realize millions of dollars in income each year and give mega gifts to favored charities do not benefit much from the ability to deduct such gifts. There have been proposals to limit, change, or only direct the charitable deduction to certain types of organizations, such as those that help the poor, and to provide a non-itemizer deduction for moderate-income people who do not itemize their deductions on their tax forms. Overseeing the implementation of those types of changes would be difficult under current conditions within the federal enforcement community. With staff attrition at high levels[23] and the audit rate remaining extraordinarily low[24] within the IRS Tax Exempt and Government Entities Division, enforcement of any new regulations will stretch current IRS resources even more markedly.

Fundraising Oversight

State charity officials are responsible for oversight of charitable solicitation within their states. Many, if not most, fundraisers are for-profit firms that raise money through the mail or telephone calls and increasingly through social media and other technological platforms such as text-to-give. Some of these firms keep most of the dollars raised to pay for their costs. In some cases, the firms allegedly set up charities as vehicles for their fundraising.[25] Because fundraising activities typically cross state lines, it is difficult for individual states to regulate their activities without cooperative relationships with other states and information from the IRS, which is difficult to orchestrate under the current statutory regime, as discussed next.

Financial Relationships with Government

Governments at all levels are more reliant on charities to deliver many human services through contracts and grants. However, for nonprofit organizations providing these services, there is often a shortage of capital and sustainable revenues to keep them solvent—a condition exacerbated by government underpayment of service and administrative costs for the programs, late payments, and matching fund stipulations. Understanding the different revenue streams and requirements is important for effective oversight, but reporting and auditing requirements are usually uncoordinated, time consuming, and duplicative.[26] Charities are trying to push for reforms, using evidence from national surveys to conduct public education and lobbying efforts led by the National Council on Nonprofits.[27] Promoting options for reforms in government contracts and grants processes is having some success. Office of Management and Budget Uniform Guidance[28] now requires government contracts to provide a minimum overhead cost reimbursement for nonprofit contractors. However, it is necessary to implement those new regulations.

Blurring Lines with Government

In addition to many nonprofits receiving significant revenues directly from government, sometimes nonprofits are created or incentivized by governments, or enter into complex financial relationships, for example, using tax-exempt bonds and other devices. Social impact bonds (SIBS) are another model of funding that generally involves foundations, charities, businesses, and government in efforts to capitalize nonprofit programs, while only providing a return to investors if agreed upon results are achieved.[29] Another example is the government's attempt to create and fund nonprofit co-ops to provide alternatives to for-profit health insurers under the ACA. Although the recent failure of several co-ops has slowed this effort, the oversight of nonprofits is complicated further by government efforts to create, use, or incentivize financing for nonprofits for policy reasons. Adequate transparency and reporting are imperative to oversee these complex activities.

Closing the Regulatory Gaps

The changes now affecting the nonprofit sector in terms of scope and structure present immense regulatory challenges, both at the federal and state levels. As Marcus Owens notes in Chapter 5, federal regulators have struggled in the last years to present a unified regulatory front because of political undercurrents and structural changes that have left the IRS hobbled in its regulatory and enforcement functions. The states also face these challenges, although in different forms. Unlike the federal regulators who have been the target of political discussion and budget cuts, state charities regulators, until very recently, have been the object of benign neglect, with lack of recognition of their role in regulation, enforcement, and resource allocation. As a result, states' charities regulators have not been able to keep up with changes in the sector because of major under-resourcing documented in a recent study.[30] The survey of state charities offices found that about a third of responding jurisdictions (31 per cent) had less than one full-time equivalent employee (FTE) dedicated to charities oversight and that more than half have fewer than three FTEs, including attorneys, accountants, investigators and support staff. As of 2013, there were 355 full-time equivalent state charity staff to oversee the more than 1.4 million nonprofits.

One of the chief mandates of state charities regulation is the oversight of solicitation on behalf of charities. The advent of new technological platforms has enabled the increase of two specific types of fundraising activities, both of which cause considerable challenges for regulators. In the past, individuals would raise money for charities door-to-door or in similarly direct ways, limiting their scope. The Internet, online vehicles such as Twitter, and cell phone "text-to-give" applications now afford individuals the ability to solicit to thousands, even millions, of potential donors simultaneously and instantaneously, with little or no documentation of the solicitation. Many of these donations reach a critical mass through crowdsourcing platforms. The Internet has also enabled the introduction of online giving platforms, such as "charity malls," which may be run either as nonprofits or for-profit entities, allowing donors to choose among multiple charities on a single online platform. Many of the charities may not even know they are listed on such sites, as charity malls may not comply with requirements to seek permission from the charities. Technology has also transformed co-ventures, which have long been a popular vehicle for donations, structured as a co-venture between a for-profit entity and a specific charity. The for-profit represents that with each sale, a certain portion of the sale will go to the specified charity. These have now become institutionalized through online giving in a way never seen before. Companies as large as Amazon have combined co-ventures and charity malls through programs that allow online shoppers to direct donations automatically with each individual purchase, sending the donation to their choice of charity from hundreds of thousands listed. Compliance with state solicitation laws across the United States (and the world) is challenging for fundraisers in this complex environment. It is also challenging for regulators who must protect the donor dollar through such technologically enabled vehicles.

From a regulatory perspective, new technologies have taken old solicitation techniques and scaled them to a degree that is difficult to regulate with current regulatory resources. To date, state charities regulators have relied on a combination of extant fundraising laws and general jurisdictional principles employed in other contexts. They are aware, however, that regulation and enforcement of charitable solicitation laws in this murky area are insufficient. At the 2001 annual meeting of the National Association of State Charity Officials in Charleston, South Carolina, the Charleston Principles were devised as jurisdictional principles to address new scenarios raised through Internet donation solicitations. At the public day during the state charity regulators' conference in 2015, a discussion was opened on the Charleston Principles. The question was whether the principles need to be revisited or are elastic enough to apply to many of the current technological innovations in charitable fundraising. Concerns from the fundraising community range from differing laws among the many states to a lack of clarity about jurisdictional reach by any single state over online donations. Further discussion by state regulators is expected in coming years as they grapple with the continuous evolution of technology impacting upon traditional solicitation practices.[31]

The Charleston Principles are not codified in any state; they are intended to be an elastic set of guidelines for applying jurisdictional law to new solicitation vehicles and platforms enabled by technology. The principles have been revisited by state regulators in light of evolving technologies, and to date, no further revisions to the principles have been developed. As regulators face challenges in addressing new giving vehicles, they are also confronting many new "hybrid" corporate forms designed for meeting dual missions of both profit (even if low profit) and charity. According to Robert Wexler, "most legal hybrids are formed as a trust, a corporation, an unincorporated association, a partnership, or a limited liability company."[32] Three different hybrid forms have been enacted in various jurisdictions in the United States, including the L3C (limited liability low-profit corporation),[33] the benefit corporation,[34] and the social purpose corporation.[35] Over 30 jurisdictions now have some form of hybrid corporate forms, and these forms raise a number of issues for regulators, including transparency requirements, governance concerns, potential false marketing, and perennial questions regarding the definition of "charity" in the mind of the public.

In addition, state regulators are at a pronounced disadvantage because of a lack of technological resources that would enable them to access and analyse data from the field, and detect and track patterns. A technological platform affording better data analysis capability and data sharing among states would enable more efficient and thorough enforcement actions, as well as more informed and consistent policy development and law making. Currently, many states rely on paper filings and storage. Even those Form 990s that are available online, are "image only" and not digitized, meaning they cannot be searched and analysed efficiently.

For the last several years, state charities regulators have been planning for a nonprofit data platform that would serve multiple stakeholders: assisting nonprofits in their annual state registration requirements, aiding regulators in their quest for shared digitized data for efficient analysis, and affording researchers access to public digitized data for use in academic and policy studies. This "Single Portal" platform, officially called the Multistate Registration and Filing Portal, is expected to be available in 2017 for an initial pilot program among roughly a dozen states, with other states to follow.[36] Once in place, the Single Portal platform will be able to pull down Form 990 filing information from the IRS's system and from any other public filing platform. The new system promises more efficiency and consistency in protecting the donor dollar at the state level. There could be multiple uses for this new platform. For example, in 2015, state regulators hailed a victory in the first multi-state lawsuit that involved all 50 states and the District of Columbia, in addition to the Federal Trade Commission.[37] The suit took four years of information gathering and sharing. With the Single Portal platform, data gathering will be simplified and analysis time for such investigations will be greatly reduced.

Another major problem involves federal statutory prohibitions against information sharing between the IRS and the state charities regulators. The Pension Protection Act of 2006 inadvertently enacted criminal penalties for states that obtain information on nonprofits from the IRS, information that is publicly available through public information returns (Forms 990) that nonprofits file with the IRS. Forty-three state attorneys general publicly remonstrated against this statutory error by writing to the Senate Finance Committee and asking for the statute to be corrected.[38] For some years, only a handful of states executed the complex information sharing agreement procedures outlined by the IRS in order to comply with the statute, and as of 2016, no states currently participate in such agreements. When the regulation of such a large and important sector is subject to statutory error, problems inevitably result. When added to the funding and political problems of the IRS, the US system of regulating the charitable sector is experiencing continuing gaps in coverage and a lack of efficacy.

In light of the lag created by decreased regulatory and enforcement activity at the federal level, and under-resourced state-level regulators, the sector continues its calls for increased self-regulation.[39] Whether the nonprofit sector will have any greater success in self-regulation than any other sector involving billions of dollars remains to be seen, but one aspect of non-governmental oversight of the sector is rising sharply. Grant makers and nonprofits increasingly provide explanations and metrics to advocate for the importance and impact of their work. As a result, more information is available to the public about many of the larger organizations in the nonprofit sector, albeit not always verifiable or from the traditional governmental sources. In response to public demands for transparency, researchers, journalists, and the public have devised "workarounds" in lieu of waiting for comprehensive and accessible data from the government about the nonprofit sector. Whether small start-ups such as CauseIQ or larger organizations such as GuideStar, entities outside the government are collecting and aggregating data on the nonprofit sector as never before, to meet demand. In addition, charity watchdog groups continue to develop and disseminate information about nonprofits.

Until the regulator and enforcement community command both a political mandate and the resources to execute their mission, the sector itself and the public will have to escalate transparency and data sharing as part of their own respective missions, all toward increasing public benefit. Self-regulation should be a part of the mission of nonprofits even in a strong regulatory environment; in the absence of a robust regulatory environment, self-regulation becomes a necessary backstop to loss of not only donor dollars but also public trust in the sector.

Looking Forward

Three major issues affect the regulation of the nonprofit sector going forward: 1) technology that is affecting the sector in myriad ways and leading to changes in regulatory oversight, 2) questioning of the unique role of state charity regulators, and 3) undermining of the efficacy of IRS oversight of tax-exempt organizations. These are complex issues that require a coordinated and systematic approach, perhaps employing a commission such as the earlier Filer Commission, to collect evidence, consider a variety of views, and propose solutions for consideration.

Impact of Technology

The nonprofit sector, as other sectors, is affected by changes wrought by new technologies that afford opportunities for the sector, particularly fundraising campaigns, and challenges for the regulators, particularly in solicitation oversight. New technologies that allow individuals to harness the Internet for fundraising have a particular impact on this sector, which relies in great part on public and media oversight. In particular, the newest online technologies allow for an individual to research and access data as never before, delivering a more immediate experience with charities: donating online, seeing videos and testimonials, viewing outcome information (when available), and making comparisons across similar organizations.

The debate over appropriate performance metrics in this sector may take on new dimensions as individuals seek outcomes tailored to particular goals for their donations. Where in the past donors or the media relied heavily on grant reports or charity watchdogs to describe or analyse the governance process or results attained by a particular nonprofit, increasingly, data are made available directly to stakeholders who wish to undertake research. As new technologies afford a more individualized capacity for "oversight," we may see changes in the interaction between government regulation and sector stakeholders.

Globalization of the Nonprofit Sector

As this book's many authors have highlighted, there are many differences in the regulation of the nonprofit sector across the world. As new technologies erase time and distance between donors in one country and beneficiaries in another, regulatory regimes will need to acknowledge differences and minimize "regulatory friction" among international jurisdictions in order to create public benefit. As sector leaders try to minimize these frictions, there will need to be more explicit and organized partnership efforts to facilitate the transfer of resources and information. Such partnering, combined with technology that allows for instantaneous data sharing, movement, and tracking of resources, certainly will lead to further shared platforms and reciprocity agreements as the sector increases both in complexity of grant making and global reach.[40]

Potential Jurisdictional Changes

As the IRS Exempt Organizations division moves toward administrative functions in lieu of regulation and enforcement, states will have to step up their efforts. In addition, it is quite possible that over the next decades, the formal jurisdictional parameters for regulating the charitable sector may change. Marcus Owens has offered one alternative, the concept of a new and independent agency that has governmental functions but is also supported in part by the sector itself.[41]

Another alternative could be the formal shift of jurisdiction to other federal agencies already charged with oversight of particular aspects of activities conducted by charitable organizations. When a nonprofit functions in a specific substantive area, federal jurisdiction overseeing that area could be enlarged beyond the current regime to incorporate further oversight of the nonprofit's activities. For example, as the line between for-profit and nonprofit business models blurs, it seems likely that the Federal Trade Commission's jurisdiction eventually may reach these hybrid corporate forms and oversee not only the for-profit aspects but also the charitable aspects of the organization. Similarly, as co-venture solicitation campaigns and other consumer-based models for charitable activity increase, the Consumer Financial Protection Bureau may find some activities of the sector in its jurisdictional reach. Because nonprofits increasingly function across sectors (government, corporate, charitable, and political), jurisdiction may also increase across sectors, particularly if the IRS role in oversight diminishes. Challenges to "diffused" jurisdiction include differing oversight cultures across federal and state agencies and likely costs incurred by nonprofits themselves in complying with multiple oversight regimes.

Regardless of whether federal oversight of the nonprofit sector in the United States becomes concentrated in one new agency or is diffused across various agencies, given the state charities regulators' increasing activity, it is unlikely that the current state of oversight can continue. The sheer size and impact of the nonprofit sector on the US economy mitigates against the status quo.

Legal Standing

One further major shift in the current legal oversight of the nonprofit sector may yet occur, as a result of combining two of the current aspects of the sector noted earlier. Currently, legal standing—that is, the legal right to challenge a specific action of a nonprofit—is held by the state Attorney General. This legal tenet survives from the Statute of Charitable Uses of 1601[42] and at the time sufficed for oversight of a specific nonprofit in that the state had the resources and the information on which to base any legal action. In 2017, neither of these bases for legal standing remains true: the regulators are resource-strapped both financially and technologically, and individuals increasingly have access to nonprofit data that rivals what is available to government agencies.[43] As individual stakeholders demand more and more accurate information on nonprofits and make their own determinations on whether a board is functioning correctly, the framework for legal standing may very well be changed to resemble a *qui tam* action, better known as a whistleblower action, whereby an individual (a "relator") seeks permission from the government to sue an entity. In the vein of public benefit and *cy près* found in charitable trust law, a relator in such an action against a nonprofit board would not receive any funds as a result of a successful suit, but could instead obtain an injunction mandating action by a board (or prohibiting a board from taking action) or monies to be returned to the nonprofit or distributed through *cy près*, if appropriate. Various protective parameters for instituting such actions would have to be in place, just as they are for *qui tam* actions currently. Certainly, such new rights for the public would be a sea change in the nonprofit sector and not welcome by many. However, with the lack of resources given to government and the increase of information given to the public, it may be only a matter of time before legal standing is afforded to individuals on a permission-granted basis.

Leadership at IRS

In the absence of any formal change in jurisdiction, the IRS will remain the touchstone for overarching policy issues in the tax-exempt arena, and the IRS must regain its stature as a leader for policy and legal issues in this sector. In the last few years, it has suffered from a perception of eroding credibility and the documented fact of decreased resources, both financial and personnel, because of political fallout. The sector, however, continues to grow in complexity of issues, dollars donated, media coverage, and political attention. These situations cry out for IRS leadership and guidance. Whether addressing perennial murky issues such as regulatory exceptions for religious organizations or cutting-edge legal and cultural changes such as the impact of legalized same-sex marriage on tax-exempt religious institutions, the dramatic growth of donor-advised funds, or the parameters of "social welfare" activities for §501(c)(4) organizations.

The controversy in the years since the 2010 Supreme Court's decision in *Citizens United v. Federal Election Commission*[44] is instructive in illustrating the problems faced by the IRS, the tax-exempt sector, and the public in grappling with evolving and complex legal and political issues as refracted through the tax-exempt prism. After *Citizens United* allowed an opening for exponentially more money to be donated to section 501(c)(4) social welfare organizations, and for those organizations to increase borderline, and at times overt political activity, the IRS maintained that it would make clear the definitions used in determining whether an organization was engaging primarily or only tangentially in political activity. After delays and then proposed regulations, a comment period that netted the highest number of public comments for any proposed regulation, and then further delay, in 2015, Congress intervened and through its appropriations bill prohibited the IRS from issuing new regulations on political activity of section 501(c)(4) organizations. For the past six years, the general public has been confounded by the flow of money through the 501(c)(4) vehicle for political activity, but the political gridlock has kept any solution from surfacing at the IRS, and Congress itself ultimately took matters into its own hands to prevent the IRS from exercising jurisdiction. This situation reflects the interplay of public dissatisfaction, IRS loss of credibility, and Congressional intervention, ultimately leading to no progress on one of the major policy issues the IRS faces currently.[45]

It is clear that the IRS must provide leadership. A lack of guidance on these and other current controversies is not neutral for the sector; it endangers the very public trust on which civil society stands. For the regulatory framework to function, all government oversight agencies, state and federal, must be able to pursue matters within their jurisdiction with appropriate mandate and support.

Conclusion

We are hopeful that oversight of the nonprofit sector will become more efficient and effective in the coming five years. Although we do not believe that major new regulations will be passed any time soon, there will be modest changes and improvements over time. The gaps in oversight are obvious, as are the solutions, but obtaining the necessary resources and training will be difficult. One bright spot is that the state charity officers are working together to become more effective. The Multistate Registration and Filing Portal initiative is gaining ground and, if funded, will provide an important tool for state oversight and will facilitate interactions between state charity offices and the IRS. This one leap into the twenty-first century will be a major step up for oversight of the sector.[46] Although we do not believe that the IRS will be able to do its oversight job effectively under the current political stalemate, over time, it too must develop more effective oversight models using technology, data, and relationships with the states. Increased visibility of the sector in the media and online on sites such as GuideStar, Global Giving, Charity Navigator, Better Business Bureau Wise Giving, and others will also allow for more scrutiny of nonprofit and foundation activities by donors, researchers, and the public. The political use of money in the elections of 2016 is likely to shine a strong light on the inadequacies of transparency for politically oriented groups, including section 501(c)(4) groups. While the IRS got burned with its first attempt to develop regulations, more focused proposals may have some traction under a new administration.

Other gaps in the regulatory structure, such as a single-focused entity to oversee and develop statistics and report on the sector, are desirable but ultimately a far off goal. Unless the major organizations of the nonprofit sector make it a priority, or some huge scandal forces a change, the sector will go on as in the past, incrementally adjusting to and never quite catching up to the changes occurring in the United States and globally.

Notes

1 See Chapter 5 in this volume, written by Marcus Owens.
2 Dennis R. Young, "Complementary, Supplementary, or Adversarial? Nonprofit-Government Relations," in *Nonprofits and Government: Collaboration and Conflict*, eds. Elizabeth T. Boris and C. Eugene Steuerle (Washington, DC: Urban Institute, 2nd ed., 2006), 37–80.

3 For more on state-level regulation of charities, see Cindy M. Lott and Marion Fremont-Smith, "State Regulatory and Legal Framework," in *Nonprofits and Government: Collaboration and Conflict*, eds. Elizabeth T. Boris and C. Eugene Steuerle, (Lanham, MD: Rowman &Littlefield, 2017). For an overview of the changes that have impacted charitable regulation, see: The Editors and Cindy M. Lott, "The Shifting Boundaries of Nonprofit Regulation and Enforcement: A Conversation with Cindy M. Lott," *Nonprofit Quarterly*, August 3, 2016, accessed September 11, 2016, https://nonprofitquarterly.org/2016/08/03/shifting-boundaries-nonprofit-regulation-enforcement-conversation-cindy-m-lott/.

4 Commission on Foundations and Private Philanthropy. *Foundations, Private Giving, and Public Policy* (Chicago: The University of Chicago Press, 1970); Commission on Private Philanthropy and Public Needs, *Giving in America: Toward a Stronger Voluntary Sector* (Washington, DC: The Commission, 1975). Panel on the Nonprofit Sector, *Strengthening the Transparency, Governance, and Accountability of Charitable Organizations: A Final Report to Congress and the Nonprofit Sector* (Washington, DC: Independent Sector, 2005).

5 Panel on the Nonprofit Sector, *Strengthening Transparency*.

6 Brice S. McKeever, *The Nonprofit Sector in Brief 2015: Public Charities, Giving, and Volunteering* (Urban Institute, 2015) 2, accessed July 18, 2016, http://www.urban.org/sites/default/files/alfresco/publication-pdfs/2000497-The-Nonprofit-Sector-in-Brief-2015-Public-Charities-Giving-and-Volunteering.pdf.

7 McKeever, *Nonprofit Sector in Brief*. See p. 2 for details on growth of charities.

8 Sarah L. Pettijohn et al., *Nonprofit-Government Contracts and Grants: Findings from the 2013 National Survey* (Urban Institute, 2013), 4, accessed July 18, 2016, http://www.urban.org/research/publication/nonprofit-government-contracts-and-grants-findings-2013-national-survey.

9 Sarah L. Pettijohn and Elizabeth T. Boris, "Contracts and Grants between Non-profits and Government," *Brief*, No. 3 (Urban Institute, December 5, 2013), accessed July 18, 2016, http://www.urban.org/sites/default/files/alfresco/publication-pdfs/412968-Contracts-and-Grants-between-Nonprofits-and-Government.PDF.

10 Bradford H. Gray and Mark Schlesinger, "Health Care," in *The State of Nonprofit America*, ed. Lester M. Salamon (Washington DC: Brookings Institution, 2nd ed., 2012), 65–106.

11 Ellen Steele and C. Eugene Steuerle, *Discerning the True Policy Debate over Donor-Advised Funds* (Urban Institute, 2015), accessed July 18, 2016, http://www.urban.org/research/publication/discerning-true-policy-debate-over-donor-advised-funds.

12 Heerad Sabeti, "The For-Benefit Enterprise," *Harvard Business Review*, 89(11) (2011): 98–104.

13 John Roman et al., *Pay for Success and Social Impact Bonds: Funding the Infrastructure for Evidence-Based Change* (Urban Institute, 2014), accessed July 18, 2016, http://www.urban.org/research/publication/pay-success-and-social-impact-bonds-funding-infrastructure-evidence-based-change.

14 See, e.g., Bloomberg Philanthropies, accessed February 28, 2016, http://www.bloomberg.org.

15 Jane Mayer, *Dark Money: The Hidden History of the Billionaires behind the Rise of the Radical Right* (New York: Penguin Random House, 2016).

16 Elizabeth J. Reid, "Advocacy and the Challenges It Presents for Nonprofits," in *Nonprofits and Government: Collaboration and Conflict*, eds. Elizabeth T. Boris and C. Eugene Steuerle (Washington, DC: Urban Institute, 2nd ed., 2006), 343–372.

17 See Marcus Owens, in Chapter 5 of this volume.

18 Cindy M. Lott et al., *State Regulation and Enforcement in the Charitable Sector* (Washington, DC: Urban Institute, 2016), accessed January 16, 2017, www.urban. org/research/publication/state-regulation-and-enforcement-charitable-sector.

19 Evelyn Brody, ed., *Property-Tax Exemption for Charities: Mapping the Battlefield* (Washington, DC: Urban Institute, 2002); see also Molly F. Sherlock et al., *College and University Endowments: Overview and Tax Policy Options* (Congressional Research Service, 2015), accessed July 18, 2016, https://www.fas.org/sgp/crs/misc/R44293.pdf.

20 See, e.g., Bradford H. Gray and Mark Schlesinger, "Charitable Expectations of Nonprofit Hospitals: Lessons from Maryland," *Health Affairs* 28 (2009): w809–w821.

21 Jon M. Bakija, Joseph J. Cordes, and Katherine Toran, *The Charitable Deduction: Economics vs. Politics* (Urban Institute, 2013), accessed July 18, 2016, http://www.urban.org/sites/default/files/alfresco/publication-pdfs/412811-The-Charitable-Deduction-Economics-vs-Politics.PDF.

22 Bajika et al., *Charitable Deduction.*

23 Exempt Organization staffing numbers fell 13.5% between 2009 and 2015: from 891 people in 2009 to 771 in 2015: Advisory Committee on Tax Exempt and Government Entities, *2016 Report of Recommendations: Exempt Organizations: Stewards of the Public Trust: Long-Range Planning for the Future of the IRS and the Exempt Community* (Washington, DC: Internal Revenue Service, 2016), accessed September 11, 2016, https://www.irs.gov/pub/irs-pdf/p4344. pdf.

24 The audit rate of exempt organization returns has remained at 0.4% for the 2011 to 2014 fiscal years. Advisory Committee on Tax Exempt and Government Entities, *2016 Report of Recommendations.*

25 See, e.g., Missouri Attorney General, "AG Koster Sues Four Sham Cancer Charities for Defrauding Donors of More than $187 million," *Press Release*, May 19, 2015, accessed July 18, 2016, https://ago.mo.gov/home/news-archives/2015-news-archives/ag-koster-sues-four-sham-cancer-charities-for-defrauding-donors-of-more-than-187-million.

26 Pettijohn and Boris, "Contracts and Grants."

27 National Council of Nonprofits, *Investing for Impact: Indirect Costs Are Essential for Success* (National Council of Nonprofits, 2013), accessed July 18, 2016, https://www.councilofnonprofits.org/sites/default/files/documents/investing-for-impact_0.pdf.

28 Office of Management and Budget, *Uniform Administrative Requirements, Cost Principles, and Audit Requirements for Federal Awards* (Washington, DC: Uniform Guidance), 2 C.F.R. 200 et seq. (2014); see also National Council of Nonprofits, *OMB Uniform Guidance*, accessed February 28, 2016, https://www. councilofnonprofits.org/omb-uniform-guidance.

29 See, e.g., Office of Management and Budget, "Paying for Success," (The Federal Budget, Fiscal year 2012), accessed February 28, 2016, https://www.whitehouse. gov/omb/factsheet/paying-for-success.

30 See Lott et al., *State Regulation and Enforcement*, discussing a survey administered by Columbia Law School's Charities Regulation and Oversight Project and the Urban Institute's Center on Nonprofits and Philanthropy, which reports on a comprehensive study of state charity offices.

31 Journalists and communications experts have explored the impact new technologies will have on the nonprofit sector in the future. Watson gives a detailed description of the ways in which social media has affected the nonprofit sector: Tom Watson, *CauseWired: Plugging in, Getting Involved, Changing the World* (Hoboken, NJ: Wiley, 2008). For more information about mobile giving and

online fundraising techniques, see Lindsay Walker, "Planned Parenthood & Tumblr: Nimble Nonprofits Need Online Engagement," *Nonprofit Quarterly* (July 28, 2016), accessed September 11, 2016, https://nonprofitquarterly. org/2016/07/28/planned-parenthood-tumblr-nimble-nonprofits-need-online-engagement/. For a brief discussion of how some nonprofit organizations are using virtual reality to engage potential donors: Nicole Wallace, "How 4 Nonprofits Use Virtual Reality to Help Their Cause," *Chronicle of Philanthropy*, February 29, 2016, accessed September 11, 2016, https://www-philanthropy-com.proxy.lib.umich.edu/article/How-4-Nonprofits-Use-Virtual/235521.

32 See Robert A. Wexler, "Attorney General Regulation of Hybrid Entities as Charitable Trusts," *Columbia University Academic Commons* (2013): 4, accessed July 18, 2016, doi:10.7916/D8Z03661.

33 See e.g., Michigan Compiled Laws Annotated § 450.4102; Vermont Statutes Title 11, Ch. 21, §§ 3001(27).

34 See e.g., California Corporations Code § 14600 et seq.; 805 Illinois Compiled Statutes Annotated 40 et seq.; see also "State by State Status of Legislation," *Benefit Corporation*, accessed February 22, 2016, http://benefitcorp.net/policymakers/state-by-state-status, noting that benefit corporation laws have been passed in 31 states and that an additional five states are working on such legislation.

35 See e.g., Washington Revised Code Annotated § 23B.25 et seq.; California Corporations Code § 2500 et seq.

36 "The Single Portal Initiative: About," Multistate Registration & Filing Portal, Inc., accessed February 22, 2016, http://mrfpinc.org/about/: "MRFP anticipates launching an operational website in phases beginning in 2016. Twelve pilot states . . . will participate in initial development of a platform that will then be expanded to include all states that require registration." See also "Single Portal," National Association of State Charity Officials, accessed February 22, 2016, http://www.nasconet.org/category/single-portal/.

37 *Federal Trade Commission, 50 States, and the District of Columbia v. Cancer Fund of America, Inc., et al.*, No. CV-15–00884-PHX-NVW (US District Court, District of Arizona, filed May 18, 2015), accessed July 18, 2016, https://www.ftc.gov/system/files/documents/cases/150519cancerfundcmpt.pdf; see also Missouri Attorney General, "AG Koster sues," *Press Release*.

38 Letter from the National Association of Attorneys General to the Honorable Max Baucus, Chairman, and the Honorable Orrin Hatch, Ranking Member, Committee on Finance, United States Senate (October 28, 2011).

39 "Principles for Good Governance and Ethical Practice: A Guide for Charities and Foundations," *Independent Sector* (2015 ed.), accessed July 18, 2016, https://www.independentsector.org/principles.

40 See e.g., "Mission," *NGOsource*, accessed February 28, 2016, http://www.ngosource.org/mission: "NGOsource, a project of the Council on Foundations and TechSoup, helps U.S. grant makers streamline their international giving. . . . simplifies the task of evaluating whether a non-U.S. organization is the equivalent of a U.S. public charity—a process known as equivalency determination."

41 Marcus S. Owens, "Charity Oversight: An Alternative Approach," *Columbia University Academic Commons* (2013), accessed July 18, 2016, doi:10.7916/D8154F1D.

42 Stat. 43 Eliz. 1, ch. 4 (1601); see also Marion R. Fremont-Smith, *Governing Nonprofit Organizations: Federal and State Law and Regulation* (Belknap Press, 2004), 28–32.

43 Similar challenges and solutions are found in shareholder suites in the private sector arena.

44 558 U.S. 310 (2010).
45 See the 2010 Supreme Court's decision in *Citizens United v. Federal Election Commission*, 558 U.S. 310 (2010).
46 Additionally, "[s]ince 2013, Foundation Center, GlobalGiving, GuideStar, and TechSoup have worked together on BRIDGE [Basic Registry of Identified Global Entities]. . . . creat[ing] a link between their databases of social sector entities . . . using the BRIDGE number and its associated APIs. Nearly 3 million BRIDGE numbers have been issued . . ." Chad McEvoy, "What Might a BRIDGE-Enabled World Look Like?" *BRIDGE: Basic Registry of Identified Global Entities* (August 11, 2016) accessed September 11, 2016, https://bridge-registry.org/what-might-a-bridge-enabled-world-look-like/.

Canada

7 The Prevention of Harm Regulator

Terry de March

Introduction

The primary purpose of the Charities Directorate of the Canada Revenue Agency (CRA), the principal charity regulator in Canada, is to protect charities, donors, and the public from harm. In making decisions based on charity common law and by enforcing the terms of the Income Tax Act (the Act) and its regulations, the Charities Directorate ensures that only those organizations that are charitable under common law, and meet the terms of the Act and regulations, are able to benefit from the tax provisions designed to help charities prosper. The Charities Directorate does not make common law, nor does it establish any of the legislated and regulatory provisions that it administers. Should it do its job well, with the many tools that it has at its disposal, the risk of harm to charities, the public, and the tax system is reduced. If it does not, the risk of harm increases. "Harm," in the charities context, manifests itself in many ways: from within charities, from without, by design, unwittingly, and by willful blindness. Charity trustees, charity staff, members of the public, taxpayers, aggressive investment firms, compliant accountants and lawyers, and, in the extreme, terrorist organizations may inflict harm. Harm may be motivated by the pursuit of financial gain, or for a variety of other purposes that benefit from the charity brand and the legitimacy that charitable status under the Act is perceived to bring. The great potential for harm in the charitable sector is accentuated by the very foundation of charity itself, a system of giving based on compassion, generosity, and trust. While temptation to turn this compassion, generosity, and trust into personal gain or to usurp it for personal motivations has always existed, there is no question that the addition of tax benefits (financial reward) for giving to charities has increased both the temptation to take unlawful advantage of it and responses by governments to deal with the risks associated with it.

While the Charities Directorate is the primary regulator of charities in Canada, it is not so by design. The Directorate is really the de facto charities regulator, as the provinces, which have constitutional jurisdiction over charities, have taken only a limited role in the oversight of them: in some provinces in the protection of charitable property and in others in the area of fundraising. Whether the placement of overall charity sector oversight in a government department is a good thing, or bad, has been extensively debated in Canada. Much of the debate has centred on the question of the independence of the regulator and whether the sector is best served by a regulator seated firmly within government. While all arguments, both in favour of maintaining the Charities Directorate as an appropriate regulator and those supporting the creation of a new and more visibly independent regulatory body, have merit (and will be discussed in greater detail later in this chapter), the system is, for now, what it is, with the Charities Director-ate charged with coping with the multitude of challenges associated with charity regulation.

This is the context in which charity regulation reform has evolved in Canada. As recent attempts at reform, both successful and unsuccessful, are explored in the pages ahead, it is important that the reader keep in mind that charity regulation in Canada is all about the prevention of harm.

Legislative Foundations

It is safe to say that were it not for the provision of tax benefits under the Income Tax Act, the regulation of charities would not have fallen to the CRA and would most likely not have fallen anywhere within federal jurisdiction. In 1930, amendments to the Income War Tax Act allowed for deductions of up to 10 per cent of total income for donations to charitable organizations with the Department of Revenue assigned as the regulatory authority.[1] In 1967, legislation was passed requiring charities to register with the Department of National Revenue and to file annual returns.[2] With this, the modern era of charity regulation in Canada began.

Significant Reform Initiatives

Since that time, changes have been made to the Act and regulations fre-quently in response to an ever-changing charitable sector environment, lobbying by the sector, lessons learned from other jurisdictions, changes in public opinion, and political agendas of governing parties as they attempt to shift the focus of regulatory oversight in accordance with their view of the place of charity in Canadian society and of the ways that charity should be both stimulated and protected.

Protection against potential harm is the primary reason behind amend-ments to the Act. Over the years, increasing threats to both charity and to the integrity of the charitable giving tax stimuli have been apparent. Those who would do harm are increasingly adept at finding new ways to inflict it, which means government must continually amend the rules to fight new risks. And so it continues in a never-ending loop with the rules becoming ever more complex and the regulation of charities ever more removed from the day-to-day good works that charities perform. These ongoing changes to charity regulation are generally minor or, if of some importance, address unique problems with unique solutions. And, yes, at times government may be persuaded to change something of significance: the removal of the 80 per cent disbursement quota is an example. (This rule required that each year a charity expend on its charitable purposes 80 per cent of income it received in the previous year for which it issued official charitable donation receipts). But, generally, most amendments to the Act have little impact on the great majority of Canadian charities, which are at little risk of falling prey to potential harm or, indeed, of causing harm to others. True "regulatory reform" in Canada occurs infrequently, and it could be argued that since the major amendments to the Act in 1967 no changes have been made that could be called true and substantial "reform." One only has to look to the creation of entirely new regulatory bodies in New Zealand, Australia, Ireland, Northern Ireland, Scotland, and elsewhere, and the enshrining of definitions of charity into primary law in such jurisdictions as England and Wales, Ireland, and Scotland to glimpse what true reform can entail.

To effect regulatory reform in Canada, there must be an alignment of interests between government and the charitable sector, and at least tacit approval of the public. A total alignment of interests between government and the sector is not necessary for reform to occur, provided that there are sufficient reform measures of interest to each party to warrant support for the entire package of reform measures. The Charities Directorate, while an interested party, is not part of the regulatory reform process beyond providing input and making its case to the government's agents of regulatory change, the Department of Finance, for changes it believes will improve its regulatory capabilities.

For regulatory reform beyond housekeeping and one-off significant amendments to the Act to reach the point of possibility, there must be some impetus, some issue, or some desired objective that is significant enough to warrant parliamentary time and attention. Above all, true reform requires a process involving the sector and government, and to some extent the public, whereby a broad spectrum of possible reform measures are considered and debated. This impetus may have two sources: one, a major coordinated public call for change by the sector on an issue or issues of compelling importance, or, two, on the initiative of the government. Government may be motivated to act on the basis of its own political agenda, or it may be moved by public calls to action. Generally, though, it is the former and not the latter that drives government to act. In the area of charity regulation, it is very difficult to get the attention of the public. We know from surveys that only about 4 per cent of those surveyed in 2008 could name the CRA as the regulator of charities in Canada—a rise from 2 per cent in 2005.[3] A few more knew that it was somewhere in government, but the great majority had no idea whatsoever.

Where there is public attention on the regulation of charities, it is usually generated by the media and nearly always relating to some harm that has been committed in the name of charity. The public reaction to such stories is almost always a call for tougher regulation to safeguard charities and the public—a call that is just as frequently relied upon by government to support efforts to tighten the regulation of charities. While there are regular calls by the charitable sector to loosen the regulatory constraints under which it must operate, such calls from the public are rare. From a government perspective (and most certainly from the perspective of the bureaucracy that advises government), any relaxation of regulatory control means an increased risk of harm, which is something to be avoided at all cost.

Traditionally in Canada, it has been coordinated action by the charitable sector that has provided the impetus for change of wide effect, focusing on broad issues that affect charities' ability to fulfil their mandates better, while still fully complying with charity laws and regulations. The charitable sector has also persistently put forward ideas for change centred on finding new pathways for advancing charity law and instituting a regulatory authority independent from government. Government, meanwhile, has commonly focused on small ongoing changes to the Act to provide additional protections against potential harm.

When looking at what regulatory reform actually is, there are different notions in the minds of the government and the charitable sector. When the government thinks regulatory reform, it thinks of strengthening the capacity of the Charities Directorate, and the government more generally, to prevent harm to charities, the public, and the tax system. When the sector thinks regulatory reform, terms such as capacity building, nurturing, easing administrative burden, and new independent regulator that will support these objectives come to mind. At the root of this divergence in thinking is a stark contrast between what the mandate and function of the current charity regulator—the Charities Directorate—is and what it could be, as envisioned by some charitable sector leaders if that mandate were either framed differently or created anew in an independent regulator outside of government.

The stated mission of the Charities Directorate is "to promote compliance with the income tax legislation and regulations relating to charities through education, quality service, and responsible enforcement, thereby contributing to the integrity of the charitable sector and the social wellbeing of Canadians."[4] We must be clear: it is not the mandate of the Charities Directorate to nurture charities, to strengthen their governance, or to improve their effectiveness and efficiency. This being said, if the Charities Directorate can support these objectives as a positive by-product of promoting compliance with and enforcing the law, then all the better: a well-run charity will not only be more capable of providing greater benefit to Canadian society but also much more likely to be able to meet its regulatory obligations, thus reducing the risk of potential harm.

So where did this divergence in thinking originate? It is clear that it comes from the observance by Canadian charitable sector leaders of the Charity Commission of England and Wales, and the perception that this regulatory model would best serve the interests of the Canadian charitable sector and, more broadly, the Canadian public. So when discussions of regulatory reform have bubbled to the surface in the past, it has been no surprise that many of the ideas for reform brought forward have been based on this model. The essence of the model that Canadian-sector leaders have found most appealing is that it is separate from the tax collection functions of government, that it is perceived to allow for the continual advancement of charity law more easily than the Canadian regulatory scheme, and that it has been seen to be a supportive friend of the charitable sector.

Voluntary Sector Roundtable and Joint Table

The most recent and serious review of the regulatory function in Canada reached its conclusion with the Liberal Government Federal Budget of 2004,[5] which introduced measures that addressed the recommendations in the report of the Voluntary Sector Initiative's Joint Regulatory Table of March 2003.[6] However, the impetus for this reform began considerably earlier with the creation in 1995 of the Voluntary Sector Roundtable (VSR), a coalition of voluntary sector umbrella organizations. This group had been created in response to a period of negative press coverage and declining public opinion regarding the health of the charitable sector, and with the goal of addressing concerns about the sector's accountability and governance.

Shortly after the creation of the VSR, the December 1996 release of the Report on the Law of Charities by the Ontario Law Reform Commission[7] added additional impetus for a regulatory review. This seminal review of charity law and its regulation, both at the provincial and federal level, included a broad range of recommendations for both levels of government to consider. While the Commission did conclude that the scheme of charity regulation under the Income Tax Act was sound and found that radical reform of the federal tax law was unwarranted, they also found that there were several areas where the regulation of charities at the federal level was seriously lacking, and therefore required a number of substantial changes and a complete redrafting of certain provisions. To raise the profile of their work, the VSR created the Panel on Governance and Accountability in the Voluntary Sector shortly after the publication of the Law Reform Commission report. The Panel was led by Ed Broadbent and was tasked with reviewing the state of the sector in Canada and making recommendations on improvements that could be made to its governance and accountability.

At about the same time as the Panel was being created, the Liberal Party of Canada, as part of its federal election campaign, released the second of its "Red Books," *Securing Our Future Together: Preparing Canada for the 21st Century.* In it, the Liberal Party pledged that, if elected (as it was), it would undertake broad engagement of the voluntary sector, including a review of the regulatory function. The book stated,

> Plans announced in 1996 to establish a Canada Revenue Agency and consequent changes to Revenue Canada offer an ideal opportunity to undertake a structural review and modernization of Revenue Canada's Charities Division. A new Liberal government will work in partnership with the voluntary sector to explore new models for overseeing and regulating registered charities and enhancing their accountability to the public.[8]

This willingness to explore new models for overseeing and regulating registered charities was a strong statement. Coming on the heels of the creation of the VSR and the Law Reform Commission Report, and at the same time as the Broadbent Panel was being created, it ensured that sufficient impetus for considering reform had been generated.

In March 1997, to honor its commitment to engage with the voluntary sector, the Liberal government launched a joint initiative with the sector creating three joint tables: Building a New Relationship, Strengthening Capacity, and Improving the Regulatory Framework. The work of these tables began following the release of the report of the Panel on Governance and Accountability in the Voluntary Sector in February 1997. In its report, titled *Building on Strength: Improving Governance and Accountability in the Voluntary Sector*,[9] the Panel delved into the regulatory oversight of the sector and made recommendations on how that oversight could be reformed and strengthened. It thus became a key backdrop to the work of the Improving the Regulatory Framework Table, helping it to focus on the issues that had been seen by the Panel as key to reforming the regulatory oversight of charities. The key recommendations of the Panel were bold and innovative:

- a legislated definition of charity;
- an open and transparent registration process;
- appeals to the Tax Court rather than the Federal Court;
- the establishment of a new Voluntary Sector Commission;
- changes to the disbursement quota and how advocacy and related business were viewed by the regulator; and
- the implementation of intermediate sanctions.

Not surprisingly, these themes (with the exception of the recommendation to enact a legislated definition of charity) were front and center in the Regulatory Joint Table's report, *Working Together*,[10] released in August 1999. It is clear from the space taken in the report, and from the amount of time taken in discussions by the Joint Table, that the themes of advocacy and new regulatory models were paramount in Table members' discussions and most certainly so in the minds of the members from the voluntary sector.

It is important to consider the charitable-sector environment at that time. Generally, there was little in the public eye in the way of harm or potential harm to charities, the public, or the tax system. These were days when abusive tax shelter programs were just beginning; there was no public outcry against perceived high charity executive salaries, and linkages between charity and terrorism were not commonly known. As a result, government and the sector representatives on the Joint Table had the freedom to consider broad-ranging system changes from a sector perspective, without focusing solely on the key driver of all charity regulation in Canada, on potential harm. It is also important to keep in mind the amount of play given to advocacy and alternative regulatory models by the first joint table when looking at what followed—namely, the work of the successor joint regulatory group established to consider reform. This was the Joint Regulatory Table (JRT) of the major Voluntary Sector Initiative, whose report in March 2003 would lay the groundwork for the 2004 Budget regulatory reform announcements.

The framework for the JRT was an equal number of sector and government members, with the members from government chosen along the lines of representation from departments that had the greatest interaction with the sector or responsibility within government for its legislative and regulatory oversight. Co-chairs were appointed, with the government co-chair being the director general of the Charities Directorate. The marching order for members was that they were to leave their work hats at home and participate in meetings as individuals, bringing with them their own ideas drawn from their own experiences rather than being representatives of their charities (in the case of sector representatives) or their departments (in the case of government representatives). This proved to be easier for sector representatives than those from government, who were constantly aware of where the power lay at the table (with the Department of Finance) and who brought with them a natural tendency to try to avoid placing the Finance representative in an untenable position on particular issues. Government representatives were there as individuals, but only up to a certain point.

There were differences, too, in the motivations of the Table members. Sector representatives had a very real agenda on key themes and were, understandably, keen to exploit the chance the Joint Table provided to make headway on those themes—it was a rare opportunity. On the other hand, with the exception of developing recommendations that would help the Charities Directorate as constituted become a better regulator, with better tools and improved processes, government representatives had no particular preconceived goals or desired outcomes. Notwithstanding these very different starting points for the sector and government Table members, there is no question that all Table members approached their task in good faith and with the best intentions of achieving results that would enhance the regulation of charities in Canada. This became evident as points of agreement and disagreement did not generally fall on sector versus government lines, as could have occurred.

In hindsight, the appointment of the head of the Charities Directorate as government co-chair was significant in the shaping of the work undertaken by the JRT. The appointment of a co-chair from the Department of Finance would have been a signal that real reform was on the table and that the work was being steered by those in a position to put into effect any recommendations that would be brought forward. The appointment of a co-chair from a more neutral department would have signalled an openness on the part of the government to consider broad changes that might have been more balanced and reflective of sector desires and needs. However, with the appointment of the regulator to co-chair the work, the path was set as one not of substantially reforming the regulator, but rather helping the regulator by providing it with the tools to do its job better. Nonetheless, there was a significant and intensive buildup to the work of the JRT, both from within government and without, and there was a palpable sense of optimism in the sector that meaningful change in the way charities were regulated was a possibility. However, over the two years that the Table met and worked, that optimism was slowly, and perhaps inevitably, dampened, as the reality of what was achievable and what was not became clear.

A significant issue was that those on the government side (with the appropriate security clearance) had access to the Cabinet document that made it clear what the mandate and scope of work of the Table was. By contrast, sector representatives had to rely on the word of government officials as to what was in or out. To some extent, this information asymmetry caused harm to the collegial atmosphere on the Table, where members were supposed to work in equal partnership. As issues about mandate and scope arose, there were those who were clearly in the know and those who were not—to the detriment of all. No one felt comfortable with this new dynamic that arose well into the process.

The work of the Table was further shaped by the actual constraints that were imposed by government. First, there would be no recommendations on regulatory models. The work had to be conducted on the assumption that the Charities Directorate would continue to be the regulator. Second, the issue of advocacy (political activities) by charities was off the table. While alternative mechanisms could be, and were, developed to ensure sector involvement in the development of guidance on advocacy, no consideration could be given to changing the rules of the game. This was a significant development and came as somewhat of a surprise to the sector. But in the context of improving charity regulation from a government perspective, or at least from the government bureaucracy perspective, it made sense. The sector's objectives with respect to advocacy were to loosen constraints on charities, and with respect to a new regulatory body, the sector saw its role as nourishing and supporting the sector. But these were themes that were unlikely to help reduce the risks of harm to charities, the public, and the tax system, and it must be remembered that reducing those risks is the primary principle of Canadian charity regulation.

The ultimate mandate provided to the Table was relatively narrow. It was asked to consider three issues and make recommendations to the government:

- increasing the transparency of the regulatory process;
- improving the system for appealing decisions made by the regulator; and
- introducing a range of penalties for non-compliance with legal requirements.[11]

With great creativity, however, the Table was able to draw linkages between its mandate and virtually everything that the regulator did in order to provide a broad spectrum of recommendations. It produced an interim report containing draft recommendations. This was taken to sites across the country in 2002 for consultation with people in the voluntary sector, their advisers, federal and provincial government officials, and those involved in regulating or supervising charities, as well as the general public. Comments and submissions received were generally supportive of the recommendations, although the weight given to each recommendation depended on the perspective of the commentator.

The final report contained 75 recommendations and, in one way or another, all served to enhance the regulator's ability to reduce the risks of harm by enhancing and augmenting the regulatory tools available to the Charities Directorate. The recommendations were pragmatic. Born of two years of intensive work and interaction between government and sector representatives, they represented an understanding by all members at the end of the process of what was likely to be accepted by the government and what would not be. This understanding resulted primarily from having a representative of the Department of Finance on the Table. It was readily apparent which way the wind was blowing. The recommendations were grouped under four headings:

- The Regulatory Framework
- Accessibility and Transparency
- Appeals
- Intermediate Sanctions

The regulatory framework recommendations were rather benign, being a mix of re-stating the mandate and the general functions of the Charities Directorate to achieve that mandate, calls for increased focus on educating the sector, public consultation, greater communication and work between the federal government and provincial governments on overlapping regulatory work, and a request for additional funding for the Charities Directorate to support the enhancements suggested in the report. Most of these recommendations were accepted by the Liberal government with additional resources committed to the Charities Directorate to carry out its enhanced activities. Discussions with the provinces were subsequently carried out; however, the provinces showed no interest, and there was little to show for the attempts to promote ongoing, regular discussions on charity regulation issues.

One key recommendation—that a Ministerial Advisory Committee be set up to provide administrative policy advice to the Minister responsible for the regulator—was accepted, and the committee was duly constituted. The creation of this committee represented a success for the sector, as it gave sector leaders a regular, ongoing forum for raising regulatory issues and discussing them directly with key Charities Directorate staff. It also allowed them to inform and advise the Minister directly when occasions for such contact arose. However, the committee was short-lived. After a successful start-up, it was disbanded in 2006 under a new minster and new Conservative government.

Accessibility and Transparency recommendations were based on common sense and were uncontroversial, notwithstanding the fact that two recommendations were not accepted by government. One was rejected primarily for practical reasons (a recommendation that the regulator publish reasons for all its application decisions on its website), while the other was rejected on privacy grounds (a recommendation that documents pertaining to the denial of registered charity status be made available to the public).

Two key recommendations were central to the appeals subcategory. The first of these was that an independent internal review body be created within the regulator to ensure a level of review before turning to a court. The second was that careful consideration should be given to making the Tax Court of Canada the site of appeals from decisions of the regulator. The sector had long maintained that appeals to the Federal Court with its rigid set of rules and high associated costs made it an inappropriate first instance appeal mechanism for charity appeals. The Tax Court, it was thought, would be accessible at a lower cost and possessed access to more informal procedures for dispute resolution.

A new review mechanism was established, but not as a stand-alone unit as envisaged by the Table. Rather, it was a small unit within the current agency-wide appeals structure within the CRA. Nonetheless, it did provide the level of independent review sought. On the other hand, although duly considered, the recommended appeals route for cases involving determinations of charitable status, through the Tax Court of Canada to the Federal Court of Appeal, was rejected. This was a major disappointment to the charitable sector. Had this recommendation been accepted, it would undoubtedly have been seen as the crowning achievement of the Table and of the work of the sector representatives in particular. However, it must be said that it appears somewhat contradictory for the sector to argue that regulation of charities is misplaced in the tax collection agency, but seek to have the first external level of appeal on questions arising from common law determinations of charity to the Tax Court, an entity mandated to deal solely with questions of tax, rather than to the more broadly mandated Federal Court of Appeal.

The final group of recommendations pertained to Intermediate Sanctions. While the form and extent of these sanctions was cause for debate, there was no debate that there was a need for some sanctions short of deregistration. The sanctions that were ultimately enacted exceeded those recommended by the Table in scope and perhaps constituted the most significant new set of tools available to the regulator. An unexpected outcome of enacting the intermediate sanctions provisions occurred several years later, when they were used creatively as primary sanctions to halt charities being used as fronts for tax shelters, prior to commencement of the more lengthy deregistration process. Some commentators suggested that this was subverting the intent of intermediate sanctions. But from a regulatory perspective of protecting against harm, a tool is a tool: if you don't have a hammer at hand and you can drive a nail just as effectively with a heavy wrench, the same result can be achieved.

Viewed through a lens of substantial regulatory reform, the Table's 75 recommendations were not earth-shattering, but no other outcome could reasonably be expected after the die was cast in the mandate it was given. That being said, there was no question that the results of the JRT's work, as reflected in the 2004 Budget announcement, were significant, at least from the perspective of the Charities Directorate. New tools were provided to the regulator, laws would be changed to create a more open and transparent regulatory environment, and systems were put in place to ensure a more interactive relationship between the regulator and the regulated. The very nature of the relationship was changing in what was anticipated to be an enduring way. The establishment of a new formal Charities Advisory Committee and a $3 million Charities Partnership and Outreach Program were novel and had the potential to entrench partnership between the charitable sector and Charities Directorate in shaping regulatory oversight and engaging the sector in educating itself on the nuts and bolts of regulation. All of this was for the goal of reducing the risks of harm and enhancing regulatory reach.

But in looking at the impetus for reform from outside government as reflected in the Ontario Law Reform Commission Report and the Broadbent Report, and the continued exploration of their ideas by the first Regulatory Joint Table, much was lost, rightly or wrongly, along the way. There was no new charities regulatory authority, no legislated definition of charity, no change to the law on advocacy, and no new avenue of appeal to the Tax Court rather than the Federal Court on matters pertaining to the registration of charities. There was no significant rewriting of complex and unclear provisions in the Income Tax Act, and nothing was done to satisfy sector demands for more work to facilitate the advancement of charity law in Canada. And certainly no bridges were built to span the gulf between the vision of a regulator with a mandate to support and nurture the sector and the reality of a regulator whose mandate is to enforce the law and nothing further.

While the results of the reform initiative may have fallen short of true and meaningful reform, and constituted something of a disappointment from the sector's point of view, the same cannot be said from the somewhat narrower viewpoint of the Charities Directorate. It was clear from the start that the overriding objective of the Table's work was to help the Charities Directorate to become a better regulator, thus contributing to the public's trust and confidence in the sector, and the 2004 Budget announcement of new legislative authorities and tools, and an injection of new funds to implement the large number of accepted reform proposals invigorated the Directorate. From the regulator's perspective, the Budget announcements were not a surprise: it is unlikely that any proposal that the Charities Directorate was not in favour of implementing would have been put forward by the Department of Finance. The opportunity was also there to use the recommendations and the Budget announcement to add further amendments that would aid the regulator, as was seen with the extension of intermediate sanctions beyond what the Table envisaged and the creation of the Charities Partnership and Outreach Program.

A special unit was set up within the Charities Directorate to manage the reform process and various teams were tasked with developing plans to put the reforms into practice. It was a time of growth, helped all the more by the belief that working closer with the sector and providing better help and service to charities to further their understanding of the law, and their compliance with it was the proper course to take. The new and more productive relationship with the sector began and, for a time, both the regulator and the regulated felt that the improvements promised in the announced reforms were being rolled out in a satisfactory way. But setbacks would come, for various reasons, not the least of which was a new government with different priorities and different views on consultation, advice, committees, and how the charitable sector in Canada should go about its business.

The Legacy of the Joint Regulatory Table

The cancellation of the Charities Advisory Committee by the Conservative government in September 2006 constituted a regression in the ongoing relationship between the Charities Directorate and the charitable sector, at least in a formalized way. The Advisory Committee had proven to be a useful body for discussing ongoing regulatory issues and approaches. However, in the spirit of the relationship that had developed, other means were developed to ensure that an ongoing exchange of ideas could continue at least in part, albeit without the stature of the Advisory Committee. Also lost, in 2012, was the Charities Partnership and Outreach Program, which was discontinued when the Charities Directorate was unable to retain funding.

This is another symptom of a different focus of a different government, in this instance, again, the Conservative government.

A question on the lips of some at the time of the 2004 Budget announcements was whether the changes announced, having fallen short of any measure of substantial reform, constituted an end to formal reform processes or the next stage in incremental reforms that would lead to further changes in the ongoing development of charity regulation. Twelve years on, it appears that the answer lies with the former. Those years have been marked by relative calm in the relationship between the sector and the government, at least until more recent Conservative government announcements of increased funding for the Charities Directorate for the purpose of political activities audits. This set off a firestorm in the sector and has galvanized it as no other issue has since the Budget announcements of 2004.

Reform Agenda Current Prospects

Any possibility of further regulatory reform in Canada will depend on what the impetus is for that reform. In 2015, the Liberal Party of Canada was elected on a platform that included the following pledge:

> We will allow charities to do their work on behalf of Canadians free from political harassment, and will modernize the rules governing the charitable and not-for-profit sectors.
>
> This will include clarifying the rules governing "political activity," with an understanding that charities make an important contribution to public debate and public policy. A new legislative framework to strengthen the sector will emerge from this process.[12]

This modernizing of the rules and development of a new legislative framework certainly appears to open the door to a fresh look at Canada's charitable regulatory system, and the sector, if it can act quickly and in a coordinated fashion, will be at the doorstep to ensure that the review is as broad as possible, with consideration of a new regulatory model being front and center on their wish list. The idea of an independent regulatory body built along the lines of the Charity Commission of England and Wales is still the Holy Grail to those who believe the charitable sector and the Canadian public are not being served as well as they could be under the current regulatory system. But what does "independence" of the charity regulator mean and, in fact, does it really exist as a model?

Much has been made of the need to have an independent regulator, free from government intervention. But can any regulator created and funded by government really be completely independent? There are two aspects to independence of the regulator: the first is independence in regulatory decision making (those decisions that the regulator is prescribed by law to make) and the second is independence in operational functions (how the regulator chooses to expend resources and go about its business). Most would agree that it is the first of these—independent decision making—that is of paramount importance. In this regard, the regulator's current placement within government has resulted in the perception among some commentators that bias is inevitable in the decision-making process, simply as a consequence of the regulator being part of a larger tax administrator with responsibility for collecting taxes and protecting the tax base. The logic appears to be that the CRA's objective of protecting the tax base must necessarily cloud the judgement of Charities Directorate employees when making decisions as to which organizations are deemed charitable, and thus eligible to issue official tax receipts that result in government revenues forgone. Comparisons are made with the Charity Commission for England and Wales, which operates at arm's length from the tax collector and thereby is free of this potential bias. While the perception of bias is understandable, given the organizational structure of the regulator, suggestions of any bias of that nature are simply not grounded in fact. Decisions by the Charities Directorate on whether organizations are charitable in law are not linked to considerations of potential outcomes in terms of effects on government revenues. This is true for decisions on both individual charities and groups or classes of charities.

The second aspect of regulator independence, independence in operational functions, does not receive as much attention as the first. Here government can and does play a major role by controlling the regulator's purse strings and by directing resources to specific tasks that would not necessarily be the regulator's priority for dedication of those resources, if it were free to choose. For example, in the recent past, the government has provided resources to the Charities Directorate specifically for the purpose of auditing charities engaged in political activities. While this has aroused ire within the Canadian charitable sector, the provision of specific task-related resources has in fact always been evident. The government has regularly provided the Charities Directorate with funds for specific activities and has taken the step in some instances to corral the funding so that the Charities Directorate could not use the funds for any other purpose (for example, resources dedicated for anti-terrorism activities and the Charities Partnership and Outreach Program). The government has also taken steps to intervene in the functions of the regulator more directly, by acts such as abolishing the Charities Advisory Committee, created by a previous government in response to the recommendations of the Joint Regulatory Table, and by discontinuing funding of the Charities Partnership and Outreach Program.

In judging how independent the Charities Directorate is in making decisions about how it carries out its work, it is reasonable to conclude that it is free to act independently, but only within certain parameters established in law or mandated by government through its provision of task-related resources. However, no charity regulator is free from this type of government control. If a government does not like the way the regulator is operating, it can change the rules. If it does not like the balance in the use of resources, it can provide additional resources to be used only to bolster those tasks that match the government's priorities. And, ultimately, the government can either enhance or diminish the regulator's presence in charity regulation by increasing or decreasing its resource base.

If we consider the Charity Commission of England and Wales, we see that even this regulator, held up as a model of independence, has increasingly become subject to government control, at least with respect to its ability to make independent decisions on where to expend its resources. In the very recent past, the government chose to decrease Charity Commission resources significantly, forcing it to change its mode of operation to match functions to the amount of resources allocated. More recently, the government has allocated additional resources to the Commission, but these funds may only be used to refocus its regulatory activity on proactive monitoring and enforcement in the highest risk areas—for example, abuse of charities for terrorism and other criminal purposes, such as tax avoidance and fraud.[13] In the past, the government has also given the Charity Commission specific funds to carry out international work, at its behest, to achieve a government objective. It also appoints all members of the Charity Commission non-executive board, which has overall responsibility for all work carried out by the Commission (the last chair, under a Labour government, was a Labour Party member; and the current chair is publicly aligned with the Conservative Party, the Party in government). The current chair of the Charity Commission has stated that charging charities for regulatory services is inevitable.[14] This could reduce direct government control over Commission resources, but in fact, it will do little to enhance its independence, merely shift the pressure. If more resources come from the sector itself, the Commission will inevitably face increased demands from the sector for a say in how and to what extent it is regulated.

All this is to say that it is governments that ultimately control the regulation of charity, whether the regulatory authority is perceived to be independent or not. In fact, the role of government is so powerful that it is surprising how much focus is placed on the regulator, which actually has very little discretion in how the charitable sector is regulated other than shifting resources between regulatory tasks to meet the priorities of the day and choosing the best means of ensuring regulatory compliance. This is not to say that the regulator cannot have an impact—it can, but not to the level of a lawmaker who can, at any time, make sweeping and dramatic changes affecting how all charities are regulated. Moreover, governments ultimately control the purse strings that can subtly, or not so subtly, evolve into puppet strings.

Would the creation of an independent regulator make a major difference in the daily lives of Canadian charities? It is unlikely to. The laws are what the laws are, and even an independent regulator would be bound to ensure compliance with them. And with regard to the primary aim of reducing the risk of harm to charities, the public, and the tax system, there has never been any suggestion that an independent regulator would be able to achieve this goal better, or be more capable than the Charities Directorate of dealing effectively with harm once it is discovered.

There remains an alternative, though, which is the creation of a body outside the regulatory sphere with the specific mandate of nurturing and building the capacity of the charitable sector. There are already organizations within the sector that fulfil this role in part, and these are funded by the sector itself. The government could create such a body—or at least allow it to be created—with permanent, stable government funding. From a government perspective, the risk would be that such an organization would become an advocate for the sector, lobbying the government to make changes to benefit the sector, possibly at the expense of creating increased risk of harm. A new Liberal government may be more willing to accept such risks than the predecessor government, which demonstrated by cancelling the Canadian Court Challenges Program, the Charities Advisory Committee, and others, that it was increasingly reluctant to fund organizations that may become critical of its actions and policies or that would take on a lobbying role.

There is an old saying that "what goes around comes around," and reading the current Liberal government's election platform pledge alongside the Liberal Red Book 2 commitments of 1997 give one a sense of déjà vu. Virtually the same commitment for a review of the regulatory function appears in both, but given the unprecedented focus and attention to the Joint Table processes in the years that followed that previous government commitment, can a different result reasonably be achieved this time? Much of the government's intentions will be read in the process by which changes to the rules and framework are explored. Are we headed down the path to another Joint Regulatory Table? If yes, one can only imagine that the work would cover much of the well-trodden ground of years past, but could prove to be more substantial if the work were to include a look at alternative regulatory models. And at least this time around, advocacy appears to be on the table.

What will become apparent to the new government in getting its mind around how to achieve its platform pledge is that the Canadian regulatory system for charities is not broken: in fact, from a purely regulatory standpoint and from the perspective of preventing harm, which is its primary purpose, it is working quite well. On top of that, there are the briefings they will receive from officials in their early days in office. One must remember that the hallmark of government bureaucracy is inertia—a natural counterbalance to the exuberance of governments that come and go. Any attempts by the government to replace the Charities Directorate with an independent regulatory body, or to hand over any legislated, charity-related decision making to such a body will be met with resistance. There is much at stake in managing charity regulation and, like an iceberg, there is much more below the surface than is visible above. From a government perspective, there is much in favour of maintaining the status quo in charity regulation and many of the following factors will undoubtedly be brought to the new government's attention.

With the regulation of charities firmly under government control, the government has a level of certainty and flexibility that it would not necessarily have with alternative regulatory models. With a well-established regulatory body in place, it has the means available through the Income Tax Act to add to and subtract from the powers of the regulator and to change the rules with which charities must comply as it sees fit. Doubtless, if an independent body were created, it would have the same ability to change the rules, but not necessarily through the same Act. And it must be remembered that all of the federal powers in charity regulation are derived from the Income Tax Act. Jurisdictional issues will surely be raised with the new government, and any suggestion of some kind of shared responsibility with the provinces in creating and maintaining an independent regulator will likely not be well received by provincial governments. With regulatory oversight being essentially provided at no cost to them, there is no advantage to their taking on any additional role or costs.

Even beyond the constitutional difficulties facing an attempt to create a new national regulator are the practical considerations of doing so. The charitable world of today is complex, and the potential for harm to charities, the public, and the tax system is increasing. A significant advantage of the charity regulator being housed within government is the economies of scale that are realized. Beyond its actual staff, the Charities Directorate has access to other resources within the CRA in areas of audit, finance, information technology, communications, public relations, legal services, human resources, and senior executive oversight. In addition, it has regular access to other government departments such as Finance, Statistics Canada, Justice Canada, Indigenous and Northern Affairs, and others essential for the effective execution of its functions. For good or for bad, and mostly for the good, it is not an island unto itself.

Another possibly significant factor in the lack of impetus to create a new regulatory model is the decline of the Charity Commission for England and Wales as a model for reform in Canada. The Charities Commission of today is a very different Charities Commission from what it was 19 years ago. No longer does it conduct charity "surgeries" that were the model for the Charities Directorate "road shows." Gone is the focus on nurturing charity and the philosophical "we are regulating angels" approach. In recent times, the Charity Commission has been criticized by both the sector and government. In 2013, the National Audit Office declared that the Commission was not auditing charities effectively, was failing to provide value for money to the taxpayer, and was in need of radical change.[15] The chair of the government's Public Accounts Committee stated that the Commission was not fit for purpose.[16] Add to this the bite of declining resources, the government's appointment of a managing board with members clearly aligned with a tougher compliance role, and the Commission's chair suggesting that charging charities for regulatory services is inevitable, and what is left appears to be an organization struggling to maintain its independence and to be the master of its own destiny.

It is possible that the government's hand may be forced by abuse in the sector such as the rampant tax shelter programs of the past decade. To a certain extent, this problem has been brought under control as a result of the coordinated actions of key directorates within the CRA and the implementation of legislative changes by the Department of Finance. However, the potential for such abuse in the future remains as new ways to cheat the tax system are developed and tested by people wishing to reap immoral and illegal gains from the lucrative charitable donation tax receipt program.

Also significant for charity regulation is the issue of abuse by those who would use the charity brand and tax donation receipts for terrorist-related purposes, not least of which are terrorist financing and radicalization. While such abuses are rare, they do exist and represent the one aspect of charity oversight governed by a no tolerance policy. Finding such instances of abuse is time consuming and resource intensive, and requires the coordinated action of many legal and regulatory bodies across Canada and internationally. The Charities Directorate plays a key role in this work and now, with a fairly long history behind it, has become an expert in the field. In light of the huge scale of abuse within the tax system wrought by promoters of tax shelters, other schemes, and outright fraud, and in light of the ever-present challenges posed by terrorism, it is difficult to imagine that the new government, even if it desired to create a new independent regulatory model, would be able to resist the bureaucracy's warnings of the potential dangers of passing on important tax-related decisions, such as the determination of charitable status, to any regulatory body independent of government.

Moreover, there is the question of whether a charity regulator can be firmly compliance oriented while at the same time nurturing charities as a friend. To many, these two roles are incompatible. And, again, one only has to look to the recent history of the Charity Commission of England and Wales to see the difficulties that can arise when the two roles compete for attention and resources. With the new Liberal government's platform pledge to clarify the rules governing advocacy, it will be addressing the most pressing sector issue of today. If a satisfactory solution is found to this issue, it may be that sector calls for a new regulatory model will be muted, especially given the uncertainty of how a new regulator would function. If advocacy as an issue is resolved, "better the devil you know" may take hold as the more prudent charitable sector position.

Notes

1 Rod Watson, "Charity and the Canadian Income Tax: An Erratic History," *The Philanthropist* 5(1) (1985): 8, accessed September 15, 2014, http://thephilan thropist.ca/original-pdfs/Philanthropist-5-1-618.pdf.
2 Watson, "Charity and the Canadian Income Tax," 11.
3 "Canada Revenue Agency: Charities Directorate Update," Canada Revenue Agency (Ottawa, November 2008), 19, accessed August 25, 2016, http://www.globalphilanthropy.ca/images/uploads/CRA_Charities_Directorate_Update_November_2008.pdf.

4 "Who We Are: Our Mission," Canada Revenue Agency, last modified June 1, 2011, http://www.cra-arc.gc.ca/chrts-gvng/chrts/bt/mssn_vsn-eng.html.

5 "Budget 2004—Budget Plan: Supporting the Voluntary Sector," Government of Canada (2004), accessed September 22, 2015, http://www.fin.gc.ca/budget04/bp/bpc4d-eng.asp#voluntary.

6 Joint Regulatory Table on Regulatory Reform, *Final Report*, accessed September 15, 2015, http://www.vsi-isbc.org/eng/regulations/pdf/jrt_final_report.pdf.

7 Ontario Law Reform Commission, *Report on the Law of Charities* (Toronto: Law Reform Commission, 1996), accessed October 2, 2015, https://archive.org/stream/reportonlawofcha01onta#page/n1/mode/2up.

8 Liberal Party of Canada, *Securing Our Future Together: Preparing Canada for the 21st Century* (Ottawa: Liberal Party, 1997), 67, accessed October 11, 2015, http://web.archive.org/web/19980423142109/http://liberal.ca/download/plan-e.pdf.

9 Panel on Governance and Accountability in the Voluntary Sector, *Building on Strength: Improving Governance and Accountability in Canada's Voluntary Sector: Final Report* (1999), accessed September 22, 2015, http://www.ecgi.org/codes/documents/broadbent_report_1999_en.pdf.

10 Joint Tables (Voluntary Sector Joint Initiative, Canada), *Working Together: A Government of Canada/Voluntary Sector Joint Initiative: Report* (Ottawa: Voluntary Sector Initiative, 1999), accessed September 22, 2015, http://www.vsi-isbc.org/eng/knowledge/working_together/pco-e.pdf.

11 Joint Regulatory Table on Regulatory Reform, *Final Report*, 4.

12 Liberal Party of Canada, *Real Change: A New Plan for a Strong Middle Class* (2015), 34, accessed January 10, 2016, https://www.liberal.ca/files/2015/10/New-plan-for-a-strong-middle-class.pdf.

13 United Kingdom, Prime Minister's Office, "New Funding and Powers to Tackle Abuse in the Charity Sector," *Press Release*, October 22, 2014, accessed October 23, 2016, https://www.gov.uk/government/news/new-funding-and-powers-to-tackle-abuse-in-the-charity-sector.

14 Rebecca Cooney, "Charging Charities for Regulation Is 'Inevitable', says Shawcross," *Third Sector* (September 17, 2015), accessed October 14, 2016, http://www.thirdsector.co.uk/charging-charities-regulation-inevitable-says-shawcross/governance/article/1364451.

15 HM Comptroller and Auditor General, *The Regulatory Effectiveness of the Charity Commission*, National Audit Office Report (HC 813, Session 2013–14, 4 December 2013), accessed October 11, 2015, https://www.nao.org.uk/wp-content/uploads/2013/11/10297-001-Charity-Commission-Book.pdf.

16 Rajeev Syal, "Charity Commission 'Not Fit for Purpose', Says Margaret Hodge," *Third Sector*, December 4, 2013, accessed October 14, 2015, http://www.theguardian.com/society/2013/dec/04/charity-commission-not-fit-for-purpose-says-hodge.

8 Reflections on the Long and Winding Road of Regulation

Bob Wyatt

Introduction

During the last quarter of a century, Canada's charities have endured a bit of a roller-coaster ride in dealings with their primary regulator—a slow rise to a peak, a sometimes wobbly ride in the upper reaches, a few ups and downs, and a sudden crash to a low point. While the regulator and the sector were responsible for some of the developments, others—including the drop to the lowest point in the relationship in that time—had more to do with the actions of "outsiders," actions that, by 2015, had led to distrust, hyperbolic rhetoric, and an unhealthy dose of silliness. The early part of the ride was complicated by the sector's own problems with its primary peak body and by a judicial system that has stilted—in fact, arguably reversed—the development of Canada's charitable sector. And, for good measure, other regulators with peripheral, but important relevance to the sector have, at times, complicated the relationships. This chapter will discuss briefly the regulatory context that exists in Canada, provide a short history of significant developments and the sector's role in them, and then examine specific issues that have existed between the regulator and the regulated. It will end with an examination of regulatory issues likely to arise in the future.

Regulatory Context

Canada is a federated state composed of ten provinces and three territories. Under the constitution, the primary responsibility for the supervision and control of charities rests with the provinces, although only one, Ontario, has a formal system that deals with the regulation of charities. (Ontario is also the largest province and the home of the largest percentage of charities.) However, the primary advantage in being a charity arises under federal law. Under the Income Tax Act, a federal law administered by the Canada Revenue Agency (CRA), charities have the privilege of issuing receipts to donors, allowing them to claim tax credits for their donations. Charities must obtain registration from CRA and are subject to CRA's ongoing supervision to ensure that they maintain their qualification as charities. Thus the government entity with which charities interact most often is CRA. The Charities Directorate of CRA supervises only charities; non-profits that are not charities are treated as businesses, although they are tax-exempt businesses. Practically speaking, in most cases, there is no regulation of non-profits, although in recent years, CRA has started making noises questioning whether some non-profits qualify for tax exemption. Individual donors to non-profits that are not registered charities do not receive any tax credit, although corporations may be able to deduct such donations as business expenses.

There is no codified definition of "charity" in the Income Tax Act. CRA and the courts rely on the common law definition, dating back to the *Pemsel* case. There are two types of charities: charitable organizations and charitable foundations. Organizations tend to be the charities that actually deliver service, while foundations are either funders or fundraisers. The primary legislative requirement is that charities use their resources for their charitable purposes and/or give money to "qualified donees" (a larger construct that includes all charities plus some other types of organizations). Although tax credit for charities has existed since the introduction of an Income Tax Act in 1918, the requirement for charities to register and maintain registration has existed only since 1967.

Throughout the last 25 years, the primary point of disagreement between the charitable sector and government has been the involvement of charities in public policy issues—so-called political activities, a theme that will be explored in more depth later in this chapter. Initially, there were no provisions in the Income Tax Act that dealt with the issue. Following some high-profile incidents, the Income Tax Act was amended in 1986 to provide that so long as a charity expends "substantially all" of its resources on charitable activities, it will not lose its charitable registration if it engages in political activities that are incidental and ancillary to its purposes. CRA considers "substantially all" to mean 90 per cent, although recent research raises the question of whether that is an accurate interpretation of judicial rulings.[1] There was (and is) an ongoing debate as to whether this provision amended the common law or simply created a "safe harbour" that provided charities with some assurances that their involvement in some types of political activities were immune from criticism.

The '90s: Discontent and the Start of Something Big

The early 1990s featured a level of discontent with the regulator, at least amongst those who spent a lot of time dealing with it. There were complaints about delays in dealing with applications for registration as well as what was seen as the regulator's narrow application of the Pemsel categories. Some in the sector looked longingly across the Atlantic Ocean and coveted the Charities Commission for England and Wales, seeing a progressive and supportive regulator—one that moved the concept of charity forward rather than keeping it in what was seen as the "stilted past" of the Pemsel era. Some of the criticism was aimed at the courts. The appeal mechanism to challenge decisions of the charities regulator is complex and expensive. Unlike other issues that flow from the Income Tax Act, charity matters are not heard in the relatively informal atmosphere of the Tax Court of Canada, but rather go to Canada's second-highest court, the Federal Court of Appeal. Criticism was (justifiably) levelled that an organization that had been refused charitable status was highly unlikely to have the resources to launch such an appeal. As a result, there is scant Canadian jurisprudence in the area of charity law.

As the '90s continued, more focus started to be paid to the question of "political activities": the engagement of charities in public policy issues. Two cases—both involving pro-life organizations that had their charitable status revoked—became the focus of much attention.[2] While not necessarily endorsing the positions or actions of the two organizations, sector leaders feared a clampdown on any involvement by charities in political activities. At around the same time, a new charity was created, the Institute for Media, Policy and Civil Society (IMPACS). Although much of its work was to be aimed at promoting a free press and democratic engagement internationally, it became a significant voice in the Canadian sector as it railed against any restrictions on a charity's ability to advocate. Throughout the latter part of the 1990s, the federal government began making significant cutbacks in funding programs, including many that supported charitable organizations. This confluence of funding issues and concerns about policy engagement prompted a number of national organizations to form the Voluntary Sector Roundtable. While it had no mandate from the broader sector (and, in fact, excluded some significant parts of the sector), the members of the Roundtable used their contacts and influence in making the sector's case to the federal government.

The year 1997 brought two significant successes for the Voluntary Sector Roundtable. The governing Liberal Party (a centre-left party) issued a policy platform document that included a commitment to developing a new relationship with Canada's voluntary sector.[3] The document recognized that the sector was responsible for delivery of many government programs and services, and that there was a need to re-examine the working arrangements between government and the sector. The other success came from the publicity surrounding the Roundtable's appointment of the Panel on Accountability and Governance in the Voluntary Sector. The Broadbent panel, (informally named after its chair, the former leader of the federal New Democrats, traditionally the left-leaning party in Parliament), delivered its report some 14 months later.[4] Amongst its other recommendations, the panel called for a statutory definition of charity that would include all of the Pemsel categories but encompass other types of organizations that provide public benefit. It also called for establishment of a commission that would take on some quasi-regulatory functions, while also providing support to charities and those wishing to become charities. Finally, of note, the Broadbent panel called for re-examination of the rules on advocacy, saying that the "10 per cent rule" should be only an approximation and that the ability of charities to engage in non-partisan political activity should be affirmed.

These two successes led to a third: the federal government announced a new type of initiative. An innovative form of policy making, the "Working Together" project, would involve three "tables" comprising equal numbers of senior public servants and senior people from the voluntary sector. Each table was co-chaired, with one co-chair coming from government and the other from the voluntary sector. The tables were given only three month to "scope out" the issues involved in their various mandates: building a new relationship, supporting capacity building, and regulatory reform. The regulatory reform table identified a number of issues that required rethinking, ranging from the form of the regulatory body, through the release of regulatory decisions, to reform of the rules relating to advocacy and the introduction of intermediate sanctions, giving the regulator some opportunity to penalize inappropriate conduct by a charity with something short of revocation of its charitable status.

Only months following the release (to generally positive reviews) of the "Working Together" report, the federal government went one step further, announcing in 1999 a five-year, $95 million project entitled the "Voluntary Sector Initiative." This was to be a longer-term, more structured version of "Working Together," this time with the creation of seven joint tables, again equally populated by senior public servants and people from the voluntary sector. One of the tables was to be known as the Joint Regulatory Table (JRT).

So while the decade of the 1990s started off with much heat and little light, the last part of the decade led to an unprecedented involvement of the voluntary sector in the development of policy recommendations, including proposals for regulatory reform affecting charities. The engagement of the Voluntary Sector Roundtable with the federal government paid significant dividends: while issues were still outstanding, there was a sense within the voluntary sector that it was at least "at the table," a partner in developing concepts that would impact the sector for years to come. In addition to the direct discussions with government, sector organizations had another venue for a review of charity law. This came in 1998, when the Supreme Court of Canada agreed to hear the first charity law case it had considered in decades. The Vancouver Society of Immigrant and Visible Minority Women had been refused charitable registration on the basis that its objects were not purely charitable. An appeal to the Federal Court of Appeal was lost. Before the Supreme Court of Canada, the Canadian Centre for Philanthropy—the leading umbrella organization of charities in the country, and now known as Imagine Canada—sought and obtained intervenor status, arguing primarily that the regulator's interpretation of "advancement of education" was impermissibly narrow. Although the Society lost its appeal before the Supreme Court (on a 4–3 split), the Court basically endorsed the Centre for Philanthropy's position and significantly expanded the law on what was "educational" for the purposes of charity law.[5]

2000–05: The Storm and the Calm

The JRT was co-chaired by the newly appointed director general of the Charities Directorate and by this author, the executive director of a private foundation based in western Canada. Its membership included six other government officials and six other sector representatives. In addition, three advisers were appointed: one from the Canadian Centre for Philanthropy (who was also the co-chair of the "Working Together" report on regulatory reform); one a lawyer specializing in charity law, and the third a senior director within the Charities Directorate.

The JRT's mandate had been set by the federal Cabinet, which, to the dismay of some in the charitable sector, restricted one aspect of the work and took another item off the table entirely. At the same time that some loud voices in the sector were calling for elimination of all or most of the restrictions on political activity, the JRT was not to examine that issue at all. Similarly, while some were calling for the creation of a new regulator along the lines of the Charity Commission for England and Wales, the JRT was allowed to examine institutional models but not to make a recommendation on which model to adopt. Despite these limitations, the Table undertook its work, looking at issues of transparency and accountability, business activities by charities, reporting, appeals mechanisms, and intermediate sanctions. There were disagreements regarding some of the issues, and the possible solutions, but the Table never split on government/sector lines. On any controversy, there were some government and some sector people on both sides of the issue.

Throughout its work, however, the issue of advocacy was never very far from the conversation. There were ongoing calls for reform, often informed by urban myths about the number of charities that had been refused registration or had lost registration because of their engagement in political activities. In fact, a study undertaken by the JRT's secretariat revealed that in the five years leading up to 2001, an average of only five charities per year had lost their registration for anything other than failure to file their annual return.

In 2002, JRT was shown a presentation that Finance officials were intending to deliver to Cabinet that discussed the advocacy issue. The one-sided nature of the presentation led to the sector members of the JRT withdrawing to a separate caucus—the first time this kind of split had happened in the Table's time together. It was apparent that the advocacy issue could not be ignored. At the same time, government officials, faced with a Cabinet instruction, could not acquiesce to allowing the JRT to discuss advocacy.

The government co-chair of JRT devised an elegant solution, something that came to be called "the alternative mechanism." A small group, partially but not fully drawn from the JRT membership, started its own set of meetings to examine the existing CRA guidance on political activities. When there were debates about wording, the sector members of the group were encouraged to draft their own text, much of which was adopted. The revised guidance was released almost concurrently with the JRT's interim report. The more permissive language and tone of the guidance eased tensions significantly, and leading sector voices praised the document, saying it provided significantly more room for them to engage in activities that they had considered foreclosed.

While the JRT could not make a recommendation on the form of the regulator, its report outlined in detail the advantages and disadvantages of several possible structures. The report provided a constitutional analysis of why an English-style commission was not a realistic possibility for Canada, omitting only the fact that when the sector co-chairs met with representatives of a number of provinces, the provincial officials indicated little interest in becoming involved in charity regulation to any significant extent. In examining the possible structures, the JRT's report focused primarily on what the regulator should do and the traits of a good regulator. Happily, many of those traits were starting to appear within the Charities Directorate, as its director general—who was also the government co-chair of the JRT—had been introducing system improvements even while the JRT was meeting, reducing processing time for applications, and identifying other efficiencies, as well as introducing more outreach programs.

The JRT consulted widely on its interim report, holding open meetings in 23 cities across the country, with various combinations of JRT members at each of the meetings. They heard agreement with many of the recommendations, disagreement with some, and questions about others, but there were few questions about either the regulatory structure or advocacy. In each city, there was a strong turnout of people who worked in the charitable sector either as employees or as volunteers, and they were not shy in offering their advice. The JRT delivered its final report[6] in mid-2003, after spending a week together finalizing the document. In early 2004, the federal government accepted 69 of the 75 recommendations.

As can be seen, throughout this process, the sector was heavily involved in helping to chart the regulatory environment within which charities must operate. Sector figures served on the JRT, but others were convening conversations and presenting briefs. A number of sector organizations were supporting IMPACS as it strove to eliminate rules restricting political activity. The acceptance of the JRT report and the internal improvements that had been made within the Charities Directorate combined to create an atmosphere of relative happiness by mid-2004, and the sector's attention moved on to other issues. But one significant change in attitude contributed to this state of harmony. Before the Voluntary Sector Initiative, the Charities

Directorate was often portrayed as evil incarnate—cloistered, uncommunicative, and the least helpful of government departments. There were closer and ongoing relationships with other departments, many of which provided funding. Post-Voluntary Sector Initiative, and with the internal changes that had been made, the Directorate was seen as more open, somewhat more transparent, and more willing to have discussions than at any time in the past—a change that was accompanied by significantly less helpful contact between the sector and other government departments.

2006–12: The Calm Before the Next Storm

In this next period, regulatory issues took an interesting change. It was, of course, a time when governments around the world were starting to implement new rules in response to global terrorism. International agreements were put in place that, amongst other measures, were intended to prevent charities from being used as vehicles for financing terrorist groups. For reasons both reasonable and unreasonable, CRA's willingness to communicate its activities in this area had a firm boundary drawn around it. It was clear that a new top-secret unit had been created within the Directorate, but no one would (or could) talk about what it did, or how it was enforcing new legislation to allow organizations to be refused charitable registration or have their registration revoked because of ties to terrorism. This remains, even at the time of this writing, an area in which there is no transparency of any kind, not even for gross data.

This period also saw the election of a Conservative government. Despite being a minority government, it began making its agenda clear relatively early, starting off by cancelling a number of programs under which charities received funding and announcing cancellation of the Canadian Volunteer Initiative because it did not align with the government's priorities. Equally relevant and disturbing was the new government's decision to end all ministerial advisory committees that had been established, including one set up to advise the Minister of National Revenue on charity issues. This was a committee that had its origin in a recommendation from the JRT. Sector attention naturally turned to issues more related to funding than regulation.

The issue of terrorism and the new government were connected in another way. Shortly after its election, the government called a public inquiry into the downing of an airplane that was travelling from Canada to India. The bombing of the aircraft took place in 1985, long before global terrorism was a hot topic, but because of criminal investigations and trials, there was no overarching inquiry until more than 20 years after the crash. The inquiry was presided over by a retired justice of the Supreme Court of Canada, and one of the issues examined was the funding of terrorism through charities. The inquiry's final report[7] outlines issues regarding the review of applications for charitable registration and discusses the potential ease with which charitable donations could, deliberately or unwittingly, end up in the hands of terrorist organizations. While the inquiry found no evidence that the particular act of terrorism had involved funds flowing through charities, it cautioned that there had been long-term suspicions that some charities had financed other terrorist activities. It noted that charities (and even more so, not-for-profit organizations that are not subject to the same level of regulation as charities) could use their status to flow funding to those who would do evil. Yet, other than suggesting that CRA be more involved in the intelligence structure looking at terrorism, the inquiry made no recommendations that would directly impact upon charities.

However, there were activities on the regulatory front that did involve charities—a crackdown that had the full support of the sector. Over the previous few years, some organizations had formed tax shelters which were registered under the Income Tax Act, but which played (at least in the view of government officials) fast and loose with the rules. The promoters of these shelters found charities to be fertile ground. Through a variety of agreements and shell companies, they promised "investors" a charitable donation tax receipt, the value of which far exceeded the amount of money the investor had put forward. A small number of charities—some naïve, some greedy—became involved and wrote the receipts or allowed the promoters to write them. CRA launched a major offensive against these tax shelters, auditing them, disallowing the claimed charitable donations, and imposing penalties on the investors. The government went so far as to announce that it would not process any tax return which claimed a charitable tax credit through one of these shelters until the shelter had been fully audited—a stance recently struck down by the courts.[8] Throughout this initiative, sector leaders spoke out in support of the CRA crackdown, recognizing that any manipulation of the process for issuing receipts for tax donations was a threat to the whole sector.

Other regulatory issues were dealt with, often after constructive consultation between the government and the sector. There were changes to the way in which ethnocultural organizations were treated when they applied for registration, making it easier for them to become charities—a step that was probably long overdue, given the increased diversity of the Canadian population. Another matter was the disbursement quota, which Canadian charities were—and still are—subject to. This is a requirement that they expend a minimum amount of money each year on charitable activities. A problematic aspect of that quota, in which donated dollars were treated less favourably than funds received from the government, was eliminated, ending a low-key but lengthy campaign by some sector leaders.

Other actions by the Charities Directorate were less well received. The Directorate issued guidance on fundraising costs, indicating that at levels of as low as 35 per cent, it would question whether a charity had ceased being entirely charitable and had engaged in fundraising to such an extent that it had become a primary purpose of the organization. The guidance raised the hackles of fundraisers and, even after amendments, some argued that it failed to take into account the variety of situations in which fundraising costs can be higher for some organizations or campaigns than for others. Issues of the constitutional authority of the Charities Directorate to enforce rules about fundraising were mooted and could still come to be tested should the Directorate ever take enforcement action on these grounds.

Sector attention turned to another proposed regulatory measure, one that came out of the blue from an unusual source. A backbench member of Parliament introduced a private member's bill that would have imposed a salary cap on anyone employed by a charity so that a charity that paid anyone remuneration of more than $250,000 per annum could lose its charitable registration. In introducing the bill, the member spoke of her father's donations to a particular charity. Recently, she said, the publication of salary levels of people working for government-funded organizations showed that the chief fundraiser for that charity had received more than $1 million in the previous year (ignoring entirely that the amount included a severance payment when he and the charity parted company). The sector's first notice of the bill came from a newspaper account, but that led to a flurry of activity as the sector tried—too late in the game—to explain the realities of the charitable sector to elected officials. Their protests about the complexities of some types of charities and the difficulties in attracting and retaining talent to the sector were in stark contrast to the simple message of the bill's promoter: money donated to charity should be used for good causes, not "outrageous" salaries. In the Canadian parliamentary system, bills introduced by backbench members—particularly those in the opposition party—usually get little attention and have no chance of passage. That was not the case here. Instead, the bill seemed to "have legs." Hearings were held before a parliamentary committee and the bill's progress towards passage appeared inevitable. Only the early prorogation of Parliament for an election saved the sector from the specter of the salary cap. The member who proposed the bill did not seek re-election, and the bill was not introduced into the new Parliament.

The sector was soon to get another surprise. For the preceding ten years or more, any significant change in charity law or policy was usually preceded by discussions with representatives of the charitable sector. Those discussions were sometimes formal, sometimes informal, sometimes with a large group, sometimes with a smaller group, usually including at least some of the peak bodies and also on-the-ground charities and affiliated professionals. But then came Budget 2011 and a provision that suddenly introduced the concept of "ineligible individuals" into the law relating to charities. Under this provision, an organization could be refused charitable registration or lose its registration if an "ineligible individual" is in a position of influence within the organization, either as an employee or a board member. The definition of "ineligible individual" is broad enough to encompass someone involved in a fraudulent tax shelter and someone convicted of shoplifting 30 years earlier. The sector—and apparently some people within the Charities Directorate—were caught totally unaware by the new provision. While the provision itself is objectionable in a number of ways (and again, constitutionally questionable), it caused a rift in the relationship that had existed between the sector and the regulatory departments within government. It was also in this period that, for the first time, the sector convened a "national summit," bringing together people from across the country to talk about an agenda for the charitable sector to promote. The national gathering followed a series of regional meetings in which Imagine Canada, the national umbrella, obtained feedback from charities in their local settings. The resulting agenda was light on issues related to regulation, perhaps a sign that things seemed to be running smoothly—but that was to change very soon after the November 2011 summit.

The sector was not the only group that was meeting. Five years earlier, in 2006, the director general of charities invited his counterparts from England, Australia, New Zealand, and the United States to meet in Ottawa to discuss issues of common concern. (This author was an after-dinner speaker at the first such gathering.) These meetings have continued every 18 months to 2 years (although in recent years, the American regulator has declined to attend), moving from country to country. The extent to which regulators are harmonizing their approaches as a result of these meetings can only be a matter of conjecture.

2012–15: No More Calm, Just Storm

The explosion hit without warning in January 2012. The federal Conservative government had been encouraging development of a pipeline that would transport oil and bitumen from Alberta across British Columbia to the Pacific Ocean, thus opening new markets for Canadian oil products. The pipeline was opposed by almost all environmental organizations, many indigenous groups, and many people in British Columbia. In mid-January 2012, the then Minister of natural resources issued an open letter, in which he wrote,

> Unfortunately, there are environmental and other radical groups that would seek to block this opportunity to diversify our trade. Their goal is to stop any major project no matter what the cost to Canadian families in lost jobs and economic growth. No forestry. No mining. No oil. No gas. No more hydro-electric dams.
>
> These groups threaten to hijack our regulatory system to achieve their radical ideological agenda. They seek to exploit any loophole they can find, stacking public hearings with bodies to ensure that delays kill good projects. They use funding from foreign special interest groups to undermine Canada's national economic interest. They attract jet-setting celebrities with some of the largest personal carbon footprints in the world to lecture Canadians not to develop our natural resources.

Finally, if all other avenues have failed, they will take a quintessential American approach: sue everyone and anyone to delay the project even further. They do this because they know it can work. It works because it helps them to achieve their ultimate objective: delay a project to the point it becomes economically unviable.[9]

The Prime Minister sought to shock Canadians with news that Canadian charities were accepting funds from donors and philanthropic organizations outside the country, something which came as no surprise to anyone, since it had been happening for decades and was, in fact, authorized by a treaty between Canada and the United States. The Minister of the environment charged, in the House and the media, that some charities were laundering "offshore money" from foreign foundations.[10] Then, the public safety Minister joined the furore, issuing a statement on the government's strategy, reported in the press, as aimed to

> target not only known terrorist groups but "vulnerable individuals" who could be drawn into politically inspired violence.
> . . . in addition to foreign threats, the government would be vigilant against domestic extremism that is "based on grievances—real or perceived—revolving around the promotion of various causes such as animal rights, white supremacy, environmentalism and anti-capitalism."[11]

Up to this point, the sector's response came primarily from environmental organizations, although Imagine Canada called upon the Environment Minister to either report evidence of money laundering to police or to withdraw the accusation. He did neither. But the rest of the sector was about to be caught up in the drama. In the 2012 budget, the federal government announced that it was giving additional resources to CRA to exercise greater supervision over political activities engaged in by charities. Included in this direction for increased vigilance was funding to conduct a "political activities audit project" that would undertake special projects to examine a number of charities to ensure that they remained within the permissible limits when they engaged in political activities. The government also announced changes to the annual reporting form, requiring charities to report on funding they received from outside Canada to engage in political activities. Finally, it required that when a foundation provided a grant to a charitable organization to undertake political activities, both the foundation and the charitable organization had to report the spending as political activities.

As the first round of audits (a total of 60 over four years) was commenced, charges were levelled that the Charities Directorate was choosing audit "targets" based on direction from politicians. The charges persisted despite denials from both elected officials and the director general of the Charities Directorate. Both the major opposition parties in Parliament accused the government of acting in bad faith and trying to intimidate charities and stifle dissent. In the run-up to the October 2015 election, both parties committed to creating more liberal rules for political activities by charities. The commentary from the sector and on its behalf was reminiscent of that in the 1990s. There were claims of advocacy chill, and some say there are now fewer charities engaged in political activities, although the statistics drawn from the annual reporting form of charities do not support this. The Charities Directorate has also been charged with becoming politicized, and there have been increasing calls for a new regulator, independent of government. In short, over the course of 25 years, the sector has come full circle.

One new development was an attempt to try to improve the "brand" of Canada's charities. Imagine Canada's Standards Program sets out 73 standards that, according to Imagine Canada, are indicators of a well-operated charity. The standards cover board governance, fundraising, financial accountability and transparency, staff management, and volunteer involvement. In some cases, there are varying degrees of compliance required, depending on the size of the charity. If an organization is able to demonstrate compliance with all of the standards, it is "accredited" and authorized to use a trust mark to indicate its status. While some greater public education of the meaning of the trust mark still needs to be accomplished, there are anecdotal reports from accredited organizations that they have found their accreditation welcomed by donors and funders. At one point, it was suggested that the Standards Program could lead to a form of self-regulation by the charity. There is little talk of that as the program develops, likely a recognition that government is unlikely to allow self-regulation of organizations which, through the issuance of donation receipts, allow taxpayers to claim income tax credits, estimated by the federal government to amount to more than $2 billion in forgone revenue.

2015 and Beyond: The Great Unknown

In the October 2015 election, the Liberal party won a majority government. In its platform document, the party said,

> We will allow charities to do their work on behalf of Canadians free from political harassment, and will modernize the rules governing the charitable and not-for-profit sectors.
>
> This will include clarifying the rules governing "political activity," with an understanding that charities make an important contribution to public debate and public policy. A new legislative framework to strengthen the sector will emerge from this process.[12]

There have been no indications of how quickly it will move on the whole of this commitment. However, a first step was taken in January 2016, when the government announced cancellation of the political activities audit project. Of the 60 audits that were to take place under the project, 6 had not yet commenced, and they were cancelled. The other 54 audits would continue in the normal course. The news release issued by the government[13] said that 30 audits had been completed, resulting in five charities being notified that CRA intended to revoke their registration. But the release also revealed that even in those five cases, involvement in political activities was not the primary reason for the intention to revoke. As of the date of this writing, none of those five charities has yet lost its charitable status; they have appeals that are proceeding within CRA. Only when revocation takes place, or an appeal is made to the Federal Court of Canada, will anyone be able to obtain any information about the identities of the five charities or their alleged transgressions.

For the remainder of the government's pre-election commitment, there is not yet any indication of what form any changes will take. The reference to "a new legislative framework to strengthen the sector" came as a surprise to many in the sector, and no one has publicly indicated knowledge of its meaning. In these early post-election days, the sector leadership is uncertain of the future, or of what it would include if the government were to ask for a list of priorities. There are, however, a few key themes, as outlined in the following sections.

Political Activities

The pre-election platform is clear that there will be some change to the rules regarding political activities. That could take the form of increasing the 10 per cent limit or it could involve following court decisions in other countries and statutorily removing the prohibition on charities having political purposes. In September 2016, CRA announced that it was starting a consultation process to examine the political activities policy. However, the consultation seems focused more on whether the existing rules are clear and understood. One of the consultation questions does ask whether the rules on political activity should be changed and, if so, in what ways. However, there has been no indication from the government that it is paying any attention to jurisprudence from other jurisdictions that has eliminated the suggestion that charities may not have a political purpose so long as it is incidental to another charitable purpose.

The Regulator

In terms of the regulator, some are predicting that some sort of independent regulator will be created, with CRA being left only to administer the charitable donation tax credit. Given that the party announced that it would go into deficit to allow for funding of infrastructure, it is questionable whether it would undertake the expenditure of creating an entirely new body, particularly when federal constitutional authority over charities is limited. Suggestions of some sort of federal-provincial arrangement for the establishment of a charities commission would seem to fly in the face of recent attempts at obtaining national agreement on issues such as securities regulation. One step introduced by the previous government and continuing under the current government is greater use of technology for charity reporting. Currently, all 86,000 charities must submit a paper report each year, and the information is then keyed in to allow some data searching. CRA has been given the resources to move to a fully electronic reporting system.

Appeal Mechanism

It might be hoped that one step the new government would be prepared to take is changing the rules for judicial reconsideration of decisions relating to charities, moving the jurisdiction to the Tax Court. In addition to providing a real option to organizations that have been refused charitable status, this would allow for Canada to develop a greater breadth of jurisprudence. It might also be hoped that hearings *de novo*, rather than on the record, might lead to the expansion of our understanding of what is charitable in the modern day, something hoped for in early charity law cases but rarely seen in Canada.

Social Finance

The phrasing in the Liberal party platform may also signal that the government will introduce legislation governing so-called social entrepreneurial activities and/or social finance. The federal government has been promising such legislation for a decade, and there are parts of the sector that believe it is a priority. Others remain more cautious about the impacts and the potential for scandal. The possibilities of new legislation were discussed as far back as the work of the JRT and Working Together. At one point, it was suggested that a Charities Act could be introduced to combine the federal incorporation rules of non-profit organizations and the necessary tax rules. In addition to creating a simpler legislative structure, such a stand-alone act could avoid one of the major pitfalls of having charities dealt with in the Income Tax Act—that is, language used for a particular situation in one part of the Act is inappropriate when it is applied to charities. A Charities Act could resolve that issue, with the Income Tax Act limited to setting out the tax credits that would apply to donations to charities. The conversation went nowhere, in part because Industry Canada, the department responsible for the supervision of federally incorporated bodies, was designing its own legislation, which paralleled the legislation applicable to for-profit corporations. After several false starts, the new legislation, the Canada Not-for-Profit Corporations Act, was finally enacted, but even Industry Canada officials have admitted this Act is designed for non-profit corporations such as airports and port authorities. Its rules are, in large part, far too complex and of questionable application for charities. But the sector was unable to stop the train that had started moving, and it now has legislation that is likely to result in massive non-compliance.

Regulation of Non-Profits

The reference in the platform document to non-profits (other than charities) could represent a huge—potentially unfathomable—change. The types of groups that are exempt from taxation because they are non-profit is vast, ranging from neighbourhood book clubs and community leagues to professional bodies such as the Canadian Medical Association. Although there are some legislative provisions requiring the largest of them to file annual returns with CRA, there has traditionally been little supervision of this. However, in recent years, CRA has questioned whether some organizations have maintained their non-profit status. It bases this on a number of tests— most of them ridiculed by observers—such as whether the organization has any surplus at the end of its fiscal year. Some of the material has suggested that a charity must plan to have no money at the end of the year, ignoring the fact that larger organizations would be operating imprudently if they did not have some form of reserve. Despite requests that CRA actually assess tax against one of these organizations so that the matter could be litigated, it appears that no such assessments have been made.

Both groups that were involved in reviewing legislation—the Working Together group and the Joint Regulatory Table—had mandates that included examining non-profit organizations as well as charities. Both groups declined to do so, reporting that the number and varying nature of non-profit groups would require a larger and more complex study than either had been given the time or resources to undertake. It is possible that the pre-election platform position anticipates the new government being able to establish rules for non-profits that are not charities, although there have been no signals as to what those rules might be. The next few years may see significant changes in the regulation of Canada's voluntary sector. Or once again we might see only tweaking at the edges.

Sector Infrastructure

One issue that is likely to work to the detriment of charities is the absence of effective and appropriately funded umbrella organizations. It can reasonably be argued that sector infrastructure is sorely lacking. Imagine Canada is seen as a leading voice on behalf of the charitable sector, and it has engaged regularly with the federal government. Some of that engagement has been successful; other attempts have allowed Imagine Canada to be heard, but its advice ignored. But like many infrastructure organizations around the world, Imagine Canada's funding is precarious at best, and its membership is a small fraction of the number of charities and other non-profits. This can be explained in part by the fact that if Imagine Canada is successful, all organizations stand to benefit: why should all of them pay membership if they are going to get the benefits of legislative and regulatory change whether they are members or not. This "freeloader" syndrome is not unique to Canada, but it has hampered infrastructure organizations at both the sector and sub-sector level. At one point, Canada was relatively generous in its government funding of sector infrastructure organizations; those days have long since passed. Some sub-sector organizations, particularly those in the area of the arts and poverty alleviation, were totally defunded and have either ceased to exist or have become a shadow of their former selves.

Government Relations

The sector has also suffered because of its concentration on relationships with the government of the day, rather than with all parliamentarians. This phenomenon was most clearly evident when the Conservative party became the government in 2006. The sector had had little engagement with the party when it was in opposition, and it was perceived (inappropriately, I would argue) as more closely aligned with the Liberal party, with some sympathies for the New Democratic Party. Its engagement with the broader group of parliamentarians of all stripes has been minimal. Although the involvement of politicians in voluntary organizations is almost mandatory if the politician is to be elected, the Canadian sector has been unsuccessful in engaging cross-party involvement. There is no "caucus" of parliamentarians who have been engaged with the voluntary sector, and there has been little in the way of relationship building with backbenchers—a problem that became painfully evident with the introduction of the bill to cap the salaries of charity employees. Comments by backbenchers during debates and committee hearings on the bill revealed a painful lack of knowledge of the basic facts of the charitable sector or its regulation.

The lack of funding—and consequent lack of capacity—of infrastructure organizations (federal, provincial, or municipal; sector wide or sub-sector in focus) is not solely the fault of governments. Indeed, the de-funding of umbrella organizations in the 1990s and in the first part of the twenty-first century demonstrated the problems with relying too heavily on government funding. The charitable sector itself—including, most particularly, foundations—have been glaring in their refusal to provide sustained funding to infrastructure; individual charities have been equally glaring in their refusal to pay even modest membership fees.

For at least the period from 2015 to 2019, Canada will be governed by a political party which has said that it will change rules to allow charities to serve their beneficiaries better. The question is whether there will be organizations in the sector who can and will help the government understand how best to do that. The alternative is to fall into the patterns of the past, when hundreds of charities would write to the government each year prior to the budget being delivered asking for small and self-interested changes that would benefit the few, but not the many. In short, the chances for regulatory reform and benefit to charities and those they serve will depend, to some significant extent, on the ability of the charitable sector to start acting like a sector, including anointing one or more infrastructure organizations with their support, both moral and financial.

Notes

1 Research commissioned by the Pemsel Case Foundation, publication pending; see www.pemselfoundation.org.
2 *Human Life International in Canada Inc v The Minister of National Revenue* 1998 CanLII 9053 (FCA), [1998] 3 FC 202; and *Alliance for Life v Minister of National Revenue* [1999] 3 FCR 504, 1999 CanLII 8152.
3 Liberal Party of Canada, *Securing Our Future Together* (Ottawa: Liberal Party of Canada, 1997), accessed February 22, 2016, http://web.archive.org/web/19980423142109/http://liberal.ca/download/plan-e.pdf
4 Panel on Accountability and Governance in the Voluntary Sector, *Building on Strength: Improving Governance and Accountability in Canada's Voluntary Sector: Final Report* (Ottawa: The Panel, 1999), accessed February 22, 2016, http://sectorsource.ca/sites/default/files/resources/files/2458_Book.pdf
5 *Vancouver Society of Immigrant and Visible Minority Women v Minister of National Revenue* 1999 CanLII 704, [1999] 1 SCR 10.
6 Voluntary Sector Initiative (Canada), Joint Regulatory Table, *Strengthening Canada's Charitable Sector: Regulatory Reform: Final Report* (Ottawa: Government of Canada, 2003), accessed February 22, 2016, http://www.vsi-isbc.org/eng/regulations/pdf/final_report_full.pdf
7 Commission of Inquiry into the Investigation of the Bombing of Air India Flight 182 (Canada), *Air India Flight 182: A Canadian Tragedy* (Ottawa: Government of Canada, 2010), accessed June 20, 2016, http://www.publicsafety.gc.ca/cnt/rsrcs/lbrr/ctlg/dtls-en.aspx?d=PS&i=85557953.
8 *McNally v. Canada (National Revenue)*, 2015 FC 767 (CanLII); appeal dismissed as moot 2015 FCA 248.
9 Joe Oliver, "An Open Letter from the Honourable Joe Oliver, Minister of Natural Resources, on Canada's Commitment to Diversify Our Energy Markets and the Need to Further Streamline the Regulatory Process in Order to Advance Canada's National Economic Interest," *The Media Room*, January 9, 2012 (Natural Resources Canada, 2012/1), accessed February 22, 2016, http://www.nrcan.gc.ca/media-room/news-release/2012/1/1909.
10 See, for example, http://www.cbc.ca/news/politics/environmental-charities-laundering-foreign-funds-kent-says-1.1165691
11 Shawn McCarthy, "Ottawa's New Anti-terrorism Strategy Lists Eco-extremists as Threats," *Globe & Mail*, February 10, 2012.
12 Liberal Party of Canada, *Real Change: A New Plan for a Strong Middle Class* (Ottawa: Liberal Party of Canada, 2015), accessed June 20, 2016, https://www.liberal.ca/files/2015/10/New-plan-for-a-strong-middle-class.pdf.
13 Canada Revenue Agency, "Minister Lebouthillier Announces Winding down of the Political Activities Audit Program for Charities," *News Release*, January 20, 2016 (Canada Revenue Agency), accessed February 22, 2016, http://news.gc.ca/web/article-en.do?mthd=tp&crtr.page=1&nid=1028679&crtr.tp1D=1?rss.

New Zealand

9   The Evanescent Regulator

Trevor Garrett

Introduction

The Charitable Uses Act 1601, commonly referred to as the Statute of Elizabeth I, was probably a dog-eared, yellowing piece of legislation when James Cook first landed in New Zealand in 1769 and made proclamations which helped ensure that Britain became New Zealand's mother country. In 1840, the Treaty of Waitangi, a treaty signed by representatives of the British Crown and Māori chiefs from tribes throughout New Zealand, gave Britain sovereignty over New Zealand and the right to govern the country, and gave Māori the rights of British subjects. Thirteen years later, the Charitable Trust Act 1853 created the first Charity Commission in Great Britain. The Britain of 1601, and indeed the Britain of 1840 and 1853, was quite different from the society that has developed in New Zealand. However, it is the definitions of charity that have flowed from those times that have helped define charitable purposes in New Zealand to the present day.

Charitable purpose is an important consideration for organizations in New Zealand for three main reasons. First, trusts for charitable purposes can be established even though they lack certain requirements of standard trusts.[1] Second, some grant givers are only able to give grants to organizations that have charitable purposes.[2] Third, and perhaps most importantly, there are significant tax advantages for organizations that are charities.[3] For many years, organizations, in a practical sense, determined for themselves whether they were charities and whether they were entitled to the tax benefits allowed to charities. The Department of Inland Revenue (IRD) had responsibility for administering the tax regulations as they applied to charities, but as there was no mandatory reporting of financial information, organizations for the most part assessed their own tax benefits. Newly forming charities would sometimes approach the IRD for a "letter of comfort," which would state that they were eligible for tax exemptions, but the letter had no legal standing, and the IRD had no procedures for ensuring that the charitable purposes were being carried out, or that the organization did not change the rules under which they operated. Further, there was no information as to how many charities there were in New Zealand and how much the cost of the tax exemptions was worth.[4] The journey to establishment of New Zealand's Charities Commission included a number of working parties and committees that considered matters such as the regulation of charities and the provision of tax benefits for organizations with charitable purposes.[5]

Charities Act 2005

The Charities Bill was introduced to Parliament in March 2004. In introducing the Bill, the Minister of Commerce noted that it would

> bring New Zealand into line with other Commonwealth countries where reporting regimes for charities are commonplace [and be] the first step towards instigating measures to satisfy New Zealand's obligations under the Financial Action Task Force's eight special recommendations relating to the financing of terrorist organizations through not-for-profit entities.[6]

The Bill was considered by the Social Services Committee of Parliament, which received a large number of submissions showing general support for the establishment of a Charities Commission.[7] The Committee recommended that the Commission should have a role in supporting and educating charities; it should be independent as an "autonomous Crown Entity," and there should be no change to the definition of charity. The IRD would retain its tax-related responsibilities.

The Charities Act was assented to in April 2005, and the Charities Commission commenced in July 2005. The Commission was, as recommended, established as an Autonomous Crown Entity (ACE). An ACE is defined in the Crown Entities Act 2004, which provides that an ACE is independent in its decision making, but it must "have regard to government policy when directed by the responsible Minister."[8] The Social Services Committee Report noted that "Particular concern was expressed at the prospect that the government might be able to directly or indirectly influence the registration or deregistration of particular charities to reflect government policy."[9] The Act makes some changes to the definition of charitable purposes, which may be unique to New Zealand. It provides that

> the purpose of a trust, society or institution is a charitable purpose under this Act if the purpose would satisfy the public benefit requirement apart from the fact that the beneficiaries of the trust, or the members of the society or institution, are related by blood. . . .[10]

This is because many Māori organizations are based around iwi or hapu (tribes), and by definition there are significant blood relationships within those structures. This wording was based on existing New Zealand tax law and provided the Commission with some challenges in terms of its interpretation. In particular, the challenges related to how small a group could become before a public benefit became a private benefit.

The Charities Commission in New Zealand

Establishing the Charities Commission as a new operating organization involved work in four general streams. These were organization development, information technology, registration systems development, and public awareness raising. While significant planning went into the establishment of these themes, in fact, the process might be most aptly described as "muddling through."

Organization Development

The life of the Commission has run through four distinct phases: establishment, registration, moving to business as usual, and disestablishment. Prior to the Commission's board being appointed, an establishment unit within the Ministry of Economic Development commenced work to set up the organization. When the board was appointed, the establishment team, who were initially consultants, became the staff of the Commission. A chief executive was appointed within several months of the board being appointed, and over a period of time, permanent staff replaced the consultants. There were significant challenges in establishing the new organization. For example, in an effort to develop and retain institutional knowledge, permanent staff replaced consultants and often had to take on a wider range of duties than was envisaged in their job descriptions. As new staff were appointed, the roles that earlier appointed staff undertook were reduced. Some staff found this constant changing of their roles unsettling. Others were uncomfortable with the absence of operating procedures and internal policies, which had not been developed because they were not a development priority. And while some people joined the Commission thinking they wanted to be a part of a start-up organization, they found the disorganization a difficult environment to work in. Established organizations have tradition, history, and culture; as with other start-up organizations, the Commission had none of that.

At the time, there were a number of charity regulators around the world, but their organizational models were not helpful in establishing the Commission, although their experience in interpreting charity law was. In 2006, the Canada Revenue Agency convened a meeting of charity regulators from common law jurisdictions, and this and subsequent meetings were very helpful in obtaining a more detailed understanding of the issues involved in the regulation of charities.

The main focus of organization development was preparing for charity registration. The key tasks for this were developing appropriate information technology, growing public awareness, and developing the registration process. The second part of organization development was setting up the organization to process a large number of applications for registration as a one-off event. Unlike some other jurisdictions, every organization that wanted to be a charity needed to be registered by the Commission before a specified date (30 June 2008) in order to retain any tax benefits. This meant that a significant but unknown number of charities needed to be registered within a short period of time, which would require a body of staff who would not be needed once the processing of those initial applications was completed. A large number of fixed-term employees, predominantly first-year law graduates, were recruited and trained. The feedback from these staff showed that the work of an analyst was interesting and challenging for a short period of time, but that it became repetitive after 12 months, and they were happy to move on to other employment. Because the decision as to whether an organization had a charitable purpose in the legal sense was a relatively complex one, it took three months to train a new employee to the point where he or she was comfortable reviewing applications without constant supervision. That created its own difficulties, as training a new staff member inevitably reduced the productivity of the trainer at a time when a high-processing throughput was required.

Once this initial processing load for registration was completed, the Commission had to move to a "business-as-usual" footing, which involved a restructure of the organization and included the recruitment of some of the fixed-term employees to permanent positions. Setting up a culture for the Commission was important. It was a regulator, dealing with some difficult legal concepts, but those being regulated were there to do things to benefit the community and wanted to get on with their work with a minimum of interference. Getting the regulatory balance right was critical. From the start, appointments from outside the public sector were made. It was considered important to recruit people who had a strong feel for the charity sector. There was also a need to have people who understood the principles of effective regulation. Given the need to interpret legislation, case law, and governing documents, it was inevitable that a core body of those employed were lawyers.

A culture of questioning and challenging was put in place. Decision makers are gatekeepers. They make determinations as to what is acceptable and what is not. In doing so, they might take a stance of being literal in applying the law, or they might be interpretive. There are three types of decision makers in charity regulation. First are those who seek to push boundaries. In doing so, they are looking at how they can reflect changes that might be happening in society more closely. Second, there are those who are most comfortable with the status quo, seeing no need to make changes. Third are those who pull away from the status quo, who look at previous decisions and want to withdraw from that position. Gatekeepers also bring their own backgrounds to the decision-making process, but the art of decision making is on the one hand to disregard particular personal beliefs, while on the other hand making use of background information that might add to an overall picture. In the case of the Commission, the chief executive encouraged the pushing of boundaries, at least to the extent that all points of view could be assessed before decisions were made. That did not necessarily mean that all staff shared that view, and it was necessary to build safeguards so that no one person could act as a final gatekeeper. Those staff having daily interactions with charities in their public awareness role were encouraged to challenge those who were developing the registration processes. Analysts considering applications were encouraged to challenge the legal views of other analysts. That culture of challenging and questioning was encouraged up to the level of the chief executive, with the intent to ensure that the best decisions were made within the Commission, that there was a high-level understanding of the whole charity sector, and that the affect of communication methods and decisions was clearly understood.

A culture of being client centred was also developed. This meant that all publications were to be in plain English, and consideration was always given to making things as easy as possible for applicants. While such a culture sounds straightforward, in reality it was not. First, a client-centred focus is not typical of public-sector organizations, which more usually expect clients to fit their behavior into the requirements of the public-sector agency. Second, such a focus means that the regulator must understand the different needs of members of the public. This can be a challenge, as those needs are varied and do not always cope with a "one-size-fits-all" approach. Further, a staff member's own personal background might mean that he or she has not been exposed to the wide variety of people that make up the New Zealand community. To help gain a better understanding of the sector, most staff were encouraged to attend public events, both in Wellington and around the country, and to interact with the people involved in the sector. Analysts were encouraged to phone applicants directly if they thought that such communication would expedite the resolution of an issue. The result of having such a culture meant that, as evidenced from regular feedback surveys, there was a generally positive relationship between the sector and the Commission.

Information Technology

Prior to the establishment of the Commission, the establishment unit commenced the development of a bespoke computer system based on a particular decision-making model for registration. That involved a fixed price fixed delivery date contract. When the Commission reviewed its legislation in terms of registration requirements, it was clear that the assumptions made for the bespoke system needed to change. Consequently, both the costs and the time frame for the system started to escalate. A staged development was introduced so that by the time registration was to commence, those components of the system that would allow for registration applications online, and application processing, would be available. This development was occurring in an environment where there were considerable external and internal pressures to get registration started. Registration commenced on the agreed date, but the system at that stage had only limited capacity. While it did allow for applications to be made online and to be processed, it did not allow for the filing of annual returns, sharing of information, or for the statutory requirement of a search of the register, and it lacked some functionality for application processing.

At that stage, the Commission decided to review its options in terms of its IT system, which resulted in a decision to replace the bespoke system with a Customer Relationship Management package system. The new project was completed within a relatively short period, and there was a transition from the bespoke system. The new system was significantly less expensive to develop, provided greater ongoing flexibility and lower ongoing costs, and was user-friendly for both applicants and registration analysts. The system allowed for online registration, notices of change, and annual returns; back office processing and search functionality; public search capacity; and information sharing.

Public Awareness Raising

When the Commission was established, there was no common database and little information on the numbers, names, or contact details of charities in New Zealand. It was also assumed that charities were not aware that they needed to register as a charity in order to retain the tax exemptions that they were eligible for. Initial internal estimates suggested that there would be 15,000 charities in New Zealand. During the awareness-raising process, it became clear that the some of the assumptions made to reach that figure were incorrect and that it was too low. A revised estimate of 25,000 was used for budgeting and planning purposes. Later figures from the Department of Statistics estimated that there were 97,000 not-for-profit organizations in New Zealand, although it was acknowledged that many of these would not qualify as charities.[11] It also became clear that the public had a poor understanding of the meaning of the word charity. For many it was confined to an organization that provided funds or services of a welfare nature.

The Commission did not have a large advertising budget to promote registration and therefore took a sophisticated, but low-key approach to awareness raising. That approach recognized the potential breadth of the definition of a charity, identified the variety of different sectors, identified the layers within each sector, and also identified all of the sources from which those sectors received information. Potential charities, professional bodies, and the media were targeted at national, regional, and local levels by way of meetings and workshops. An extensive email list was developed, and regular updates were sent out, with the feedback revealing that these were shared in turn with a larger number of people. The feedback also showed that people were receiving the same information from multiple sources. At the end of the initial registration period, the Commission was satisfied that the majority of charities would have been aware of the requirement to register and of the registration process.

Registration

One of the biggest challenges faced by the Commission was development of the registration process. This started with the preparation of an application, either on paper or online, then came processing of an application, including developing knowledge on charities law, and decision making concerning registration. As noted earlier, one of the challenges, and difficulties, was the development of an application and review process that would work, while at the same time developing an IT system that reflected those processes. This proved not to be an easy task. As the application forms were being drafted, the wording of the draft forms was tested in workshops in several centres around New Zealand to satisfy the Commission that they were easily understood and user-friendly. It was mindful that its public ranged from people who had a high level of skill in understanding the processes, through to people with very low skill levels, generally those in smaller organizations. There was a motivation to target the application process to a level at which applications could be completed simply, with no need for a high level of skill, particularly in legal matters.

While the application process was being developed, it was also necessary to develop guidance for, and train registration staff on, charities law so that by the time the first application was received, registration staff had a sufficient understanding of the legal criteria for registration. The guidelines were developed using the Charities Act 2005,[12] extensive reviews of New Zealand and international case law, and reviews of the major textbooks on charity and trust law. Further refinement was carried out by reviewing the guidance material and decisions of the UK Charity Commission. However, because the charities legislation in the United Kingdom had recently been amended, direct comparisons became more problematic. An important early action was a statement from the IRD's chief legal adviser that there would be no second-guessing by the IRD of registration decisions made by the Commission. His view was that any registration decision would be accepted for the purpose of making decisions relating to tax. This meant that the Commission could make decisions without needing to consider any fiscal implications.

Through consultation exercises, other issues were identified. For example, there was some concern—particularly from the private schools sector, charities that were involved in business activities, and philanthropists who wished to retain their anonymity—about the requirement for information to be displayed on the Register. A policy to underpin the Commission's power to withhold information was developed: essentially, the Commission took the view that when an organization went to the public for funding, then they should expect their information to be made public. Once registration started, several other key issues started to emerge and required time to resolve. These included whether or not sports organizations qualified as charities, political advocacy, organizations established for economic development purposes, membership organizations where public benefit was an issue, and disposition of funds on winding up.

Pressure to have a high level of throughput, as well as maintaining accurate decision making, encouraged several reviews of the registration process. To ensure that the processes were as efficient as they could be, several changes were made including separating legal analysis from application administration. One review also recommended developing a balance between a legalistic view of registration, whereby communication with applicants was formal, and providing assistance to applicants and communicating with them directly. It considered how an environment could be established where legal process risks were minimized rather than eliminated. In order to maintain consistency of decision making, a random selection of decisions was subjected to both internal and external legal reviews. In addition to these refinements of the internal processes of registration, there was a constant management of expectations, particularly around the delays that inevitably occurred with a rush of applications. Some applicants expected that registration would happen very quickly, whereas in fact an application took about six months to process. One major difficulty was attempting to forecast how many applications would be received and when they would come. Only half the forecast numbers had been received a month before the statutory deadline for registration, and no one knew whether the forecast was wrong or whether a large number of applications would be received at the last minute. The latter is what happened, resulting in a great deal of pressure to process those numbers. By the final date on which initial registration had to be applied for, over 25,000 applications had been submitted. Once staff were trained, about 70 per cent of applications resulted in registration, after an initial review.

Dealing with such a large number of applications in such a short period of time meant that at times a factory mentality prevailed. Experience had shown that a trained analyst could process about six applications per day. Multiplying that by the number of analysts employed showed how many applications could be processed in a day and, importantly, when any backlog of applications might be cleared. Staff resignations and new recruits could also be factored into calculations.

The Board's Role in Registration

It is important to discuss the role of the board of the Commission in the registration process. The function of making decisions on registration was given to the Commission through the board by virtue of the Charities Act 2005. The Crown Entities Act 2004 gave the board the power to delegate to the chief executive, among others. The initial board comprised seven appointees, all of whom had extensive experience in the charitable sector with one being a lawyer who specialized in trust law. Some initial board members had been involved with the earlier inquiries and with providing advice on the establishment of the Commission.

The board essentially had two roles. The first was to oversee the establishment and operation of the organization and the second was to act in a quasi-judicial capacity. Before the first applications were received, the board spent some time reviewing the guidance material being developed for analysts. It was also provided with discussion papers on key subjects, such as sport and political advocacy, that were considered to be matters that might be contentious, and it developed a decision-making tree that would guide it through the consideration of applications. When the first applications were received, the board adopted a hands-on approach to decision making, because it wanted to ensure that correct decisions were being made and that it educated itself on the decision-making process. After a period of time, some decision making became standardized, and the numbers of applications meant that it was no longer practicable for the board to see them all without overwhelming the process. So the board delegated to the chief executive the capacity to make decisions within categories that it felt it no longer needed to see.

For some time, the board continued to make the final decision on all applications that might result in a rejection. It also needed to be confident that the chief executive would continue to submit applications to the board for consideration; it did not want to be excluded from the process. This required careful management, as taking applications to the board naturally slowed the process and required more work from analysts, as they had to prepare detailed papers for the board. However, that also meant that analysts needed to be more disciplined in their work, knowing that it might come under board scrutiny. As board members were replaced, it was important to ensure that their replacements could quickly develop an understanding of charities law, which was achieved most effectively by providing them with an effective induction program and including them in the decision-making process. Experience showed that it took up to 12 months for a new board member to become comfortable with that process.

All board decisions were made on the papers presented to it, which included all information provided by applicants. Analysts attended to provide any additional information that was required, but there were no face-to-face meetings between the board and the applicants. All decisions to decline registration were provided to applicants and were published on the Commission's website. While there was no political interference in the board's decision making, there were occasions when applicants, who might have been facing a decline of registration or de-registration, carried out a debate in the media and it became necessary to explain the decision-making process to politicians or the media. This was done by the chief executive so that the board's independence was not compromised. Where there were contentious decisions, the Minister and other politicians would be advised after the decision had been made.

Registering as a Charity

As already indicated, with the enactment of the Charities Act 2005, the major challenge was to register all eligible charities in New Zealand before the deadline so that they could retain their tax-exempt status. The challenge for charities, apart from being aware of the need to register, and complying with registration requirements, was the need to ensure that rules documents were up to date and met the new requirements of having a charitable purpose. For many, the legal concept of charitable purpose was a new one. It differed from the popular understanding of what a charity was, and for some it was archaic. Trying to comprehend a piece of legislation from 1601 that talked about "marriages of poor maids" and relating it to modern times was a challenge. To complicate the matter further for many smaller charities, rules generally set out what their organizations did without contemplating the requirements of qualifying with a charitable purpose. Having navigated the definition of charitable purpose, the next challenge was to understand the public benefit test. Most organizations believed that what they were doing was for the good of the public—after all, that was why they did it. They were surprised when the law did not see it that way, and this was particularly the case for some economic development agencies, social enterprises, community housing agencies, and ratepayers' organizations, some of which had their applications tested in court.[13] Despite the challenges, the registration process proceeded reasonably smoothly, and while some organizations did need to spend time to get their rules sorted, and others discovered that they had never in fact been charitable, the majority of applications for registration were approved.

Education

One function of the Commission which the Parliament considered important was education, specifically including effective use of charitable resources, good management, and governance. The role of a regulator in providing education is complicated because the two roles may at times be in conflict. In such cases, the primary function must continue to be that of a regulator. There are good reasons for having a role in education. First, the regulator has access to all charities, because they are on the Register. Second, the regulator develops a good technical understanding of issues concerning the sector because of the information that it receives and can share these with the sector. Third, whether or not they agree with the regulator, charities will listen because they feel that they need to.

Expanding on the final point, it is relatively easy for a regulator to have access to groups in the sector because those groups feel that they have to listen in case they miss something that is critical to their continued registration. This is probably easier for a regulator to achieve than for an organization whose sole purpose is education. The danger is that the agent for the regulator cloaks itself with an authority that might not be available to a non-regulator. Faced with this apparent authority, charities may feel an obligation to do what the educator says, even if they might not agree with it. Conversely, the second danger is that the intent of the educator is at odds with that of the regulator, even though they are a part of the same organization. In this scenario, the educator may encourage a charity to a particular course of action, which the charity finds is contrary to the requirements of the regulator. Notwithstanding the potential difficulties, it would be unfortunate if a regulator were to identify good practice during the course of their work and not share that practice with organizations that were failing. Some regulators take the view that to share a practice might be seen to endorse it and for that reason decide against taking on a role in education.

Therefore, developing a role in education was not a simple task. Early on it was clear that many agencies, private and public, were already doing excellent work assisting charities in a wide range of matters. The Commission took the view that it should not duplicate this work. Apart from its registration awareness-raising programme, the Commission was required to hold an annual meeting. The initial meetings were very popular. The observation from these meetings was that people wanted to get together, they wanted information and ideas, and between them they recognized that they had skills and knowledge that they could share. Further, the general skills required to run a charity were not sector specific. Using these principles, the education team developed half-day programmes, based on feedback from charities, and took these to locations around the country. The programmes included information from Commission staff but often included sessions run by people from the sector. There was often surprise expressed at the wide range of organizations that were present at the meetings, and it allowed for the further development of local networks. Because the Register allowed for targeted communications to all charities within a particular region, the meetings were representative of the organizations operating in those regions. The meetings also provided an opportunity for key government departments to be available to meet with participants. An observation was that some government departments were not practised at this type of interaction, and some were uncomfortable with it, but because the Commission could demonstrate what was achievable, it encouraged them to continue to participate.

A second initiative was a programme involving chief executives of charities. This was based on an idea of looking at ways by which chief executives could be supported and could share issues that they had before them. These could range between human resource issues, dealing with boards, fundraising climates, and impacts of changes of governments. Although the education programme had been going for a short time before the Commission was abolished, it was clear that the events provided did require leadership and resources for them to happen. It is doubtful that they would continue without it.

The Register

Perhaps the most important role that the regulator can take is that of providing access to information provided by charities. The Register is a relatively simple collection of all information provided for the purposes of registration or for fulfilling their requirements with regards to annual returns. However, the Act takes the next step of ensuring that any person is able to search the register for all information held on it, apart from information that the secretary has agreed to withhold.[14] Because of the value of the information on the Register, and because the data on it is "live," the Commission undertook a project to make all of the data accessible by searching using any of the criteria under which information was held. Further, an "open data" facility allowed people to use the data within their own computer applications for whatever legal purposes they wished. This meant that all up-to-the-minute data was fully available to the public for whatever use they wanted to put it to. The "open-data" project was not easy to sell. The Commission's monitoring agency was opposed to it because it believed the Commission would not be able to control how people would use the information. It also had a concern that the information might be used in a way that might embarrass the Minister. Some Commission staff were concerned that open data might make the IT system vulnerable. There was also a concern that the actual data, which was coming directly from charities through their annual returns, might not be accurate. The advantage of making the Register accessible in this way was that people could ask any question relating to charities that the data might provide for and get answers to those questions without having to contact the regulator.

The Commission was mindful that charities had interactions with many other agencies, such as government departments and funding organizations, that required the submission of financial information. It took the view that information made available on the Register should have been sufficient for those organizations and that they should not require a separate submission of that information from those charities. It was felt that the agencies should be educated to use the Register to obtain as much additional information as they could about the charities that they worked with so as to minimize duplication of effort. In practice, this was a slow process, as it took government agencies time to change their approach and systems.

Because it also had a role of promoting and stimulating research, the Commission saw the Register as a way of encouraging research into charities. It could do this by making universities aware of the significant data set available for students and staff and encouraging them to use it. It gave government agencies, as well as others, the opportunity to send targeted information to individual charities. For example, if IRD was changing tax rules for businesses, it would be able to send that information out to all charities that had been identified as being involved in business. This was the most advanced "open-data" project within the New Zealand government. While that was a significant achievement, it also meant that as potential users were not aware of either the data or the opportunities that they might present, it was necessary to actively promote its use. This was done by educating government departments and universities about the possibilities, and it was achieved in part, but with the demise of the Commission, the active promotion of the project ceased.

Annual Returns

Every registered charity has a duty to prepare an annual return, which is required six months after the charity's balance date.[15] The requirements of the annual return are prescribed by regulation.[16] The aim was to have forms submitted online, although provision also had to be made for paper returns. Because of the substantial differences between charities in terms of how they prepared their annual financial statements, along with a desire to have a single annual return form, it was necessary to test drafts of the proposed form with a wide range of organizations. As with registration, workshops were held around the country to educate people about completing annual returns. This was a much easier exercise than the earlier awareness raising, as registered charities could be contacted more easily, guidance could be provided online, and people expected to have to file an annual return.

Charities expressed two areas of concern with the annual return process. The first was the filing fee. Although registration as a charity was free, government expected that there would be a fee for filing an annual return: $50 for an online return and $75 for a paper return—encouraging online filing with the lower fee. It was later decided that no fee would be imposed on charities with an income less than $10,000. Charities were annoyed that they were required to use their funds to pay for something that they saw as a government requirement. The Commission itself saw the fee as a costly administrative issue because of the need to follow up on returns that did not include the fee and matching online returns with cheques sent by mail. In 2014, the Department of Internal Affairs advised charities that it would not process annual returns if the fee was not paid.[17] The second concern arose because charities had to provide financial details on the annual return form as well as attaching their financial statements, which they regarded as a duplication of effort. The reason for it was so that the information on the Register was rich in data, meaning that it could be searched using financial variables and statistics could be compiled about the sector, thus giving a much better understanding of the sector. When charities realized that this was going to advantage them, and was not just being done for the regulator, there was a higher level of acceptance. In practice, the annual return process has proceeded relatively smoothly. For example, in 2011–12, 62 per cent of registered charities filed their annual returns either early or on time, compared to 38 per cent filing late; 931 charities were deregistered for not filing a return.[18] These results have largely been maintained.

Financial Reporting Standards

Transparency of charities to the public requires financial information to be accurate and comparable. It was clear from the initial annual returns that the financial statements from charities were extremely variable, from a handwritten page of numbers to statements meeting international reporting standards. There were several problems for charities and other not-for-profit organizations. First, they differed greatly in size, so no one standard could fit all. Second, there were no accepted standards that were available specifically for not-for-profit organizations. Third, financial reporting standards for commercial organizations were ill suited to not-for-profit organizations. Rather than develop its own standards, and because it did not see its role as being a financial reporting standards body, the Commission worked with the External Reporting Board to develop both standards and auditing requirements for charities. Four different tiers for reporting standards have been developed for charities, ranging from a simple format cash report for charities with annual operating payments under $125,000 through to full standards for those with over $30 million in annual expenses or that have public accountability. These new standards came into effect after 1 April 2015.[19]

Financing of Terrorism

In introducing the Charities Bill, the Minister of Commerce stated that regulating the charities sector would bring New Zealand in line with its obligations under the Financial Action Task Force's (FATF) special recommendation relating to the funding of terrorism through not-for-profit entities. The FATF obligation was met partly by establishing a register of all charities so that their existence was known, office bearers were identified, and their financial positions were transparent. The Register also allowed the identification of any charity that sent money overseas. Consequently, the Commission was able to send targeted information to more than 2,000 charities setting out its views on their need to be clear as to where funds sent overseas were going and how those funds were to be used. The Commission formed links with agencies such as the New Zealand Police and the Security Intelligence Service. One difficulty related to the security of classified information sourced from both international and domestic intelligence agencies. The Commission was subject to the Official Information

Act, which is intended to increase the public accessibility of official information,[20] meaning that it was difficult to guarantee that classified information could be kept secure. Ways needed to be found to achieve this in a way that the Commission could be kept informed and provide assistance without compromising the integrity of the classified information.

Definition of Charities

Charity law is complex because of its reliance on analogies between current activities and the intent of legislation passed long ago. Court decisions relating to activities carried on in times past are expected to provide guidance for activities being provided in a modern setting. Further, common law anticipates that changing circumstances will inevitably bring about incremental change to the law. The Social Services Select Committee considered the definition and was aware of the difficulty with the legislation, but took the view that changing it may well have unintended consequences.[21] It felt that any changes might disrupt the extensive case law that existed which would guide decision making. There are several general areas where the current definition has caused difficulties. These include economic development agencies which are designed to provide a public benefit by developing employment opportunities, community housing agencies which are seeking to provide affordable housing, residents' associations which are working to provide community amenities and also ensure that local governments are responsive to their needs, and professional organizations that support members but also seek to ensure that their members provide a benefit to the community. All of these have unsuccessfully had decline of registration applications tested in court.[22]

Two other subject matters which have tested the definition of charitable purpose are sports organizations and advocacy by charities. These are discussed in more detail in the following sections.[23]

Sport

Sport presented possibly the most difficult area to deal with in terms of the definition of charitable purpose as it involves a significant part of the population and plays such an important role in the nation's identity. Sports clubs are the way by which most people participate in sport, with more than 273,000 adults belonging to sporting clubs in New Zealand. Historically, these clubs have gained income tax exemption through the Income Tax Act 2007 CW46 and have not needed to rely on charitable status. However, with the passing of the Charities Act 2005, with the possibility of tax exemptions for charitable donations, there was a greater reason for sports clubs to seek registration as charities. Notably, if sport was not considered to be a charitable purpose, it would become more difficult for funders, particularly those that were registered charities, to grant money to sports organizations—if it meant they were spending their monies on non-charitable purposes, they would be risking deregistration. Many funding bodies that sports organizations had traditionally relied on were in this category. Moreover, donee status was not available to sports organizations if they were not registered charities, making it more difficult to attract donations.

The Charities Commission spent some time considering whether sports organizations could become registered charities. On the one hand, it was aware of previous court decisions, and on the other hand, it was aware of the role that sport played in New Zealand and the community benefits that accrued. Meanwhile, in New Zealand's High Court, *Travis Trust v Charities Commission*[24] confirmed the restricted view taken by *Re Nottage*[25] that mere sport or recreation was not a valued charitable purpose. *Travis Trust* was a case where the gift was for the purpose of providing funds to support the New Zealand racing industry by the anonymous sponsorship of a group race known as the Travis Stakes. The Court stated,

> In the area of sport and leisure, the general principle appears to be that sport, leisure, and entertainment for its own sake is not charitable but that where these purposes are expressed to be, and are in fact, the means by which other valid charitable purposes will be achieved, they will be held to be charitable.[26]

This was not a helpful decision. As with *Re Nottage*, it took the giving of a prize for a professional sport and from that made assumptions about sport in general. Consequently, it raised questions about the validity of charitable registration of sports organizations in New Zealand. Given this uncertainty, an amendment was made to the Charities Act[27] to provide more clarity on the circumstances in which amateur sports could be charitable purposes. The Associate Minister of Justice, in moving the amendment, said,

> The Amendment to the Charities Act 2005 includes a proposed change to the definition of "charitable purpose" to clarify the circumstances in which amateur sports are indeed charitable. This amendment is meant to address uncertainty amongst sports groups, funders, and the legal community about the charitable status of amateur sports and the consequent confusion about funding eligibility.[28]

However, the amendment did not lead to any greater clarity. In 2012, Swimming New Zealand filed changes to its constitution for approval by Charities Services (the successor to the Charities Commission). That led to a review of the organization and to deregistration by the Charities Registration Board. Swimming New Zealand is the national body for swimming and had been registered as a charity by the Charities Commission. It runs learn-to-swim programmes, swimming competitions and a high-performance programme. As a national organization, it works to deliver its programmes through regional centres and local clubs. The Board's decision appeared to reverse the trend of registering sports organizations and threatened the registered charity status of other sports clubs:

> It seems clear that this new position will result in few, if any, national or regional sports organizations becoming or remaining registered charities. Every time a rule amendment is filed (whether minor or otherwise), existing sports organizations that are charities will be up for review. . . . The application of this position could go further to local club level if clubs exist to promote their sport, which is the case for many. Can it be said, for example, that rugby clubs exist to promote health, or to promote rugby?[29]

In 2015, the Board again deregistered a sports organization, New Zealand Rowing, because of its involvement with elite sport.[30] The issue for sport is that historically it has been set up to provide organized competitions. Those competitions inevitably lead to higher level competitions and to elite levels of performance. Leaving aside professional sport, which most would consider would never qualify for charitable status, the problem for sports organizations is having to decide at what point they are charitable and when they cross a boundary to non-charitable. The Swimming New Zealand and the New Zealand Rowing decisions appear to make that decision more difficult. Adding to the confusion, in some circumstances, such as in an education environment, the promotion of sport is seen to be charitable.[31] What is required is a more definitive test of the law in New Zealand by a mainstream sports organization, such as Swimming New Zealand, to provide more certainty about the parameters of when sport is a charitable purpose in this country.

Advocacy

If dealing with sport as a charitable purpose was difficult, then the subject of political advocacy was highly contentious. Submissions on the Charities Bill expressed a concern that any political advocacy by charitable organizations had the potential to strip them of their charitable status, because political advocacy was not seen as a charitable purpose, and since a charity had to be exclusively charitable, any political advocacy could lead to deregistration. Charities were mindful that a previous Prime Minister, angered at the political activities of one organization—CORSO—had stripped it of its charitable tax exemptions.[32] The Social Services Select Committee was sympathetic to the submissions, and a clause was inserted into the Bill that acknowledged this.

> (3) To avoid doubt, if the purposes of a trust, society, or an institution include a non-charitable purpose (for example, advocacy) that is merely ancillary to a charitable purpose of the trust, society or institution, the

presence of that non-charitable purpose does not prevent the trustees of the trust, the society, or the institution from qualifying as a charitable entity.[33]

Note that the more general term, advocacy, was used in the legislation, not political advocacy. For registered charities, there was a concern that any advocacy that they were doing as a normal part of their work would be of concern to the regulator. The Commission was guided by significant case law on the subject. The Court in *Re Collier (deceased)* discussed three categories of trusts which were traditionally considered invalid.[34]

1. Charitable trusts to change the law, because it would go against the notion of a coherent system of law to accept as charitable, that which goes against its own provisions
2. Trusts to support a political party, "because it is thought undesirable for the advantages of a charity to be conferred on trusts which overtly 'secure . . . a certain line . . . of political administration and policy' "[35]
3. Trusts for perpetual advocacy of particular points of view or propaganda trusts, because such political agitation could become dangerous

In *Latimer v Commissioner of Inland Revenue*,[36] a distinction was made between a main purpose and the means to attain those purposes:

> The distinction is between ends, means, and consequences. The ends must be exclusively charitable. But if the non-charitable benefits are merely the means or the incidental consequences of carrying out the charitable purposes and are not the ends in themselves, charitable status is not lost.[37]

Importantly, in New Zealand, there has been no move to quantify an allowable level of political advocacy. While suggestions as to what level of public benefit may be acceptable has been given in other areas,[38] this has not been done for political advocacy. The practical advantage of this is that from time to time an organization will spend considerable time and resources on a particular issue, but once that issue has been resolved, it settles back into its normal activities. It would be unfortunate if a particular quantum were to be applied on an annual basis.

While advocacy was the subject of much general discussion by organizations about the extent to which they might be permitted to be involved, the matter came to a very public head when the Charities Commission deregistered the National Council of Women (NCW). The NCW was a longstanding organization that was established to "serve women, the family, and the community at the local, national, and international level." It was registered as a charity but because of initial concerns about its political advocacy activities was later investigated. In making its decision to deregister the NCW, the Commission gave the following reasons:

The Society submits that it is involved in political advocacy, but that this is a tool as a means of fulfilling or supporting its primary purpose of promoting progress for women and not a purpose of the Society.

However, information provided on the Society's website and in its submissions indicate that the Society is "urging" and lobbying the government to change the laws on a wide range of issues that are not restricted to furthering particular charitable purposes, and is not ancillary to any charitable purposes or activity. The Commission is of the view that the object of the Society, "to promote political change is so pervasive and predominant as to preclude its severance from other charitable objects."[39]

The decision caused a great deal of anger and anxiety within the charitable sector and raised the question as to whether legislation should be changed to allow greater flexibility in terms of political advocacy. The NCW made a fresh application for registration two years later, which was successful before the Charities Registration Board despite NCW stating that its activities were "materially indistinguishable from the nature of its activities at the time of the Commission's deregistration decision."[40]

The most significant decision relating to advocacy was delivered by the Supreme Court in a case brought by Greenpeace.[41] Greenpeace had been declined registration by the Commission.[42] That decision was subsequently upheld by both the High Court[43] and the Court of Appeal.[44] A final appeal was then made to the Supreme Court—the first appeal under the Charities Act that had gone this far and therefore a decision of significance. The majority of the Supreme Court concluded,

> A "political purpose" exclusion should no longer be applied in New Zealand: political and charitable purposes are not mutually exclusive in all cases; a blanket exclusion is unnecessary and distracts from the underlying inquiry whether a purpose is of public benefits within the sense the law recognizes as charitable.[45]

By allowing that political advocacy and charitable purposes could coexist in a charitable organization, this decision appeared to open up the possibility of greater political advocacy,[46] but the Court qualified this by saying, "Advancement of causes will often, perhaps most often, be noncharitable."[47] However, it held that "it may be accepted that the circumstances in which advocacy of particular views is shown to be charitable will not be common, but that does not justify a rule that all non-ancillary advocacy is properly characterized as non-charitable."[48]

Following that, a further decision related to advocacy was decided in the High Court. In *Re Family First*,[49] Collins J explained the Supreme Court decision further, pointing out that the majority had said,

> There was no basis for a distinction between general promotion of social attitudes and advocacy directed at government activities, and

that political and charitable purposes were not mutually exclusive. The Supreme Court explained that whether advocacy of a particular purpose was charitable or not depended on the need advocated, the means used to achieve that end and the manner in which the cause was promoted in order to determine whether the purpose was a public benefit within the spirit and the intendment of the Statute of Elizabeth I.[50]

The ramifications of these two decisions have yet to flow through to subsequent decisions by the Board. However, to put this into some perspective, the Commission and the Board have declined to register or have deregistered about ten organizations for having political purposes, out of more than 30,000 registered.

Dis-establishment of the Charities Commission

The Charities Commission was dis-established in 2012.[51] Its functions were merged into the DIA as Charities Services, and a Charities Registration Board, serviced by the DIA, was established. The Act remained essentially intact, with the chief executive of the DIA being responsible for all Commission functions apart from those decision-making functions undertaken by the Board. However, in the year before the transition, there was a 35 per cent turnover of staff, as people sought certainty of employment elsewhere; others left after the dis-establishment. The prime reason given for dis-establishment was to reduce costs. The appropriation for the Commission in 2011–12 was $4.844 million, compared to $5.22 million appropriated for Charities Services in 2015–16. The decision was controversial, particularly among charities that had previously campaigned for a politically independent Commission. Moving the functions into a government department was seen as compromising that independence. The passage of the Bill to enact the changes was highly contentious, as evidenced by the Bill passing by only one vote in parliament. The new Charities Registration Board comprises three members. Its functions were reduced to having "the functions, duties, and powers relating to the registration and deregistration of charitable entities that are conferred or are imposed on it" by the Act.[52] Independence appears in the Act's stipulation that each member of the Board "must act independently in exercising his or her professional judgment; and is not subject to direction from the Minister" when performing the functions, duties, and powers.[53]

Emerging Issues

Reflecting on the period since the enactment of the Charities Act, there are a number of matters that warrant further consideration. The first relates to decisions of the regulator that are appealed in court. Legislation properly makes provision for a person aggrieved by a decision of the regulator to appeal to the High Court. Failure at that court may then lead to appeals to the Court of Appeal and finally to the Supreme Court. As the Charities Commission, and later the Charities Board, make the decisions that are being appealed, it is not their role in the court to defend their decisions. Those decisions stand on their own. However, in the absence of a party that can take a contrary position from the appellant, and to assist the court, it has been usual for the decision maker to appear as contradictor. It means, though, that where the court decides in favour of an appellant, there is no further possibility of an appeal because there is no respondent to appeal that decision. This means that if there is a view that the judge has made the wrong decision, or that other affected agencies, such as the IRD, believe that there are significant consequences as a result of the decision, the matter must be dealt with in a different way. Certainly, not every decision adverse to a regulator should be challenged, but it would seem that there should be some avenue by which a "rogue" decision could be.

The second issue relates to commercial entities. There is some debate about commercial entities being able to be registered as a charity. Most charities need to raise funds in order to achieve their charitable purposes and seek ways to do this, traditionally, by relying on donations and grants, but increasingly they also seek more commercial means of generating funds, including through property investments, public share portfolios, and owning unrelated businesses. For the most part, these are relatively uncontroversial, as there is an incentive on the part of the charity to maximize returns on these operations to return funds to what they do. In other words, there is an incentive for these funds to be used for charitable purposes. The issue can become problematic when a business is put into trust, with trustees having the discretion to use any income for charitable distributions. The question then is whether the incentive is for trustees to grow the business, or to maximize charitable distributions—in fact, whether there is any incentive to actually make any charitable distributions.

To illustrate this issue, it is useful to consider the Joan Fernie Charitable Trust Board.[54] This was a bequest of a farm to a trust for which grants could be given for specified charitable purposes. A review of the 2014 accounts shows that the total assets of the trust were around $63 million, and the surplus for the year was $1.76 million, but only $70,000 was paid in grants to meet the Trust's charitable purpose. If, for the sake of argument, tax forgone by government on the surplus was $500,000, then a benefit of $430,000 provided by government has been lost.[55] The question in cases like this is whether the value of the tax exemption is greater than the public benefit that is obtained by the community.[56] The issue, then, insofar as commercial entities are concerned, is what incentives should be put in place to ensure that a reasonable public benefit is given from any commercial organization that has charitable status.

Conclusion

The development of a regulatory regime for charities in New Zealand was generally welcomed by the sector, and its implementation went relatively smoothly. It is clear that establishing a regulatory regime of this nature takes a number of years to become business as usual, and that time frame does not always fit with changing political environments. Further, the sector's expectation of a politically independent regime is sometimes challenged depending on how politicians see regulation in action, or in some cases where individual charities take exception to decisions made. The experience in New Zealand is no different from that experienced in other jurisdictions. Charities operate within dynamic societies and regulators need to be aware of how that dynamic impacts on definitions of charity in a way that charitable organizations retain their relevance in that changing society. The regulator itself must also review the manner in which it regulates so that charities feel that their work continues to benefit the public rather than working to the constraints imposed by a regulator. Those are the ongoing challenges.

Notes

1 For example, charitable trusts are exempt from the aspect of the perpetuity rule that is termed the "rule against inalienability," and courts can, pursuant to their cy-près jurisdiction, modify charitable purposes that have become impossible or impracticable to carry out.

2 For example, if a grant giver is a registered charity it is not able to make grants for non-charitable purposes.

3 Susan Barker, Michael Gousmett and Ken Lord, *The Law and Practice of Charities in New Zealand* (Wellington: Lexis Nexis New Zealand, 2013), 27–409.

4 On July 25, 2016 there were 27,799 registered charities in New Zealand, with a total income in 2015 of NZ\$16.44 billion: Charities Services, Live Stats, accessed July 24, 2016, https://www.charities.govt.nz/view-data/#. By comparison, New Zealand's top export earner to the end of March 2015 was dairy with NZ\$14.1 billion, followed by tourism with receipts of NZ\$11.7 billion: Grant Bradley, "Tourism Earnings Almost Trump Dairy," *New Zealand Herald*, October 28, 2015, accessed July 24, 2016, http://www.nzherald.co.nz/business/news/article.cfm?c_id=3&objectid=11535941.

5 Barker et al., *Law and Practice of Charities*, 418–419.

6 New Zealand, *Parliamentary Debates*, 30 March 2004, 12108 (Margaret Wilson, Minister of Commerce), accessed July 24, 2016, https://www.parliament.nz/en/pb/hansard-debates/rhr/document/47HansD_20040330_00001284/charities-bill-first-reading.

7 New Zealand Parliament Social Services Committee, *Charities Bill: Government Bill: As Reported* (Charities Bill 108–2, 17 December 2004), accessed July 24, 2016, https://www.parliament.nz/en/pb/sc/reports/document/47DBSCH_SCR2973_1/charities-bill-108-2.

8 Crown Entities Act 2004, s. 7(1)(a).

9 Social Services Committee, *Charities Bill Report*, 2.

10 Charities Act 2005, s 5(2)(a).

11 Statistics New Zealand, *Country Non-Profit Institutions in New Zealand 2005*. Cat 51.904 Set 06/07–154, accessed July 24, 2016, http://www.stats.govt.nz/

browse_for_stats/people_and_communities/Households/Non-ProfitInstitutions SatelliteAccount_HOTP2005.aspx.

12 One issue encountered was that the definition of a charity in the Charitable Trusts Act 1957 differed slightly from that in the Charities Act 2005. This meant that, potentially, an organization incorporated as a charitable trust might not qualify for registration as a charity.

13 *Canterbury Development Corporation v Charities Commission* [2010] NZHC 331; *Re Draco Foundation (NZ) Charitable Trust* [2011] NZHC 368; *Re Queenstown Lakes Community Housing Trust* [2011] NZHC 617.

14 Charities Act 2005 s. 27.

15 Charites Act 2005, s. 41.

16 Charities (Fees, Forms, and Other Matters) Regulations 2006.

17 Charities Services, "Important Change from 1 July 2014: Filing Your Annual Return," *Charities News Alert*, June 5, 2014, accessed July 24, 2016, https://www.charities.govt.nz/news-and-events/newsletters/.

18 New Zealand Parliament, *Charities Commission Annual Report 2011/2012*, 13, accessed July 24, 2016, https://www.parliament.nz/en/pb/papers-presented/current-papers/document/50DBHOH_PAP23920_1/charities-commission-komihana-kaupapa-atawhai-annual. *Charities Act 2005*, s 32, Grounds for removal from register.

19 Accounting Standards for Not-For-Profit Entities applying after 1 April 2015 are published by the External Reporting Board, accessed July 24, 2016, https://www.xrb.govt.nz/Site/Accounting_Standards/Current_Standards/default.aspx.

20 Official Information Act 1982, s. 4.

21 Social Services Committee, *Charities Bill Report*, 3.

22 *Canterbury Development Corporation v Charities Commission* [2010] NZHC 331; *Re Draco Foundation (NZ) Charitable Trust* [2011] NZHC 368; *Re Queenstown Lakes Community Housing Trust* [2011] NZHC 617.

23 Other areas have also been the subject of debate. For example, religion, which has an income of NZ$1.19 billion and totals 17.7% of registered charities, as of 3 November 2015. See an example of the discussion in Sally Blundell, "The God Dividend," *New Zealand Listener*, February 2, 2008, accessed July 24, 2016, http://www.listener.co.nz/commentary/the-god-dividend/.

24 [2008] NZHC 1912, (2009) 24 NZTC 23, 273.

25 *In re Nottage* [1895] 2 Ch 649.

26 *Travis Trust v Charities Commission* [2008] NZHC 1912 [52].

27 Statutes Amendment Bill (No. 2) 2011.

28 New Zealand, *Parliamentary Debates*, 12 April 2011, 17981, (Nathan Guy, Associate Minister of Justice), accessed July 24, 2016, https://www.parliament.nz/en/pb/hansard-debates/rhr/document/49HansS_20110413_00000214/guy-nathan-statutes-amendment-bill-no-2-first-reading.

29 Maria Clarke, "Is Sport Charitable Anymore?" *LawTalk*, April 10, 2015, accessed July 24, 2016, https://www.lawsociety.org.nz/lawtalk/lawtalk-archives/issue-862/is-sport-charitable-any-more.

30 Charities Services, *Deregistration Decision: New Zealand Rowing Association Incorporated*, No. D2015–3, September 11, 2015, accessed July 24, 2016, https://www.charities.govt.nz/assets/Uploads/New-Zealand-Rowing-Association-Incorporated.pdf.

31 *Kearins v Kearins* (1957) SR NSW 286.

32 David Sutton, Carolyn Cordery and Rachel Baskerville, *Paying the Price of the Failure to Retain Legitimacy in a National Charity: The CORSO Story* (Victoria University of Wellington, Governance and Taxation Research Working Paper No. 47, 2007).

33 Social Services Committee, *Charities Bill Report.*
34 *Re Collier (deceased)* (1998) 1 NZLR 81, 89–90.
35 (1998) 1 NZLR 81, 90, quoting *Re Hopkinson (dec'd)* [1949] 1 All ER 346, 352.
36 [2004] 3 NZLR 157.
37 [2004] 3 NZLR 157, 170.
38 For example in education: see *Re Education New Zealand Trust* [2010] NZHC 1097.
39 Charities Commission, *Deregistration Decision: Re National Council of Women of New Zealand Inc.*, No. D2010–9, July 22, 2010, [76]—[77], quoting from *Public Trustee v Attorney-General of New South Wales* (1997) 42 NSWLR 600, at 621, accessed October 24, 2016, https://www.charities.govt.nz/assets/Uploads/national-council-of-women-of-new-zealand-incorporated.pdf.
40 See *National Council of Women of New Zealand Inc. v Charities Registration Board* [2014] NZHC 3200, [16].
41 *In re Greenpeace of New Zealand Inc.* [2014] NZSC 105.
42 Charities Commission, *Re Greenpeace of New Zealand Incorporated*, April 15, 2010, [74].
43 *Re Greenpeace of New Zealand Incorporated* [2010] NZHC 77, per Heath J. The matter was considered further in the judgment of the New Zealand High Court in *Re Draco Foundation (NZ) Charitable Trust* [2011] NZHC 368, which considered the High Court of Australia decision in *Aid/Watch Incorporated v Commissioner of Taxation* (2010) 241 CLR 539.
44 *Re Greenpeace of New Zealand Incorporated* [2012] NZCA 533.
45 Charities Commission, *Deregistration Decision: National Council of Women of New Zealand Inc.*, July 22, 2010.
46 See *In re Greenpeace* [2014] NZSC 105, [59]—[76].
47 *In re Greenpeace* [2014] NZSC 105, [73].
48 *In re Greenpeace* [2014] NZSC 105, [74].
49 *Re Family First New Zealand* [2015] NZHC 1493.
50 *Re Family First New Zealand* [2015] NZHC 1493, [78]—[79].
51 Charities Amendment Act (No. 2) 2012.
52 Charities Act 2005, s. 8(3).
53 Charities Act 2005, s. 8(4).
54 Joan Fernie Charitable Trust Board, Registration No. CC28680, June 30, 2008.
55 By comparison, a similar organization, Hillview Trust, Registration No. CC27344, June 30, 2008, with assets of $15,540,053 had a surplus of $368,491 and made distributions of $297,023 in 2014.
56 For a further discussion, see Michael Gousmett, "Is Trading by Charities Charitable?" *LawTalk*, September 25, 2015, accessed July 24, 2016, https://www.lawsociety.org.nz/lawtalk/lawtalk-archives/issue-874/is-trading-by-charities-charitable.

10 Reflections on Regulatory Accountability

Sue Barker[1]

Introduction

The Charities Act 2005 (the Charities Act) heralded a new era in charities regulation in New Zealand. This chapter examines the aims and objectives of the new regime, whether these have been met in the decade since its enactment, and suggests a productive regulatory path for the future.

New Zealand's Charitable Sector

As of 19 September 2016,[2] New Zealand has 27,605 registered charities, with total assets under management exceeding NZ$61 billion. There are a number of active umbrella bodies in the sector, including Hui E! Community Aotearoa,[3] Fundraising Institute of New Zealand,[4] Philanthropy New Zealand *Tōpūtanga Tuku Aroha o Aotearoa*,[5] New Zealand Trustees' Association *Aotearoa Whakapono*,[6] Community Networks Aotearoa,[7] and Community Housing *Nga Wharerau o Aotearoa*.[8] Most New Zealand charities are very small, with almost two-thirds having gross annual income under NZ$100,000. However, the combined gross annual income of all registered charities totals over NZ$20 billion, representing approximately 8 per cent of New Zealand's gross domestic product (broadly equivalent to that of New Zealand's largest company, Fonterra). Of this income, the largest proportion, NZ$7.3 billion or 36 per cent, is earned from "government grants and contracts," followed by "service trading income" of NZ$6.8 billion, or 33 per cent. Donations and bequests total approximately NZ$1.8 billion (9 per cent), with "other grants and sponsorship" totalling NZ$1.1 billion (5.5 per cent). Registered charities' paid staff contribute 7,886,836 hours of work weekly and volunteers an additional 2,639,086 hours of work each week. These figures are only an approximation. Charitable registration is voluntary, and New Zealand charities are not required to register to call themselves a charity or collect funds from the public.[9] The number of unregistered charities and other not-for-profit entities is unknown, with some estimates as high as 97,000.[10] To date, the quality of data on the charities register has also been highly variable.

Pre-charities Act Regime for Charitable Tax Privileges

Charities in New Zealand are eligible for a number of fiscal privileges,[11] including:

- an exemption from income tax for entities that meet the requirements of the charitable income tax exemptions;[12] and
- donee status, which provides tax relief for donors to organizations whose funds are applied "wholly or mainly to charitable, benevolent, philanthropic, or cultural purposes within New Zealand," or that otherwise meet the criteria in section LD 3 of the Income Tax Act 2007 (known as "approved donees" or "donee organizations").[13]

Registration for Tax Exemption

Prior to the Charities Act, there was no requirement, nor any formal process, for registering charities.[14] Charities were required to "self-assess"[15] their eligibility for the charitable income tax exemptions, with no application to the New Zealand tax authority, the Inland Revenue Department (IRD), required. In practice, many charities voluntarily sought IRD's opinion to gain "comfort" that the charitable income tax exemptions applied.[16] However, IRD "comfort letters" were neither compulsory nor binding: whether an entity's purposes were charitable was ultimately a matter for the Courts.[17] Lack of registration meant there was no complete list of entities claiming the charitable income tax exemptions: IRD did not publish a list of recipients of "comfort letters" because of strict taxpayer secrecy requirements,[18] and self-assessment also meant that charities could claim the exemptions without IRD knowledge.

In administering the income tax legislation, IRD might decide that an entity's purposes were not charitable. An entity wishing to dispute such a decision could enter the elaborate tax disputes procedures in part 4A of the Tax Administration Act 1994.[19] Importantly, where these procedures did not resolve the issue, the entity could issue challenge proceedings before the Taxation Review Authority or the High Court.[20] In such proceedings, the entity was entitled to a full oral hearing of evidence, in which the Commissioner of Inland Revenue took the role of an active protagonist.[21]

Reporting for Tax Exemption

Reporting requirements under the pre-Charities Act regime were minimal.[22] Charities performing services under government contracts, or receiving grants or gifts from philanthropic funders, were generally required to provide some form of reporting, such as audited accounts, to ensure that public monies or charitable funds were being used for the intended purposes. However, no such accountability was required to access the charitable tax exemptions. Section 58 of the Tax Administration Act 1994 enabled IRD to require "gift-exempt bodies" to file income tax returns on request.[23] However, this power was "rarely used,"[24] and charities were generally not required to file income tax returns. Charities structured as incorporated societies were required to file basic financial statements under the Incorporated Societies Act 1908,[25] but no standards governed this reporting, and a wide variety of practices were used.[26] Charitable trusts were not required to file any financial statements at all.[27]

Monitoring of Charities

There was also very little government monitoring of whether a charity continued to pursue its charitable purposes over time.[28] IRD has wide powers of audit,[29] but lack of reporting requirements meant little information was available to make a decision to conduct an audit. The audit process also had its limitations:[30]

> . . . the Commissioner of Inland Revenue's role is to ensure that income not entitled to an exemption is taxed. The role is not about ensuring that the charitable sector is generally accountable to the public. Holding the officers of a charitable organization to account for an organization's administration expenses, for example, is well beyond the ambit of the commissioner's current responsibilities.

IRD doubted its legislative authority to challenge an entity that was established for, but no longer pursuing, charitable purposes in any event.[31] As the Privy Council noted,[32]

> In New Zealand (unlike the United Kingdom) the relevant tax exemption does not depend on income actually being applied for the intended charitable purposes. Any alleged deviation from the terms of the Trust would be a matter for the Attorney General. . . .

Instead, the statutory mechanism for IRD was to inform the Minister of revenue under section 89 of the Tax Administration Act.[33] It is not clear to what extent section 89 was ever used.

The Attorney General has power to inquire into any charity and to enforce a charitable trust.[34] However, these powers also have practical limitations and were rarely used,[35] as one member of Parliament commented, ". . . by the time a complaint is laid with the Attorney General . . . all the evidence has gone, all the money has gone, and it is far, far too late."[36] The lack of practical regulatory control over charitable trusts had been of concern since at least the 1970s, when Rev. RM O'Grady commented publicly, "The public has no protection against charities in New Zealand. It would not be difficult for a skilled promotional person to raise $10,000 or more for almost any appeal one cares to name."[37] The Property Law and Equity Reform Committee considered these comments in 1979, and noted

> . . . the whole of the Charitable Trusts Act 1957 called for a general examination. . . more effective means of control of charitable trusts [would be desirable], perhaps by means of a charities commission along the lines established in the UK.[38]

Accountability Issues

Concern at the absence of structural transparency or accountability for New Zealand charities was widespread across the charitable, state, and private sectors.[39] Many expressed concern about charities being engaged, knowingly or unknowingly, in fraud, corruption, or other criminal activities.[40] Complaints were made that "fly-by-nighters . . . [were] getting a free ride under the guise of being charitable organisations."[41] There was also concern that charities were being set up or used for tax avoidance or evasion purposes.[42] For example, the Trinity Foundation Charitable Trust was implicated in a complex forestry tax avoidance scheme involving almost $4 billion in potential tax losses.[43]

Lack of registration and monitoring meant the reputation of the entire New Zealand charitable sector was vulnerable to "rogue" charities.[44] The charitable sector overwhelmingly supported the establishment of a Charities Commission so that "bad" charities could be "weeded out" and the public could have trust and confidence in those that remained.[45] The government was also concerned to meet New Zealand's international obligations in terms of countering money laundering and financing of terrorism,[46] noting that other comparable jurisdictions, such as the United Kingdom, Australia, the United States, and Canada, all had "significantly more developed registration and reporting arrangements."[47]

Aims and Objectives of the New Regime

To address all these concerns, the government agreed to introduce a Charities Bill to establish a Charities Commission[48] to administer a registration, reporting, and monitoring system for New Zealand charities.[49] The existing regulatory framework would remain essentially unchanged, but to access the charitable income tax exemptions, charities would have to register with the Commission.[50] The registration system was intended to improve the accountability and transparency of the charitable sector to the donating public, funders, and regulators, as well as the government,[51] and to help foster a culture of philanthropy and giving in New Zealand by increasing the public's trust and confidence in charities.[52] To this end, the Commission would have power to monitor registered charities to ensure they acted,[53] and continued to act,[54] in furtherance of their charitable purposes over time.

To assist with this monitoring process, registered charities would have to notify changes to the Commission and to file annual returns,[55] although key reporting requirements were to be developed later.[56] A stated aim of the Bill was to "strengthen [the government's] relationship with the community and voluntary sector," and help ensure New Zealand's charitable sector "is able to operate effectively and efficiently to deliver important services for . . . our communities."[57]

Gestation of the Charities Act 2005

By the time the Charities Bill was introduced in March 2004, it had been at least 16 years in gestation. The process began in December 1987, under a traditionally social democratic Labour government. The Minister of Finance at the time, Hon Roger Douglas, had announced an intention to impose a "flat tax" of 15 per cent, including on the income of charities.[58] The proposal was very controversial: then Prime Minister Rt Hon. David Lange wrote that it was an "unaccustomed addition to the burdens of office to have the Finance Minister take leave of his senses."[59] Ultimately, the proposal to tax charities did not proceed and was "kicked into touch" through the appointment of a working party to conduct a major review of New Zealand charities law.[60] The Working Party on Charities and Sporting Bodies reported in 1989, recommending a Commission for Charities be established to register, advise, and supervise charities, and to increase the accountability of charities to the public.[61] This report was not well received by the sector, and the initiative did not proceed following the change of government in 1990:[62] the new traditionally conservative National Government deferred the recommendation indefinitely, on the basis that further consultation was required.[63]

However, the charitable sector continued to ask governments for greater support,[64] for example, through an increase in tax relief for donations. At that time, the maximum tax relief for donations was capped at $500 per year.[65] Successive Ministers of Revenue made agreeable noises about "lifting the cap," but continually verbalized unease about doing so because of anecdotal evidence that "some charities were involved in tax avoidance arrangements."[66] The lack of robust information about the charitable sector also made it difficult for governments to assess how much lifting the cap would cost.[67] In addition, there was no specific law, standard procedure, or government department concerned with ensuring the accountability of entities receiving donations.[68] In the meantime, media concern about the accountability of charity fundraisers led to the creation in 1995 of the Accountability of Charities and Sporting Bodies Working Party, a voluntary group led by two charities.[69] The Working Party proposed a self-regulatory system, employing a code of practice for voluntary organizations, with oversight from a consortium from the charitable sector.[70] However, the Working Party's proposals were not adopted by the sector, perhaps because of sector diversity or lack of funding.[71]

In March 1998, the National Government appointed a Committee of Tax Experts to consider the robustness of the tax system. The Committee reported in December 1998,[72] recommending, among other things, a review of the tax treatment of charities' commercial activities that were unrelated to their charitable purposes. The Committee was concerned about competitive advantage, given the ability of charities to earn business income free of tax.[73] Although there was some community concern about the charitable business tax exemption being "inappropriately used,"[74] with Seventh-day Adventist breakfast cereal maker Sanitarium often cited as an example, there was also concern to protect charities' ability to earn income for their charitable purposes in this way.

Before the recommended review could take place, nine years of National Party Government were brought to an end in 1999, in the second election under the new Mixed-Member Proportional electoral system, by a minority coalition of Helen Clark's Labour Party and the smaller, left-leaning Alliance Party, with confidence and supply support from the Green Party. This Labour-led government would introduce legislation bringing about the Charities Commission during the second of its three terms.

In 2000, then Minister of Finance Hon Dr Michael Cullen expressed a willingness to consider a more generous donations regime, provided a means could be found to ensure the benefits extended only for *bona fide* charities.[75] A government review of the tax treatment of charities followed, drawing on all of the aforementioned work.[76] The ensuing 2001 discussion document, *Tax and Charities*,[77] contained a range of proposals for improving the accountability of organizations receiving government assistance.[78] More than 1,600 submissions on the discussion document were received—a majority of which supported or accepted the need for registration.[79] This, in turn, persuaded the government to set up a Working Party on Registration, Reporting and Monitoring of Charities. Reporting in 2002, the Working Party recommended that a Charities Commission be established, with responsibility for establishing and maintaining a registration, reporting, and monitoring regime for New Zealand charities. The government accepted those recommendations,[80] and after a two-year period of review, consultation, and drafting, the Charities Bill was finally introduced in 2004.[81] The Bill was described as the "climax . . . of a 16-year attempt by the charitable sector to bring about a fundamental change in its status in New Zealand society."[82] After such a long gestation process, "[o]ne would have hoped that . . . they would have got it right," but concern was expressed that that was not the case.[83]

The Parliamentary Process on the Charities Bill

The Charities Bill had its first reading in Parliament in March 2004 and was referred to the Social Services Select Committee. The Committee received 753 submissions from submitters collectively representing thousands of

New Zealand charities.[84] Conceptually, the Charities Commission had overwhelming support, but there was considerable concern with specific provisions in the Bill.[85] Described as a "Trojan horse" that could allow the government to "colonise and control" the charitable sector,[86] the Bill was widely seen as "fundamentally flawed."[87] It was virtually rewritten at Select Committee stage.[88] One area of concern related to charities' appeal rights. The Bill gave charities a right of appeal against registration decisions of the Commission to the District Court, whose decision was to be final.[89] The Select Committee changed this formulation to the following:

59. Right of appeal

    (1) A person who is aggrieved by **a decision** of the Commission under this Act may appeal to the **High** Court.

    . . .

61. Determination of appeal

    (1) In determining an appeal, the High Court may:
        (a) confirm, modify or reverse the decision **of the Commission** or any part of it.

The rationale for this change was described as follows:[90]

> . . . charities **should not be limited to appealing decisions relating to registration** . . . it should be possible to appeal from **all** decisions of the Commission that adversely impact on a particular entity.
>
> [Further,] given the experience of the **High Court** in considering matters relating to charitable entities, it would be the most appropriate forum for hearing appeals [and] **the initial appeal to the High Court should not be the final resort for charities.**
>
>   [Emphasis added]

Charities fought hard to achieve this change.

Another area of concern related to the "Crown agent" classification of the Commission. Of the three types of statutory entity created by the Crown Entities Act 2004 (Crown agents, autonomous Crown entities, and independent Crown entities), Crown agents have the closest connection to government: they must *give effect to* government policy when properly directed to do so.[91] Submitters were concerned that this classification might allow the government to control the Commission, for example, by directly or indirectly influencing the registration or deregistration of particular charities to reflect government policy. This would not reflect the charitable sector's independence from government.[92]

In response, the Select Committee changed the Commission's classification to an autonomous Crown entity (ACE).[93] Although not as independent as an independent Crown entity,[94] this classification was a significant improvement. The Select Committee also removed the requirement for the Commission to administer a register of approved donees, stating it would be "inappropriate" to have an ACE responsible for "making decisions that will impact on the revenue base."[95] Therefore, IRD continued to administer donee status under the income tax legislation.

Significantly, none of the Select Committee's many changes were subject to full consultation. Ministry of Economic Development (MED) officials wrote to "approximately 25"[96] selected entities to seek their views on the proposed amendments. Members of the Committee from the National Party, then in opposition, expressed concern at the lack of consultation on such substantial changes:[97]

> The consultation process was inadequate with the original bill and we have major concerns that the redrafted sections of the bill should have been made available for a further period of sector wide consultation. We all know the devil is in the detail and if the bill gets it wrong, as the first draft definitely did **the charitable sector will pay the price and we will see many charitable organisations close.** There is the possibility that there are a number of structural issues in the bill remaining unaddressed and without a further period of consultation with the sector it is difficult to fully identify these.
>
> [Emphasis added]

There do indeed appear to be several structural issues in the Charities Act for which the New Zealand charitable sector does indeed appear to be paying the price, as we will discuss further.

The final amendments to the Charities Bill (including further minor, but extensive, changes made by Supplementary Order Paper) were passed through under urgency, with all final stages occurring on one day (12 April 2005). The comment was made that "we do not really know what we are passing tonight, or what the implications are."[98]

> The community and voluntary sector has seen this bill as a really significant piece of legislation . . . the fact that we are dealing with the bill with such unnecessary dispatch . . . typifies the whole unsatisfactory process on the bill from its conception to its delivery. The facts that the bill was conceived, evidently in Treasury, and was designed by the Ministry of Economic Development show just how out of touch the originating . . . Ministers were with the realities of the community sector in this country today . . . The bill should not have been the responsibility of a ministry far more accustomed to working with "for profit" business than with the vast diversity that comprises the world of non-government organisations.

The Bill was also criticized for containing no regulatory impact or compliance cost statement:[99]

. . . there has not been, at any point, comprehensive analysis of the genuine need for or real cost of the proposed legislation, nor has the Government really ever had a clear understanding of what the bill seeks to achieve and how.

Concerns were assuaged, however, by a clear understanding that the Charities Act would be subject to a thorough post-implementation review.

The Charities Bill became law on 20 April 2005, and the Commission was formally established on 1 July 2005, some 16 years after the initial Working Party recommendation. The charities register opened in February 2007 and, from 1 July 2008, charities had to register with the Commission (or otherwise meet the definition of "tax charity")[100] to access the charitable income tax exemptions.

To What Extent Have the Aims and Objectives Been Met?

In most respects, the initial user experience for charity customers of the Commission was excellent. The digital register was (or became) very user-friendly, and the Commission is to be congratulated on its open-data project. The educational outreach of the Commission was highly valued: Commission staff were friendly and approachable, and the Commission was clearly very well led. The only real difficulty, in the writer's view, related to the Commission's legal interpretations of the definition of charitable purpose.

The Definition of Charitable Purpose

Section 5 of the Charities Act imported the definition of "charitable purpose" from the income tax legislation,[101] which defined "charitable purpose" by reference to the four heads of charity from *Pemsel's case*—relief of poverty, advancement of education, advancement of and religion, and any other matter beneficial to the community.[102] It is well established that this definition imports the common law of charities,[103] which sets out a two-step test for whether a purpose is charitable:[104] (1) is the purpose for the public benefit and (2) if so, is it charitable within the spirit and intendment of the Preamble to the Statute of Charitable Uses Act 1601 (43 Eliz c4). The first step, the "public benefit test," is not directly referred to in the statutory definitions, but is imported as a key element of the charitable purposes test through the common law. Whether a purpose meets the public benefit test is a question of fact to be answered "by forming an opinion on the evidence."[105]

In the 2001 discussion document, the government expressed concern that the definition of charitable purpose had "broadened over the years"[106] and that the charitable income tax exemptions may have become "too widely available."[107] The government cited the New Zealand Council of Law Reporting and the New Zealand Medical Council as examples,[108] implying that their contribution to the community may be only "incidental."[109] Although the absence of information about the sector made it difficult to tell whether this problem was real or one of "perception only,"[110] the government put forward three options for changing the definition[111] so that the "fiscal privileges" accorded to charities would be limited to those charitable purposes that "[accord] with society's current objectives":[112]

- maintaining the current definition, but allowing the government to "deem" a particular entity not to be charitable so that "decisions about government resources [could] be made in a manner consistent with evolving views on what constitutes a charitable purpose";[113]
- replacing the current definition with a new definition to "move away from existing case law, which may have expanded the boundaries of what is charitable to such an extent that it is now too easy to become a charity";[114] and
- limiting the definition to the relief of poverty.

The government acknowledged that the last of these would exclude a significant number of charities that had community support and did not proceed with this option.[115] By contrast, the sector was concerned that, despite the courts' broad interpretations, IRD was interpreting the definition of charitable purpose very narrowly, particularly in the area of sport.[116] Although sport plays a key role in New Zealand culture, IRD was resolute that "sport is not charitable," on the basis of cases such as *Re Nottage*.[117] Importantly, IRD's interpretations in this regard had not been the subject of contemporary judicial consideration.

Another key area of sector concern related to advocacy. In the 1980s, former National Party Prime Minister Rt Hon Robert Muldoon famously attacked CORSO (Incorporated), then a highly regarded international relief and development charity. In response to CORSO speaking out against the South African apartheid regime, particularly attacking the 1981 Springbok rugby team's tour of New Zealand, Muldoon had legislated to remove CORSO's donee status by Supplementary Order Paper.[118] An annual grant to the organization was also ended. These actions brought a once-strong organization to its knees: although CORSO has now had its donee status reinstated,[119] the organization remains a shadow of its former self. The legitimacy or otherwise of these actions, as a matter of charities law, or natural justice, was not tested in any court. Nevertheless, the CORSO example influenced concern that the Bill would "open the way for Government to control and possibly kill off groups that carry out any kind of political advocacy."[120]

The Definition Was Not Changed

In introducing the Charities Bill, the government again expressed an intention to ensure "those entities receiving tax relief continue to carry out charitable purposes and provide a clear public benefit."[121] Importantly, however, none of IRD's suggested options for changing the definition were accepted:[122] the Committee considering the Charities Bill specifically did not amend the definition of charitable purpose, stating that this might be "interpreted by the Courts as an attempt to widen or narrow the scope of charitable purposes, or change the law in this area, which was not the intent of the bill."[123] The courts have confirmed the Charities Act did not alter the definition,[124] meaning that the definition of charitable purpose, recognized by IRD in 2001 as being very broad, should have survived the passing of the Charities Act.

The Charities Commission's Approach to the Definition

The advent of the Charities Commission as a guardian of the definition of charitable purpose was much anticipated.[125] However, the Commission's approach to the definition took the sector by surprise—with the possible exception of sport, its interpretation of the definition was so narrow that many hundreds of "good" charities that were run well and were carrying out important work in the community were controversially rejected for registration.[126] The charities register had, unfortunately, been misconceived as analogous to the register of companies, requiring simply a box-filling exercise. As all charities had to seek registration in the transition to the new regime, this inevitably led to a large backlog of initial registrations and political pressure to reduce it.[127] The Commission may have responded to this pressure by initially registering charities but identifying them for subsequent investigation. This in turn may have increased the number of deregistrations. As of 3 September 2015, 6,388, or nearly 25 per cent of New Zealand's 27,000 registered charities, had been deregistered. While some had genuinely ceased operating, and a large proportion were deregistered for failure to file an annual return, only three were deregistered for "serious wrongdoing,"[128] ostensibly the original rationale for the regime. By contrast, the number deregistered as a result of narrow jurisprudential interpretations of the definition of charitable purpose seems very high. Hundreds of other charities have been declined registration,[129] or will have voluntarily deregistered or withdrawn their application to pre-empt an adverse decision on the charities regulator's website, on the basis of similarly narrow interpretations. The situation is particularly noticeable in relation to international charities, many of which have struggled with registration in New Zealand despite having the equivalent of registered charitable status around the world.[130]

The Public Benefit Test

Much of the difficulty arose in relation to charities' apparent inability to satisfy the public benefit test.[131] This difficulty was exacerbated by changes made to the appeal right at the Select Committee stage. In changing the appeal mechanism from the District Court to the High Court to allow charities a fuller right of appeal, the Select Committee did not clarify the nature of the hearing on appeal. As a result, the usual rules have been held to apply.[132] District Court appeals are normally first instance *de novo* hearings, which allows a full oral hearing if any party so insists.[133] By contrast, High Court appeals are generally conducted as "appeals on the record," with only limited power to admit further evidence[134] and with the impugned decision maker not permitted to take an active role. The High Court rules are premised on the first instance decider having already held a full oral hearing. However, under the Charities Act, the charities regulator does not adjudicate a dispute between two parties, and it does not conduct an oral hearing.[135]

Therefore, a significant unintended consequence of changes made to the appeal right at the Select Committee stage is that charities' ability to have a full oral hearing of evidence has effectively been removed by a "side wind," under urgency and without notification or proper consultation.[136] The removal puts charities at a significant disadvantage in proving that their purposes operate for the "public benefit,"[137] particularly given the charities regulator's apparent reluctance to recognize "new" charitable purposes. Proving that a purpose is charitable can be difficult. To have to do so without the benefit of a hearing of evidence significantly exacerbates this difficulty. In early decisions, the courts also appear to have deferred to the charities regulator as the specialist adjudicative body rather than embracing a role as the source of the law on the definition of charitable purpose.[138] Fortunately, this trend now appears to be reversing.[139] However, the cost and formality associated with an appeal to the High Court present a barrier to many charities' ability to access justice.

Consequently, charities face significant hurdles in holding the charities regulator to account for its decisions. The net result is that many good charities are facing closure through no fault of their own. Registered charitable status has increasingly become the gateway, not only to an increasing number of tax and other privileges[140] but also to funding and credibility, and therefore to survival. These difficulties highlight a significant structural issue for which New Zealand charities do indeed appear to be "paying the price."

What Led to the Commission's Narrow Approach?

It is not clear what led to the Commission's narrow approach. In contrast to IRD, the Commission seemed refreshingly able to find public benefit in sporting purposes, which seemed entirely appropriate in contemporary New Zealand society and was welcomed by the sector. However, in other areas, including social housing,[141] advocacy,[142] economic development,[143] member organizations,[144] education,[145] and many others, the Commission issued lengthy written decisions that seemed to strain not to find public benefit. The result was perplexing as, in many cases, a decision that the purposes were charitable would arguably have been readily available under the broad approach mandated by the courts prior to the Charities Act.

Lifting the Cap

Questions arose as to whether perceived fiscal consequences might be driving the Commission's narrow approach, particularly given IRD's clear desire in the 2001 discussion document to limit access to tax benefits, which was only reinforced by the "lifting of the cap" in 2008. As part of its confidence and supply agreement with the centrist United Future Party, the Labour-led government ultimately delivered on its promise to lift the cap on donee status:[146] from 1 April 2008, claims for tax relief for donations to donee organizations became limited only by the donor's net income. This change was intended to encourage philanthropy;[147] however, it has unsurprisingly resulted in a significant increase in claims. Further, as donations tax credits are refundable, it has in turn resulted in a significant cash outflow for the revenue and a significant IRD audit focus on donee organizations. Donee status is administered by IRD under the income tax legislation. There is no legal requirement for donee organizations to have charitable registration, and the Charities Commission has no mandate in respect of tax as a matter of law. Consequently, even if IRD might have wanted to reduce the number of donee organizations, it is not clear that this would have driven the Commission's narrow view of charitable purpose.

Whatever the reason, the Charities Commission's approach was very controversial within the charitable sector. For example, the Commission's decision to deregister the National Council of Women of New Zealand Incorporated on the basis of their work making submissions on parliamentary bills in furtherance of their charitable purposes, which was work they were contracted by the government to carry out, caused such widespread consternation[148] that it may ultimately have been a factor in the Commission's disestablishment.

The Crown Entities Reform Bill

In November 2008, nine years of Labour-led government were brought to an end by a minority government of John Key's National Party, with support on confidence and supply from United Future, the classic liberal ACT Party, and the indigenous rights-based Māori Party. At the time of writing, this National-led government is in its third term, with another general election due in 2017. Initially, this government seemed supportive of the Commission. Tariana Turia, then co-leader of the Māori Party, was appointed Minister for the Community and Voluntary Sector, a minister outside Cabinet, under the Māori Party's confidence and supply agreement. In November 2010, in her speech to the Charities Commission Annual General Meeting, Tariana Turia announced that a first principles review of the

Charities Act would be conducted, to be completed by 2015.[149] However, in May 2011,[150] less than three years after the Charities Act had fully come into force, and without apparent consultation, the government announced a proposal to disestablish the Charities Commission. The stated reason was that, in the current period of "fiscal and economic restraint," the government wished to reduce the number of government agencies, to get better value for money, "improve the delivery of services to the public," "reduce duplication of roles," and allow "reprioritisation of spending."[151] It was not clear that disestablishing the Commission would achieve any of these objectives, raising the question of whether the controversy surrounding its decisions was perhaps an unstated reason for its disestablishment.

Whatever the reason, the proposal was to transfer the functions of the Commission to the Department of Internal Affairs (DIA), while keeping registration decisions separate from Ministers by means of a statutory Charities Registration Board (the Board). The Board would comprise three members, appointed by the Minister, with board members required to act independently in exercising their professional judgment.[152] The Board would be permitted to delegate its functions to the DIA, which would be required to supply secretarial and administrative services to the Board.[153] This structure appears to have been based on the Gambling Act 2003, under which the Gambling Commission considers applications for gambling licences, and receives secretarial support from the DIA in doing so.[154] Class 4 gambling, otherwise known as "gaming machines," provides valuable grant funding to communities (approximately $250 million in 2015),[155] but has been subject to widespread abuse.[156] As an aside, one wonders to what extent the DIA's experience of regulating the gambling industry may have coloured its approach to the charitable sector generally.

That point aside, the process of disestablishing the Charities Commission moved quickly. Following confirmation of the proposal in August 2011,[157] the Crown Entities Reform Bill was introduced the following month. Parts 1 and 2 of the Bill proposed to disestablish a number of bodies unrelated to the Commission.[158] Part 3 proposed to amend the Charities Act to disestablish the Commission, establish the new Board, and set out the respective functions, duties, and powers of the Board and the DIA (referred to as "the chief executive"). Schedule 8 of the Bill then made consequential amendments to over 40 sections of the Charities Act, replacing each reference to "the Commission" with either (i) the Board, (ii) the chief executive, or (iii) the Board or the chief executive.

Schedule 8 dealt with charities' appeal rights by replacing the word "Commission" with the word "Board" in section 59. Because the Board would only be able to make a limited number of decisions, principally relating to registration,[159] on its face, this amendment would have removed charities' ability to appeal any other decision. However, schedule 8 also proposed to replace the word "Commission" in section 61 with the words "Board or the chief executive." The two amendments were inconsistent: section 59 allowed charities to appeal decisions of the Board only, but in determining "the appeal," the High Court could modify the decision of the "Board or the chief executive." As discussed earlier, the 2004 Select Committee had clearly stated that charities should be able to appeal *all* decisions of the charities regulator, not just those relating to registration. There was also no mention in the Crown Entities Reform Bill explanatory note, or in any publicly available material, of any intention to restrict charities' rights of appeal. The proposed amendment to section 59 therefore seemed to be a mistake—one of a number contained in a Bill that was clearly written in haste.[160]

Following its first reading in October 2011, the Bill was referred to the Government Administration Select Committee. However, a general election took place in November 2011 and the Bill lapsed. Although the Bill was reinstated by the new Parliament, submissions were not clearly called for. Despite this, many submissions were made, and those that did comment on Part 3 were overwhelmingly opposed to it: while many disagreed with many of the Commission's decisions, getting rid of the fledgling regulator was seen as premature, shortsighted, and unlikely to address any of the problems being experienced. The Committee acknowledged submitters' strong opposition to the proposed disestablishment and noted that the legislative safeguards provided in the Bill might be[161]

> . . . insufficient to maintain the degree of independence that the Charities Commission provides. We also believe that the charities-related functions will be less accessible to the public, and that the charities sector work will be carried out less transparently if the commission's functions are transferred to the [DIA]. . . .

However, Government Committee members considered the proposed transfer to the DIA would create a "more robust, resilient agency" and endorsed the intention to do so before the review of the Charities Act.

The remaining stages of the Bill occurred quickly over 22 to 29 May 2012. Part 3 was hotly contested, passing its second reading by only 61 votes to 60. A supplementary order paper was put forward proposing to defer commencement of Part 3 to allow the government to fulfil its commitment to review the Charities Act before any decision was made.[162] However, the government had the numbers, and the motion was rejected. Part 3 became the Charities Amendment Act (No. 2) 2012 and passed into law on 6 June 2012. The Charities Commission was disestablished from 1 July 2012.

As expected, changing the decision maker has not alleviated the previous problems. The narrow, strict approach has continued and in fact appears to have tightened further, particularly in areas such as sport[163] and advocacy. Echoing concerns of "colonisation and control," charities appear to be actively punished for engaging in the democratic process, causing an enormous "chilling effect."[164] There are reports of a strict hands-on approach to governance matters, particularly in areas of conflict of interest.[165] Such an approach has no legal mandate[166] and is particularly surprising given disclosure requirements in the new financial reporting rules to be discussed next.

The narrow approach may effectively corral the definition of charitable purpose into a nineteenth-century paternalistic concept of handouts to the poor. The approach seems hostile to innovation and risks deconstructing the New Zealand charitable sector. Rather than exercising an independent check, the Board appears in practice largely to rubber-stamp lengthy formulaic decisions written by the DIA.[167] Charities are still denied an oral hearing of evidence. Functions relating to charities do indeed appear less transparent and less accessible, and it is not clear that any money has been saved. The net result is that, despite clear opposition from the charitable sector, the Charities Commission's functions have been absorbed into an entity that is even closer to government than the Crown agent classification originally rejected.

The Review of the Charities Act

Then, in November 2012, only four months after disestablishing the Charities Commission, and precisely 21 minutes after the Court of Appeal delivered its decision in *Greenpeace*,[168] the National-led government unilaterally and controversially announced that the promised first principles review of the Charities Act would not take place.[169] Three reasons were given: (1) that the definition of charitable purpose was "working reasonably well"; (2) that a review might lead to more charities being eligible for registration, which "could result in increased fiscal costs;" and (3) with the disestablishment of the Commission, a first principles review was "no longer appropriate."[170] These reasons do not bear critical examination.[171] While the definition of charitable purpose has the potential to work well, as demonstrated by its longevity over hundreds of years, the current narrow interpretation of the definition could not be said to be "working reasonably well" for the many hundreds of good charities that are currently being excluded from the regime. Further, it appears to be assumed that interpreting the definition of charitable purpose in a manner more consistent with the community's expectations would result in a widening or a liberalization of the definition. This assumption overlooks the fact that the interpretations of the charities regulator have arguably narrowed the definition, without mandate.

Further still, the definition of charitable purpose is surely not an appropriate tool for addressing fiscal costs. As the High Court has noted, Parliament has seen fit to adopt the common law definition of charitable purpose in section 5 of the Charities Act. To the extent that Parliament has elsewhere legislated so that taxation consequences are determined by reference to charitable status, "those consequences must follow the application of the common law principles which govern charitable status. The taxation consequences should not play a part in the application of those common law principles."[172]

Further, while registration as a charity is a gateway to the charitable income tax exemptions, many charities do not earn significant income. The impact of interpreting the definition of charitable purpose in a manner more consistent with the community's expectations may in fact be small from the perspective of fiscal cost. At the same time, the benefits to the public that charities provide appear to have been overlooked, as has the loss to the public of those benefits if non-registration forces charities to close. Similarly, the fiscal consequences involved in providing legislative fix ups, such as those that followed the controversial deregistration of the Queenstown Lakes Community Housing Trust,[173] appear to have been overlooked. The net fiscal effect from interpreting the definition of charitable purpose in a manner more consistent with the community's expectations may in fact be positive. The point is that the empirical analysis has not been done.

Finally, to not conduct the much anticipated review on the basis of a controversial and hotly contested decision to disestablish the Charities Commission was merely to add insult to injury. The net result is a framework of regulation that appears, in practice, to be materially frustrating rather than facilitating[174] charitable work in New Zealand, while the need for charities' services is as high as ever.[175]

The Charities Amendment Bill

The relationship between the government and the community and voluntary sector was further strained when a Statutes Amendment Bill was introduced in October 2015.[176] The Bill proposed to make technical and non-controversial amendments to 28 Acts, including the Charities Act. However, the proposed removal of the words "or the chief executive" from section 61 of the Charities Act would put it beyond doubt that charities' hard-won rights of appeal were indeed removed when the Commission was disestablished in 2012. Following its first reading in December 2015, the Bill was referred to the Government Administration Select Committee, with submissions closing shortly following the Christmas break on 29 January 2016. There was no specific notification to charities that such a significant amendment was being made. Fortunately, the issue was noticed and raised with the Committee, which agreed that the proposed amendment was not "technical and non-controversial." The Committee removed the proposed Charities Act amendments to a separate Charities Amendment Bill, with a short further period for submissions.[177]

As word spread, the charitable sector expressed considerable concern. In response, the charities regulator issued a news alert[178] to every registered charity in the country to "assure" them that the proposed amendment to section 61 would have "no impact" on their appeal rights, and that "all **current** avenues" [emphasis added] for charities to seek a review of the charities regulator's decisions would "**remain open and unaffected by the amendment**" [emphasis in original]. What the news alert did not make clear was that these statements were based on a view that charities' rights of appeal had already been removed in 2012. Whether such a view is correct is subject to significant doubt, as discussed earlier. Despite the news alert, many charities expressed their strong opposition to the amendment, and fortunately, the Select Committee listened. In September 2016, the Select Committee recommended the proposed amendment to section 61 be struck out because of "community concern."[179] At the time of writing, the Bill is awaiting its second reading.

New Financial Reporting Rules

Finally, in 2013, the government enacted financial reporting reform,[180] which has been described as the most significant change to the financial reporting requirements imposed on New Zealand's charities in history.[181] From 1 April 2015, the annual returns of all registered charities must be accompanied by financial statements prepared in accordance with financial reporting standards issued by the External Reporting Board.[182] These financial statements must be publicly available on the charities register (unless the charities regulator has approved a restriction on public access in the public interest, which is rarely given).[183] Larger charities must also have their financial statements audited or reviewed.[184] Included among the requirements is a service performance report, under which non-financial information, such as why a charity exists and what it is trying to achieve, must be presented and, if necessary, audited. Although a four-tier structure is intended to tailor the new rules to a charity's size, and significant efforts have been made to make the transition process as smooth as possible, the new rules represent a significant increase in compliance burden for many charities. Key issues in this context include the requirement to prepare consolidated financial statements covering all entities "controlled" by a charity and the treatment of related party transactions,[185] which are often unavoidable in a small country such as New Zealand. There is concern that these and other requirements, such as the new regime for health and safety,[186] together with associated high penalties for non-compliance, are fuelling a trend towards "big charity," where resources are available to meet the requirements. Such a trend would not augur well for the bulk of New Zealand's charities.

The Need for Future Reform

The decade since the passing of the Charities Act highlights the importance of consultation and of ensuring that objective empirical analysis is carried out before changes are made. If the objective of the Charities Act regime was to strengthen the charitable sector, it is not being met. Even if the objective was to reduce "fiscal cost," the regime does not appear to be succeeding. It is to be hoped that the government will listen to the concerns of the charitable sector and finally conduct the post-implementation review of the Charities

Act that was originally promised. Such a review is urgently required and must be conducted thoroughly, with full consultation, so that a framework for New Zealand charities regulation that is fit for purpose can be devised in the interests of all concerned.

Notes

1 I would like to acknowledge the assistance of the following people: Dave Henderson, external relations manager, Hui E! Community Aotearoa; Ros Rice, executive officer, Community Networks Aotearoa; Gabrielle O'Brien, CEO, Birthright NZ; Joan Isaac, ComVoices administrator; Grace Collett and Raina Ng, law clerks at Sue Barker Charities Law; and my daughters, Imogen and Ella.
2 "The Charities Register," Charities Services (New Zealand), accessed September 19, 2016, https://www.register.charities.govt.nz/AdvancedSearch.
3 Hui E! Community Aotearoa, accessed October 7, 2016, http://www.huie.org.nz/; Social Development Partners, "New National Body for Community Sector," *Scoop Politics*, July 16, 2014, accessed October 7, 2016, http://www.scoop.co.nz/stories/PO1407/S00262/new-national-body-for-community-sector.htm.
4 Fundraising Institute of New Zealand, accessed October 7, 2016, http://finz.org.nz/.
5 Philanthropy New Zealand, accessed October 7, 2016, http://philanthropy.org.nz/.
6 New Zealand Trustees Association, accessed October 7, 2016, http://www.nzta.org.nz/.
7 Community Networks Aotearoa, accessed October 7, 2016, http://communitynetworksaotearoa.org.nz/.
8 Community Housing, accessed October 7, 2016, http://communityhousing.org.nz/.
9 Charities Bill 108–1, Explanatory Note, 1, accessed October 18, 2016, http://www.nzlii.org/nz/legis/hist_bill/cb20041081114/.
10 Donald Poirier, *Charity Law in New Zealand* (Wellington: New Zealand Department of Internal Affairs, 2013), [1.1.1], accessed October 7, 2016, https://www.charities.govt.nz/assets/Uploads/Resources/Charity-Law-in-New-Zealand.pdf.
11 Susan Barker, Michael Gousmett, and Ken Lord, *The Law and Practice of Charities in New Zealand* (Wellington: LexisNexis New Zealand, 2013), chapter 3.
12 Income Tax Act 2007 (NZ), ss. CW 41 and CW 42.
13 Income Tax Act 2007 (NZ) ss. LD 1—LD 3, DB 41, DV 12.
14 Inland Revenue Department, Policy Advice Division, *Tax and Charities* (IRD, 2001), [8.3].
15 Tax Administration Act 1994 (NZ) s. 92.
16 Inland Revenue Department, "Interaction of Tax and Charities Rules, Covering Tax Exemption and Donee Status," Operational Statement OS 06/02 (2006), [7]—[9] and [16]; New Zealand House of Representatives, *Parliamentary Debates*, Vol. 616, 12110 (March 30, 2004, Richard Worth, National).
17 IRD, *Tax and Charities*, [6.2] and [6.3].
18 Tax Administration Act 1994 (NZ) s. 81. Following the passing of the Charities Act in 2005, a list of approved donees became publicly available: http://www.ird.govt.nz/donee-organisations/donee-X.html, accessed July 28, 2016.
19 *Latimer v CIR* [2002] 1 NZLR 535 (HC), *Latimer v CIR* [2002] 3 NZLR 195 (CA), and *Latimer v CIR* [2004] 3 NZLR 157 (PC).
20 *Foundation for Anti-Aging Research v Charities Registration Board* [2015] NZCA 449, [44].

21 *Re Foundation for Anti-Aging Research* [2016] NZHC 2328, [13].

22 IRD, *Tax and Charities*, [6.2]—[6.3], [7.1]—[7.4].

23 Tax Administration Act 1994, s. 3, definition of "gift-exempt body."

24 IRD, *Tax and Charities*, [8.18]; New Zealand House of Representatives, *Parliamentary Debates*, Vol. 625, 19951 (April 12, 2005, Gordon Copeland, United Future).

25 Incorporated Societies Act 1908, s. 23.

26 Ministry of Business, Innovation and Employment, *Exposure Draft: Incorporated Societies Bill: Including Consultation on Agricultural and Pastoral Societies Legislation: Request for Submissions* (Wellington: MBIE, 2015), [102]).

27 Even if their trustees were incorporated as a board and registered under the Charitable Trusts Act 1957.

28 IRD, OS 06/02, [2]—[4]; IRD, *Tax and Charities*, [2.12]—[2.13].

29 New Zealand, *Parliamentary Debates*, Vol. 625, 19942 (April 12, 2005, Judith Collins, National).

30 New Zealand, *Parliamentary Debates*, Vol. 625, 19973 (April 12, 2005, Judith Tizard, Associate Minister of Commerce).

31 IRD, *Tax and Charities*, [4.4].

32 *Latimer v CIR* [2004] 3 NZLR 157 (PC), [20].

33 *Dick v CIR* [2003] 1 NZLR 741, [51]; IRD, *Tax and Charities*, [6.6].

34 Charitable Trusts Act 1957, ss. 58, 60; *Morgan v Wellington City Corporation* [1975] 1 NZLR 416; *Mendelssohn v Centrepoint Community Growth Trust* [1999] 2 NZLR 88.

35 New Zealand, *Parliamentary Debates*, Vol. 625, 19946–19948 (April 12, 2005, Rodney Hide, ACT).

36 New Zealand, *Parliamentary Debates*, Vol. 625, 19952 (April 12, 2005, Dail Jones, NZ First).

37 New Zealand, *Parliamentary Debates*, Vol. 616, 12111 (March 30, 2004, Dail Jones).

38 New Zealand, *Parliamentary Debates*, Vol. 625, 19952 (April 12, 2005, Dail Jones).

39 New Zealand, *Parliamentary Debates*, Vol. 625, 19946–19948 (April 12, 2005, Rodney Hide); Vol. 616, 12113 (March 30, 2004, Sue Bradford, Green).

40 New Zealand, *Parliamentary Debates*, Vol. 616, 12116 (March 30, 2004, Richard Prebble, ACT); Vol. 625, 19943 (April 12, 2005, Judith Collins); Vol. 625, 19945 (April 12, 2005, Bill Gudgeon, NZ First); Vol. 625, 19946–19948 (April 12, 2005, Rodney Hide); Vol. 625, 19950 (April 12, 2005, Sue Bradford).

41 New Zealand, *Parliamentary Debates*, Vol. 625, 19953 (April 12, 2005, Dail Jones); Vol. 625, 19945 (April 12, 2005, Bill Gudgeon).

42 New Zealand Parliament, (Charities Bill 108–2, December 17, 2004), Select Committee Report, 19; New Zealand, *Parliamentary Debates*, Vol. 616, 12118 (March 30, 2004, Gordon Copeland).

43 *Accent Management Limited v CIR* (2007) 23 NZTC 21,323 (CA), *Ben Nevis Forestry Ventures Ltd v CIR* [2009] 2 NZLR 289 (SC), *Muir v CIR* [2016] NZSC 113 (August 26, 2016).

44 New Zealand, *Parliamentary Debates*, Vol. 625, 19980 (April 12, 2005, Jill Pettis, Labour).

45 New Zealand, *Parliamentary Debates*, Vol. 625, 19982 (April 12, 2005, Gordon Copeland); 19967 (April 12, 2005, Judith Tizard, Minister of Consumer Affairs).

46 Charities Bill 2004, explanatory note, 2; New Zealand, *Parliamentary Debates*, Vol. 616, 12109 (March 30, 2004, Margaret Wilson, Minister of Commerce).

47 IRD, *Tax and Charities*, [2.14].

48 Charities Bill 2004, 108–1, Explanatory Note, 1.
49 New Zealand, *Parliamentary Debates*, Vol. 616, 12108 (March 30, 2004, Margaret Wilson, Minister of Commerce).
50 Charities Bill 2004, Explanatory Note, 1.
51 Charities Bill 2004, Explanatory Note, 1; New Zealand Parliament, *Report of the Select Committee*, Charities Bill 108–2, December 17, 2004, 1.
52 New Zealand, *Parliamentary Debates*, Vol. 616, 12108 (March 30, 2004, Margaret Wilson, Minister of Commerce).
53 Charities Act 2005, s. 18(3).
54 Charities Act 2005, s. 50.
55 Charities Act 2005, ss. 40–41.
56 New Zealand, *Parliamentary Debates*, Vol. 616, 12113 (March 30, 2004, Sue Bradford).
57 New Zealand, *Parliamentary Debates*, Vol. 625, 19974 (April 12, 2005, Judith Tizard, Associate Minister of Commerce).
58 New Zealand, *Parliamentary Debates*, Vol. 616, 12117–12118 (March 30, 2004, Gordon Copeland); Vol. 625, 19950 (April 12, 2005, Gordon Copeland).
59 David Lange, *My Life* (Auckland: Viking, 2005).
60 New Zealand, *Parliamentary Debates*, Vol. 616, 12118 (March 30, 2004, Gordon Copeland).
61 Sir Spencer Russell, *Working Party on Charities and Sporting Bodies* (Wellington, 1989).
62 New Zealand, *Parliamentary Debates*, Vol. 616, 12118 (March 30, 2004, Gordon Copeland).
63 David McLay, "Regulation of Charities," *New Zealand Law Journal* 78 (2002): 55–56, cited in Carolyn J. Cordery, and Rachel F. Baskerville-Morley, *Charity Financial Reporting Regulation: A Comparison of the United Kingdom and Her Former Colony, New Zealand*, School of Accounting and Commercial Law Working Paper No. 20 (Wellington: Victoria University of Wellington, 2005), 19.
64 New Zealand, *Parliamentary Debates*, Vol. 625, 19973 (April 12, 2005, Judith Tizard, Associate Minister of Commerce).
65 Barker et al., *Law and Practice of Charities*, [3.677]; New Zealand, *Parliamentary Debates*, Vol. 625, 19950 (April 12, 2005, Gordon Copeland).
66 New Zealand, *Parliamentary Debates*, Vol. 616, 12118 (March 30, 2004, Gordon Copeland).
67 IRD, *Tax and Charities*, [7.2].
68 New Zealand, *Parliamentary Debates*, Vol. 625, 19973 (April 12, 2005, Judith Tizard, Associate Minister of Commerce).
69 David Robinson, "Self-Regulation Report: New Zealand," *International Journal of Not-for-Profit Law* 1(1) (1998).
70 IRD, *Tax and Charities*, [1.5]—[1.7]; Barker et al., *Law and Practice of Charities*, [4.12]; New Zealand, *Parliamentary Debates*, Vol. 616, 12108 (March 30, 2004, Margaret Wilson, Minister of Commerce).
71 Cordery and Baskerville-Morley, *Charity Financial Reporting Regulation*, 19.
72 Committee of Experts on Tax Compliance, *Tax Compliance: Report to the Treasurer and Minister of Revenue by a Committee of Experts on Tax Compliance* (Wellington: New Zealand Government, 1998).
73 IRD, *Tax and Charities*, [1.5]—[1.7].
74 IRD, *Tax and Charities*, foreword, [4.2], [7.1]—[7.3].
75 New Zealand, *Parliamentary Debates*, Vol. 616, 12118 (March 30, 2004, Gordon Copeland).
76 IRD, *Tax and Charities*, foreword, [1.1], [1.5]—[1.7].
77 IRD, *Tax and Charities*.

78 IRD, *Tax and Charities*, foreword, [1.1]—[1.4].
79 David McLay, "Charities Commission: The Gestation Continues," *New Zealand Law Journal*, 80 (2004): 73–75, cited in Cordery and Baskerville-Morley, *Charity Financial Reporting Regulation*, 19.
80 New Zealand, *Parliamentary Debates*, Vol. 616, 12118 (March 30, 2004, Gordon Copeland).
81 New Zealand, *Parliamentary Debates*, Vol. 616, 12113 (March 30, 2004, Sue Bradford).
82 New Zealand, *Parliamentary Debates*, Vol. 616, 12118 (March 30, 2004, Gordon Copeland).
83 New Zealand, *Parliamentary Debates*, Vol. 616, 12113 (March 30, 2004, Sue Bradford).
84 Charities Bill 2004, 108–2, *Select Committee Report*, 1; New Zealand, *Parliamentary Debates*, Vol. 625, 19944 (April 12, 2005, Georgina Beyer, Labour); Vol. 625, 19982 (April 12, 2005, Gordon Copeland).
85 Charities Bill 2004, 108–2, *Select Committee Report*, 1; New Zealand, *Parliamentary Debates*, Vol. 625, 19982 (April 12, 2005, Gordon Copeland).
86 New Zealand, *Parliamentary Debates*, Vol. 616, 12108 (March 30, 2004, Sue Bradford).
87 Charities Bill 2004, 108–2, *Select Committee Report*, 21; New Zealand, *Parliamentary Debates*, Vol. 625, 19980 (April 12, 2005, Sue Bradford).
88 New Zealand, *Parliamentary Debates*, Vol. 625, 19944 (April 12, 2005); Charities Bill 2004, 108–2, *Select Committee Report*, 21.
89 Charities Bill 2004, 108–1, cll. 67 and 69(6).
90 Charities Bill 2004, 108–2, *Select Committee Report*, 13–14.
91 Crown Entities Act 2004, ss. 7(1)(a), 103(1) [emphasis added].
92 Charities Bill 108–2, *Select Committee Report*, 2.
93 Charities Act 2005, as originally enacted, s. 9(1); Crown Entities Act 2004, s. 104 and Sch. 1 Part 2.
94 Barker et al., *Law and Practice of Charities*, [3.1411]—[3.1416].
95 Charities Bill 2004, 108–2, *Select Committee Report*, 2.
96 Charities Bill 2004, 108–2, *Select Committee Report*, 1; New Zealand, *Parliamentary Debates*, Vol. 625, 19940 (April 12, 2005, Judith Tizard, Associate Minister of Commerce).
97 Charities Bill 2004, 108–2, *Select Committee Report*, 20.
98 New Zealand, *Parliamentary Debates*, Vol. 625, 19981 (April 12, 2005, Sue Bradford); Vol. 625, 19948 (April 12, 2005, Sue Bradford).
99 New Zealand, *Parliamentary Debates*, Vol. 616, 12113 (March 30, 2004, Richard Worth); Vol. 625, 19981 (April 12, 2005, Sue Bradford).
100 Income Tax Act 2007, s. CW 41(5).
101 Income Tax Act 1994, ss. OB 1, OB 3B.
102 Charities Bill 2004, cl. 4(2).
103 *Latimer v CIR* [2002] 1 NZLR 535, [5].
104 *Latimer v CIR* [2002] 3 NZLR 195 (CA), [32].
105 *Molloy v CIR* [1981] 1 NZLR 688 (CA), 695.
106 IRD, *Tax and Charities*, [3.8].
107 IRD, *Tax and Charities*, [4.1].
108 *CIR v New Zealand Council of Law Reporting* [1981] 1 NZLR 682; and *CIR v Medical Council of New Zealand* [1997] 2 NZLR 297.
109 IRD, *Tax and Charities*, [4.2] and [4.4].
110 IRD, *Tax and Charities*, [4.1].
111 IRD, *Tax and Charities*, chapter 5.
112 IRD, *Tax and Charities*, [4.3].

113 IRD, *Tax and Charities*, [5.7].

114 IRD, *Tax and Charities*, [5.11], [5.15].

115 IRD, *Tax and Charities*, [5.19]—[5.20].

116 Charities Bill 2004, 108–2, *Select Committee Report*, 3.

117 *In re Nottage; Jones v Palmer* [1895] 2 Ch 649.

118 David Sutton, Carolyn Cordery, and Rachel Baskerville, *Paying the Price of the Failure to Retain Legitimacy in a National Charity: the CORSO Story*, Centre for Accounting, Governance and Taxation Research Working Paper No. 47 (Wellington: School of Accounting and Commercial Law, Victoria University of Wellington, 2007).

119 Income Tax Act 2007, Schedule 32, Recipients of Charitable or Other Public Benefit Gifts.

120 New Zealand, *Parliamentary Debates*, Vol. 616, 12108 (March 30, 2004, Sue Bradford).

121 Charities Bill 2004, Explanatory Note, 1.

122 *Re Greenpeace New Zealand Incorporated* [2013] 1 NZLR 339, [42].

123 Charities Bill 108–2, *Select Committee Report*, 3; New Zealand, *Parliamentary Debates*, Vol. 616, 12108 (March 30, 2004, Gordon Copeland); Vol. 625, 19941 (April 12, 2005, Judith Tizard, Associate Minister of Commerce); Vol. 625, 19949 (April 12, 2005, Sue Bradford).

124 *Greenpeace of New Zealand Incorporated* [2015] 1 NZLR 169, [16]; *Re Greenpeace New Zealand Incorporated* [2011] 2 NZLR 815, [40].

125 David Brown, "The Charities Act 2005 and the Definition of Charitable Purpose," *New Zealand University Law Review* 21 (2005): 598, 631, 633.

126 See Charities Services, "Declined to Register" decision type, accessed October 7, 2016, https://charities.govt.nz/charities-in-new-zealand/legal-decisions/view-the-decisions/. From information obtained under the Official Information Act and from the media, there are many hundreds of other charities not included on this list.

127 New Zealand National Party, "Charities Commission Chokes on Backlog," *Scoop Parliament*, October 12, 2007, accessed October 7, 2016, http://www.scoop.co.nz/stories/PA0710/S00228/charities-commission-chokes-on-backlog.htm.

128 Charities Services, "We're Putting the Record Straight," *Charities News Alert*, September 4, 2015, accessed July 28, 2016, http://createsend.com/t/j-5B3C7BF2DAD54E9E.

129 See "Declined to Register," https://www.charities.govt.nz/charities-in-new-zealand/legal-decisions/view-the-decisions/, which contains only a selection of the charities deregistered or declined registration.

130 *Greenpeace of New Zealand Incorporated* [2015] 1 NZLR 169 and *National Council of Women of New Zealand Inc. v Charities Registration Board* [2015] 3 NZLR 72.

131 *New Zealand Society of Accountants v CIR* [1986] 1 NZLR 147 (CA) at 152; *Commissioner of Taxation v The Triton Foundation* [2005] FCA 1319 at [21]—[22], and *Tasmanian Electronic Commerce Centre Pty Ltd v Commissioner of Taxation* [2005] FCA 439 at 50, referred to with approval in *Queenstown Lakes Community Housing Trust* [2011] 3 NZLR 502 (HC) at [63]—[67], and *Canterbury Development Corporation v Charities Commission* [2010] 2 NZLR 707 (HC) at [42]—[43] and [61]—[65]. See also *Education New Zealand Trust* (2010) 24 NZTC 24354 (HC) at [25].

132 *Foundation for Anti-Aging Research v Charities Registration Board* [2015] NZCA 449, [43].

133 *Shotover Gorge Jet Boats Ltd v Jamieson* [1987] 1 NZLR 437 (CA), 440, line 15.

134 *Foundation for Anti-Aging Research v Charities Registration Board* [2015] NZCA 449, [42].

135 *New Zealand Computer Society Inc.* (2011) NZTC 20,033, [32].

136 Susan Barker, "Appealing Decisions of the Charities Regulator," (presented at ADLSI Seminar "Charity Begins At . . . Developing Perspectives on Charity Law," Auckland, New Zealand, April 1–3, 2014).

137 New Zealand, *Parliamentary Debates*, Vol. 625, 19950 (April 12, 2005, Sue Bradford).

138 See Susan Barker, "Canterbury Development Case," *New Zealand Law Journal* (2010): 248.

139 See *Foundation for Anti-Aging Research v Charities Registration Board* [2016] NZHC 2328.

140 Securities Act (Charity Debt Securities) Exemption Notice 2013 exempts only registered charities from certain financial markets disclosure requirements, accessed October 7, 2016, http://www.legislation.govt.nz/regulation/public/2013/0471/latest/DLM5761759.html?search=ts_act%40bill%40regulation%40deemedreg_Securities+Act+(Charity+Debt+Securities)+Exemption+Notice+2013_resel_25_a&p=1. See also the proposal to exempt registered charities from the requirement to pay for police vetting: United Future NZ Party, "United Future Secures Better Deal for Charities—Dunne," Scoop Parliament, September 14, 2016, accessed October 7, 2016, http://www.scoop.co.nz/stories/PA1609/S00235/unitedfuture-secures-better-deal-for-charities-dunne.htm.

141 Susan Barker and Grace Collett, "Fiscal Consequences," *New Zealand Law Journal* (2016): 102.

142 *Draco Foundation (NZ) Charitable Trust* (2011) 25 NZTC 20–032 (HC); *Greenpeace* [of] *New Zealand Inc.* [2011] 2 NZLR 815 (HC); *National Council of Women of New Zealand Inc. v Charities Registration Board* [2015] 3 NZLR 72 (HC).

143 *Canterbury Development Corporation & Ors v CC* [2010] 2 NZLR 707 (HC).

144 *Grand Lodge of Antient Free and Accepted Masons in New Zealand* [2011] 1 NZLR 277 (HC); *New Zealand Computer Society* (2011) 25 NZTC 20–033 (HC); *Plumbers, Gasfitters and Drainlayers Board v Charities Registration Board* [2013] NZHC 1986; *Liberty Trust v CC* [2011] 3 NZLR 68 (HC).

145 *Education New Zealand Trust* (2010) 24 NZTC 24,354 (HC).

146 Taxation (Business Taxation and Remedial Matters) Act 2007, ss. 340, 348 and 440, following the government discussion document: Policy Advice Division, Inland Revenue Department, *Tax Incentives for Giving to Charities and Other Non-profit Organisations* (Wellington: Inland Revenue Department, 2006).

147 Taxation (Annual Rates, Business Taxation, Kiwisaver, and Remedial Matters) Bill 2007, explanatory note 2.

148 See for example "National Council of Women May Lose Charity Status," *Radio New Zealand News*, July 2, 2010, accessed October 7, 2016, http://www.radionz.co.nz/news/national/34565/national-council-of-women-may-lose-charity-status; and *National Council of Women of New Zealand Incorporated v Charities Registration Board* [2015] 3 NZLR 72.

149 Tariana Turia, "Charities Commission Annual General Meeting," *Beehive. govt.nz: The Official Website of the New Zealand Government*, accessed November 30, 2010, www.beehive.govt.nz/speech/charities-commission-annual-general-meeting-0.

150 "Government Reviews More State Agencies," *Scoop Parliament*, May 31, 2011, accessed October 7, 2016, http://www.scoop.co.nz/stories/PA1105/S00611/government-reviews-more-state-agencies.htm.

151 Tony Ryall, "Reduction in State Agencies Confirmed," *Beehive.govt.nz: The Official Website of the New Zealand Government*, August 11, 2011, http://www.beehive.govt.nz/release/reduction-state-agencies-confirmed. See also "Government Reviews More State Agencies," *Scoop*.

152 Charities Act 2005 (NZ) s. 8(4).

153 Charities Act 2005 (NZ) ss. 8(5), 8(6), 9.

154 Government Administration Committee, *Crown Entities Reform Bill: Report of the State Services Commission* (2012), [137]—[142], accessed October 7, 2016, https://www.parliament.nz/resource/en-NZ/50SCGA_ADV_00DBHOH_BILL11083_1_A224561/e33ab0c076c62c387bc0a2b51d231285d030125d.

155 New Zealand, Department of Internal Affairs, *Discussion Document: Review of Class 4 Gambling* (Wellington: Department of Internal Affairs, 2016), 4, accessed October 7, 2016, http://www.ttcfltd.org.nz/wp-content/uploads/2016/06/Class-4-review-discussion-document-2016.pdf.

156 Barker et al., *Law and Practice of Charities*, [3.1656]—[3.1657].

157 Tony Ryall, "Reduction in State Agencies Confirmed."

158 Crown Entities Reform Bill 332–1 (2011).

159 See Charities Act 2005, s. 8(3). Other decisions able to be made by the Board all clearly relate to registration and deregistration, see ss. 14(1), 15(e), 16(4)—(9), 19, 20, 31, 32, 35, 36, 44, 46, 48, 49, and 55.

160 Other mistakes were contained in ss. 48, 56, 57 and 60(3), see Sue Barker, Charities Law, "Supplementary Submission on the Charities Amendment Bill," 71–2B, September 7, 2016, https://www.parliament.nz/en/pb/bills-and-laws/bills-proposed-laws/document/00DBHOH_BILL69365_1/tab/submissionsand advice.

161 Government Administration Committee, *Crown Entities Reform Bill: Government Bill: As Reported* (Wellington: NZ House of Representatives, 2012), 4–5.

162 Crown Entities Reform Bill (332–2), Supplementary Order Paper 2012 (32).

163 See, for example, the decisions to deregister Swimming New Zealand: https://charities.govt.nz/charities-in-new-zealand/legal-decisions/view-the-decisions/view/swimming-new-zealand-incorporated and the New Zealand Rowing Association: https://charities.govt.nz/charities-in-new-zealand/legal-decisions/view-the-decisions/view/new-zealand-rowing-association-incorporated.

164 See, for example, "Relationships Aotearoa—Our Story," *Scoop Politics*, May 19, 2015, accessed October 7, 2016, http://www.scoop.co.nz/stories/PO1505/S00207/relationships-aotearoa-our-story.htm; and Eric Crampton, "Problem Gambling Foundation Loses Govt Funding: Service Provision vs Service Advocacy," *National Business Review* (March 22, 2014).

165 "Conflict of Interest," *Charities Services*, accessed October 7, 2016, https://charities.govt.nz/im-a-registered-charity/officer-information/officer-kit/conflict-of-interest/; and New Zealand Trustees Association, *NZ Estate & Trust Bulletin*, accessed September 2, 2016, http://www.nzta.org.nz/ETB.html.

166 See New Zealand Law Commission, *A New Act for Incorporated Societies*, Report 129 (Wellington: Law Commission, 2013), [6.132]—[6.134], accessed October 7, 2016, http://www.lawcom.govt.nz/sites/default/files/projectAvailable Formats/NZLC%20R129.pdf.

167 See *Foundation for Anti-Aging Research v Charities Registration Board* [2016] NZHC 2328.

168 *Greenpeace of New Zealand Incorporated* [2012] NZCA 533.

169 Jo Goodhew, "No Review of the Charities Act at This Time," *Beehive.govt.nz: The Official Website of the New Zealand Government*, November 16, 2012, accessed July 29, 2016, http://www.beehive.govt.nz/release/no-review-charities-act-time.

170 Background Paper to SOC Min (12) 24/3 (November 7, 2012), [5], [29(7)].
171 Barker et al., *Law and Practice of Charities*, [10.14]—[10.22].
172 *Queenstown Lakes Community Housing Trust* [2011] 3 NZLR 502, [78].
173 *Queenstown Lakes Community Housing Trust* [2011] 3 NZLR 502 (HC), and Income Tax Act 2007, ss. CW 42B and LD 3(2)(ac), as inserted by the Taxation (Annual Rates, Employee Allowances, and Remedial Matters) Act 2014, and associated consequential amendments.
174 *National Council of Women of New Zealand Incorporated v Charities Registration Board* [2015] 3 NZLR 72, [53].
175 Susan Barker, "Let Them Eat Cake—What Brexit Should Tell Us about Charity Regulation in New Zealand," *LinkedIn*, July 9, 2016, https://www.linkedin.com/pulse/let-them-eat-cake-what-brexit-should-tell-us-charity-susan-barker?trk=prof-post.
176 Statutes Amendment Bill 2015, 71–1, accessed October 7, 2016, https://www.parliament.nz/en/pb/bills-and-laws/bills-proposed-laws/document/00DBHOH_BILL66162_1/statutes-amendment-bill
177 Charities Amendment Bill 2016, 71–2B, accessed October 18, 2016, https://www.parliament.nz/en/pb/bills-and-laws/bills-proposed-laws/document/00DBHOH_BILL69365_1/charities-amendment-bill.
178 Charities Services, *News Alert*, July 7, 2016, accessed October 7, 2016, https://charities.govt.nz/news-and-events/hot-topics/news-alert-details-of-the-charities-amendment-bill/.
179 Government Administration Committee, *Charities Amendment Bill: Government Bill: As Reported*, 2, accessed October 7, 2016, https://www.parliament.nz/resource/en-NZ/51DBSCH_SCR71066_1/49133708d9e276b2d84335918472e48d372e6422.
180 Financial Reporting (Amendments to Other Enactments) Act 2013, ss. 19 and 20.
181 Craig Fisher, "New Charity Financial Reporting and Audit Requirements: An Opportunity for Alignment," *Newsroom*, RSM New Zealand, August 20, 2015, accessed October 18, 2016, http://www.rsm.global/newzealand/news/new-charity-financial-reporting-and-audit-requirements-opportunity-alignment.
182 Charities Act 2005, ss. 41(2)(b), 42A and 42B; External Reporting Board, "Standards for Not-for-profit Entities After 1 April 2015," accessed October 18, 2016, https://www.xrb.govt.nz/Site/Accounting_Standards/Current_Standards/Standards_for_Not-For_Profit_PBEs/Stds_for_Not-For-Profit_T1–4.aspx.
183 Charities Act 2005 s. 25; see also "Restricting Information," *Charities Services*, accessed October 18, 2016, https://www.charities.govt.nz/im-a-registered-charity/restricting-information.
184 Charities Act 2005, ss. 42C—42F, as inserted by the Charities Amendment Act 2014.
185 "Related Party Transactions for Tier 3 and Tier 4 Charities," *Charities Services*, accessed October 18, 2016, https://charities.govt.nz/new-reporting-standards/tier-3/related-party-transactions-for-tier-3-and-tier-4-charities/.
186 The Health and Safety at Work Act 2015 came into force on April 4, 2016.

Australia

11 The Digital Regulator

Susan Pascoe

Overview

The story of the establishment of Australia's first independent charity regulator is an epic tale spanning decades, enlivened by a cast of colourful characters, and played out on contested terrain. Yet the Australian Charities and Not-for-profits Commission (ACNC) is unique in the level of sustained advocacy and support it garnered from the not-for-profit (NFP) sector, and in its establishment as a digital-first agency. This chapter is written by a participant observer in the final chapters of this saga. The author was the head of the taskforce created to establish the ACNC and is its inaugural commissioner. The chapter will provide the context in which Australia's first fit-for-purpose charity regulator was established, the stormy passage of the legislation, the work of the taskforce which oversaw the establishment of the ACNC, the early days operating in uncertainty, the role and functions of the regulator, and the eventual political settlement which saw the embryonic body given a lease of life.

Policy Context

Australia's history from 1788 is one of British settlement and stable democratic government. The continent was previously occupied solely by Indigenous peoples. Since 1901, the country has enjoyed stable democratic governments in a federated structure comprising a Commonwealth government with six state and two territory governments. NFPs are regulated at all three levels—Commonwealth, state or territory, and local government. The Australian Constitution came into effect in 1901 and formed the federation. It set out the fields over which the Commonwealth had power, leaving NFP regulation to the states, with the income taxation power gravitating to the Commonwealth after the Second World War. This dichotomy of state responsibility and Commonwealth financial capacity ensured the Commonwealth taxation authority, the Australian Taxation Office (ATO), held a de facto role as NFP regulator as it was the arbiter of what was a charity and what was not. In practice, the states and territories are responsible for fundraising regulation, the collection of jurisdictional taxes, and NFP oversight, much of which causes duplicative regulation and reporting for charities, especially those operating in more than one jurisdiction.[1] The British legacy has left an enduring commitment to the rule of law and sound parliamentary process. In addition, there is an appetite for moderate and proportionate regulation to ensure probity, safety, and fairness, which over time creates ongoing pressures for deregulation and administrative simplification. From the earliest times of colonization, this legacy also resulted in the transfer of ideals of charity and mutual support which formed the basis for Australia's modern NFP sector. Indeed, the colony of South Australia was the first Australian jurisdiction to establish a legal framework specifically to enable the incorporation of associations in order to undertake NFP activities.

The NFP sector has considerable political and policy influence despite being largely organized into industry groupings.[2] A number of the peak bodies are adroit and experienced advocates sought out by the media for opinion and consulted by ministers on key policy matters. While there is no umbrella peak body such as the UK's National Council of Voluntary Organisations, Imagine Canada, or the USA Independent Sector, there are a number of highly influential organizations impacting policy such as the Australian Council for Social Services (ACOSS),[3] the Community Council for Australia (CCA),[4] Philanthropy Australia,[5] and the Australian Council for International Development (ACFID).[6] Religious denominations, particularly the Catholic and Anglican Churches, have an important historical legacy and continue to influence the political process in education, health, community services, and charity regulation.

The Size and Importance of the NFP Sector

There are some 54,000 registered charities in Australia. They are an increasingly important part of the economy. Official data shows that NFP organizations hold $176 billion in assets and employ over one million Australians—8 per cent of the nation's workforce. To put these figures in perspective, NFP income is larger than that of the agriculture sector, and NFPs collectively employ five times as many people as the mining sector.[7] Some two million people volunteer in charities.[8] Australia's NFPs are, on average, growing at a faster rate than for-profit or public sector organizations. This growth is the outcome of a number of factors, primarily the result of governments continuing to outsource services to NFP providers, including those in education, welfare, disability, housing, and health. Of the $103 billion income earned in 2014, around $42 billion was from government grants, with approximately $54 billion from earned income and nearly $7 billion from donations and bequests. Australia differs from other similar countries in that NFPs enjoy substantial government and commercial income but relatively low levels of philanthropy.[9]

Policy Contest

The emergence of the ACNC highlighted significant philosophical and policy differences between the major parties in their approach to civil society and public administration. Before winning office in 2013, the Coalition parties signalled that they opposed regulation of the NFP sector, arguing it was an unwarranted interference by government into civil society where there was a low incidence of reported wrongdoing. Labor and the Greens took the view that the NFP sector was a significant part of the economy, as well as civil society, and supported the sector's advocacy for a dedicated regulator. Key sector opinion leaders and peak bodies wanted a regulator to promote trust and confidence in charities, and put them on a comparable regulatory footing with government and business.

Three separate parliamentary inquiries during the Bill's passage delayed the implementation of the ACNC until December 3, 2012. Despite winning government in September 2013, the Coalition was unable to progress a bill to repeal the ACNC Act because of opposition from Labor, the Greens, and some independents in the Senate. On March 4, 2016, the government announced it was not proceeding with the ACNC Repeal Bill. Australia's first national charity regulator now has parliamentary and political authorization.

A Fit-for-Purpose Regulator

Until the establishment of the ACNC, the ATO operated as the de facto charity regulator and determined charitable status for the purpose of applying tax concessions. However, the ATO did not require charities to submit annual returns. It relied on self-assessment of tax status and showed limited interest in the conduct of NFPs prior to the introduction of Australia's consumption tax in the year 2000. There was a dominant perception in the NFP sector that the ATO was conflicted as both assigner of charity status and collector of the national revenue. Further, there was a view that a dedicated regulator could provide guidance and support, and protect the reputation of the sector by dealing with mischief. Key NFP advocates lobbied that the inevitable increase in administrative requirements for the purposes of transparency and accountability would be offset by the regulator overseeing a reduction in red tape. The notion of data being provided once to government and used multiple times ("report once, use often") became both a policy promise of government and a mantra for the sector's red tape reduction drive.

Calls for a fit-for-purpose NFP regulator were formalized in six national inquiries stretching over 15 years:[10]

- 1995 Industry Commission Report, *Charitable Organisations in Australia*
- 2001 Report of the Inquiry into the Definition of Charities and Related Organisations (Charities Definition Inquiry)
- 2008 Senate Standing Committee on Economics, Inquiry into the Disclosure Regime for Charities and Not-for-Profit Organisations

- 2010 Productivity Commission Report, *Contribution of the Not-for-Profit Sector*
- 2010 Australia's Future Tax System Review (the Henry Review)
- 2010 Senate Economics Legislation Committee, Inquiry into Tax Laws Amendment (Public Benefit Test) Bill

All these inquiries recommended some form of independent regulation of charities. The inquiries attracted some 2,029 submissions, a considerable investment by the sector. Following the 2010 inquiries, the Labor government was persuaded to act and allocated funding in its 2011 Budget for the creation of a taskforce to oversee the establishment of the ACNC. I was approached to lead the Taskforce and was later appointed as the inaugural commissioner.

Regulatory reform in the NFP sector was part of a broad suite of social policy reforms, including a National Compact with the sector, a national volunteering strategy, improvements to contracting with government, and legislation on advocacy. These reforms were largely based on the recommendations of the 2010 Productivity Commission Report. To steer these reforms, the former Labor government created a pair of operational and advisory mechanisms: the Office for the Not-for-profit Sector in the Department of Prime Minister and Cabinet (DPMC) to administer the reforms, and the Not-for-profit Reform Council (comprising key NFP stakeholders and opinion leaders) to advise the Minister. Treasury had the role of investigating the feasibility of a stand-alone regulator, and in January 2011, it released a scoping study for consultation and a final report six months later.[11] The Treasury scoping paper argued,

> Recent trends have seen higher levels of governance and accountability requirements of both the commercial and government sectors in Australia; however, the NFP sector has been ignored. The overall governance and accountability arrangements in the NFP sector have not kept pace with international trends to improve governance in the sector.[12]

Treasury took the lead in instructing on the exposure draft of the ACNC Bill (and later the Charities Bill) and in managing the consultation. As ACNC Taskforce leader, I was physically located in, and supported by, Treasury from July 2011. There was a complicated set of relationships for this broad reform agenda. In practice, Treasury had the lead on regulatory and taxation matters, while the DPMC led other aspects of the reforms.

ACNC Taskforce and Stakeholder Engagement

The ACNC Taskforce operated from July 2011 to November 2012. Staff members were seconded from the ATO, Treasury, and the DPMC. From the outset, the Taskforce sought genuine engagement with all stakeholders. Relationships were built with key government, NFP, and community entities, and alliances forged through cognate initiatives such as the government's NFP Reform Council where I, as taskforce leader, was given observer status. Leading the work of the ACNC Taskforce was challenging, as the careers of ATO personnel who had hitherto had the de facto function were affected. It required a capacity to relate credibly to central government agencies and to NFP peak bodies, with significant minorities in both groups not persuaded of the benefits of an independent regulator. Against this backdrop, certain lobby groups actively campaigned to undermine key elements of the proposed regulatory framework such as the requirement for financial reporting and the inclusion of broad enforcement powers for the regulator.[13]

The work of the ACNC Taskforce to establish the regulator progressed alongside the work of the Treasury to develop an exposure draft of the ACNC Bill. From the perspective of the sector and the community, we are all seen as undifferentiated aspects of government, and every effort was made to combine and phase consultations where possible. A discussion paper was released and feedback documented from community meetings held across Australian in January and February 2012. The Taskforce released an Implementation Report in June 2012 and an Update in January 2013.

Broader stakeholder engagement was more difficult to achieve, as the Taskforce had a confined role to establish the new regulator, while policy and legislative development was conducted by the DPMC and Treasury. The states and territories were engaged through the established national forum for political dialogue in the Australian federation, the Council of Australian Governments (COAG). A COAG sub-group comprising jurisdictional Treasury officials was created which curiously did not involve those responsible for regulating NFPs in the states and territories. There was disquiet from states and territories about the potential for regulatory and reporting duplication, and a perception of insufficient early consultation by the Commonwealth. Independent research was commissioned by the COAG Working Party to quantify the impact of proposed regulatory reforms, and a regulatory impact assessment was completed.[14]

Being positioned at the sidelines of these inter-jurisdictional debates had longer term consequences for the ACNC. Worthwhile red tape reduction in Australia's federation requires harmonization with the states and territories. In 2012, most jurisdictions had rejected key elements of the Commonwealth's regulatory reforms—only South Australia and the Australian Capital Territory agreed to harmonize. The difficulty for the ACNC was that it was seen as a part of the Commonwealth bureaucratic machine, irrespective of its status as an independent regulator. It took time for these relations to soften.

The Australian Charities and Not-for-profits Commission Act 2012

A sub-plot within the grander narrative of the establishment of the ACNC was the passage of the enabling legislation. The main characters for this part of the story were the Treasury officials responsible for developing instructions for the parliamentary drafters, and the peak body representatives from the NFP sector.[15] Officials scrutinized legislation from other common law jurisdictions and sought to integrate the best elements into the ACNC Act. These officials were highly capable, but they had little experience consulting with the NFP sector. Powerful lobby groups such as universities, churches, and financial services bodies advocated competently with politicians and senior staff in central government agencies. They briefed the media and exerted influence in the political sphere. The process was marked by tensions about consultation time frames,[16] suspicion as to the authenticity of the Treasury engagement, and concerns regarding key aspects of the Exposure Draft of the ACNC Bill. The main concerns expressed were as follows:

1. The regulator would increase rather than reduce red tape.
2. The scope and range of enforcement powers could result in a heavy-handed regulator.
3. The media could mischievously and destructively use data on the register.

The NFP adviser to the then assistant treasurer became involved in the negotiations with peak NFP bodies and key opinion leaders to resolve unease on aspects of the ACNC Bill and to broker resolutions with Treasury. Sector representatives lobbied successfully for an expansion to the objects in the draft Bill. The version circulated on December 9, 2011, had a single object: "to protect and enhance public trust and confidence in the not-for-profit sector." The Cabinet had agreed to this and a budget was allocated accordingly. However, key advocates believed that this single object began from an assumption of deficit in the sector and lobbied not only to add "maintain" to the first object but also to add two further objects. The objects became[17]

1. to maintain, protect, and enhance public trust and confidence in the Australian not-for-profit sector;
2. to support and sustain a robust, vibrant, independent, and innovative Australian not-for-profit sector; and
3. to promote the reduction of unnecessary regulatory obligations on the Australian not-for-profit sector.[18]

The two additional objects had a dramatic impact on the kind of regulator the ACNC would be. Not only did it need to stretch its modest resources to add two functions but also it needed to be concerned about the sustainability of the sector it regulated and to actively promote initiatives to reduce unnecessary administrative burdens on the NFP sector.[19] After nearly two decades, the sector was finally getting the kind of regulator it wanted, but the regulator needed to manage the tension between its keenness to engage with and support the sector, and its responsibility to supervise and regulate it.

An additional challenge for the ACNC commissioner was that the umbilical cord joining the new regulator to the ATO was not severed. The model chosen by legislators was for an independent statutory office holder, the commissioner, to be supported by an office that was required to purchase its operational services from the ATO. However, core elements of independence were protected: independence of decision making regarding charitable status is written into the ACNC Act; the new regulator has its own appropriation; its delegations on staffing and budget management have been negotiated with the ATO; it reports directly to Parliament. This efficient model was likely one of the protective factors for the ACNC following the change of government in 2013, as there would have been only modest savings if the expanded regulatory functions had been returned to the ATO. However, it has put an onus on the ACNC to protect its independence and to make this independence clear to a sector that retains some suspicion of a revenue agency standing at the gateway to charity concessions.

To achieve its objects, the ACNC has functions that include[20]

- maintaining a public register of Australian charities;
- registering new charities and deregistering those which are no longer eligible;
- collecting information on charities annually and updating the register;
- receiving and acting on complaints about registered charities;
- monitoring charities for compliance with legal requirements;
- providing advice and guidance to charities and the public to enhance the transparency and good governance of the sector; and
- driving the reduction of unnecessary or duplicative regulation and reporting.

The legislation and regulations impose new obligations on registered charities[21]

- to report annually to the ACNC in an Annual Information Statement;
- to comply with Governance Standards; and
- to maintain up-to-date register entries including details of their responsible persons (generally formal office bearers such as company secretary or board members).

The work to establish these functions and educate charities on their new obligations was considerably enhanced by the involvement of overseas charity regulators.

Contribution of International Charity Regulators

One motif in the narrative of the ACNC's creation is the generosity of charity regulators in common law countries. For a neophyte organization operating against a backdrop of contested policy development and a precarious future, it was comforting to receive the active support of other regulators from the "Grandmother" of us all, the Charity Commission of England and Wales (CCEW), and neighbours near and far. Soon after I was appointed to the Taskforce, I was introduced to Trevor Garrett, the then chief executive of the New Zealand Charities Commission (NZCC). The NZCC had been formally established in 2005, and Garrett had overseen its start-up. He conducted sessions for the Taskforce in Australia and participated in roundtables, reflecting on lessons learned from the NZCC's experience in building a charity regulator from scratch. His insights were invaluable, as were the many material supports his office provided. Ironically, he was with the ACNC Taskforce when the NZ government announced it was integrating the NZCC functions into the Department of Internal Affairs. A generous offer was made by the Charity Commission of England and Wales to provide its director of Charity Services, David Locke, for a three month secondment to the ACNC Taskforce. He arrived in October 2011 and had his stay extended. He later successfully applied to become one of the two assistant commissioners of the ACNC, bringing invaluable operational expertise. Locke's mantra that the ACNC "surprise and delight" its clients sat oddly with the Australian vernacular, but has been embraced by staff and earned the ACNC ongoing plaudits for its client-oriented services.

The Compliance function got off to an early start, drawing on the expertise of the recently retired director of compliance from the Charities Directorate in the Canada Revenue Agency, Donna Walsh. She contributed to discussion on regulatory requirements and information and enforcement powers in the Exposure Draft of the ACNC Act. In addition, she assisted in the profiling and hiring of compliance staff, and the development of the ACNC's regulatory approach. Not only did this external expertise strengthen the work of the ACNC Taskforce but also it assisted in creating the perception of an informed, independent, emerging new regulator. The ACNC is delighted now to be providing assistance to the Charities Regulatory Authority in the Republic of Ireland and to be forging stronger collegial relations with state regulators in the United States.

Moving from Taskforce to Regulator

As already signalled, the parliamentary debate around the ACNC establishment legislation was protracted and disputatious during 2012. The then assistant treasurer, Hon. David Bradbury MP, tabled Exposure Draft 3 of the ACNC Bill and immediately referred it to a House of Representatives Economics Committee on July 5 for an inquiry over the winter recess. The committee's report was tabled on August 14. However, this scrutiny did not prevent two further inquiries in September 2012: one by the Senate Community Affairs Committee and another by the House of Representatives Joint Committee on Corporations and Financial Services. The Bill passed the House of Representatives on September 18, 2012. There were further delays in the Senate because of scheduling, and the ACNC Bill finally passed the Senate on November 1, 2012. These delays meant that the life of the ACNC Taskforce, which was meant to finish its work on June 30, 2013, for a July 1 start, was extended by five months. This was not unduly problematic, as the Taskforce began to assume the role of the regulator, enabling a phased introduction. My appointment as commissioner designate began in December 2012.[22]

Key Tasks in Establishing the ACNC

The work schedule for the establishment of the ACNC continued in 2012, despite the slow passage of the ACNC Bill. The delays were used as an opportunity to provide full staff training and develop policies and procedures. The first task was to appoint staff, beginning with senior staff. An organizational structure was developed based on the requirements in the ACNC Bill, the available budget, and an investigation of organizational models in cognate charity regulators. The commissioner is supported by two assistant commissioners, general counsel, and Charity Services. There were originally eight directorates with approximately 100 staff. Two outstanding senior appointments were made of individuals with established reputations: Murray Baird as general counsel and David Locke leading Charity Services. As noted, Locke was a respected and experienced regulator from the United Kingdom. Baird has a deserved reputation as one of Australia's pre-eminent charity lawyers and joined the ACNC after a distinguished career in private practice advising in a number of high-profile cases, including as solicitor instructing on the *Word Investments* case in the High Court.[23]

Once appointed, senior staff were involved in interviews for their own teams. We were resolute that the staff know, understand, and respect the NFP sector and deliberately appointed a mix of people from government and regulatory agencies, the NFP sector, and the private sector. Most of the directors were able to start by early March 2012, and there was a high level of excitement about being involved hands-on in the start-up venture. Attention was paid to developing a client-oriented work culture and work practice, in particular providing a responsive, useful, timely service to charities and the broader community. There was a general sense of pride and moral purpose in the work. With key staff in place, a slow phased handover from the ATO began. There were tensions as people formerly responsible for particular roles worked with newly appointed staff. However, these were worked through with some personnel changes and goodwill. Intensive training was provided to staff, with experienced ATO staff working with newly appointed ACNC staff. It is noteworthy that this work occurred against a backdrop of sustained public and private lobbying from those who wanted the then opposition to retain its commitment to abolish the ACNC, as well as from those advocating for its existence. Staff members at the ACNC were advised to ignore the policy uncertainty, to focus on their work, to and do the best job possible. This approach has had a positive impact.

The ACNC's Object to Educate

The objects of the ACNC Act require the regulator to assist charities to comply by providing guidance and education.[24] The ACNC has had the immense advantage of commencing in a digital era. A national regulator physically located on one site in a country as vast as Australia needs to provide equitable access to the Register, educational materials, and advice. Establishing an attractive website,[25] a portal for charities, and an online register were foundation tasks. As inaugural regulator, the onus was on the ACNC to build charities' capacity to meet their new obligations and also to support the sustainability of the sector. We prioritized the development of materials to help charities meet regulatory and reporting obligations, and have since produced a range of practical resources on good governance and sound financial management. Both as a taskforce and as the new regulator, we also conducted national "roadshows" and regional information sessions, visiting major centres across Australia offering free interactive briefings for charities. These were always well attended, often requiring multiple sessions to accommodate demand. It was important that people heard directly from the commissioners; this helped quell fears and gave the opportunity for the nervous, the disgruntled, and the supportive to voice their issues. Over time, many detractors became advocates for an independent charity regulator.

New products and services are continually being developed. We have produced booklets on topics such as good governance and on protecting your charity from fraud. Reporting fact sheets, compliance checklists, policy papers, and template constitutions are all freely available on the website. We have conducted invitational roundtables, webinars, and *Ask ACNC* sessions,[26] and we speak at conferences regularly.

Advice Services

The companion work to the education and guidance function is the advice provided via phone and email. This is generally the first point of contact that charities and the community have with the ACNC. We decided to have an in-house contact centre, took a conscious decision not to use scripts for standard calls, and recruited staff with interest in the sector. Staff were coached to be responsive, timely, and helpful. During *Ask ACNC* sessions, these staff took laptops to the remotest settings, connected to ACNC systems, and fixed registration and reporting issues on the spot. This certainly "surprised and delighted" our clients! The helpfulness of Advice Services staff ensures that 99 per cent of charities interact with the ACNC online, including filing Annual Information Statements. These staff regularly analyse the contents of calls and provide feedback to the Education and Guidance team so they can develop fact sheets or other materials where there seems to be a knowledge gap. Two-thirds of the concerns about charities come through phone calls and emails from charities and the public. Advice Services staff handle around 65 per cent of complaints by directing the complainant to materials on the ACNC's website or other publicly available materials. The remaining 35 per cent are passed over to Compliance staff.

Compliance

Establishing the Compliance function[27] was a complicated and sensitive task, even with the early advice of experts. There was fear that the information-gathering and enforcement powers were unnecessarily interventionist and heavy-handed; there was general nervousness from a sector unused to monitoring and accountability, and there was uncertainty as to how the regulator would treat slipshod and forgetful, versus negligent and reprobate charities—a critical issue given the reliance by charities on volunteers. The ACNC Taskforce released a discussion paper on its regulatory approach and sought feedback. Some 90 per cent of respondents supported the draft regulatory approach, and their feedback helped shape the final framework. A variant of the classic regulatory advice pyramid was developed (Figure 11.1).

Figure 11.1 Regulatory Pyramid of Support and Compliance.
© Commonwealth of Australia.

The ACNC assumes that charities are acting honestly and gives them opportunities for self-correction. We use the least intrusive powers that are sufficient to address a particular issue and act quickly in cases where evidence of gross negligence or serious misconduct has been established, or where vulnerable people or significant charitable assets are at risk. When deciding whether to use our powers, we consider the type of problem, who or what is at risk, the nature and degree of potential harm, and the likelihood and frequency of an occurrence or recurrence. We develop a risk profile of the charity (factors such as size, existing accountability mechanisms, and history of compliance) and consider the behaviour of responsible individuals. We work cooperatively with Commonwealth, state, and territory regulators, and with intelligence, enforcement, and security agencies. Key concerns raised about charities include allegations of fraud and other misuses of money, charities used for private benefit, harm to members, scam charities, poor governance, illegal activity, and support of terrorism. Approximately 700 concerns are raised annually. Consistent with our proportionate approach, only 14 charities had their registration revoked in the first three years. The vulnerability of charities as potential conduits for funding terrorism is a significant concern. The Financial Action Taskforce (FATF), which addresses international anti-money-laundering and counter-terrorism measures in member countries, has found Australia only partially compliant. FATF has recommended regulatory coverage of all NFP entities (not just charities) and greater outreach to counter the support of terrorism.

The very tight secrecy provisions in the ACNC Act prevent details from being provided publicly when the ACNC takes action against a charity, thereby diminishing its educative and deterrent effect. To counter this, we published an overview of the first two years of compliance activity,[28] and this will now be published bi-annually. Initially, compliance was the area of ACNC activity most prone to staff volatility, with tensions and early staff departures. This reflects a mix of factors, including the attempt to blend intelligence, enforcement, and policy personnel in a small staff group; the lack of active cases in the first few months; and the organizational drive for a proportionate (not punitive) regulatory approach. The implementation of agreed policies and operational procedures, and some staff changes, helped resolve these issues.

Reporting, Group Reporting, and Bulk Lodgement

When the ATO was the de facto regulator, charities were not required to file an annual return. This set Australia apart from other common law jurisdictions. Charities must now complete an Annual Information Statement within six months of the end of their reporting period[29] and comply with ACNC Governance Standard 5, which requires them to act with due diligence and sound financial management. The ACNC maintained a high level of engagement with the sector in the development of the Annual Information

Statement, not only because this remains the preferred regulatory practice but also in recognition of fears about burdensome red tape. For some, those fears did not abate until they completed their first Annual Information Statement. As noted earlier, about 99 per cent of charities engage with the ACNC online. Second and subsequent statements are pre-populated and simply require updating for the year. On an international comparison, these reports are minimalist in their requirements. At the time of this writing, the compliance rate for the first year of reporting (the 2012–13 financial years) was 99.8 per cent, and for 2014, it was 94 per cent. Given the high levels of uncertainty about the future of the ACNC, this is a good achievement. We are tracking to higher compliance levels for the incomplete 2015 reporting year.

Streamlined reporting is available to those charities that operate in groups. A group of registered charities can submit just one collective Annual Information Statement and one financial report, instead of one for each registered charity. In 2014–15, the ACNC approved 47 grouping applications comprising approximately 450 charities. Bulk lodgement is another option for those multiple registered charities who wish to reduce red tape by submitting their Annual Information Statements on a single form. In 2014–15, 15 per cent of 2014 Annual Information Statements were filed using bulk lodgement. Examples included corporate trustees or denomination offices for religious charities.

Engagement with the Sector

One of the hallmarks of a good regulator is that it knows the sector it regulates. The second object in the ACNC Act ensures that the charity regulator adopts this disposition. However, the ACNC has always been mindful that high levels of engagement could result in regulatory capture. Clear protocols for staff, and formalized mechanisms for engagement, help ensure that staff maintain proper professional relationships. Social media presented great opportunities to reach across age and interest groups, and across the sparsely populated continent. Given the diverse and geographically distributed regulated community, we were very fortunate to have senior personnel immersed in social media and communications staff who are young and have revelled in being ahead of the broader public service in the use of YouTube, Twitter, Facebook, LinkedIn, and the like. The ACNC was formally recognized for its excellence in this area, winning the Institute of Public Administration's 2016 Digital Transformation Award.

There are three formalized mechanisms for regular feedback to the ACNC: the Advisory Board, the Professional User Group, and the Sector User Group. The membership and role of the ACNC Advisory Board is set out in the ACNC Act.[30] The Board is not a decision-making board and exists to advise the commissioner. It comprises highly expert general and *ex officio* members, and it has been a source of wise counsel and sound judgement for me as commissioner. Both the Professional and Sector User Groups were established by the ACNC to provide a structured means of engaging with peak bodies and key sector groups as well as practitioners—typically specialist lawyers and accountants. They each meet three times a year with the commissioners in attendance. Briefings are provided, issues identified, and advice is sought. The advice of these groups is also sought out of session.

The ACNC continues to engage with the sector. Its senior managers speak at conferences and workshops, visit charities to see their work first-hand, and maintain personal contact with peak bodies and sector leaders. We retain the belief that authentic engagement is at the heart of good regulatory practice and sound policy and legislative development. Happily, this view is also embedded in the government's *Regulator Performance Framework*,[31] putting the ACNC at the forefront of expected regulatory practice in Australia.

Red Tape Reduction

In a similar vein, the ACNC has spearheaded initiatives consistent with the government's deregulation agenda. Amongst the policy drivers for the establishment of the ACNC was that it develop a "report once, use often" mechanism so that charities could be relieved from repeatedly providing the same information to various governments and departments within governments. Many charities that supported the establishment of a charity regulator did so believing they had entered into an informal compact where the increase in accountability and transparency was offset by reduced red tape.

The problem for the ACNC was that we had the object "to promote the reduction of unnecessary regulatory obligations on the Australian NFP sector,"[32] but neither explicit powers nor the budget to achieve administrative simplification. As already noted, an additional two objects were added to the ACNC Bill after the Cabinet had approved the proposal and budget. So the new regulator had the statutory object but limited leverage with Commonwealth agencies, and none at all with state and territory governments. Moreover, research commissioned from Ernst & Young by the ACNC in 2013 provided evidence that the overwhelming red tape impost was from the governments' tendering, contracting, monitoring, and acquittal requirements. The ACNC contributed just 0.01 per cent of the regulatory burden.[33] In fact, the ACNC had relieved potential duplication by accepting reports developed for states and territories as meeting its requirements for the first three years of operation. Undeterred, the ACNC developed a "Charity Passport": an electronic compilation of key corporate data required by governments in their dealings with charities which was drawn from the information charities had provided at the point of registration with the ACNC, or in their Annual Information Statements. This information is then freely available to government agencies in all jurisdictions to ensure that the data, provided once, is used often. Government agencies that use the Charity Passport simply need a charity's legal name or unique identifier when interacting for multiple purposes, thus avoiding the repeated requests to provide the same information. The ACNC is also home of the National Standard Chart of Accounts devised as a data dictionary for NFPs that reduces acquittal costs of different agency contracts with charities. The uncertainty regarding the ACNC's future slowed implementation, but adoption should accelerate following the government's decision to retain the ACNC.

Similar work is under way for states and territories to harmonize their reporting requirements with the ACNC to reduce duplication for charities.[34] These bilateral negotiations slowed dramatically with the change of government in September 2013, but gained new momentum with the decision in July 2015 of Consumer Affairs Commissioners to harmonize jurisdictional reporting requirements for ACNC-registered charities. Similarly, the state revenue commissioners agreed in December 2015 to establish a working party to investigate alignment with the ACNC. It is noteworthy that these initiatives anticipated the government's decision to preserve the ACNC. The key drivers are reducing the administrative burden on charities and the potential savings to agency budgets.

The ACNC Register—A One-Stop Shop

The reduction in administrative burden is generally measured on community, business, or government entities. However, the impact can be as dramatic for members of the public. The provision of free, accessible, up-to-date information on a credible register of charities has dramatically reduced the time required for community members to undertake their due diligence when considering donating or volunteering. The Register is at the heart of the ACNC, and its elements are set down in legislation.[35] There is no ACNC without a Register, and conversely there is no Register without a regulator. The story behind the creation of this Register is one of dogged resolve. At its inception, the ACNC was handed a paper-based list of 56,400 charities by the ATO. We were determined to ensure easy equitable access by digital means. We regularly repeated a contact cycle that began with mail outs and then winnowed the numbers down by identifying potentially inoperative charities from return-to-sender lists with follow-up desktop searching and data matching. Since the launch of the Charity Register in July 2013, some 13,500 charities have had their status revoked, as they were no longer operating or had not met their obligations for two years (the latter category including nearly 8,000 charities). The Charity Register now holds detailed information about Australia's 54,000 charities.

Research and Use of Data

In keeping with our "report once, use often" commitment, the information provided by charities in their Annual Information Statements has been used to create the first comprehensive analysis of charities in Australia.

Having an online database allowed us to easily provide data to an independent agency for analysis. The ACNC commissioned Curtin University to analyse the 2013 Annual Information Statement data, and the resulting *Australian Charities 2013* Report[36] was very positively received. We then commissioned Curtin University to undertake further analysis on religious organizations and overseas aid organizations.[37] Importantly, charities themselves quickly saw the utility of the data—a peak body in one state analysed the data and used it in its budget negotiations with government. The Centre for Social Impact and the Social Policy Research Centre at the University of New South Wales won the contract to analyse the 2014 Annual Information Statements. With financial information included for the first time, its analysis, *Australian Charities Report 2014*,[38] constitutes Australia's first authoritative and comprehensive analysis of charities' finances. There is a dedicated website which enables users to interpret the data in multiple ways, such as by location, activity and size.[39]

The ACNC has also actively promoted and commissioned research to provide an empirical base for our work. A companion research project undertaken during 2015 by Deloitte Access Economics has investigated the material benefits to the states and territories of aligning with the ACNC.[40] This has provided a concrete base on which to progress discussions with those jurisdictions. In addition, we have been active participants in the key academic researchers group, spoken at academic and professional conferences, provided a research award, and commissioned surveys into trust in charities. The ACNC is committed to closing the feedback loop and providing data back to charities and the Australian community. There has never before been a census analysis of charities in Australia. In addition to analysing the data, we have made it available to the general public on data.gov.au and on australiancharities.acnc.gov.au. This use of data models good practice to the sector and provides information that can be used for advocacy, planning, and program development.

The Charities Act 2013 (Cth)

Many Australians see charity as the provision of free services to those in necessitous circumstances. However, the Charities Act 2013 (Cth) gives a more contemporary definition and defines a charity and charitable purposes. This Act is based on the heritage of the Statute of Elizabeth of 1601 and *Pemsel's* case,[41] and is informed by recent Australian High Court cases that have generally extended the conventional understanding of the limits of charity, such as the decisions associated with *Central Bayside*,[42] *Word Investments*,[43] and *Aid/Watch*.[44] The Charities Act 2013 came into effect on January 1, 2014, and it affirms that a charity must have charitable purposes that are for the public benefit.[45] Any other non-charitable purposes must be incidental or ancillary to, and in furtherance or in aid of, these charitable purposes. The Act requires a charity to be not-for-profit, not have a disqualifying purpose,[46] and not be an individual, a political party, or a government entity.[47] This Act uses familiar concepts from the common law and modernizes them by including additional charitable purposes, such as the promotion or protection of human rights and the promotion of reconciliation, mutual respect, and tolerance within Australia. It also affirms that a charity may itself advance public debate about a charitable purpose as an independent (non-ancillary) charitable purpose in itself.

Managing in a Time of Uncertainty

Uncertainty attended the establishment of the ACNC from its inception. While the ACNC Taskforce had the benefit of supportive Ministers, the fledgling ACNC operated in an environment where the polls pointed decisively to a change of government, and the opposition at the time (a coalition of Liberal Party and National Party) was opposed to the regulation of charities. During the election, I sought advice from the Australian government solicitor as to my duties and responsibilities as commissioner should the Coalition Parties win the government and retain their resolve to abolish the ACNC. This advice was necessary given the likelihood that the new government would not control the Senate (the Upper House), which is necessary in the Australian Parliament in order to pass most types of legislation. This, combined with the likely ongoing support of Labor and the Greens for the ACNC, meant that simply repealing the ACNC Act was likely to be unavailable to the government, and the ACNC would operate within considerable policy tension.[48]

Statutory office holders, such as commissioners, are servants of the Parliament, not the government of the day. I am appointed to administer an Act (or Acts) of Parliament. The advice was concise and clear. As the commissioner appointed to administer the ACNC Act, I was legally required to do so until, and unless, the Parliament amended or repealed the Act. The executive of the ACNC (the commissioner and two assistant commissioners) consulted with the Advisory Board chair, Commissioner Robert Fitzgerald AM. We were all committed to robust charity regulation and respectful of the democratic process. We determined it was our responsibility to concentrate on core tasks such as building the Register and providing advice to charities on their new obligations as registered entities.

Our relationship with government was also ambiguous, as the ACNC Act sat within the Treasury portfolio and the Charities Act between Treasury and Social Services. Following the change of government in 2013, the lead Minister, the Assistant Treasurer, ceded policy leadership to the Minister for Social Services, who was committed to abolishing the ACNC. He was frustrated in this, with the Senate staunchly opposed to abolishing the new charity regulator. The Minister's department severed all communication with the ACNC in July 2014, creating a difficult operational environment. The two subsequent ministers for social services softened the government's stance and then reversed the policy position.

For charities as well, this was a very confusing time. After the 2013 election, the Minister spoke of his intention to abolish the ACNC, but the ACNC itself was continuing to provide guidance on how charities should meet their regulatory commitments. Should charities just ignore the ACNC advice and wait for the repeal of the ACNC Act? The initial slow submission of 2013 Annual Information Statements was treated sensitively by the ACNC, as we gave charities the benefit of the doubt for the first reporting period, in light of the prevailing confusion.

For the ACNC, this uncertainty slowed the rate at which we could progress key initiatives such as reducing red tape by harmonizing reporting requirements with the states and territories. Like the charities, these governments and their agencies asked themselves whether they should commit resources to a national regulator which would be gone as soon as the Commonwealth government could marshal the votes in the Senate. For most, the initial answer was in the negative. However, as the comments from the Commonwealth government softened, the state and territory jurisdictions moved to positive re-engagement with the ACNC, collaboration on regulatory and reporting harmonization, and administrative simplification. Senior ACNC staff quietly but actively engaged in bilateral discussions with senior officials across the states and territories. With policy certainty, momentum is building for harmonization within the national regulatory architecture that the ACNC affords.

For the ACNC staff, the ongoing uncertainty and the sustained hostility from the government wore some down. We had a high attrition rate in the six months after the change of government in September 2013, but, significantly, this was not from amongst senior staff. The two assistant commissioners and I declared to staff that we would see it through, whatever the outcome. I committed to being there for the duration of the ACNC Act and personally taking down the shingle if we got to that point! Similarly, most of the eight directors remained committed to the new regulator they had moved jobs to help create. The stability of senior staffing had a calming effect on the general staff. In addition, we undertook to keep the staff informed. What had been informal Friday morning teas catered by staff became more sober events with weekly updates on developments. We consistently delivered the same message: our job was not politics, and the only thing we could do was to do a good job and provide an effective service to the community and charities. In the early days, the anxiety on staff faces was palpable, but as time passed, the faces relaxed. Sector support remained high; the government did not develop the necessary second Repeal Bill;[49] the Senate determination to reject any ACNC repeal remained;[50] ministerial changes saw a softening in rhetoric, with relevant new ministers indicating it was low on the government's priorities;[51] and successive budgets were not cut. And on top of that, we received many plaudits from users of our services for the professionalism, timeliness, and friendliness of the staff. The announcement made to staff on our assured future on March 4, 2016, elicited both excitement and relief.

Concluding Comment

At the time of this writing, the ACNC had its fourth assistant treasurer and fourth Minister for social services in three years. The change resulted from a ministerial reshuffle in September 2015 following internal party-room voting to change Prime Minister (Australia's fifth leadership change in five years). The July 2016 election resulted in a modest change to the ministerial personnel involved. The ACNC Act will continue to sit within the Treasury portfolio, but it will be overseen by the Minister for Small Business. This unusual arrangement is likely driven by the pragmatics of ministerial workloads rather than political rationales. The Charities Act will continue to be overseen by both Treasury and Social Services, requiring the ACNC to relate to two Ministers. The unstable political backdrop is a key sub-plot to the story of the establishment of the ACNC. The steadfastness of the NFP sector in support of the regulator they fought to establish is another deep strand of this narrative. As noted earlier, the NFP sector in Australia has a track record of effective advocacy—undoubtedly related to the esteem with which charities are generally held in the community and the political capital which that carries. Peak bodies and key sector leaders retained their support for the ACNC and lobbied to ensure its survival. It is indeed noteworthy that the ACNC was not created in response to a regulatory scandal, but at the initiative of the sector itself.

The continued existence of this initially contested regulator is testimony to the willingness of the overwhelming majority of Australian charities to do the right thing, to increase accountability and transparency, and to work with the regulator. We at the ACNC respect their various missions and are committed to providing them with a secure, manageable, and enduring regulatory environment.

Notes

1 Deloitte Access Economics, *Australian Charities and Not-For-Profits Commission, Cutting Red Tape: Options to Align State, Territory and Commonwealth Charity Regulation: Final Report* (Deloittes, 2016), accessed September 5, 2016, http://www.acnc.gov.au/ACNC/ACNC/Publications/Reports/CuttingRedTape.aspx.
2 In his 2009 report of observations of the not-for-profit (NFP) sector in Australia, the CEO of the Muttart Foundation, Bob Wyatt, lamented the fragmentation of Australian charities and NFPs into industry groups and the resultant diminished capacity for coordinated lobbying.
3 ACOSS describes itself as the peak body of the community sector and the voice for low-income people in Australia, http://www.acoss.org.au/, accessed September 5, 2016.

4 CCA is a member-based peak body focused on building communities by enhancing the work of Australia's not-for-profit sector: http://www.communitycouncil.com.au/, accessed September 5, 2016.

5 Philanthropy Australia is the national peak body for philanthropy. It describes its mission as leading an innovative, growing, influential, and high-performing philanthropic sector in Australia, http://www.philanthropy.org.au/ accessed September 5, 2016.

6 ACFID is an independent national association of Australian non-government organizations working in the field of international aid and development, https://acfid.asn.au/, accessed September 5, 2016.

7 Australian Bureau of Statistics, *Australian Industry 2013–14*, Cat.no. 8155.0 (Canberra: ABS, 2015), released June 29, 2015 http://www.abs.gov.au/AUSSTATS/abs@.nsf/allprimarymainfeatures/A1C2F9FF5A38EFC9CA257FBF00114070?opendocument.

8 N. Cortis et al., *Australian Charities Report 2014* (Sydney: Centre for Social Impact, and Social Policy Research Centre, 2015), accessed August 13, 2016, https://www.acnc.gov.au/ACNC/Pblctns/Rpts/CharityReport2014/ACNC/Publications/Reports/CharityReport2014.aspx.

9 The *Australian Charities Report 2014* summarizes sources of income for charities in 2014–15.

10 Industry Commission, *Charitable Organisations in Australia*, Report No. 45 (Melbourne: Industry Commission, 1995); Commonwealth of Australia, Inquiry into the Definition of Charities and Related Organisations, *Report* (Canberra: Treasury, 2001); Parliament of the Commonwealth of Australia, Senate Standing Committee on Economics, *Disclosure Regimes for Charities and Not-for-Profit Organisations* (Canberra: Senate, 2008); Productivity Commission, *Contribution of the Not-for-Profit Sector: Research Report* (Melbourne: Productivity Commission, 2010); Australia's Future Tax System Review Panel, *Report to the Treasurer* (Canberra: Treasury, 2009); Parliament of the Commonwealth of Australia, Senate Economics Legislation Committee, Tax Laws Amendment (Public Benefit Test) Bill 2010 (Canberra: Senate, 2010).

11 Treasury, *Final Report: Scoping Study for a National Not-for-profit Regulator* (Canberra: AGPS, 2011), accessed August 13, 2016, http://archive.treasury.gov.au/documents/2054/PDF/20110706%20-%20Final%20Report%20-%20Scoping%20Study.pdf.

12 Treasury, *Scoping Study Final Report*, 57.

13 The Australian Catholic Bishops' Conference successfully lobbied for the inclusion of a new category of NFP body in the ACNC Act, a *Basic Religious Charity*. To be classified as such, a body must have its sole purpose as religious, must not have a legal form or tax deductible status for its donations, and must not be in receipt of government grants over $100 000 in a three-year period. Most local parishes would fit this profile.

14 Council of Australian Governments, *Regulatory Impact Assessment of Potential Duplication of Governance and Reporting Standards for Charities* (Canberra: COAG, 2013), accessed August 13, 2016, https://www.coag.gov.au/sites/default/files/COAG%20Regulatory%20Impact%20Assessment%20of%20Potential%20Duplication%20of%20Governance%20and%20Reporting%20Standards%20for%20Charities.pdf.

15 Highly influential over a sustained period of time were David Crosbie, CEO of the CCA and his chair, Reverend Tim Costello; deputy CEO of ACOSS, Dr Tessa Boyd-Caine, and CEO, Dr Cassandra Goldie; and Father Brian Lucas, general secretary of the Australian Catholic Bishops' Conference.

16 The first version of the Exposure Draft was released by Treasury on December 9, 2011, with a closing date for feedback of January 16, 2012, to allow for the Australian Christmas shutdown period.

17 Australian Charities and Not-for-profits Commission Bill 2012 (Cth), cl. 15–5(1).

18 The Bill included "Not-for-profits" in its title, despite the contents confining the role to charities. This retained the policy aspiration of the government to eventually include all NFPs with a legal form, while recognizing the contested environment within which the Bill was being debated.

19 The inherent tension between the transparency and red tape reduction imperatives has had to be managed carefully.

20 Australian Charities and Not-for-profits Commission Act 2012 (Cth), Ch. 2 Part 2–2; Ch. 5.

21 Australian Charities and Not-for-profits Commission Act 2012, Ch. 3.

22 The position was widely advertised and the interview panel comprised the public service commissioner, the secretary of treasury, and the secretary of the Department of Human Services.

23 *Commission of Taxation of the Commonwealth of Australia v Word Investments Ltd* (2008) 236 CLR 204.

24 Australian Charities and Not-for-profits Commission Act 2012, s. 15–5(2)(b).

25 Australian Charities and Not-for-profits Commission, accessed October 23, 2016, www.acnc.gov.au.

26 The *Ask ACNC* sessions were developed after the deadline for the first year of reporting had passed and some 10,000 charities had failed to submit their first Annual Information Statement. We conducted 36 sessions in 32 locations across Australia, improving the submission rate.

27 Australian Charities and Not-for-profits Commission Act 2012, Ch. 4.

28 Australian Charities and Not-for-profits Commission, *Charity Compliance Report December 2012—December 2014 and Beyond* (Melbourne: ACNC, 2015), accessed August 13, 2016, https://www.acnc.gov.au/ACNC/Publications/Reports/ComplianceRpt2012_2014.aspx.

29 The default reporting period in the ACNC Act is the financial year, but a significant minority of charities operate on a calendar year, or on a different cycle.

30 Australian Charities and Not-for-profits Commission Act 2012, Ch. 6.

31 Australian Government, "Regulator Performance Framework," (2014), accessed August 13, 2016, https://www.cuttingredtape.gov.au/resources/rpf.

32 Australian Charities and Not-for-profits Commission Act 2012, s. 15–5(1)(c).

33 Ernst & Young, *Research into Commonwealth Regulatory and Reporting Burdens on the Charity Sector: A Report Prepared for the Australian Charities and Not-For-Profits Commission* (Canberra: Ernst & Young, 2014).

34 South Australia and the Australian Capital Territory agreed to harmonize with the ACNC in 2013, but other jurisdictions were not prepared to commit because of the uncertainty regarding its future.

35 Australian Charities and Not-for-profits Commission Act 2012 s. 40–5.

36 Penny Knight and David Gilchrist, *Australian Charities 2013: The First Report on Charities Registered with the Australian Charities and Not-for-profits Commission* Report for the ACNC (Perth: Curtin University Not-for-profit Initiative, 2014), accessed September 5, 2016 http://www.acnc.gov.au/ACNC/Pblctns/Rpts/Curtin_Report/ACNC/Publications/Reports/Curtin_Report.aspx.

37 Penny Knight and David Gilchrist, *Australia's Faith-based Charities* (Melbourne: ACNC, 2015), accessed August 13, 2016, http://www.acnc.gov.au/ACNC/Pblctns/Rpts/Faith/ACNC/Publications/Reports/Faith.aspx?hkey=d726a00b-acef-4dbc-b603-f66bf3d42567.

38 Cortis et al., *Australian Charities Report 2014.*

39 "Information on the ACNC Register," accessed October 23, 2016, http://www.acnc.gov.au/ACNC/FindCharity/About_Register/ACNC/Reg/Info_Reg.aspx?hkey=9497ea1e-1885–4f6f-bb73–1676e875ddbc.

40 Deloitte Access Economics, *Australian Charities and Not-For-Profits Commission, Cutting Red Tape.*

41 Statute of Charitable Uses 43 Eliz. 1, c. 4; and *Commissioners for Special Purposes of Income Tax v Pemsel* [1891] AC 531.

42 *Central Bayside General Practice Association Limited v Commission of State Revenue* [2006] HCA 43.

43 *Commissioner of Taxation of the Commonwealth of Australia v Word Investments Limited* [2008] HCA 55.

44 *Aid/Watch Incorporated v Commissioner of Taxation* [2010] HCA 42.

45 Charities Act 2013 (Cth), ss. 5, 6.

46 Charities Act 2013 (Cth), s. 11.

47 Charities Act 2013 (Cth), s. 5.

48 In the Australian electoral system, the Senate is voted for fixed terms and the House of Representatives for up to three years with the election date set by the government of the day.

49 The government tabled the ACNC Repeal Bill (No. 1) on its first Repeal Day on March 19, 2014. This was a brief document that foreshadowed Repeal Bill (No. 2), which would detail the arrangements for a successor agency. On the second Repeal Day on October 23, 2014, Repeal Bill No. 2 was not tabled.

50 The government scheduled Repeal Bill No. 1 for two days of debate in the House of Representatives on December 3–4, 2014, the last sitting week. A journalist from the *Sydney Morning Herald* phoned each of the independent Senators on December 3 and asked them how they intended to vote—the Repeal Bill would not have passed. It was withdrawn from debate the next day. On June 24, 2015, a motion that the government withdraw the ACNC Repeal Bill to give certainty to the ACNC was passed by the Senate on the voices with no debate, with the government choosing not to speak against the motion.

51 There was a ministerial reshuffle on December 19, 2014, and a new assistant treasurer, Hon. Josh Frydenberg MP, was announced along with a new minister for social services, Hon. Scott Morrison MP. Both ministers made statements that the abolition of the ACNC was a low policy priority for the government.

12 Reflections on Birthing a Regulator

Ursula Stephens

Introduction

Australia's charitable and nonprofit sector is unique in several respects. Its development throughout the twentieth century has reflected the combined political fortunes of conservative and progressive governments. Despite persistent efforts, the sector has never been able to come together under a unified national peak body and as a consequence has suffered from a crisis of identity, which is yet to be fully resolved. This chapter examines how the sector has organized itself in response to significant government reforms in Australia since the 1990s. The creation of an Australian charity regulator emerged from two competing, yet complementary, agendas: the sector sought respite from burgeoning compliance regimes, whilst the government of the day recognized opportunities for broader regulatory and taxation reform emerging from the sector's willingness to support recommendations of a report by the Productivity Commission.[1] The chapter also reflects on the impact of the new regulator, the Australian Charities and Not-for-profits Commission (ACNC), on the sector and explores challenges the ACNC may face in regulating a sector that has worked hard to "save" it. The author was an elected member of the Australian Parliament during the period of 2002 to 2014 and brings perspectives of the sector, the government, and the political environment from within which the ACNC emerged.

Australia's colonial history, forged from convict settlements in a landscape devoid of built infrastructure, shaped the development of many institutions. Religious organizations played an important role in social welfare provision, supported through philanthropic donations from home and abroad. The country's oldest charity, the Benevolent Society, was founded in 1813 as the New South Wales Society for Promoting Christian Knowledge and Benevolence. Post-World War II immigration influx brought many skilled migrants from non-English speaking countries, triggering the creation of formalized multicultural groups and associations advancing the welfare of these migrants and their families. Importantly, at this time, while other countries sought to nationalize their social services, Australia did not, although social services continued to be subsidized and supported by government.

Nonprofits, therefore, have a long history of delivering services to their members, their clients, or to the wider community through the provision of education, sports, arts, culture, worship, welfare, and community services. And Australia's charitable institutions and nonprofits have enjoyed strong public trust over many decades.

Under the Australian Constitution, the regulation of charities has primarily fallen to state and territory governments, with the exception of taxation, which is deemed a federal (national) government responsibility. State governments oversee incorporation of most nonprofit organizations and license them to raise funds. The emergence of New Public Management (NPM) in the 1980s began to shape conservative governments' approaches to free-market models and created major upheaval in traditional economic sectors, including the nonprofit sector. In Australia, the national conservative government commissioned the Hilmer Review into national competition approaches.[2] It introduced administrative reforms based on ideas of contestability, user choice, transparency, and incentive structures. Governments pursued alternative forms of service delivery to identify the "least-cost" methods.[3] Improvements in technology facilitated the disaggregation of the costs of providing services and provided new ways for services to be packaged. Service delivery options included funder-purchaser-provider agreements, outsourcing, and privatization. Australia's state governments embraced NPM in different ways and at different rates. The capacity of the national government to influence this shift was via the Commonwealth Grants Commission, through which the federal government makes payments to the state and territory governments. Financial incentives and penalties are a potent lever for policy reform. The introduction of NPM, therefore, led to massive public-sector disruption and the introduction of new contracting provisions for "non-essential" government services. These were incorporated into a National Competition Policy framework (NCP), which created a market mechanism for tendering for public services.

Public choice theory rejects an advocacy role for nonprofits, promoting a more narrow view of their role as merely a function of the private market. There were few national peak organizations to identify and promote common interests across the sector, which was organized (for government purposes) into industry classifications such as education, health, housing, arts, each with its own sphere of influence. Larger charities organized and lobbied state governments on issues that impacted on them, while smaller nonprofits, operating outside the nationally developed NCP framework, continued oblivious to these reforms. However, The NCP framework drove rapid reform across the economy, creating a challenging environment for nonprofit organizations required to compete for government funding of services, not only with each other but also with the private sector. As the industry, business, and financial sectors were scrambling to respond to the expectations of the government in this new policy framework, so too the public sector struggled to manage this reform agenda. The nonprofit sector, perceived to be operating mainly under state jurisdiction, was not considered significant.

As Australia's economy grew, the nonprofit sector expanded, both in service delivery and in wider political and policy influence. The government adopted the Australian System of National Accounts in 1993 to expand the core national accounts for selected areas of interest and as part of this process referred the structure and complex taxation treatments of charities to the Industry Commission for consideration. Large charities working across a range of services (housing, poverty alleviation, international aid, community services, and aged care) were alert to the impact of "unrelated business" provisions in their organizations and lobbied hard against any change. The Industry Commission Inquiry into Charitable Organisations[4] determined that nonprofits did not seek to compete on price to gain market share and therefore should continue to enjoy income tax exemption on their unrelated business income. By 1996, many new organizations had emerged in the community arts, environment, international development, aged care, and migrant services arenas, and with them, a number of national peak bodies. The federal government provided funding for peak organizations and funded a range of consultative mechanisms with the sector. The sector's role was broadly accepted as including legitimate advocacy for policy influence and promoting change on social, cultural, and economic issues.

The election of conservative governments across the world in the 1990s signalled a renewed commitment to NPM and a re-emphasis on economic reform through tighter controls of public policy. In Australia, the conservative government elected in 1996 acted quickly to rein in the influence of nonprofit organizations. Following that, an international summit on Non Profit Leadership in 2001 and a second summit in 2004[5] focused on the importance of financial stability, strategic challenges of leadership, forging relationships and partnerships, advancing philanthropy, governance, mission, role of trustees, financial constraints, changing expectations of governments, and philanthropy.[6] Organizations identified many challenges for the sector as the government introduced regulatory and accountability mechanisms to manage risks associated with competitive tendering. These included policy fragmentation, loss of expertise within government, and lack of contract management skills within government and the sector. Many struggled with the introduction of the Goods and Services Tax (GST) in 2000 and the transaction costs of competitive tendering processes.

Different parts of the sector responded to this environment in the way most suited to their relationship with government. Following claims that CARE International (chaired by former conservative Prime Minister Malcolm Fraser) had links to the Global Relief Foundation, which had been found in the United States to have funded terrorist activities and was listed as among "Designated Charities and Potential Fundraising Front Organizations for Foreign Terrorist Organizations,"[7] the International Aid sector organized itself through the Australian Council for International Development

(ACFID). ACFID developed codes of conduct to create a framework for working with government through the Foreign Affairs portfolio. The Fundraising Institute Australia, whose membership comprised fundraisers for large charities, also developed codes of conduct and began lobbying for harmonization of state-based fundraising legislation.

The federal government also tried to organize the sector to suit its own purposes, creating several peak bodies. In 1999, 30 women's organizations funded under a national grants program were replaced by three funded "secretariats," the YWCA, the Business and Professional Women's Association, and the National Council of Women Australia (NCWA). The government also created Volunteering Australia to promote volunteerism in Australia. Its membership was unclear, and it had no mandate. As Melville and Perkins argue, a peak organization can only be created by the sector it represents, "meaning such decisions cannot legitimately be made by governments."[8]

Battle Lines Were Drawn

Following the 2001 election, when the Howard government won its third term, the relationship between the government and the sector became more fractious. Conservative think tanks challenged the advocacy role of nonprofits that were critical of government, singling out environmental organizations for scrutiny and criticism.[9] The Report of the Charities Definition Inquiry (CDI) noted, "That the existence in the tax provisions of a number of categories that entities may fit into under the tax legislation can be a cause of confusion."[10] It also noted,

> Much of the confusion in the sector is related to what tax or other concessions attach to what type of entities and what the boundaries arc between different types of entities. This is not surprising given the wide range of categories of entities that can access the concessions.[11]

Unlike the United States and Canada, in Australia (as in New Zealand), the Australian Taxation Office (ATO) imposed no annual or financial reporting requirements on charities and nonprofit organizations. Prior to 2000, Australian charities and nonprofits undertook self-assessment of their taxation status. The introduction of the Goods and Services Tax (GST) in 2000 brought charities and nonprofits into a reportable system for the first time.

Following the release of the CDI Report, the government proceeded with a draft Charities Bill in 2003. Nonprofit organizations in receipt of public donations to fund their advocacy found their charitable status being challenged. An organization endorsed to access tax concessions—including tax exemption as a charity and deductible gift recipient (DGR) status—would need to be endorsed by the ATO, have its charity status attached to its Australian Business Number, and have its information accessible to the public through the Australian Business Register. The Treasurer also announced that the draft legislation had been referred to the Board of Taxation for consultation with the charitable sector to determine "whether the public benefit test in the exposure draft should require the dominant purpose of a charitable entity to be altruistic, as recommended by the [CDI Report]."[12] There was widespread criticism of the proposal, which made the ATO responsible for administering this legislation while also having the authority to determine if an organization was in breach of it. Organizations argued that defending their charitable status through the judicial system could be "potentially devastating to charities in terms of the financial costs."[13]

The government then appointed the Institute of Public Affairs (IPA) to audit how nonprofit organizations lobby or work with government departments. The IPA had already published a series of papers calling for greater disclosure and accountability by organizations receiving funding from and working with government agencies, arguing that nonprofits represent a challenge to elected governments in democracies,[14] because the electorate has no direct control over these organizations, their activities, or their finances. It was particularly critical of environmental groups and those involved in foreign aid delivery. The IPA audit[15] covered eight government departments and agencies with substantial dealings with non-government organizations (NGOs). Seven government departments, including those responsible for immigration and multicultural affairs, families and community services, health and ageing, and environment, along with AusAID, participated in the study.[16] It was to produce a comprehensive assessment of the links between key Commonwealth government departments and their client NGOs—a framework for assessing the role and standing of NGOs based on the information requirements of those departments and ministers, a framework for a database of NGOs, including their standing, and a proposed trial protocol that requested NGOs to supply information about their organization that would be available publicly.[17] This IPA report and the draft Charities Bill 2003 led to further escalation of tensions between the government and the sector.

The debate about the accountability, funding and the ability of NGOs to lobby for their causes without losing their charity status was now squarely on the public agenda. The redefinition of a charitable organization and proposal to redefine the traditional notion of the public benefit test, as well as the IPA audit designed to allow government to reshape its relations with NGOs, triggered widespread debate and criticism. The draft Charities Bill was heavily criticized in parliamentary debates and was withdrawn prior to the 2004 election. The government announced it would not proceed with the draft Bill. Instead it would maintain the status quo on the common law meaning of a charity, while extending the current meaning of a charity to include certain child care and self-help groups, and closed or contemplative religious orders. The government also announced the delayed introduction of changes requiring charities to be endorsed in order to access relevant tax concessions until July 2005. However, it continued to press for changes through regulation and Tax Office rulings; more punitive clauses were included in contractual agreements, and funding levels were cut.[18] Sector leaders recognized the cumulative impact of these measures, combined with broader reforms occurring in the national regulatory environment, the lack of consultative measures, and "gagging clauses" being included in contracts. The deterioration in relations between the federal government and nonprofits had reached the point where many believed they had been "frozen out" and feared having their funding withdrawn. Maddison and colleagues outlined the extent to which the government undermined dissenting and independent opinion. Referred to by sector leaders as "taming or training," no organization or individual was immune to the tactics of bullying and intimidation, public denigration and harassment.

> It's done very cleverly—by selectively destroying organisations, defunding, public criticism, ministerial interference and criticism, excessive auditing and "review."
> This perception of the diverse range of tactics adopted by governments [demonstrates] how the Federal Government seeks to bully, demean and challenge the credibility of its critics, something it does both publicly and privately.[19]

Organizations were threatened with defunding if they did not come out in support of the government's policies. Government agencies even drafted media statements for them. Stricter controls on media contact were imposed through compliance measures as the government attempted to stymie public debate.

The first attempts to bring the sector together to address these and other strategic issues came in the formation of the National Roundtable of Non-Profit Organisations (NRNO) in 2004, under the chairmanship of Robert Fitzgerald, then president of the Australian Council of Social Service (ACOSS). The NRNO's ambition was to enhance the recognition and promote support for the work of Australia's nonprofit sector and to contribute to the development of research, exchange of ideas, sound policies, and capacity of the nonprofit sector overall to benefit the public.[20] The concept of a peak body implies a level of organization and coordination that was just not possible at that time in the nonprofit sector. Changes in funding arrangements made the coordination task even more difficult. There were tensions from the outset. The NRNO comprised national organizations, many of which had their base in either Sydney or Canberra. Philanthropy Australia in Melbourne acted as host and secretariat in the initial stages, but tensions existed about membership, particularly from members based outside of Victoria (the state with the strongest philanthropic presence in Australia linked directly to conservative politics). Some mid-sized organizations felt excluded. Some faith-based charities chose not to participate, believing they were able to influence government better if they "went it alone."[21]

Sponsored and supported by the participating organizations, the NRNO announced a Nonprofit Regulation Reform Program calling for a fundamental overhaul of the existing legal and regulatory environment to provide a clear, consistent, and coherent framework based on sound public policy considerations.[22] The Howard government had created the Prime Minister's Community Business Partnership in 1999, appointing a group of prominent business and community leaders to provide advice on community business collaboration, philanthropy, and corporate social responsibility.[23] This group developed strategies to promote philanthropy in Australia and lobbied successfully for significant tax concessions for philanthropy. The Community Business Partnership devised a new peak, Non Profit Australia (NPA), which was successful in attaining DGR status in 2006 and was funded by the government for its activities.[24] The governance of this limited liability company was to include an Advisory Board representative of the sector.[25]

Brokering the Peace

In December 2006, in preparation for the federal election, the Labor opposition convened a two-day policy summit in Canberra, where the nonprofit sector was widely represented. Workshops identified key policy issues and recommendations for action by a new progressive government, including the need to address how public debate and dissent had been stifled.[26] It was clear that repairing the relationship between government and the nonprofit sector would be a valuable election commitment. A policy working group began to consider regulatory and taxation issues. Another group was charged with building relationships across the sector, identifying, developing, and testing policy proposals. The sector was fractured, fragmented, and suspicious, as well as intimidated by government threats. Formal meetings, community forums, informal briefings, and confidential consultations proceeded throughout 2007 to build trust and working relationships with different parts of the sector. This work was influenced by advisers from the UK government who had implemented a range of progressive "third-way" reforms. In the lead-up to the 2007 election, with a new opposition leadership team, Labor signalled a series of social policy reforms in its Social Inclusion Policy Statement.[27]

The policy statement included a series of commitments: creating a Social Inclusion Board and an Office for Social Inclusion, developing a Productivity Commission Inquiry, funding for the Australian Bureau of Statistics (ABS) to produce a Non-Profit Institutions Satellite Account in the National Accounts, developing a new and respectful relationship with the sector through the development of a National Compact, removing gagging clauses from funding agreements, considering taxation treatments for nonprofits, shifting the emphasis back to people-centred services, reducing red tape and duplication, addressing anomalies in state-based fundraising regulation; and developing a nonprofit sector workforce strategy.

Sector leaders met to discuss how coherent nonprofit policies could be shaped and how best to improve relationships with government. The NRNO was under-resourced and many of its original membership had moved into different roles. The conservative government had funded NPA to become the representative body through its Advisory Council, but it struggled to find a way to operate as a for-profit company to the nonprofit sector. Its main emphasis was on trying to establish a clearinghouse to leverage the sector's purchasing power in telecommunications and equipment contracts, seeking to duplicate systems already established by the Catholic sector, and attempting to drive competition within the sector.[28] NPA also sought to promote the potential for partnerships and corporate sponsorships. It was perceived by many smaller organizations as distant from the sector itself, and whilst it had an active board, the Advisory Council did not eventuate.

After its election in October 2007, the new Labor government set about reshaping the Australian political landscape. Community expectations were high. An early initiative with limited bipartisan support was the Australia 2020 Summit, held to "help shape a long term strategy for the nation's future."[29] The summit brought together 1,000 participants from across all sectors of society to consider 10 key policy streams, and while dismissed by conservatives and media as a PR stunt, many of the recommendations have been acted upon since the final report was released in May 2010. In the "Stronger Families, Communities and Social Inclusion" stream, for example, there was active debate about the need for a charity regulator and reducing the burden of red tape, as well as the need for the sector to have an independent voice.[30]

The Labor government's administrative orders created complicated cross-portfolio arrangements in an effort to bring together a more coherent policy framework. The outgoing secretary of the Department of Prime Minister and Cabinet, Dr Peter Shergold, left to establish the Centre for Social Impact,[31] another initiative of the former government's Community Business Partnership. The new government also recruited senior bureaucrats from beyond the Australian public service, including policy advisers to the Blair government in the United Kingdom, and seconded employees from the private and nonprofit sectors, to help build the social inclusion framework.

However, enacting the government's social inclusion agenda was very difficult. The narrative of social inclusion had not been tested, and the policy lacked clarity in defining how "social inclusion measures" might be initiated and evaluated for impact. The term "social inclusion" was an adaptation of the "social exclusion" narrative of the UK Blair government, but it had little resonance across government and became so open to interpretation as to lose its policy intent. In fact, it was dropped after the 2010 election. At the time though, this author was appointed parliamentary secretary for the Voluntary Sector and Parliamentary Secretary for Social Inclusion,[32] working across the portfolio areas of Prime Minister and Cabinet, Families and Community Services, and Employment and Workplace Relations. Many agencies struggled to apply a lens of social inclusion to the complex contracting arrangements that were already in place. The sector was equally perplexed. It was as if the social inclusion framework was working in parallel to the "business as usual" agenda of the public service. Treasury, in particular, resisted efforts to engage in consideration of harmonization of fundraising and dismissed the concept of a national regulator as an unjustifiable and unnecessary expense to government. Advisory groups and working parties were appointed, drawing on expertise from the community and business sectors. The Australian Social Inclusion Board was formed, and the coordinating office for social inclusion initiatives was established within the Prime Minister's Department. Funding for NPA was withdrawn, and the company was wound up. The sector may have hoped the funding would be redirected to a more representative body, but it did not exist. The NRNO was not able to gain traction with the sector. Personality conflicts among its membership had irreparably damaged their initial impetus for collaboration, in part because of the divisive nature of the conservative government's competitive tendering processes.

Regulatory and taxation reform were also dominant themes emerging from the Australia 2020 Summit. A Review of the Taxation System was initiated in 2008[33] to take a "root and branch" approach to examine Commonwealth and state government taxes, and interactions with the transfer system, to position Australia to deal with the demographic, social, economic, and environmental challenges that lay ahead.[34] The Senate Economics Committee conducted a parliamentary inquiry into disclosure regimes for charities and the nonprofit sector which reported in 2008, recommending a national regulator for the sector.[35] In March 2009, the government formally requested the Productivity Commission to "undertake a research study on the contributions of the not for profit sector with a focus on improving the measurement of its contributions and on removing obstacles to maximising its contributions to society."[36]

Treasury identified that the best way to ensure that the nonprofit sector was able to benefit from red tape reduction measures was through the work of the Council of Australian Governments (COAG), formed to deal with the split constitutional responsibilities of the Australian federation. The COAG Business and Regulation Competition Working Group of federal and state officials began to include the nonprofit sector in their deliberations and agreed that the states and territories would adopt a Standard Chart of Accounts (SCOA) as an initiative to reduce duplication in reporting by organizations. The SCOA would mean one financial reporting method would be used across all state and federal agencies. Efforts to gain state harmonization of charity treatments proved more difficult. Handing over powers to the federal government for registering charities and nonprofits would eliminate one of the few sources of revenue available to the states and territories, which had agreed to eliminate most state-based taxes with the introduction of the GST in 2000. There was also resistance to what was perceived as regulatory creep.

In 2008, the government commissioned the development of a National Compact. By the end of 2009, work had concluded on the consultations and drafting, and the Compact was formally launched in March 2010 by the Prime Minister, who described it as setting

> benchmarks for an active partnership between Government and the Third Sector . . . where those who advocate on the part of the vulnerable and the dispossessed are not silenced and gagged, but where their opinions are heard and respected. . . .[37]

By the end of 2010, more than 500 organizations had signed on to the Compact.

Managing Expectations

While the Compact was welcomed by the sector, government agencies felt little ownership of its content or its implications for how they engaged with the sector. The government moved quickly to instruct agencies to remove "gagging clauses" from funding agreements, which many resisted. When the Productivity Commission Report was released in 2010,[38] the sector had been immersed in deep consultations and submissions for almost three years, and there was evidence of "consultation fatigue," notwithstanding the goodwill that remained. The government was also dealing with the fall-out of the global financial crisis and concentrated its efforts on maintaining economic stability. Several large charities suffered losses of their investments in the Lehman Brothers collapse, and the government was required to provide emergency funding to ensure contracted services could continue. The energies of the sector were also focused on the wider impacts of the global financial crisis. The Productivity Commission recommended wide-ranging reforms to remove regulatory burdens and costs, and improve accountability of the nonprofit sector. The presiding commissioner, Robert Fitzgerald AO, was supported by Professor Myles McGregor-Lowndes; both were uniquely placed to undertake the analysis required and deeply respected by the sector and by government. McGregor-Lowndes was Australia's pre-eminent academic on charity accounting and regulation, while Fitzgerald had served as a commissioner on the Charities Definition Inquiry and was actively engaged with the sector through his involvement in several significant charities. Fitzgerald considered that "the proposed reforms would directly address concerns about the multiplicity of regulatory requirements, poor collaboration between the sector and governments and emerging capacity constraints. They would thereby create a much stronger foundation for this expanding sector."[39] To consolidate regulatory oversight and enhance transparency, the Commission proposed a "one-stop shop" for Commonwealth-based regulation in the form of a registrar. It also recommended smarter regulation, including a more coherent endorsement process for tax status, to be administered by the proposed Registrar; a new definition of charities; and reforming government purchasing and contracting arrangements.[40]

The Productivity Commission's Report was regarded as a seminal work in the continuing development of the nonprofit reform agenda. The Commission's working papers and consultations were invaluable in educating the public sector about the reach and complexity of the sector. The Report provided a road map for reform which allowed organizations big and small to understand where they fit and how they would benefit from the reform agenda. For the first time, there was a coherent, dispassionate, systematic case for a national regulator presented to the government. The sector overwhelmingly endorsed the position, with ACOSS, the national peak body for social service, later describing the situation as being one in which mission-driven organizations which just wanted to get on with addressing their clients' needs had progressively become subject to both over-regulation and ineffective regulation. "Whether or not organisations should have been pushing back on the regulatory burden that has been imposed on them, the question is: how do we now fix that system?"[41] The Productivity Commission Report summarized the benefit that would come from a national regulator:

> [Not-for-profits'] compliance costs are minimised when they have to face a single clear set of requirements—whether in regard to registration, tax endorsement or fundraising—with common reporting standards and requirements, and where one report satisfies most, if not all, obligations. The public benefits from this when it can easily access information on an NFP from a trustworthy source, as do philanthropists and government agencies. The challenge is to provide a regulatory system that offers these advantages.[42]

The sector welcomed the recommendations and anticipated that the government would adopt them quickly. However, the political environment had shifted. The government's popularity was waning. There was no cabinet minister championing the reforms, and the government had little appetite for further changes in the lead-up to an election. It had attempted a major social reform agenda in health, education, climate change, and aged care, and a massive stimulus program during the global financial crisis of 2008. Although Australia had weathered the financial crisis, policy implementation mistakes and challenges by state governments across a range of fronts made the administration an easy target for public criticism. The political upheaval of 2010, and subsequent leadership change in late 2010, led to the re-election of a minority Labor government.

This government gave stronger focus to administrative accountability and Cabinet processes. It created the National Office for the Non-Profit Sector in the Prime Minister's Department, and a Not-for-Profit Reform Advisory Council was appointed to oversee the whole-of-government reform agenda, including establishing a dedicated nonprofit regulator. High-performing sector leaders were recruited to the public service and embedded in the reform working parties. Paul Ronalds, formerly deputy CEO of World Vision Australia, was appointed to the Department of Prime Minister and Cabinet to implement the government's not-for-profit reform agenda and oversee the establishment of the Office for the Not-for-profit Sector. His team included Sue Woodward seconded from the Victorian-based Public Interest Law Clearing House (now Justice Connect) as a specialist adviser on the sector's legal and regulatory framework. The government appointed a Not-for-Profit Sector Reform Council, comprising sector members and a former state Attorney General to support the work of the office. Ronalds outlined the reform agenda as having three broad aims:

> The first is to improve the way the government and the not-for-profit sector work together. Initiatives under this goal include the National Compact, an extensive work around streamlining funding and grant arrangements. The second goal goes to the streamlining and simplification of regulation, and here the Australian Charities and Not-for-profits Commission is the hallmark reform, along with a range of other tax reforms. The third goal of the not-for-profit reform agenda is to promote the long-term sustainability of the not-for-profit sector. This includes initiatives such as better workforce planning, a comprehensive volunteering strategy, and work on social investment and philanthropy.[43]

Treasury wanted responsibility for developing the scope and reach of a sector regulator. The strongest advocate for the ACNC was the parliamentary secretary to the Treasurer (David Bradbury). Whereas in the previous government, the nonprofit reforms had been the responsibility of social policy Ministers, Parliamentary Secretary Bradbury recognized that for the ACNC to have the independence envisaged by the Productivity Commission, it needed to be within a finance portfolio rather than with the prime minister's own department.[44] The government then established a taskforce to oversee the establishment of the ACNC. Susan Pascoe AO, former Victorian State Services commissioner, was appointed to lead the Taskforce, and Robert Fitzgerald AO as chair of the advisory body for the ACNC, was an ex officio member.

The year 2011 was one of consolidation. Significant progress had been made in streamlining contracts, eliminating rolling one-year funding agreements, and simplifying applications for funding; there was a renewed commitment to the Compact, and Compact champions were recruited within the senior ranks of the public sector. The Not-for-Profit Reform Council continued to advise government on regulatory and taxation reform. However, by the second anniversary of the National Compact, there was growing criticism about the lack of action on sector reform. ACOSS complained that, although it included the right sentiments and words about partnership, respectful relationships and reducing red tape burdens," in fact, there was little concrete improvement in dealings between government and nonprofits, apart from "eliminating so called 'gag' clauses in government contracts."[45]

> Sure the Government has led the way with a raft of proposed legislative and other reforms relating to the regulation and treatment of Charities and NFPs. . . . Much of this reform was highlighted in the 2010 Productivity Commission Report and has been signaled by NFPs for several years as being highly desirable. However what has been noticeable in the manner in which this is being managed is that in many ways the Government really doesn't get it when it comes to working with the NFP sector.[46]

The criticism was harsh, given how much had been achieved since 2007. Sector critics did not acknowledge how much work was being done with state and territory governments, the depth of public sector reform that was being undertaken, or the difficulties of minority government. The irony of arguing that reforms were placing sector organizations under pressure, while complaining about the lack of progress on the reform agenda, was not lost on the key players in the reform process. There was a deep sense of frustration from within the ministerial and advisers' offices that their efforts would never be enough to satisfy the sector. Such commentary also fed into the criticism by the conservative opposition parties that the non-profit reforms were more rhetoric than reality.

Fortunately, not all of the sector agreed. The collapse of Australia's largest childcare provider, ABC Learning (a for-profit company), in 2008, provided an opportunity for government, nonprofit sector, and business to work quickly to resolve what was recognized as a catastrophic corporate failure. The childcare sector had consolidated as government-subsidized private providers such as ABC Learning bought up small, private, and community-based centres, driving up enrolments through incentives and fee discounts. Caught by the global financial crisis, ABC Learning defaulted on loans, and the federal government had to inject $22 million into the company to keep its childcare centres open until the end of 2008, securing the 72,000 childcare places that were at risk.[47] A rescue package to take over 570 ABC Learning centres was developed by a consortium of Mission Australia, the Benevolent Society, the Brotherhood of St Laurence, and Social Ventures Australia, who negotiated additional finance arrangements from the government.[48] The government was quick to give credit to the consortium members for their innovative response to the crisis, while the consortium members were able to provide direct input to Treasury and officials of the Office for the Not-for-Profit Sector about the regulatory challenges of the solution.

Armed with the recommendations of the Productivity Commission, the sector acted to create a new body, the Community Council for Australia (CCA) "to facilitate collaborative relationships and advocate for the not for profit sector on key issues that impact the viability and effectiveness of the sector."[49] The Council elected Rev. Tim Costello as chair and appointed David Crosbie, formerly CEO of the Mental Health Council, as CEO. The CCA positioned itself as a moderate voice for reform and undertook a series of consultations across the sector. Many of its members were in key advisory roles on government policy, including the ACNC working group, and were determined to bring a collective perspective to the reform work being undertaken. Another important factor in helping the sector to establish its independent voice was the emergence of Pro Bono Australia[50] as an independent media source for the sector. Pro Bono Australia aggregated local and international media stories about the sector and provided an active platform for disseminating information using social media and partnering with peak organizations to undertake surveys of the sector on a range of issues.

Meanwhile, the work of the ACNC Taskforce in shaping the national regulator continued. The team recruited to establish the practices of the regulatory functions were chosen for their experience in working with the sector, and the environment in which they operated was one of education and facilitation rather than compliance and regulatory impost. This approach was in stark contrast to the sector's experiences with the ATO. In July 2011, Treasury released its final report on the Scoping Study for a national regulator.[51] The exposure draft of the ACNC Bill followed in early December 2011. It was necessarily complex, given the wide range of existing legislation that would be impacted by the introduction of a new regulator. Opponents were quick to complain that the timing of the release was a ploy to reduce scrutiny of the draft legislation.[52] Intense political lobbying from the sector resulted in the objects of the Bill being expanded and, with that, the proposed role and jurisdiction of the regulator.

The government could not have anticipated that the passage of this Bill, which had so much support from the sector, would be delayed for a full 12 months. The election of the minority government had shifted the balance of parliamentary power and debate in an unforeseen way. The government had to negotiate with independents in the House of Representatives to gain support for critical government legislation including appropriation bills. It was in constant negotiations on a range of fronts, and trade-offs were made to meet the demands of the independent members' support. The legislative program was huge and controversial, especially in relation to climate change, health reforms, and national security issues. Treasury used an inexperienced assistant treasurer to introduce measures to "better target" the tax concessions given to nonprofit organizations following a High Court decision in *Commissioner of Taxation v Word Investments Ltd*.[53] The *Word Investments* decision confirmed that charities were able to use tax concessions intended to support altruistic activities for unrelated commercial activities in their pursuit of funds for charitable purposes. The timing of the new tax measures was poor, the wording clumsy, and its implications were significant, although not understood by the Minister. It was followed closely by another Tax Amendment Bill to limit tax concessions to activities "in Australia," another contentious issue arising in the *Word Investments case*. Some in the sector felt ambushed by the propositions. Consultation on both issues was limited and created a distraction from the work of the Office of the Not-for-Profit Sector.[54]

The draft ACNC legislation emerged from Treasury and was added to the list of controversial legislation. The legislation was subject to intense parliamentary scrutiny, first by the Joint Statutory Committee, which recommended amendments.[55] Then a set of three bills was referred for further inquiry by two Senate Committees: the Australian Charities and Not-for-profits Commission (Consequential and Transitional) Bill 2012, the Australian Charities and Not-for-profits Commission Bill 2012, and the Tax Laws Amendment (Special Conditions for Not-for-profit Concessions) Bill 2012.[56] In the Lower House (the House of Representatives), the bills were referred to the Parliamentary Joint Committee on Corporations and Financial Services. Witnesses appearing before the committees included the interim commissioner of the ACNC Implementation Taskforce, Ms Pascoe, who outlined the work of the Taskforce charged with establishing the ACNC, and assistant commissioner and general counsel Murray Baird,[57] as well as senior staff from the Department of Treasury and Mr Ronalds from the Department of Prime Minister and Cabinet. Opposition committee members challenged the witnesses on several points of regulatory oversight including the intersection between the requirement of the Australian Securities and Investment Commission and the ACNC, potential directors' liabilities of volunteer boards, and the impact of the regulation on philanthropic giving. The legislation was due to come into effect on October 1, 2012. Fr Brian Lucas, representing the Australian Catholic Bishops Conference, summarized the sector's view of the legislation:

> What would be very unfortunate, as this legislation makes its way through the House and the Senate, would be a serious political divide and the risk—should there be a change in government—of repeal. That would leave the sector with a great deal of anxiety and uncertainty.[58]

The opposition had already announced its intention to repeal the legislation when they regained government,[59] and it used submissions from the sector to hone their narrative that the minority government was adding to the regulatory burden and was out of touch with the sector. They quoted sector submissions to argue that the bills were unworkable; would create a heavier regulatory burden on charities, "many of whom are already struggling to meet the demands of government in this area";[60] and there would be uncertainty until agreement was reached with state and territory governments to hand over their powers to the Commonwealth regulator and harmonize their laws.[61] This was a potent argument—one that the government relied upon its public servants to rebut.[62] The difficulty lay in explaining the complexities of the bills; while good work was being undertaken with state and territory governments to harmonize legislation, not one jurisdiction had agreed to hand over powers to the Commonwealth before the bills were introduced. The opposition was able to capitalize on what was described as a great "leap of faith."

> Before the government introduced this new level of regulation, chari-
> ties and not-for-profits in this country were travelling along perfectly
> well. . . . The Catholic sector and the independent schools have stood
> up and said: "We already comply with 50 state bills; we already comply
> with about 20 Commonwealth bills. All you are doing is introducing a
> new level of regulation with which you expect us to comply."[63]

The bills were passed with further amendments following negotiation with the Australian Greens and independent members and came into effect on December 3, 2012. The ACNC was now established and operational, although its demise under a future Coalition government was clear.[64] Within the sector, there was relief and a naïve faith that once established, it would be difficult to overturn the ACNC. The first tranche of the charities register was launched in July 2013, with 57,600 charities transferred from the Australian Securities and Investments Commission's (ASIC's) register. Research undertaken revealed wide public support for the ACNC Register and that the sector was overwhelmingly supportive of the ACNC and its work.[65]

The government's reform agenda continued: promoting social enterprise, encouraging a diversification of financing options, streamlining and refining the regulation of nonprofits and charities, and developing a clearer definition of charities. In 2012, the Not-for-Profit Reform Council's Tax Concessions Working Group released a discussion paper which incorporated recommendations of the Henry Review.[66] The government then released the Charities Bill, which introduced a statutory definition of charity and provided greater certainty over charitable status eligibility.[67] During the parliamentary debate, the opposition announced they would not only oppose the Bill, but if elected, they would seek to repeal it, referring to their earlier legislative achievement with respect to the Extension of Charitable Purpose Act 2004 and arguing "why create a statute where the common law has and does serve us well? Why depart from 400 years of clarity and consistency?"[68]

The sector supported the Bill. In a widely reported statement, the Community Council for Australia outlined its benefits.[69] Of importance to the sector as a whole, the Act made provision for peak bodies within the definitions.[70] The Bill also addressed a presumption of public benefit,[71] another issue that had been subject to parliamentary scrutiny.[72] The Charities Bill was eventually passed with amendments in June 2013. Amid fears of impending electoral defeat, political turbulence continued within the government. The Prime Minister was replaced again, Parliament rose for the winter recess, and the 2013 general election was called in September 2013. On September 7, 2013, Australia elected a new conservative Coalition government.

Back to the Future

Although it did not have control of the Senate (the Upper House), the new government announced, "The adults are back in charge," and it moved to reinstate the Prime Minister's Community Business Partnership[73] and abolish more than 70 advisory bodies, including the Not-for-Profit Sector Reform Council.[74] Policy responsibility for nonprofit regulation and the ACNC was placed with the Treasurer. While some in the sector believed the reforms were embedded, the new government was committed to disbanding the ACNC and returning its regulatory functions to the ATO and ASIC and other bodies. The ACNC Repeal Bill was introduced into the House of Representatives as one of its first pieces of legislation. The ACNC commissioner reflected on the uncertainty about the regulator's future in her second report to Parliament:[75]

> The ACNC has lived in a climate of uncertainty since its inception, and this is likely to continue until Parliament votes on the ACNC Repeal Bills. . . . Despite the confusion and frustration this policy of uncertainty generates for charities, the ACNC will continue to implement its Act as we are legally required to do.

The government believed it had a strong mandate for change (restoring the natural order[76]) and, having opposed campaigns for climate action, also initiated an inquiry into environmental groups eligible to receive tax-deductible donations. The sector recognized the tactics being employed by government MPs, with the support of conservative organizations such as the IPA, which was used by the government to run media commentary about how the sector, and particularly advocacy organizations, were out of control.[77] Ministers implemented measures that restricted access to information and limited the engagement of nonprofits in policy changes. The government imposed unprecedented secrecy about its blockade of refugee boats coming to Australia;[78] nonprofit organizations providing advocacy services to refugees in offshore detention had contracts terminated; the Refugee Council of Australia was defunded.[79] The Drug and Alcohol Council lost its funding and wound itself up,[80] and community legal centres across Australia were forbidden to use Commonwealth money for advocacy or to campaign for law reform.[81] Ronalds observed,

> Environmental groups who had previously sought to constructively engage the Federal Government now saw little prospect of progress. The Chief Executive Officer of the Australian Conservation Foundation, one of Australia's most influential environmental groups, declared

there was "not a lot of point lobbying for policy in Canberra now." Henceforth, the organisation would abandon its "insider" strategy and seek to engage the community directly.[82]

He went on to observe that "Funding cuts to peak bodies were interpreted by many in the sector as a way to reduce nonprofits' policy influence."[83] ACOSS suggested, "Cutting support for vital community expertise and voices is a major mistake. Community voices play a crucial role in providing on-the-ground advice and an important link connecting communities with government decision-making processes."[84] While the government said it was not going to repeal the Not-for-profit Sector Freedom to Advocate Act 2013, enacted by the previous Labor government, ACOSS argued, "You don't get a bigger gag clause than completely defunding community advocacy."[85]

The speed with which the new government acted galvanized the sector to move quickly to defend the role and effectiveness of the ACNC. The CCA and Pro Bono Australia commissioned research to investigate attitudes to the extensive sector reform that had taken place in recent years and to the future of that reform, finding that the ACNC "is seen as the key actor in addressing a number of the areas of concern identified in the survey, including governance, accountability, transparency, and streamlining reporting."[86] The Australian Charities and Not-for-profits Commission (Repeal) (No. 1) Bill was introduced in December 2013 but not brought on for parliamentary debate until December 2014,[87] coinciding with the second anniversary of the ACNC. In defence of the ACNC, opposition members argued that the Repeal Bill provided no alternative arrangements for regulating charities: "The ACNC is more efficient than the Government regulators it replaced, is doing good work and deserves a chance to achieve its three goals of reducing red tape, increasing public trust and strengthening the charities sector."[88] Organizations within the sector were encouraged to speak out in support of the ACNC, but some feared the government's swift retribution. In a public statement, ACNC Advisory Board Chair and Productivity Commissioner Robert Fitzgerald advised the government that

> . . . the key beneficiaries of the repeal of the ACNC are really only those organisations who do not want independent public accountability or transparency but which seek to continue to receive large benefits from the Australian community. All of the failings in the past regulatory regime identified so often and in so many inquiries would remain and be entrenched . . . The opportunities offered by the establishment of a one-stop regulator would be forgone. Independence from the Australian Taxation Office will be abandoned, allowing identified conflicts to persist. The sound, well-functioning and efficient agency, highly respected by much of the sector with considerable expertise and experience will be abolished.[89]

As the debate proceeded in Parliament, David Crosbie, CEO of the CCA, observed that the government was out of touch with the charities sector.[90] Government members appeared to ignore the evidence from surveys of the sector that the ACNC was seen by the majority as a positive development. Uncertainty continued, and parliamentary debate on the Repeal Bill was suspended. Then, after a Cabinet reshuffle in December 2014, the government confirmed that abolishing the ACNC was still its policy, but it was now low on its list of priorities[91]

The sector stepped up its lobbying in support of the ACNC throughout 2014, described by one Canberra journalist as a "tenacious campaign."[92] The government released a discussion paper on options for replacing the ACNC,[93] and the Senate held its own inquiry into the ACNC Repeal Bill. Both of these were inundated with submissions in support of the Commission. Hassan observed,

> It's a lesson too in how to get and sustain reform. The charities regulator was not imposed but born of the sector. It was also recommended by the highly-credible Productivity Commission. It was in incubation a long time. Good things worth fighting for take time and when threatened need a multitude of voices. . . . The charities commission will face tougher times as it steps up to be a regulator with all that that implies. But the sector's successful fight to defend it puts the ACNC in a stellar position to get on with the job.[94]

In 2015, the Senate moved a motion calling on the government to withdraw the Australian Charities and Not-for-profits Commission (Repeal) (No. 1) Bill 2014 to provide certainty to Australia's charities. The motion was passed unopposed, effectively putting the government on notice that the Repeal Bills would not pass through the Senate if put to a vote. After more than two years of uncertainty about the future of the ACNC, and following the 2016 election, the government announced that it would not proceed with the ACNC Repeal Bills and that it would retain the ACNC to progress regulatory reform and improve the nonprofit sector.

Conclusion

A decade of nonprofit sector reform has changed the landscape of Australian nonprofits. Information technology has served to improve links and provide unprecedented resources for galvanizing support and campaigns within and across the sector. Yet the future is as uncertain as ever while a government can unilaterally gag public comment about public policy. The nonprofit sector has gained significant expertise and advocacy skills borne in no small measure of support from progressive Labor governments. It will require tenacity to retain that expertise and influence in coming years. Having fought so hard to achieve a charity regulator in Australia and done so much to champion its continuation, the challenge for the sector will be to ensure that the value of the ACNC's work is measured far beyond compliance reporting to the important educational role that sets it apart from the ATO or ASIC as regulators. As well, the important taxation changes, as recommended by the Productivity Commission, and which form a continuing part of the nonprofit reform agenda, may well bring the ACNC into conflict with the sector. The challenge will be for the sector, having emerged from a period of capacity building, to maintain the goodwill required to achieve strong regulatory reform without retreating to the default position of protecting self-interest.

Notes

1 Productivity Commission, *Contribution of the Not-for-Profit Sector: Research Report* (Melbourne: Productivity Commission, 2010).
2 National Competition Policy Review, *National Competition Policy* (Canberra: AGPS, 1993), accessed October 2, 2016, http://ncp.ncc.gov.au/docs/National%20Competition%20Policy%20Review%20report%2C%20The%20Hilmer%20Report%2C%20August%201993.pdf.
3 Christopher Hood, "The 'New Public Management' in the 1980s: Variations on a Theme," *Accounting, Organizations and Society* 20 (1995): 93.
4 Industry Commission, *Charitable Organisations in Australia*, Report No. 45 (Melbourne: Industry Commission, 1995).
5 *Summit on Non Profit Leadership* (2nd, 7–9 July 2004, Melbourne); *International Summit on Non Profit Leadership* (1st, 2–4 October, 2001, Melbourne).
6 "Not for Profit Leadership Summit—Advertorial," *Pro Bono Australia*, May 24, 2004, accessed September 19, 2016, https://probonoaustralia.com.au/news/2004/05/not-for-profit-leadership-summit-advertorial/.
7 US Department of the Treasury, "Treasury Department Statement Regarding the Designation of the Global Relief Foundation," *Press Release*, October 18, 2002, accessed September 19, 2016, https://www.treasury.gov/press-center/press-releases/Pages/po3553.aspx.
8 R. Melville and R. Perkins, *Changing Roles of Community Sector Peak Bodies in a Neo-Liberal Policy Environment in Australia* (Wollongong: Institute of Social Change and Critical Inquiry, University of Wollongong, 2003).
9 See, e.g., Gary Johns, "Why Champions of Causes Need Close Scrutiny," *The Australian*, January 30, 2002, accessed September 19, 2016, http://ipa.org.au/news/266/why-champions-of-causes-need-close-scrutiny/pg/7; Gary Johns, "NGO Way to Go: Political Accountability of Non-government Organizations in a Democratic Society," *IPA Backgrounder*, 12(3) (2000), accessed September 19, 2016, http://www.ipa.org.au/library/IPABackgrounder12–3.pdf.
10 Commonwealth of Australia, Inquiry into the Definition of Charities and Related Organisations, *Report*, (Canberra: Treasury, 2001), 34 (CDI Inquiry).
11 CDI Inquiry, 34.
12 Australian Board of Taxation, "Terms of Reference," *Consultation on the Definition of a Charity* (2003), accessed September 20, 2016, http://taxboard.gov.au/consultation/definition-of-a-charity/; see also Peter Costello, Treasurer, "Release of Charities Definition Exposure Draft," *Media Release*, No. 059, July 22, 2003, accessed September 20, 2016, http://ministers.treasury.gov.au/DisplayDocs.aspx?doc=pressreleases/2003/059.htm&pageID=003&min=phc&Year=2003&DocType=0.

13 Australian Council for Overseas Aid, *Submission to the Board of Taxation on the Draft Charities Bill* (Canberra: ACFOA, 2003) 8, accessed September 20, 2016, http://taxboard.gov.au/consultation/definition-of-a-charity/.

14 For example, see Johns, "NGO Way to Go"; Mike Nahan, "The Green Movement: Time to Get Serious," *IPA News*, July 22, 2003, accessed September 19, 2016, http://www.ipa.org.au/sectors/food-environment/news/895/the-green-movement-time-to-get-serious/pg/26; Mike Nahan and Don D'Cruz, "NGOs Undermining Democracy," *IPA Review*, December 2004, accessed September 19, 2016, https://ipa.org.au/library/56-4-NGOs%20Undermining%20Democracy.pdf

15 Gary Johns and John Roskam, *The Protocol: Managing Relations with NGOs: Report to the Prime Minister's Community Business Partnership* (Melbourne: Institute of Public Affairs, 2004), accessed September 19, 2016, https://www.ipa.org.au/library/ProtocolWeb.pdf.

16 Johns and Roskam, *The Protocol*, 2.

17 Sid Marris, "Think Tank Accused of 'Sneer and Smear'," *The Australian*, August 4, 2003, 2; Dennis Shanahan, "Howard Tightens Screws on Charities," *Weekend Australian*, August 2, 2003, 5.

18 J. Staples, *NGOs Out In the Cold: Howard Government Policy towards NGOs*, University of New South Wales Faculty of Law Research Series, No. 8 (Sydney: University of New South Wales, 2007).

19 S. Maddison, R. Denniss, and C. Hamilton, *Silencing Dissent: Non-Government Organisations and Australian Democracy* (Canberra: Australia Institute, 2004) quoting from responses to a 2004 survey of NGOs.

20 National Roundtable of Nonprofit Organisations, "Public Statement," 2004: "The Program will be progressed through a consultative process involving the Not for Profit sector, its members, funders, donors and the wider community. It will cover reforms in areas including: National Law and Regulation; Fundraising and Capital Raising; Corporate Structures; Accounting Standards; and Taxation The objective of the Program is to promote organisations and their activities leading to increased employment, volunteerism, capacity building, enhancing efficiency in the delivery of services, integrity and donor confidence."

21 Author's discussions with Mark Lyons and David Thompson.

22 "Calls for Urgent Charity Reform," *Pro Bono Australia*, June 25, 2004, accessed September 13, 2016, http://www.probonoaustralia.com.au/news/2004/06/calls-urgent-charity-reform#sthash.Pt5KOFsm.dpuf.

23 John Howard, Prime Minister, "Announcement of Members of the Prime Minister's Community Business Partnership," *Media Release*, No 11259, August 19, 1999, accessed September 20, 2016, https://pmtranscripts.dpmc.gov.au/release/transcript-11259

24 In 2004–05, $500,000 was provided and $350,000 in 2005–06 under the Community Business Partnership; once the CBP was discontinued, funding for NPA was continued under the Families, Community Services and Indigenous Affairs portfolio.

25 Conversations with Elaine Henry (2015). Diary notes on file with author.

26 Notes of summit on file with author.

27 Australian Labor Party, *Social Inclusion Agenda* (2007). See Emily Long, "The Australian Social Inclusion Agenda: A New Approach to Social Policy?" *Australian Journal of Social Issues* 45 (2010): 161.

28 One organization, Church Resources, had already expanded beyond its original faith-based sector to assist other nonprofits with purchasing equipment and IT: "Church Resources: NFP Savings," *Pro Bono Australia*, February 12, 2007, accessed September 20, 2016, https://probonoaustralia.com.au/news/2007/02/church-resources-nfp-savings/.

29 Kevin Rudd, Prime Minister, "Australia 2020," *Media Release*, February 10, 2008, accessed September 20, 2016, http://trove.nla.gov.au/work/8481427?q=rudd+an d+2020+summit&x=0&y=0&c=book; "Australia 2020 Summit Participants," *Media Release*, March 23, 2008, accessed September 20, 2016, http://parlinfo. aph.gov.au/parlInfo/search/display/display.w3p;query=Id%3A%22media/ pressrel/PLZP6%22.

30 *Australia 2020 Summit: Final Report* (Canberra: Department of the Prime Minister and Cabinet, 2008), accessed September 20, 2016, http://apo.org.au/files/ Resource/2020_summit_report_full.pdf.

31 "Our History," Centre for Social Impact, accessed September 20, 2016, http:// www.csi.edu.au/about-csi/history/.

32 "A Rudd Labor Government and the Third Sector," *Pro Bono Australia*, December 3, 2007, accessed September 20, 2016, https://probonoaustralia.com.au/ news/2007/12/a-rudd-labor-government-and-the-third-sector/.

33 Australia's Future Tax System Review Panel, *Report to the Treasurer* (Canberra: Treasury, 2009).

34 "Australia's Future Tax System," accessed September 20, 2016, http://taxreview. treasury.gov.au/Content/Content.aspx?doc=html/home.htm.

35 Senate Standing Committee on Economics, *Inquiry into the Disclosure Regimes for Charities and Not-For-Profit Organisations: Report* (Canberra: The Senate, 2008), Recommendation 3, accessed September 20, 2016, http://www.aph. gov.au/Parliamentary_Business/Committees/Senate/Economics/Completed%20 inquiries/2008-10/charities_08/index.

36 Julia Gillard, Chris Bowen, Ursula Stephens, "Productivity Commission to Review the Contribution of the Not-for-profit Sector," *Joint Media Release*, No. 017, accessed September 20, 2016, http://ministers.treasury.gov.au/DisplayDocs. aspx?doc=pressreleases/2009/017.htm&pageID=003&min=ceb&Year=&DocT ype=0.

37 Kevin Rudd, "Launch of the National Compact with the Third Sector," March 17, 2010, accessed September 23, 2016, http://pmtranscripts.dpmc.gov. au/release/transcript-17138.

38 Productivity Commission, *Contribution of the Not-for-Profit Sector: Research Report* (Melbourne: Productivity Commission, 2010), accessed September 12, 2016, http://www.pc.gov.au/inquiries/completed/not-for-profit.

39 Productivity Commission, "Wide Ranging Reforms Needed to Strengthen the Not-for-profit Sector," *Media Release*, accessed September 20, 2016, http:// www.pc.gov.au/inquiries/completed/not-for-profit/report#media-release.

40 Productivity Commission, *Research Report*, "Summary of Recommendations."

41 House of Representatives Standing Committee on Economics, Australian Charities and Not-for-profits Commission Bill 2012 and an Associated Bill, Official Committee Hansard (Dr Boyd-Caine, ACOSS, July 26, 2012) 2.

42 Productivity Commission, *Research Report*, 115.

43 Parliamentary Joint Committee on Corporations and Financial Services, Australian Charities and Not-for-profits Commission Bill and Related Bills, *Official Committee Hansard* (Mr Ronalds, September 3, 2012), 1.

44 Conversation with David Bradbury (2015). Diary notes on file with author.

45 "National Compact Two Years On," *Pro Bono Australia*, March 22, 2012, accessed September 23, 2016, https://probonoaustralia.com.au/news/2012/03/ national-compact-two-years-on/.

46 "National Compact Two Years On," *Pro Bono*, March 22, 2012.

47 Alexandra Kirk, "Government Injects $22m Bailout into ABC Learning," *PM*, ABC Radio National, November 7, 2008, accessed September 23, 2016, http:// www.abc.net.au/pm/content/2008/s2413919.htm.

48 Andrew Main, "Goodstart Clears up ABC Learning Mess," *The Australian*, December 4, 2012, accessed September 23, 2016, http://www.theaustralian. com.au/business/wealth/goodstart-clears-up-abc-learning-mess/story-e6frgac6– 1226529122258.

49 "Policy Work," Community Council for Australia, accessed September 23, 2016, http://www.communitycouncil.com.au/content/policy-work.

50 See https://probonoaustralia.com.au/who-we-are/.

51 Australian Treasury, *Final Report: Scoping Study for a National Not-for-profit Regulator* (Canberra: AGPS, 2011), accessed August 13, 2016, http:// archive.treasury.gov.au/documents/2054/PDF/20110706%20-%20Final%20 Report%20-%20Scoping%20Study.pdf.

52 For example, the Catholic Health Network suggested many of its members were unable to review and comment on the exposure draft because of its release during the Christmas/ New Year period: Catholic Health Australia, *Exposure Draft Australian Charities and Not-for-profits Commission Bill: Response to Treasury Consultation* (Canberra: Catholic Health Australia, 2012), 4, accessed October 11, 2016, http://www.cha.org.au/~chaorg/images/submissions/CHA%20 submission%20Exposure%20Draft%20NFP%20Commission%20Bill%20 Jan%202012.pdf. Catholic Social Services Australia expressed similar concerns: see http://www.cssa.org.au/storage/270112_CSSA_Governance_requirements. pdf, accessed October 11, 2016.

53 *Commission of Taxation of the Commonwealth of Australia v Word Investments Ltd* (2008) 236 CLR 204.

54 Paul Ronalds, "Australia: Federal Government and Nonprofit Relations in Australia," in *Rebalancing Public Partnership: Innovative Practice between Government and Nonprofits from Around the World*, ed. John Brothers (Surrey: Gower Publishing, 2015), 109.

55 Parliamentary Joint Committee on Corporations and Financial Services, accessed September 23, 2016, http://www.aph.gov.au/Parliamentary_Business/Committees/ Joint/Corporations_and_Financial_Services/Completed_inquiries/2010–13/ charities/index.

56 Senate Standing Committee on Community Affairs, accessed September 23, 2016, http://www.aph.gov.au/Parliamentary_Business/Committees/Senate/Community_ Affairs/Completed_inquiries/2010–13/charitiescommission/index.

57 Murray Baird had been the solicitor who ran the successful *Word Investments* case to the High Court.

58 Parliamentary Joint Committee on Corporations and Financial Services, Australian Charities and Not-for-profits Commission Bill and Related Bills, *Official Committee Hansard*, (Rev. Lucas, September 3, 2012), 27.

59 Kevin Andrews, "Empowering Civil Society: Major Policy Address: The Coalition's Approach to the Charitable Sector," (Speech delivered at the Menzies Research Centre, Melbourne, June 15, 2012), accessed September 23, 2016, https://www.menziesrc.org/events/item/coalition-policy-announcement-empow ering-civil-society; "Coalition Opposes Charity Definition," *Pro Bono Australia*, June 18, 2013, accessed September 23, 2016, https://probonoaustralia.com.au/ news/2013/06/coalition-opposes-charity-definition/.

60 Parliament of Australia, House of Representatives, *Hansard*, (Mr McCormack, September 18, 2012) 10977.

61 "The bills do not meet their objects. . . . These bills introduce complexity, uncertainty and further regulation to a sector that is already struggling with high administrative costs and red tape. These additional burdens distract charities and NFPs from their primary community role": Senate Standing Committee on Community Affairs, *Australian Charities and Not-for-profits Commission*

Bill and Related Bills: Coalition Members and Senators Dissenting Report (September 12, 2012), 45–46, accessed September 23, 2016, http://www. aph.gov.au/Parliamentary_Business/Committees/Senate/Community_Affairs/ Completed_inquiries/2010–13/charitiescommission/report/index.

62 Ministers are not required to attend Parliamentary Committee hearings. Public servants represent the government's view.

63 Parliament of Australia, House of Representatives, *Hansard*, (Mr Pyne, September 18, 2012) 10978.

64 "Coalition Unveils Plans for Charity Commission," *Pro Bono Australia*, June 15, 2012, accessed October 10, 2016, https://probonoaustralia.com. au/news/2012/06/coalition-unveils-plans-for-charity-commission/; "Federal Opposition Slams Charity Regulator Bill," *Pro Bono Australia*, July 25, 2012, accessed October 11, 2016, https://probonoaustralia.com.au/news/2012/07/ federal-opposition-slams-charity-regulator-bill/; Royce Millar, "Church Lobby in 'Win' Over Charities Watchdog," *Sunday Age*, September 1, 2013, 1.

65 Australian Charities and Not-for-profits Commission, *Six-Month Progress Report*, (Melbourne: ACNC, 2013).

66 Not-for-profit Sector Tax Concession Working Group, *Fairer, Simpler and More Effective Tax Concessions for the Not-for-profit Sector: Consultation Paper* (Canberra: Treasury, 2012), accessed September 19, 2016, http://www.treasury.gov.au/ConsultationsandReviews/Consultations/2012/ Tax-concessions-for-the-not-for-profit-sector.

67 Charities Bill 2013 (Cth); see Bills Digest, No. 160 2012–13, http://www.aph.gov. au/Parliamentary_Business/Bills_Legislation/bd/bd1213a/13bd160; and Explanatory Memorandum, https://www.legislation.gov.au/Details/C2013B00135/ Explanatory%20Memorandum/Text

68 Parliament of Australia, House of Representatives, *Hansard* (Mr Andrews, June 17, 2013), 5876.

69 Greater certainty about what constitutes a charity and what activities are charitable is key to growing high-impact philanthropy in Australia. The money foundations spend on legal advice to work out what they can legitimately fund could be better spent on organizations doing good works, https://probonoaustralia. com.au/news/2013/06/nfps-urge-mps-to-pass-charity-bill/.

70 Charities Bill 2013 (Cth) and Charities (Consequential Amendments and Transitional Provisions) Bill 2013 (Cth), Explanatory Memorandum, 14.

71 Charities Bill 2013 (Cth) s. 7 Certain purposes presumed to be for the public benefit.

72 A private member's Bill had been introduced by Senator Xenophon, an independent: Tax Laws Amendment (Public Benefit Test) Bill 2010.

73 Prime Minister's Community Business Partnership [membership announcement], November 20, 2014, http://www.communitybusinesspartnership.gov.au/ prime-ministers-community-business-partnership/ "First meeting of the Prime Minister's Community Business Partnership," December 12, 2014, http://www. communitybusinesspartnership.gov.au/prime-ministers-community-business-partnership-2/, accessed October 10, 2016.

74 "ACNC—Surviving One Year On," *Pro Bono Australia*, December 3, 2013, accessed October 10, 2016, https://probonoaustralia.com.au/news/2013/12/ acnc-surviving-one-year-on/.

75 Australian Charities and Not-for-profits Commission, *Annual Report 2013– 14* (Melbourne: ACNC, 2014), 8, accessed September 19, 2016, http://www. acnc.gov.au/ACNC/About_ACNC/Corporate_info/Annual_Reports/ACNC/ Publications/ARlanding.aspx.

76 "It's the Debate that Now Follows Every Major Election," *Western Advocate*, September 11, 2013, 2.

77 John Butcher, "Not for Profit Reform 'Back to the Future'?" *Pro Bono Australia*, February 13, 2014, accessed October 10, 2016, https://probonoaustralia.com. au/news/2014/02/not-for-profit-reform-back-to-the-future/.

78 Minister for Immigration and Border Protection, "Operation Sovereign Borders, Press Conference," September 30, 2013, accessed September 23, 2016, http:// pandora.nla.gov.au/pan/143035/20131003-1143/www.minister.immi.gov.au/ media/sm/2013/sm208372.htm.

79 Refugee Council of Australia, "Government Removes Refugee Council's Core Funding," *Media Release*, May 30, 2014, accessed September 23, 2016, http:// www.refugeecouncil.org.au/media/government-removes-refugee-councils-core-funding/.

80 Tanya Nolan, "Alcohol and other Drugs Council of Australia in Voluntary Administration After Coalition Cuts Funding", *ABC News*, November 27, 2013, accessed September 23, 2016, http://www.abc.net.au/news/2013-11-27/ alcohol-and-other-drugs-council-adca-administration-funding-cut/5119744.

81 Carolyn Bond, "Legal Aid Cuts a Worrying Sign from the Abbott Team," *The Age*, September 19, 2013, 31; Nicola Berkovic, "Not a Lot Left to Cut from Aid: Report," *The Australian*, August 8, 2014, 27.

82 Ronalds, "Australia: Federal Government and Nonprofit Relations," 118, quoting Mike Seccombe, "Cousins of the Green Movement," *The Saturday Paper*, November 8, 2014, 14.

83 Ronalds, "Australia: Federal Government and Nonprofit Relations," 118.

84 Australian Council of Social Service, "Shutting down Community Voices Will Weaken Government's Ability to Make Effective Reforms," *Media Release*, December 23, 2014, accessed October 11, 2016, http://www.acoss.org.au/ media_release/shutting_down_community_voices_will_weaken_governments_ ability_to_make_effe/.

85 Australian Council of Social Service, "Collective Community Sector Call for Government Halt to 'Devastating' Funding Cuts," *Media Release*, December 31, 2014, accessed October 10, 2016, http://www.acoss.org.au/media_release/collective_ community_sector_call_for_government_halt_to_devastating_funding/.

86 "Red Tape & Compliance Key NFP Issues—Sector Survey Results," *Pro Bono Australia*, August 15, 2013, accessed September 20, 2016, http://www.probono australia.com.au/news/2013/08/red-tape-compliance-key-nfp-issues-sector-survey-results#sthash.AlxKKcDf.dpuf.

87 The Bill was structured to require enactment of Repeal (No. 2) Bill before it could commence.

88 Parliament of Australia, House of Representatives, *Hansard*, (Dr Leigh, December 3, 2014) 14150, quoting David Crosbie, CEO of CCA.

89 Robert Fitzgerald, quoted in: Parliament of Australia, House of Representatives, *Hansard*, (Dr Leigh, December 3, 2014), 94.

90 Xavier Smerdon, "Feds Move Again to Abolish ACNC," *Pro Bono Australia*, December 4, 2014, accessed September 23, 2016, https://probonoaustralia.com. au/news/2014/12/feds-move-again-to-abolish-acnc/.

91 Timna Jacks, "Charity Watchdog to Stay for Now," *The Age*, February 7, 2015, 16, quoting Minister for Social Services Scott Morrison.

92 Lina Caneva, "Saving the ACNC," *Pro Bono Australia*, May 26, 2015, accessed September 23, 2016, https://probonoaustralia.com.au/news/2015/05/saving-the-acnc/.

93 Department of Social Services, *Australian Charities and Not-For-Profits: Options Paper* (Canberra: Department of Social Services, 2014).

94 Toni Hassan, "Significant Victory for the Charities Sector," *Canberra Times*, May 22, 2015, 5.

Conclusion

13 Conclusion

Myles McGregor-Lowndes and Bob Wyatt

The previous eleven chapters record the narratives of regulators and charity sector leaders of five Anglo-centric jurisdictions about how they make sense of the last 25 years of charity regulation. The sense-making of their career experiences at the front line of regulation is a rich source for analysis about charity regulation and its surrounding policy environment. Unlike the usual process for comparative studies, the narrators were not given a pre-determined template, but had freedom to decide how to construct their narratives. It was anticipated that this would allow for discourse which was meaningful for them. Readers will apply their own lens, extracting clues from the accounts, making sense of the narratives, and informing their views of past lessons and what the future may hold.

As editors, we offer our lens to make sense of charity regulators' and sector leaders' views. We first convey how we broadly understand the expressed rationale of charity regulators for their work and its implications for charities and their regulation. Then we examine some other themes that arise out of the chapters—international relations and policy sharing, regulatory strategies, charity regulation and risk of terrorism, calling charity regulators to account, political muddle, independence and structure of the charity regulator, and how the future of charity regulation is perceived.

The Narrative of Charity Regulation

How do charity regulators make sense of the core purpose of their own organizations and what impact does this have on how they and charities go about their business? The phrase "trust and confidence" is ever present in the regulators' contributions from England and Wales, Australia, and New Zealand. This is echoed loudly by sector leaders. It describes the desired regulatory outcome to have the general public place trust in regulator-monitored charity organizations. Such public trust is over and above the accountability that individual charities give to their stakeholders. The regulator is akin to an independent third-party referee with a responsibility to champion the charity brand. The language of both US contributors departs from this, preferring to use terms such as transparency, accountability, and oversight.

Their focus is on the individual charity giving evidence of its trustworthiness to those who care to inform themselves about such issues. Donors and beneficiaries in these jurisdictions appear to have less assistance from the state in their decision making about charities. The Canadian regulator uses the phrase "protecting charities and the public from harm," and the sector contributor describes the 25-year-long hankering of the sector for a shift to a "trust and confidence" model. It is making sense of these differences within the context and history of the different regulatory environments that gives us an insight into the possible path of charity regulation.

The notion of trust and confidence appears to connect with a widely acknowledged theory propounded by Henry Hansmann.[1] There are many other theories about nonprofit organizations and their existence, but he shares these regulators' emphasis on public trust.[2] He offers an explanation of why nonprofit organizations arise in a market economy and appear to survive and prosper in the face of possible competition by the government, for-profit organizations, and family groupings. It is that nonprofit organizations have immutable organizational attributes that are clear signals of trustworthiness to those who deal with them. The main attribute is a non-distribution constraint that prohibits the distribution of residual earnings (profit) to individuals who exercise control over it. Any surplus must be devoted solely to the organization's purposes. This signalling allows nonprofits to prosper in the market by conducting certain transactions with less friction and cost. An example of such a transaction is where the consumer of a good or service is unable to evaluate its quality, or to do so for an acceptable price. In the for-profit market this could lead to the organization producing a lower quality good or service to maximize residual earnings, cheating the consumer. The constraint is also a signal of trustworthiness for gifts by donors of time, goods, and money for the organization's purposes. Donors need to trust the organization to use their gift as directed, without the cost of specific contracts or monitoring. The non-distribution constraint acts as a very clear signal of trustworthiness to funders, donors, and beneficiaries without the full costs of searching, assessing, and monitoring. Not all nonprofits are charities, but those with charitable status also signal that they are exclusively public benefit organizations.

The theory is challenged by a few issues. First, those dealing with charities must realize they are dealing with a charity, not just any other type of firm, and understand the meaning of the non-distribution constraint signal, and, second, the reputation of for-profit firms generally must not be reliable (the reputational ubiquity challenge).[3] It appears that for-profit firms may be able to earn a reputation with consumers for trustworthiness where there is significant consumer engagement. The third issue is that, with no owners demanding a surplus, nonprofit managers have lower incentives to impose strict cost minimization, and costs may rise to outweigh the value of the consumer protection signal.

Charity regulators who express their foremost goal as ensuring "trust and confidence" in charities are promoting confidence of funders, donors, and beneficiaries (public) in the signal of the non-distribution constraint and the exclusive charity brand. Through activities such as sector education, capacity building, compliance, scrutiny, consumer protection, and, more recently, facilitating public access to the financial and other accounts of charities, regulators give the trustworthiness signal and charity brand extra credibility in the marketplace. They are taxpayer-funded government certifiers of charity trustworthiness. It is also critical that the regulators are trusted as well, or their credentialing and promotion will be severely tainted. This appears to be a robust explanation of the situation in Australia, New Zealand, and, until recently, England and Wales. However, there are signs that change is afoot in these jurisdictions. They appear to be moving towards emulating the North American regulators located in taxation agencies, where the US discourse of individual charity transparency, accountability, and oversight prevails.

The discourses of US regulator and sector leaders appear almost identical, stressing transparency, accountability, and oversight. In comparison to other jurisdictions, US charities appear to receive less overt bolstering of their trustworthiness signals by the regulator. Its location in a tax agency, where its prime mission is to administer taxes, is the starting point for explaining the difference. Despite this, IRS registration of a charity is still a signal to the public that the charity has been vetted and has government recognition. Our sense is that a weakening signal from the regulator has resulted from a combination of the IRS's regulatory retreat, having its credibility publicly questioned over an extended period, and critical public opinions of charities fed by public scandal, amplified in the traditional press and recently joined by social media. Perhaps the nonprofit organizations' signal of trustworthiness has itself been so besmirched that it is no longer an effective signal in the eyes of the public.

Owens, Lott, and Boris point a way forward that does not rely on rebuilding the signal power of the IRS, instead requiring the charitable sector to create trustworthiness through transparent metrics of outcomes and accountability, be it by private watchdog analysis, benchmarked impact metrics, or individualized forms of accountability to stakeholders. Much of this has been occurring for some time, but they argue for more and better accountability. There are other forces driving this increased accountability such as the trend towards an audit society and the development of New Philanthropic Management—the transposed clone of New Public Management (NPM), adopted by private funders of charities. Industry regulators of both for-profit and nonprofit firms in health and education also give trust signals to the public. So charities are now presumably bearing more of the cost of providing assurance to donors, funders, beneficiaries, and the public, which is what the non-distribution constraint signal was designed to avoid, and probably with limited capacity to pass on costs. Could this contribute to making some uncompetitive?

The Canadian contributions show the regulator, the Charities Directorate of the Canada Revenue Agency (CRA), concerned with protecting the public. This does not go as far as having an objective to enhance the charity brand generally. The sector clearly desires more signalling support from the regulator and has won some meagre gains, but the support falls far short of the aspirational English model. The Charities Directorate is located in a tax agency with a non-charity prime mission that helps to explain why it is not a full trust and confidence, charity brand, defending regulator. There has not been a funding crisis for CRA, only a slight reputational reversal during the Harper Conservative government and some minor scandals, but the path to increased individual accountability of charities is possible if such events occur. It should be noted that a world-class, self-regulatory scheme, arranged for charities by Imagine Canada, is in place and may not have developed so quickly if there had been a trust and confidence regulator in place.

If we return to the description of recent events in England and Wales, we see the Charity Commission (CCEW) being redirected towards greater command and control compliance functions as it weathers budget cuts, reputational damage, and political reaction to scandals, which is threatening public confidence in the trustworthiness of charities as a whole. Again, is the nonprofit signal and charity brand itself no longer regarded as a good mark of trustworthiness? The rhetoric of the National Council for Voluntary Organisations (NCVO) in calling for the sector to take its future into its own hands is not new, but it is now a necessity for individual charities to demonstrate accountability and trustworthiness to their stakeholders. It appears to us to be going briskly down the US path and may continue in that direction, even if the CCEW re-balances its regulatory strategy.

Charities have the wit and wisdom to use tools, old and new, to demonstrate accountability and build trusting relationships with their immediate stakeholders, either alone or by self-regulatory clubs. This will incur a cost, and many feel it will divert scarce resources from their mission. Donors could pay third parties to assess trustworthiness but appear reluctant even to spend relatively little on accessing free evaluations.[4] It may be increasingly difficult for charities to demonstrate and maintain their trust—at least in a cost effective way—with the general public who have a claim as stakeholders, being the ones who ultimately pay for charity tax concessions.

In both the United Kingdom and the United States, the popular press and social media have been a significant forum to call charities to account and have been decisive in the collective public judgement on the trustworthiness of charities. The narrative of a fallen saint, a disgraced charity, is of intense interest to the populace and elevates the sense of ordinary wickedness of transgressions to incensed moral outrage. It is one thing to be cheated by a business, but another to be taken down by a supposedly trusted pillar of society. We simply observe that if such a forum is to replace a charity regulator completely, there is a risk of public opinion, reflected and moulded by the popular press and social media, imposing a capital sentence on a charity without the procedural protections of the rule of law. Despite efforts in all jurisdictions featured in this book to educate the public about fundraising costs, administrative costs, use of professional staff, and market-based remuneration of executives, the public's opinions appear only marginally altered in relation to any realistic, logical, and proportionate view of these issues. Such negative signals appear not to drive the majority of ordinary funders to greater search and analysis of charities.[5] Is opinion generated by traditional and new media effectively crowding out charity regulators' signals in any case? Again, the costs of being accountable in such an environment, particularly when the costs cannot be passed onto the beneficiaries or funders, may threaten the competitive advantages of trust signals as theorized by Hansmann.

Other issues are also contributing to sector instability. For example, new technologies allow consumers to redress asymmetrical information deficits and bypass charity intermediaries through donors dealing directly with beneficiaries. Hybrid enterprise forms and isomorphism within industries such as health care are also contributing to the fading of the organizational non-distributional signal in the market. Perhaps industry regulators in health, education, and community service now provide a specialist signal of trustworthiness for all organizational forms (for-profit, nonprofit, and hybrid) involved in that industry. For-profit firms may also be earning a reputation with consumers, thus diminishing the effect of charities trumpeting the non-distribution constraint as a signal of trustworthiness. The implication for Australia and New Zealand is that this may be their path as well, if triggered by similar events. It may not occur as dramatically as in the United States. An example of a more gradual path is shown by Canada, where increased individual accountability has been achieved partly through a self-regulatory accreditation scheme that provides the public with a signal of trustworthiness, or through specific industry regulators.

We are not predicting the imminent demise of charitable organizations. The support for their trustworthiness signal once provided by regulators in some jurisdictions has been greatly diminished. Charities will have to find new cost-effective ways to signal their supporters in a market that appears to crave clearer metrics of performance and relishes putting the fallen saint to the public sword of retribution. Having described our macro view of the regulatory environment, we now descend to a closer view of issues that are apparent from the contributions. The first to receive our closer examination is that of recently established but already challenged charity regulators, who clearly chose the trust and confidence path modelled by the CCEW.

New Players

New Zealand and Australia came late to creating a modern charity regulator. Their inaugural commissioners tell of their struggles, triumphs, learnings, and disappointments in the journey to establish a new regulator, which in both cases was intensified by later threats to their organizations' very existence. Sector representatives, a politician, and a charity lawyer recount the experience of seeking to shape the policy decisions made about the regulator's formation and the debate about their continuation under incoming conservative governments. There are some valuable insights, both shared and to be drawn from their reflections about founding a charity regulator in the twenty-first century. One line of questions is, how do you make sense of why these regulators were established at this particular time? Why would a sector with minimal regulatory imposts and not facing any significant public controversy about their conduct seek a central regulator? Why did governments finally act at this time after decades of public inquiries about the matter in both countries? And then what drove conservative governments to advocate reversing the initiatives?

The classic academic response to such questions is to use Kingdon's policy windows framework, focusing on public problems requiring attention, policy interests, and policy entrepreneurs.[6] Alternatively, there is the advocacy coalition framework by Sabatier and Jenkins-Smith, which is a perpetual policy process of shifting coalitions forming alliances that either move to converge on a position or in the direction of polar extremes.[7] Both can be applied to explore the events. A detailed application is beyond the space available in this concluding chapter, but some observations can be drawn from the narratives provided by our contributors. Clearly, there was a convergence of political and administrative windows with policy entrepreneurs in strategic positions of influence.

The timing of policy execution came after literally decades of inquiries in both countries that largely recommended a central charity regulator. A major barrier was conservative governments that had no appetite for creating new regulatory bodies unless there was a compelling political reason to do so. This was unlike the UK conservatives who followed the sector meta-policies of Blair with a Big Society narrative. Implementation had to await the coming to power of a progressive party in the political cycle. Both countries had progressive governments in power with a largely willing sector and active sector-policy entrepreneurs.

New Zealand and Australia both cited the Financial Action Task Force (FATF) and terrorism obligations as a formal reason for enhanced charity regulation, but this was not the reason that occupied the attention of the sector or the public discourse. The narrative of both jurisdictions' sectors was that it sought a competent government agency to proactively defend against "rogues" that would affect trust and confidence in the sector. The Australian sector was also able to influence the legislative objects of the Australian Charities and Not-for-profits Commission (ACNC) at a late stage to insert two additional objects. One was that the regulator was "to support and sustain a robust, vibrant, independent and innovative Australian not-for-profit sector" and the other was to reduce unnecessary red tape in the sector.[8] As Susan Pascoe laments, both objects were unfunded in its initial budget and had a potentially wide scope. In neither country was the initiative a reaction to a sector scandal demanding a political response. The New

Zealand government did venture down the path of pointing to potential mischiefs of "rogue" charities, but in Australia, any hint of the sector needing reform because it currently fell short of the expected level of conduct was fiercely challenged by sector leaders.

When the political cycle changed and conservative governments came to power, they both proposed changes to the new regulatory regime. In New Zealand, the narrative was to reduce government costs as part of a bonfire of separate government agencies and merge the commission into a Department. Susan Barker suggests that the Commission's controversial decision to deregister the National Council of Women of New Zealand Incorporated may be another factor. Despite sector advocacy, the amendments passed by the narrowest of margins: one vote. The former NZ commissioner notes, with the benefit of hindsight that, over three years, the cost of the new arrangements increased by nearly half a million dollars and over a third of the staff of the young regulator departed.

In Australia, the incoming conservative government sought to abolish the ACNC and return regulation to the taxation authority, hinting also at American charity watchdog in the image of Charity Navigator and the establishment of a special largely sector-funded body to improve charity governance. Like New Zealand, a bonfire of unnecessary regulation was championed as a major election policy, being a direct policy transfer from UK conservative parties, and included the ACNC. The conservatives' arguments were ideologically based but in no sense a clearly developed meta-policy for the sector. It was opposed by a significant proportion of the sector and more importantly by independents holding the balance of power in the Upper House. The regulator took an approach of business as usual and tried to mitigate the flight of staff and reluctance of other agencies to engage with an agency marked for extinction. Finally, after nearly two years of failed attempts to progress a bill, a change of Prime Minister and supervising Ministers, and lack of significant support for a change from both the public and the sector, the decision was reversed.

The two commissioners' contributions reveal some common themes that are worth considering for those embarking on establishing a charity regulator. They both received valuable guidance from other national charity regulators, particularly the CCEW. This was through the global regulators' meetings, secondment, and actual poaching of staff, but again, the CCEW appears to be the most plundered regulator for inspiration. Trevor Garrett reflected that hearing other charity regulators' experiences in charity law decision making was invaluable, but both Australian and New Zealand regulators had their own ideas about organizational design and culture. Both recruited heavily from outside the public service (particularly outside tax agencies) for those who had a strong feel for the charity sector and intentionally built a client-centred culture. This was bolstered by frontline staff being encouraged to be involved in the sector and build empathy for volunteer charity officers. Such staff were encouraged to pick up the phone to charities and try to resolve minor paperwork issues quickly without bureaucratic formalism. The ACNC lived this out during their early years of public engagement with the sector by being accessible at "town hall" meetings across Australia with Internet-connected laptops that could be used to correct the register on the spot. Both were digital-by-default regulators, and the sector appears to have embraced this without issue. The cost savings and the usefulness of the public register, as a result, is significant, but managing IT appears to have been a major issue for both regulators. Apart from the ongoing revision costs of a digital register, both are still grappling with some parts of the sector being uneasy about the digital publication of charities' affairs and in particular personal information of office bearers. New Zealand has made significant advances in developing appropriate charity accounting standards for public reporting that are fit for purpose and comparable, whereas Australia still lags well behind with little short-term prospect of reform in this area.

Our sector contributors are largely happy with the outcomes. Sue Barker concludes, overall, the New Zealand Commission has largely achieved its goals except appropriate decision making about the boundaries of the definition of charity. Ursula Stephens predicts that the sector's honeymoon with the ACNC may be tested with future government implementation of taxation concession reforms and that the two ACNC objectives inserted at the behest of the sector need to be guarded and funded. The two new charity regulators were greatly assisted by being part of a global community of charity regulators and we now turn to considering global issues.

International Relations and Policy Sharing

We expected that the forces of globalization, which have created an economy and civil society that stretches beyond the fixed geographic boundaries of the nation-state system, would have touched charity regulators. Our sense, from what regulators have written, is that while issues such as terrorism, money laundering, fraud, and charities adopting cross-jurisdictional legal forms and accounting standards are international in scope, there is no movement towards an international police force for charity such as an INTERPOL, or a UN-style agency, or even international conventions. Rather, charity regulators react to international issues within their jurisdictions and share their knowledge and expertise. This sharing has led to the transfer of administrative and policy ideas, and Australia and New Zealand have benefited significantly, particularly with input from the CCEW. Charity regulators have been steadily increasing their mutual contact across national boundaries over the last 25 years. The inception of this book was only possible because regulators were gathered together in an international forum and already had working relationships and so were at ease with each other. Such trusting relationships happen neither by chance nor overnight, but they have been aided by the international forum of charity regulators held approximately every 18 months. These forums, which include the jurisdictions covered in this book and others such as Singapore, Scotland, and Ireland, have continued to meet in a different jurisdiction since 2006. The forum provides a valuable means to maintain relationships among regulators, addressing practical and varied agendas including best practice administration and regulation.

By the time Australia and New Zealand were establishing their commissions, regulators and governments were open to assisting other nations with human and intellectual charity capital partly given the relationships that had been formed across borders and also as a means of building the capacity to deal with international terrorism. The new regulators attracted staff from other jurisdictions, both on secondment and as permanent officers. The ACNC has been particularly influenced by having the ex-director of CCEW Charity Services become one of its assistant commissioners, as well as by having experienced start-up staff from New Zealand and old hands from Canada. Such staff brought detailed inside knowledge of their former agencies and ideas for greenfield regulatory environments that might be difficult to implement in older legacy regimes. This was critical administrative systems knowledge transfer.

The new regulators' descriptions of broad policy transfers are from the United Kingdom rather than from North America. This is in contrast to the previous century's major nonprofit reforms, when both Australia and New Zealand embraced the US version of the nonprofit corporation as its main legal structure for associations rather than the English charitable trust or company limited by guarantee. This has been a relatively successful policy import, becoming the most popular nonprofit legal structure. More recently, Australia has also successfully adopted policies about volunteer indemnity protections and family foundations from the United States.

Our sense as to why the shift towards the United Kingdom occurred is that both these jurisdictions began closer to the English common law. Adopting the English statutory definition of charity approach provided an incremental way forward in updating the definition of charity. This was politically sustainable. It did not unduly interfere with the court's ability to continue providing precedents. The US statutory definition had become far removed from the English flow of decisions, and Canada offered no model for reform because there had been little. Further, both jurisdictions finally settled on an independent regulator rather than one located in a taxation agency. The charities sector in both countries had advocated for an independent regulator, having been at the receiving end of government actions designed to curb their public criticisms. In Australia, Treasury favoured the Canadian model, but the sector made strenuous representations that it wanted a regulator independent of the taxation agency.

Canada appears to have had little in the way of general policy exports or imports in the last 25 years, and as noted earlier, the United States' domestic tale has little reference to outside influences or external engagement.

This is in contrast to that country's long history of exporting civil society and the US brand of regulatory infrastructure to the countries of the former Soviet sphere of influence and Asia. Our sense-making is that the IRS may be crowded out by the many foundations, think tanks, and capacity building organizations, such as the International Center for Not-for-Profit Law, operating overseas in legal and regulatory capacity building. This is facilitated by the ease with which US organizations are able to operate externally compared to many other jurisdictions.

While charity boundary cases have different outcomes in some jurisdictions, this has not created conflict between regulators. Precedents from other jurisdictions are often cited, analysed, and even adopted on a regular basis. One instance of strained international relations revealed by the narratives occurred in 2003, when the CCEW disagreed with the United States' view of the charity Interpal's link to terrorism. The Commission came to a different conclusion from the Americans and acted in what it believed was a proportionate and impartial response to the issue. An NCVO report in 2006 argued that existing regulation was sufficient to deal with the threat of terrorism and that the Commission's independence from government must be protected to shore up confidence in its ability to take a proportionate and impartial response.

Regulatory Strategies

The nature of regulation provokes a significant level of disagreement between theorist and practitioners alike, having aspects of political and ideological battles, and the disagreement encompasses issues about the purpose, form, and implementation of regulation. We may expect that the nature of regulatory activities undertaken by charity regulators would be influenced by the outcome of such political contests. Theory might predict the path according to whether the political decision is to create the regulator as an independent agency or to locate it within a taxation agency.[9] The objectives expressed in the statutory instruments establishing the regulator, and how it is made accountable and resourced may all play a part in how it conducts its regulatory functions. The environment in which the regulator operates, including public expectations and the characteristics of regulated parties, might also play a role.

Our contributing regulators provide a rich narrative of their regulatory strategies, why they adopted them, and their impact. Many issues stand out, but our sense is that certain key matters should be considered. First is the detailed observations made by Richard Fries and Lindsay Driscoll about how the CCEW developed its regulatory strategy and tools in the context of the unfolding UK agenda of NPM and its abrupt about-face more recently. Second is the regulatory limitations of the US and Canadian models, which place the regulator within a tax agency. Third is the regulatory strategies of newly established regulators in Australia and New Zealand. And, finally, we see charity governance as an emerging area of regulatory interest common to all jurisdictions.

The regulatory journey of the CCEW over these 25 years warrants a detailed analysis that is far beyond the constraints of this publication—it appears to have travelled the full gamut of regulatory styles and philosophies, from being the charities' friend to being the enforcer and may be on the way back again. Some assert that it is impossible to be simultaneously friend and police officer. Richard Fries's explanation of the development of charity regulation in England and Wales proceeds from an understanding that the Charity Commission was initially established as a quasi-judicial body, tasked with being quicker and cheaper for charities than full engagement with the courts of equity. It provided legal support and was dominated by lawyers with a strong legal culture, but without any real connection to the sector. It was not a regulator in the contemporary sense. Further, regulation was not a concept that featured in the early English reform reports. Charity was perceived as essentially an independent activity of private individuals that were free to experiment with solutions to wicked social issues. It was not a government or public function. Richard explains the purpose of tax concessions as "encouragement for such activities," whereas currently they may be perceived more in the nature of grants, for which the state wishes a public benefit return. At the time, there was concern that public funding was making charities increasingly dependent on government, thus challenging their independence. This appears to presage the current inescapable commentary that charities are now public organizations, with public accountabilities, subsidized by tax concessions, delivering contracted public services on behalf of government agencies, and open to market competition. This is despite the fact that in all jurisdictions, the vast bulk of charities do not receive significant government funding or contracts.

Under the Charities Act 1960, the CCEW began a very incremental journey towards becoming a regulator of charities, with the establishment of a public register that was eventually digitized, naming and shaming of defaulters, and the addition of Summary Information Returns with information beyond the annual report. A telephone help line, with guidance in plain English and multiple languages, joint sector codes of governance, comic videos, and sector education forums were all experimented with to boost the capacity of the sector to meet their legal obligations and responsibilities. Compliance actions were aimed at remediation rather than imposing sanctions, and in 2003, the CCEW publicly set out its view of charity regulation, with its goal being increased public trust and confidence. Sector bodies such as the NCVO argued that the CCEW should have a primary function of compliance, and they ought to distinguish between "musts" and "shoulds" in their advice. This was particularly in the context of charity governance. Then, after a series of budget cuts and regulatory defaults by the CCEW beginning in 2011, the Strategic Plan for 2012–2015 set out two clear priorities: developing the compliance and accountability of the sector and developing the sector's self-reliance. The support and advice work would be met primarily by web-based advice to promote good governance. The mission was based on a threefold concept: charities know what they have to do; the public knows what charities do; charities are held to account. Priority compliance areas included are now serious financial loss, criminality and misuse for terrorist purposes, and serious harm to vulnerable beneficiaries. The CCEW had dramatically changed its regulatory philosophy not only to reflect its diminished staff capacity but also its board appointed in a party political process. It has moved to look far more like the charity regulators located in tax agencies.

The charity regulators located in tax agencies perhaps understandably have a different regulatory philosophy, shaped by their situation and difficulty in accessing adequate and fit-for-purpose resources. Marcus Owens states flatly that the IRS's function is to ensure that taxpayers, whether individuals or businesses, pay the appropriate amount of federal income tax, and IRS systems and procedures are designed to support that tax collecting role. The regulation of charities is not perceived as having a unique character— charities being just another taxpayer, subject to the same classic command and control punitive tax tools. Developments such as digitization of annual returns is merely an offshoot project of corporate tax digitization, which has hampered charity-specific modification. Apart from intermediate sanctions, the IRS Exempt Organizations Division's (EOD) charity regulation toolbox is limited to classic tax tools with ironclad taxpayer privacy provisions. In 1941, the United States introduced the charities' annual return, the Form 990. It is the information on this form that triggers most regulatory action. Marc points to two troubling issues with such an approach: achieving a timely response and managing with a less than sophisticated regulatory response.

In terms of the first issue, a return can be filed as much as 10 months and 15 days after the close of the year in which it occurred and could be nearly 2 years after the actual event inciting attention. In the case of charities involved in political campaigning, that will typically be after the relevant election is over. The IRS has attempted regulatory co-option and co-production by enabling charity watchdogs to access the returns for analysis and digital public access. However, while there has been a measure of success, as the chapter by Elizabeth T. Boris and Cindy M. Lott indicates, the analysis is only for a limited number of organizations, metrics are contested, and their business model is parlous. Strict privacy provisions restrict the IRS's ability to share information and other resources with similarly tasked federal regulators and with states (except state revenue authorities). So regulatory cooperation, critical in a federation, is closed off.

Second, the regulatory tools are fraught with difficulties. For example, excise taxes, a penalty intended to discourage egregious behaviour, are applied to tax-exempt organizations. But this is often a disproportionate response, and rather than punishing the managers who caused the default, it ultimately punishes the beneficiaries of charities through reduced distribution of public goods. Marcus Owens also sheds light on why the IRS EOD produces relatively little, compared to other regulators, in terms of educational guidance and rulings. It is the Department of the Treasury that is responsible for tax law guidance, including regulations, notices, announcements, revenue rulings, and revenue procedures, and it has only a single attorney assigned to tax-exempt organization matters. While the larger staff in the IRS Office of Chief Counsel assists in the development of guidance, all guidance must cross the desk of the single attorney in the Treasury Department assigned to the area. To compound this situation, Elizabeth T. Boris and Cindy M. Lott believe that state charities regulators have been the object of benign neglect, with lack of recognition of their role in regulation, enforcement, and resource allocation. About a third of responding jurisdictions had less than one full-time equivalent employee dedicated to oversight of charities, and more than half had fewer than three.

Similar themes are also apparent in Canada, but not to the same extent in relation to resourcing. Terry de March notes that the mission of CRA's Charities Directorate is "to promote compliance with the income tax legislation and regulations relating to charities through education, quality service, and responsible enforcement, thereby contributing to the integrity of the charitable sector and the social well being of Canadians."[10] This is not a mandate for charity capacity building in the style of the CCEW or the ACNC, unless that occurs as a by-product of promoting compliance with and enforcing the law. CRA does provide ample education materials for charities through its website and does allow public access to charities' annual returns where those have been digitized (and has preparations for fully digital filing well advanced). But Terry suggests that a regulator cannot be firmly compliance oriented while at the same time nurturing charities as a friend, pointing to recent events at CCEW as an example. The Canadian response to non-compliance is largely the tax audit accompanied by intricate and specific rules. For example, the requirement to keep books and records means international development charities must retain at their Canadian offices the original invoices, receipts, and emails of foreign transactions, translated into French or English. Terry concludes that a strong reliance on such a classic tax regulatory approach leads to

> [t]hose that would do harm [becoming] increasingly adept at finding new ways to inflict it, which means government must continually amend the rules to fight new risks. And so it continues in a never-ending loop with the rules becoming ever more complex and the regulation of charities ever more removed from the day-to-day good works that charities perform.

It seems to us that charity regulators in these large national tax agencies are not given space to apply a regulatory strategy that fits with the characteristics of charities, or to adopt a mission and strategy fit to regulate charities and their controllers. It appears their and the sector's voice for provision of adequate resources is lost in the politics of such a large agency. We also suspect that the culture of tax agencies, their taxpayer privacy provisions, and command and control regulatory tools combine to hamper effective charity regulation.

The two new regulators in Australia and New Zealand were initially independent agencies modelled on the CCEW and could be expected to have regulatory strategies similar to CCEW's. This is largely borne out with bespoke digital charity registers, proportionate reporting levels, engagement with social media, a significant investment in sector education and capacity building, and regulatory tools that take account of the sector's characteristics. They both appear to have been resourced adequately, compared to the situation in the United States and that of CCEW more recently. Both are digital-by-default regulators with almost total digital uptake by the charity population. In New Zealand, the charity register was the most advanced "open-data" project within the New Zealand government, and the Australian register was formally recognized for its excellence, winning the Institute of Public Administration's 2016 Digital Transformation Award. Both engaged with universities to promote the register as a research vehicle, which has resulted in significant data analysis to inform the regulator, suggestions to improve data collection, and provide charities with data and analysis to inform their strategies and evidence-based advocacy. The ACNC's youthful communications staff have revelled in being ahead of the broader Australian Public Service in the use of YouTube, Twitter, Facebook, and LinkedIn, and formalized mechanisms for engagement via social media help ensure that staff maintain proper professional relationships.

The narratives of both of these fledgling regulators highlight the importance of establishing an appropriate organizational culture for the regulator. This has involved an openness to engage meaningfully with charities, umbrella organizations, and advisers about sector issues, proposed regulatory initiatives, and regulator performance feedback. Both deliberatively built a client-centred culture, departing from the public service norm—as Trevor Garrett expressed it, "a client-centred focus is not typical of public-sector organizations, which more usually expect clients to fit their behavior in to the requirements of the public sector agency." Frontline staff were recruited from the sector or with sector empathy and encouraged to participate in sector activities and to take calculated risks to solve charity issues quickly via email or telephone. In Australia, regional ACNC forums were conducted by senior staff, accompanied by their registry staff and representatives from other federal and state departments to become a one-stop shop for questions and concerns. After public consultation, the ACNC also adopted a compliance strategy informed by responsive regulation, assuming that charities are acting honestly and giving them opportunities for self-correction. The ACNC intends to use the least intrusive powers that are sufficient to address a particular issue and acts quickly in cases where evidence of gross negligence or serious misconduct has been established, or where vulnerable people or significant charitable assets are at risk. They have an armoury of regulatory tools including intermediate sanction-style undertakings as to future behavior, removal of officer bearers, and appointment of an administrator. One glaring deficiency for the ACNC is its strict privacy provisions. These provisions do not prevent it from sharing intelligence with other federal and state regulators, but they do make it more difficult to respond adequately to public and political concerns.

It is perhaps too early to fully assess the success of these agencies, but the level of on-time filing of annual returns reported by both regulators is impressive. Time will tell whether their regulatory strategies have been successful, including whether the registers are fit for purpose and whether abusive behaviour is promptly and appropriately addressed. Both regulators noted that they were alive to being captured by sector interests and diverted from their mission. Sue Barker's contribution outlines the many adverse decisions made by the New Zealand regulator and the significant number of charity cases before the courts, which is good evidence that capture was not occurring to any great extent. It is a little more difficult to establish that the ACNC has not been subject to some form of capture, particularly considering the lengthy period when it was threatened with abolition and relied upon sector voices to advocate for its continuance. The Australian Taxation Office and Treasury have not objected to the ACNC's registration decisions or its educational guidance material, which seems a good indication that its conduct is viewed as appropriate.

Charity governance is the regulatory sweet spot that all regulators consider important to influence. Even the United States has managed to address the issue with a revised Form 990 which asks a range of questions designed to prompt good governance. Charity governors are a key point for regulatory supervision, given the high numbers of them recorded in charity registers. Governors of charities are the closest and most timely accountability forum for the management of charities; they are generally volunteers, and a high proportion of them are replaced regularly. Soft regulatory tools are available to build the capacity of this group—for example, education, agreed codes of conduct, and co-option of umbrella bodies to assist with governance capacity building. These tools appear to be targeted better for impact rather than relying on post-factum audits or sanctions. At the apex of the regulatory tools pyramid is removal of those in control of charities if they are persistently engaging in abusive behaviour. While exercise of such a power by a regulator needs to be monitored carefully (for example, to ensure due process), it has the advantage of preserving the organization's assets for the public good. The alternative may be de-registering the organization from charity status and tax concessions, resulting in loss of the assets for the designated public purpose. Removing defaulting office bearers enables reform of the organization's soul rather than merely kicking the body.

This is responsive regulation and has much to recommend it in an environment in which scarce regulatory resources must be used responsibly, for maximum impact and with minimal interference. It is not so much a choice between being a friend or an enforcer as choosing to be a community police officer. Traditional crime-control policing with its accompanying centralized bureaucratic command structure has its place at the top of the regulatory response pyramid. Community policing as an inclusive philosophy, based on encouraging partnerships between the police and communities to address problems of crime and disorder collaboratively, appears more appropriate for the bottom tiers of the regulatory pyramid.[11] By contrast, regulatory responses to the prevention and detection of terrorism financing appeared initially to buck the trend towards responsive regulation.

Charity Regulation and the Risk of Terrorism

The evidence of terrorists using or duping charities across these jurisdictions varies. Given the consequences, heightened political rhetoric and specially directed funding, it remains an important issue for regulators to manage, and for the charity sector to mitigate excessively burdensome and heavy-handed regulatory interference. FATF, an international self-regulatory scheme for member jurisdictions, has addressed the issue in a blunt fashion with little regard for the disruption of legitimate charitable activities or effectiveness of the regulatory tools used. Non-democratic nations have relished the opportunity to use its broad and uncompromising principles to stifle dissenting civil society organizations in their own domestic spheres. Other jurisdictions have simply been disproportionate in their response, in arguably symbolic public gestures, to have politicians seen to be doing something. A couple of years after initial reaction to the global terrorist threat, responsive regulation and self-regulatory tactics were introduced into the regulatory mix. A CRA unit specializing in terrorism and charities was formed after the attack on New York, but little is known publicly about its activities. Other parts of CRA gradually produced soft education materials. In the United Kingdom, the CCEW published its first guidance about terrorism by 2003. CCEW's response to FATF principles was to actively assist regulators in other high-risk regions to improve their charity regulation using teams of senior officials travelling to different countries and explaining the CCEW model of regulation.

In New Zealand and Australia, terrorism was cited as a corollary reason for creating new charity regulators and the establishment of a charity register to meet FATF requirements. Unlike regulators located in tax agencies with inbuilt secrecy provisions, these agencies found it difficult to provide a level of comfort about the compromise of shared intelligence to other government agencies. New Zealand required lengthy negotiations to come to suitable agreements, although in Australia, where the privacy provisions for charities were stronger, the delays were largely occasioned by the uncertainty about the ACNC's future.

Calling Regulators to Account

Charity regulators may have quasi-judicial powers, and all have some discretionary administrative powers that in effect help determine what purposes and activities are charitable and other disputed boundary issues. But perhaps more importantly, the regulator can wield soft power through its guides and educational materials to influence sector expectations and behaviours. It is common for all regulators to be called to account, not only by the executive or politicians but also by aggrieved parties in court. Charity regulators' accountability often serves a dual purpose of moving the definitional boundaries of charity when decisions are disputed. The Australian and New Zealand judicial decisions in relation to political advocacy are examples. This attribute sets charity regulation apart from many other accountability regimes. In a common law jurisdiction, an independent agency regulator without fiscal protection objectives can be an effective forum for the development of new law.

Appealing regulators' decisions appears as a significant issue in several jurisdictions and has been identified by both regulator and the sector. In some jurisdictions, for various reasons, the regulator's contentious decisions have not been challenged; in others, structural issues in the appeal process are causing problems. The New Zealand regulator has experienced a lively set of appeals against its decisions. The former commissioner reflects that once a judgement has been given in favour of a charity litigant, there is no possibility of appeal by the regulator, leading to the possibility of what he calls a "rogue" decision that will stand without challenge until a similar point of law proceeds to a higher court in another factual situation. The sector has a different view. It identifies a serious structural issue with the appeals mechanism that is exacerbated by the regulator taking a narrow approach to construing the definition of charity and rejecting any quasi-judicial capacity to determine such matters. There is a disconnect between the narratives here, as former commissioner Trevor Garrett claims that internally pushing the boundaries was encouraged. Structural hindrance flows from unintended drafting that has the High Court hearing charity definition appeals in New Zealand, but it is severely restrained from receiving evidence, apart from the record of the regulator. Charities rarely prepare an application for registration with supporting materials as if they were going to trial, and in any case, the regulator is not bound by the strict rules of evidence in reaching a decision. The result is that courts do not have the best evidence available to make decisions, often having to remit the decision back to the regulator.

In Canada, there is also discontent with appeals from the regulator's decisions. The expense and complexity of appeals to Canada's second-highest court, the Federal Court of Appeal, deters applicants. The suggestions are for the tax courts to hear appeals in a more relaxed and cost effective environment. As Richard Fries notes, in England and Wales, the cost of reviewing the CCEW's determinations was historically a major barrier to new case law being made. Although the idea of a suitors' fund was floated, it was rejected by the government. It was not until 2008, after the 2006 reforms, that a tribunal for charities was established as a low-cost arbiter of charity issues and a forum to hold the CCEW to account. Initially, however, the Tribunal attracted silks and counsel and only now is self-representation occurring. Lindsay Driscoll's assessment of the new Tribunal is that the Commission has been held to account and has improved its due process procedures accordingly. It is remarkable that a case on the political purpose and advocacy activity boundary has not been squarely litigated in the United Kingdom, given the number of legal opinions, successive sector reviews, and reports on the issue.

In Canada, Australia, and England and Wales, there is evidence that regulators can also affect the flow of cases to the judiciary. They can use other means to avert matters going to court on substantive issues. In Canada, the prescriptive books and records offence offers an easier, cheaper, and effective path for dealing with charities than messy litigation on political purpose, and in England and Wales, the CCEW has sought to broker compromises on any number of contentious legal issues. In Australia, both sides of the coin are seen, with the ATO funding test case litigation[12] and the ACNC having no litigation during its threatened disestablishment and little afterwards. It is a difficult balance for a regulator to achieve. It can make decisions that invite litigation to clarify the law but run the risk of charities turning down the opportunity to litigate or appeal all the way to the highest court. A hard decision may be entrenched. Alternatively, does the regulator engage with the sector to find mitigating workarounds? This may be a less risky process but does not provide a case to develop the law, such as Aid/Watch in Australia or Greenpeace in New Zealand. Judicial appeal mechanisms that are cost proportionate and fit for purpose are essential to alleviate such tensions for regulators.

The United States has a richer history of charity litigation, with a constant flow of superior court cases. Marcus Owens illustrates the point with the *Bob Jones University* case.[13] Charities must serve a public purpose that is not contrary to public policy and so the university's racially discriminatory policies could not stand. The Exempt Organizations Division of the IRS found itself in one of the most controversial cases of the time, with a conservative president who refused to allow the Department of Justice to argue the case. After appointing a private litigator to pursue the case on behalf of the IRS, history was made in the face of considerable protest.

Marcus Owen makes the case that the IRS has historically been underfunded to perform its role adequately, including matching a professionalized charity law bar with a penchant for litigation. The current parlous state of IRS funding leaves little room for expensive litigation. Judicial challenges are regularly being taken from state regulators' decisions about property tax exemptions. Well-endowed charities in older cities of the northeast United States are finding that financially challenged states are winding back charity exemptions, leading to disputes or negotiated payments instead of taxes. Cindy M. Lott and Elizabeth T. Boris suggest that pressure is building for new ways of tackling this problem.

Regulators not only call others to account, but they also need to be called to account adequately for their actions or inaction. As Marcus Owens succinctly puts it, the benefits of a common law definition of charity are that the notions of charitable purpose are sufficiently flexible so that they can evolve to reflect social change. Charity regulators have a vital role to play as they are often the key to progressing a matter for judicial determination, or may be a quasi-judicial decision maker or a wielder of soft power through administrative practices, sector guidance, and education. The flexibility can be accompanied by ambiguity and inconsistent interpretations that offer compromising workarounds or bloody-minded intransigence by a regulator.

The Political Muddle

Making sense of the relationship between charities and the government is, on one level, simple. Each side attempts to use the other to assist in achieving their ends or prevent the other from confounding their plans. When they collaborate and play nicely in the sandpit, the coalition is formidable, for good or ill. An informed public debate involving government, charities, and others is one mark of a liberal democratic system. If there is a jostle, governments have both soft and coercive power to bring to bear on charities. Charities are not powerless in the contest. They use their trusted brand in the forum of public opinion, extensive networks, expertise, thwarting government administrative decisions through litigation, and sheer dogged determination that cannot be shaken in any contest. Governments have used their influence on charity tax status to bring charities to heel, and this has played out in a number of ways in our jurisdictions—from a dog-whistle tactic to scare risk-averse volunteer charity officers, to a legislative amendment removing tax concessions. Our sense is that some charities and governments are resorting increasingly to blunt influence levers, such as creating their own captive charities, and character attacks in the popular press.

As Richard Fries points out, the English law's concern with charity and politics was not rooted in ancient case law, but is a twentieth-century development. In the previous century, lobby groups concerned about slavery, penal reform, and Sunday observance laws, and the Charity Organisation Society, were commonly regarded as charitable. In 1917, Bowman's case[14] transformed a previously obscure case authority denying charitable status to an activity contrary to public policy[15] into authority for denying charitable status to party political purposes or even for seeking to alter the law and government policy. The essence was that the Court had no means of judging whether a proposed change in law or policy would be for the public benefit.

This was judicially confirmed in 1981 by the Amnesty International decision[16] and administratively adopted by the CCEW's response to a complaint about Oxfam's campaigning.

Over the years, the NCVO and UK International Development Organisations produced numerous reports to promote alternative legal interpretations of the case law to encourage the CCEW to be flexible in its enforcement. Enforcement action was minor, with only the most flagrant breaches being pursued and none reaching the courts for determination. The sector's concerns are with the chilling effect on office bearers. The chill occurs when charity officers react by adopting an overly risk-averse position often avoiding an activity completely, not just restricting it to non-contentious aspects. More cautious charities shy away from supporting sector campaigns. At one time, even a report of the Cabinet Strategy Unit recommended that the CCEW tone down the cautionary tenor of its guidance.

The various legal contortions to resolve the issue revolve around a determination of an organization's purpose or purposes and then whether they are political. Are political purposes divined only from a charity's written constitution, or from an examination of its activities and the utterances of its supporters? How do you identify a "political" activity and does the quantity or context matter? If you have multiple purposes, are subservient political purposes permissible? This is a muddle for both the regulator and charity officers, where a bright line can only be provided by an arbitrary metric unless judicial review provides a reconceptualisation of the legal principles.

The English policy path has followed a pattern of incremental relaxation of the political purposes guidances in the absence of any new case law on the matter. One might expect the new judicial review arrangements will eventually result in a case that will go to a superior court for determination—one case is already showing the way.[17] The issue is unlikely to rest. Since 2014, the Conservative government has enacted separate lobbying legislation to mitigate mischiefs, catching charities within its wide scope. And as Sir Stuart Etherington points out, the voices of single-issue campaigning organizations play an increasingly prominent role in a democracy, as the public disengages from political parties and traditional methods of political participation—a trend that can also be seen in the United States.

The Canadian account of charities has politics as a central theme throughout all 25 years. It is less muddled, with a hard metric adopted early to try to definitionally solve issues. The taxation legislation was amended in 1986 to require "substantially all" of a charity's resources to be expended on its charitable activities. CRA considered this to be 90 per cent. The Joint Regulatory Roundtable mandate from federal cabinet excluded the issue, but a separate departmental paper during this period was influenced by the sector to allow more flexibility. The 2012 Conservative federal government's railing against environmental and indigenous organizations opposed to an extensive oil pipeline revived the chill effect. Government Ministers spread the chill to all who opposed government policy, to restrict foreign funding of organizations deemed counter to Canada's national interests, and then to domestic terrorism. The chill became a freeze for many charity officers when the budget announced generous funding for the CRA to conduct special charity audits of political activities. One might have expected litigious environmental organizations to relish their day in court to put the CRA 90 per cent guidance to the test. However, the constraining appeal system and CRA's preference to pursue other non-political violations for de-registrations have not yet provided such a case. The election of a progressive government in 2015, with a mandate to free charities from such political harassment thawed the permafrost back to a chill, with the promise of possible further reform in this term.

Superior court decisions in Australia and New Zealand have rejected the restrictive English precedents and returned to the pre-Bowman position. The Australian High Court expressly rejected the English cases in its Aid/Watch decision, so there is no general doctrine which excludes political objects from charitable purposes.[18] The "contrary to public policy" argument from Bowman case was dismissed. The Court had previously found that the basis of the Australian Constitution and system of law relied upon communication between electors and legislators and the officers of the executive, and between electors themselves, on matters of government and politics. It followed that the generation of public debate was a charitable purpose because its activities contributed to public welfare, and were, therefore, charitable within the fourth head of *Pemsel*. The Australian Charities Act 2013, enacted after the decision, declared that a disqualifying "purpose" (not "activity") was "the purpose of promoting or opposing a political party or candidate for political office"[19] and that it was charitable to have a purpose "of promoting or opposing a change to any matter established by law, policy or practice . . . if the change is in furtherance; or in aid of one or more of the [charitable] purposes."[20] The Australian regulator's narrative is silent on such matters indicative of its relative ranking of regulator issues. The issue has not disappeared completely, as the ACNC regularly grapples with elected political representatives and mining lobby group complaints about advocacy by charitable organizations, and it has issued guidances for charities. Our sense is that after judicial and legislative clarification, it is not of the same order of importance as in the United Kingdom, the United States, or Canada, but tensions remain.

This may not be the end of the story about charities entering into public policy debates. There are other levers that governments can use to impede charities entering into a public debate as illustrated by the UK lobbying legislation. The narrative of former Senator Ursula Stephens about sector relations leading to the establishment of the ACNC and passing of the Charities Act also graphically bears this out. Governments can de-fund charities, include gag or no public comment clauses in grant agreements, create their own charities, restrict charities' access to information and consultation processes, fund contrary think tanks, and even publicly attack their trustworthiness by funding research to produce adverse reports on charity advocacy. The very encouragement of NPM and competitive markets for charitable services dampens critical voices, particularly if it includes for-profit competitors with comparatively little restraint on directly funding political candidates and parties.

Unlike Australia, New Zealand had case law endorsing the later English cases. Also, in the 1980s, a conservative Prime Minister de-funded a large respected international aid organization, and revoked its registration for tax purposes, because of its advocacy against a South African football team playing in New Zealand. Against this backdrop, the drafting of New Zealand's Charities Act included a reference that advocacy could be a non-charitable secondary purpose.[21] Both Trevor Garrett and Sue Barker agree that advocacy issues were fraught for the regulator and for charities, but their agreement appears to end there. They found themselves on opposite sides of the bar table in the National Council of Women (NCW) case.[22] NCW had a long tradition of making submissions on parliamentary bills—in fact, the government had funded them to do so. The Commission initially found that its primary charitable purpose was promoting progress for women, and it was deregistered for advocacy deemed to be far wider than merely supporting its charitable purpose. A fresh application appeared to tick the boxes for re-registration with the Charities Registration Board, despite there being no material change in its activities. The New Zealand Greenpeace decision[23] endorsed the tenor of the Australian High Court decision in Aid/Watch and noted the difference between using political activities to support purposes which are recognized as primarily charitable and pursuing purely political purposes. Although the regulator claims that a mere 10 applicants out of 27,000 were rejected for having political purposes, Sue Barker points to a large number of organizations that voluntarily deregistered to pre-empt an adverse decision being published on the regulator's website.

The US approach appears muddled as well, but presents a very different confusion. US charities have ample opportunity compared to other jurisdictions to engage in advocacy to pursue their purposes either on their own or through well-established workarounds. However, a mixture of exacting tax laws and organizations with a healthy risk appetite for pushing the boundaries requires patrolling by an effective regulator. There has always been tension created by the philosophic divide between church and state, creating issues for political comment by religious charities, but the *Citizens United* decision is central to the discourse of the US contributors.[24] This constitutional decision has allowed civic leagues or organizations not established for profit but operated exclusively for the promotion of social welfare (section 501(c)(4)) to participate in politics, so long as politics does not become their primary focus. Up to 50 per cent of their revenue may be spent on political activities, often partisan political advertising. Since 2010, a flood of registrations for such organizations and partisan funding have occurred. Political figures openly use high-profile charities and foundations to affect their political fortunes indirectly. The public and political ructions following scrutiny of IRS's vetting of such organizations led to large-scale IRS staff changes and reduced funding. A failed attempt to provide revised regulations has left the area largely unregulated. Our commentators reflect that only when a future administration with political mandate for the issue comes to power will there be any chance of addressing the matter.

Our sense is that charities and government will continue to be sparring partners. This is so even in jurisdictions that have a most liberal drawing of the advocacy boundaries. Using charities for service delivery on the basis of NPM, eventually moving them into contrived markets of formerly public goods and services, will continue to cause friction. Individual disengagement from political parties will result in greater engagement with single-issue charities. The growing reputational capital of such single-issue charities, compared to governments and business, appears to be gathering pace, and this shift can be expected to cause a reaction. Governments have policy levers other than the definition boundaries enforced through charity regulators, and these are appearing in several jurisdictions as an alternative strategy to reduce the irritating voice of charities.

Independence and Structure of the Charity Regulator

Independence is an issue that surfaces in most of the narratives, either as the regulatory agency's independence from political direction, its capture by sector influences, or as a rationale for policing the sector-politics charity boundary. Terry de March refers to the apparent structural separation of CCEW as a "Holy Grail" that the Canadian sector has been hankering after for 25 years. New Zealand and Australia both had this prize firmly in view when structuring their regulators. In federations such as the United States, Canada, and Australia, where charity regulation is constitutionally given to the states and provinces, the locus of national tax powers offers the logical location for charity regulation. However, the strong sector perception in some jurisdictions is that locating the regulator in a tax agency diminishes independence for critical decisions about charity boundaries in favour of the fisc. Australia chose a riskier constitutional basis for its regulator and located it outside the tax regulator, following the CCEW model. As several regulators agree, the crux is that decision making is, and is perceived to be governed, by the rule of law not by the rule of the figure in power. Terry de March flatly denies that positioning the Charities Directorate in CRA means it does not exercise its regulatory discretions according to law. He explains that adverse perceptions appear to be aggravated when a regulator's independence in operational matters, such as how it spends its resources and goes about its business, is compromised. While the Canadian sector may aspire to a CCEW vision of structural independence, recent events in England and Wales indicate that real independence requires more than just structural separation.

Richard Fries states unequivocally that his independence was never directed by political actors or financing departments, but recent events in and surrounding the CCEW give cause for concern. Both Lindsay Driscoll and Sir Stuart relate actual and perceived challenges to the independence of the CCEW. There was sufficient concern for a specific provision as to its independence to be inserted into the Charities Act 2006, and later in 2015, the NCVO produced a paper on the issue. It pointed to the potential politicization of the selection process of its chair and board members, and the board's extended involvement in management, affecting its ability to hold CCEW managers to account. The unfortunate CAGE matter, where the CCEW was seen to be acting outside its powers in attempting to pressure two foundations to cease funding an organization, thus fettering the discretion of trustees, did not assist a favourable public perception. Opening up regulator meetings to the public was a reform that did not attract public interest and was discontinued, but Sir Stuart offers suggestions about reforming the appointment process to involve bipartisan parliamentary approval and non-renewable fixed terms.

In Australia and New Zealand, there was considerable angst from the sector about the independence of any regulator from political interference and the taxation authorities. The sector looked to the CCEW as a model, rather than following Canadian or US examples. In New Zealand, the form initially chosen from several alternatives was the one with the closest connection to government: "independent Crown entity," which must give effect to government policy when properly directed to do so. The sector was concerned about the choice, but Trevor Garrett, like others, flatly rejects any suggestion of political pressure. The subsequent movement of the Commission into a government department also caused concern within the charitable sector about the future of its independence, but the Act did finally refer specifically to the relocated entity's independence from the responsible minister in its decision making.

In Australia, there was a considerable public debate about the independence of the regulator. As former senator Stephens notes, the previous Conservative government had acted to curb sector voices in politically sensitive areas by a number of means, and again, the sector championed the virtues of an English-style independent regulator. The first Treasury paper on the structure of the regulator argued that federations such as Canada and the United States had regulators embedded in tax authorities, but this was stoutly resisted by the sector. The model finally chosen was for a commissioner who was an independent statutory officeholder with a fixed term; independence of decision making regarding charitable status was written into the legislation, and the regulator reported to Parliament with its own budgetary appropriation. However, for the sake of operational efficiencies, it was required to purchase backroom services such as human resources and information technology from the taxation agency. With the election in 2013 of a new government, whose policy was to roll the ACNC back into the tax authority, legislation had to be amended to achieve this. With the prospect of being blocked by the Senate, only modest savings, and the sector's advocacy for retaining the ACNC, the government finally backed down.

All of the US contributors are dissatisfied with the structural arrangements of charity regulation they have at present, and our sense is that change may well occur in that jurisdiction, but not via the usual avenues seen in other jurisdictions. The United States appears to be facing the prospect of regulatory failure with the current state of the IRS and growing issues that require attention. The IRS is plagued by ongoing political controversy, digesting budget cuts, challenged leadership, old legacy IT platforms, and rapidly innovating hybrid structures. It may not be a matter of waiting for a change of political masters, as both sides are reluctant to tackle the issue. A regulatory vacuum is fast developing from the stepping back of the IRS and a raft of emerging intertwined issues. The United States has had a fundraising culture that pushes the boundaries and a section of the industry that is fraudulent, and whose impact is now amplified by digital platforms, social media, and hybrid legal forms. As our US contributors from the sector note, new technologies have taken old solicitation techniques and scaled them to the degree that is difficult to regulate with current regulatory resources.

It is the US states that may step up to perform a greater role in regulation, along with private watchdogs. Before the IRS issues, private watchdogs had risen to offer comparative metrics by placing IRS data into user-friendly Internet platforms. They were financed by foundations and donors who were willing to pay for the service. After an initial chorus of public approval, their progress has been stalled by a lack of data and funding. It simply appears that donors are unwilling to pay in sufficient numbers for the vetting service. Transparency alone cannot deal with outright fraud and deception for donors who do not want to invest any effort in checking a website before donating. Like states and provinces in Canada and Australia, most US state regulators have been free riding on the efforts of the central regulator and other states. As Elizabeth T. Boris and Cindy M. Lott point out, the state charity regulators are the object of benign neglect, with the lack of recognition of their role in regulation and enforcement. However, they report promising evidence of cooperation, as state regulators hailed a victory in the first multistate lawsuit against a national fundraising fraud, involving all 50 states and the District of Columbia, in addition to the Federal Trade Commission. There is also cooperation to bypass the IRS's IT issues and inability to share intelligence with the creation of a new fit-for-purpose reporting database to enhance transparency and reduce the red tape proliferation from multiple filings. This platform, officially called the Multistate Registration and Filing Portal, is expected to be available in 2016 for an initial pilot program among roughly a dozen states, with other states to follow. Marcus Owens proposes a more radical policy solution to the structural malaise, suggesting decoupling charity oversight from the IRS and the federal government itself. The function would be shifted to a commission jointly overseen by federal and state agencies concerned with charity behaviour, but with funding from the charitable sector rather than from government sources, thus lessening the constraints imposed by civil service rules and the Internal Revenue Code. Again parts of the exalted CCEW model looms large in his vision.

Looking into Crystal Balls

So what is in the contemplation of regulators and sector leaders for the future? In Australia, New Zealand, and the United States, matters dealing with the regulator's form and daily existence predominate. For the new charity regulators in Australia and New Zealand, their immediate concerns are consolidating their operations and managing revision of their legislation to correct unintended consequences of the initial legislative drafting. The sector contributors in Australia and New Zealand are intent on pursuing these legislative revisions. In Australia, Ursula Stephens warns that the sector will need to protect the ACNC's role as a capacity-building agent from conservative forces trained against it, and it also faces a taxation reform agenda that is yet to be implemented. On the other hand, the IRS is not expected to regain its former place in the regulatory environment anytime soon, if ever. In the vacuum, US state regulators are stepping up to complement private watchdogs and self-regulatory schemes. One can imagine a scenario requiring a national policy response in the United States, such as a series of high-profile scandals involving the conversion of charitable assets to the for-profit sector. But it is difficult to foresee whether the IRS will be reinvigorated or whether in fact a new national regulatory structure, as proposed by Marcus Owen, will overtake it.

In Canada, the former regulator notes despairingly that "what goes around comes around," and the new government may achieve no more than ploughing old ground unless it seeks boldly to examine alternative regulatory models. Terry de March concedes that advocacy rules may be reviewed, but otherwise fears that inertia is likely to prevail, given the constitutional difficulties, the useful role that CRA plays in anti-terrorism, and the CCEW's rapid decline tarnishing its position as an aspirational regulatory model. Bob Wyatt from the Canadian sector is also cautious about the prospects of policy movement under the new government but comes with a shopping list of reforms, most of which have been canvassed previously. The lack of effectively funded sector umbrella groups will hamper the advancement of these reforms. He also points to the hitherto neglected category of non-charitable nonprofit organizations as likely to attract the attention of taxation policy makers.

Lindsay Driscoll indicates that the future of the CCEW and the sector in England and Wales is uncertain. The Commission's resourcing is clearly inadequate for its stated objectives, and charging charities fees for registration and filings seem inevitable with public backing, effectively transferring costs from public taxpayers to beneficiaries. She hints that criticism of the Commission and the sector's scandals reported by the press have tarnished both institutions with little short-term prospect of clawing back all of this fall from grace. Sir Stuart Etherington identifies the British press as the new regulatory force influencing the public's notions of what is charitable and the appropriate standard of conduct. This is compounded by charities being more visible because of the NPM agenda. For him, the path of the sector is clearly not reliant on a benevolent taxpayer-funded regulator being a community police officer or even a tough compliance-based regulator, but on the charitable sector being accountable in the forum of public opinion, swayed by popular press. He exhorts the sector in the following words,

> Charities, therefore, need to show their supporters that they exist to make a difference, and they can be trusted to do so. This is not something that can be achieved simply by increasing the level of regulation. The onus must be on charities themselves to become more transparent, being clearer about what they do, how they do it, and how well they do it.

So what is the sense of the editors for the future of the regulators, sector, and charity regulation? As we elaborated at the beginning of this chapter, those that have modelled themselves on the "trust and confidence" CCEW regulator face a slide to becoming a purely command-and-control compliance regulator if their credibility as a certifier wanes. For-profit firms and hybrids are now in traditional charity markets and, as indicated earlier, their quality and reputational signals may be convincing to the public in the absence of scandals. Has the non-distribution trust signal reached its "use by" date altogether? Are new signals needed by charities? Charities faced with operating in such an environment may move to replace traditional signals and support that comes through the regulator's credibility with a range of other signals to their stakeholders and the public—for example, self-regulation, enhanced metrics for reporting, and closer engagement with supporters and beneficiaries. It will be critical for them to manage public opinion cost effectively, or the signal inherent in being nonprofit will become worthless in the marketplace.

We expect that charity regulators will develop and hone new regulatory tools driven by fiscal restraints, increasing performance metrics, and new technologies. Behavioral nudging that some regulators are starting to experiment with is cheaper, better, and faster than current command-and-control regulation, and holds great promise for achieving desired behaviours with minimal disruption. Digital technologies will be critical for regulators to drive efficiencies in their regulatory functions. It will be central to their communications with charities and the public, and for gathering intelligence to detect wrongdoing, but will require significant ongoing investment. Who will pay for this investment: taxpayers, charities, donors, or beneficiaries?

Those regulators caught in the IT legacy systems of tax agencies face significant challenges to transfer paper-based systems to fit-for-purpose IT platforms. At the same time, digital technologies provide new avenues for fraudulent charity behavior and new objects of regulation. If social media platforms and the financial system can remove the need for a nonprofit intermediary to complete gift transactions, this may have a profound effect on both charities and regulators. For charities, it may mean oblivion, unless they can demonstrate how they add value over and above social media's person-to-person contact. For regulators, the challenge of patrolling numerous episodic individual transactions in the wilderness of jurisdictions covered by the Internet is enormous and requires ever more novel and dynamic approaches.

We see the early signs of charitable tax concessions being wound back in the United States. The narrative gaining traction is that of taxpayer fairness. Why should taxpayers subsidise the ultra-wealthy, at best to indulge their whimsical vision of public goods and at worst to engage in political advocacy with a tax break or tax-abusive behavior? As Phillips and Smith note, at present, this narrative is largely confined to the United States.[25] They point to the UK sector being able to withstand a similar attempt to reduce access to tax concessions, but it is doubtful whether such a campaign would have been successful if it had occurred after the series of tax-abusive, fundraising, and regulator scandals. If tax concessions are rolled back in the United States, then we predict it will embolden treasuries in other countries to seek to rein in charitable tax expenditures

The last 25 years have seen a widening in the boundaries for viewing purposes as charitable, and we expect that the fitful, incremental expansion will continue. Advocacy and the political-charitable boundary will continue to be contested terrain in our view and are likely to be problematic in the near future, as we suggested earlier. Even in jurisdictions that appear to have settled the issue in a sensible fashion, governments of all colours will be tempted to interfere, particularly to thwart the powerful networked grassroots forces that are increasingly difficult to contain. Amateur sport is probably the next barrier to fall in many jurisdictions. With the exception of the United States, our regulators' scope is charities, and this leaves other nonprofit organizations outside their reach. It is hard to make a case in fiscally constrained times for increasing a regulator's jurisdiction to encompass democratically directed self-regulating organizations which have little public benefit other than binding social capital. Governments in some jurisdictions may move to tax nonprofit organizations' income, which has been left untaxed thus far. However, some non-charitable nonprofits are producing public benefits, often receiving tax concessions with little transparency. Social enterprises illustrate this point. In our view, the current fever-pitched experimentation with social impact, social enterprise, and other alternative models of financing and operating will eventually settle into niche tools. But regulation of the area may be problematic, particularly given the dangers of crowdfunding and other mass financing. Further, new hybrid forms of both government and for-profit firms are clearly producing public benefits and raise questions about whether they should be regulated by charity regulators or others, and whether organizations with charitable purposes which are wholly funded by government are in fact charitable. Perhaps we will see a trend towards greater influence by industry-specific regulators.

There appear to be no signs of globalization slowing, and it will inevitably draw charities further into achieving their missions across state boundaries. Will regulation follow and what form will it take? International commerce has developed sophisticated standard trade protocols through self-regulation; international conventions can be enforced through international courts or commercial arbitration; the tax regulation of multinational corporations is developing rapidly. By contrast, the infrastructure for charities and nonprofits operating internationally is meagre, with merely the odd tax treaty dealing with gift concessions or exemptions, and quality standards for development aid. This is despite some of the oldest charity "brands" being international, such as the Red Cross, the Catholic Church and its agencies, Greenpeace, and Amnesty International. Charity regulation to address international fundraising fraud, a legal form that transcends state boundaries, international accounting and reporting standards, and mutually recognized philanthropic charity tax concessions are all possibilities. These developments may be in the form of self-regulatory schemes, such as the embryonic Basic Registry of Identified Global Entities, referred to by Elizabeth T. Boris and Cindy M. Lott, which enables comparison across approximately three million nonprofit organizations.[26] But this may not be enough for the global challenges that will confront charities, and national regulators must be drawn to cooperate more vigorously. However, here, too, the growing social media revolution allowing donors to connect directly with beneficiaries may spell the end for charities as intermediaries. A donor in the developed world may already choose to bypass charities by using digital platforms to transfer resources directly to beneficiaries. Unfortunately, this is yet more fertile ground for fraud and deception, but will the most effective measures to address the problems be self-regulatory, government-based regulation, or a mixture of both?

Whatever the future holds for charity regulation, the last 25 years is likely to be regarded as merely the prelude to an era of increasing change and development. Those who were involved on the frontline have recounted the story, and now a new generation of regulators and sector leaders will have to face the next 25 years of challenges. We hope that lessons may be drawn from the experiences narrated in this book to assist future regulators as they guide charities and other organizations in their efforts to provide public benefits for the greater good of their communities.

Notes

1 Henry Hansmann, "The Rationale for Exempting Nonprofit Organizations from the Corporate Income Tax," *Yale Law Journal* 91 (1981): 54, 92; Henry Hansmann, "Reforming Nonprofit Corporation Law," *University of Pennsylvania Law Review* 129 (1981): 500; Henry Hansmann, *The Ownership of Enterprise* (Cambridge, MA: Harvard University Press, 1996).

2   Other theories include public goods theories: see B.A. Weisbrod, *The Non-Profit Economy* (Cambridge, MA: Harvard University Press, 1988); entrepreneurship theories: D.R. Young, *If Not for Profit, for What? A Behavioural Theory of the Nonprofit Sector Based on Entrepreneurship* (Lexington, KY: Lexington Books, 1983); stakeholder theory: A. Ben-Ner, "Nonprofit Organizations in the Mixed Economy: A Demand and Supply Analysis," *Annals of Public and Cooperative Economics* 62 (1991): 519; and independence theory: L.M. Salamon, *Partners in Public Service: Government—Nonprofit Relations in the Modern Welfare State* (Baltimore, MD: Johns Hopkins University Press, 1995).

3   A. Ortmann and M. Schlesinger, "Trust Repute and the Role of Nonprofit Enterprise," in *The Study of Nonprofit Enterprise Theories and Approaches*, eds. H.K. Anheier and A. Ben-Ner (New York: Kluwer Academic/Plenum, 2003), 77–114.

4   R.A. Cnaan et al., "Nonprofit Watchdogs: Do They Serve the Average Donor?" *Nonprofit Management and Leadership* 21 (2011): 381, doi:10.1002/nml.20032; R. Szper and A. Prakash, "Charity Watchdogs and the Limits of Information-based Regulation," *Voluntas: International Journal of Voluntary and Nonprofit Organizations* 22 (2011): 112.

5   M.F. Sloan, "The Effects of Nonprofit Accountability Ratings on Donor Behavior," *Nonprofit and Voluntary Sector Quarterly* 20 (2008): 1; Cnaan et al., "Nonprofit Watchdogs"; Szper and Prakash, "Charity Watchdogs."

6   J.W. Kingdon, *Agendas, Alternatives and Public Policy* (Boston, MA: Little, Brown, 2nd ed., 1995).

7   P.A. Sabatier and P. 7 Jenkins-Smith, "The Advocacy Coalition Framework: An Assessment," in *Theories of the Policy Process*, ed. P.A. Sabatier (Boulder, CO: Westview Press, 1999), 117–166.

8   Australian Charities and Not-for-profits Commission Act 2012 (Cth), s. 15–5.

9   Paul Pierson, "Increasing Returns, Path Dependence, and the Study of Politics," *American Political Science Review* 94 (2000): 251.

10 "Who We Are: Our Mission," Canada Revenue Agency, last modified June 1, 2011, http://www.cra-arc.gc.ca/chrts-gvng/chrts/bt/mssn_vsn-eng.html.

11 T. Williamson, "Preface," in *The Handbook of Knowledge Based Policing: Current Conceptions and Future Directions*, ed. T. Williamson (Sussex: John Wiley, 2008), xxi–xxv.

12 For example *Commissioner of Taxation of the Commonwealth of Australia v Word Investments Ltd* (2008) CLR 204; [2008] HCA 55.

13 *Bob Jones University v. United States*, 461 U.S. 574 (1983).

14 *Bowman v Secular Society Ltd* (1917) AC 406.

15 *De Themmines v de Bonneval* (1828) 5 Russ. 288.

16 *McGovern v Attorney-General* [1882] 1 Ch 1.

17 *The Human Dignity Trust v The Charity Commission for England and Wales* [2014] UKFTT (First Tier Tribunal (Charity).

18 *AID/Watch Incorporated v Commissioner of Taxation* (2010) 241 CLR 539; [2010] HCA 42.

19 Charities Act 2013 (Cth) s. 13(b).

20 Charities Act 2013 (Cth) s. 12(l).

21 Charities Act 2005 (NZ) ss. 5(3) and (4).

22 *National Council of Women of New Zealand Incorporated v Charities Registration Board* [2015] 3 NZLR 72; [2014] NZHC 3200.

23 *Re Greenpeace of New Zealand Incorporated* [2011] 2 NZLR 815; [2011] NZHC 77.

24 *Citizens United v. Federal Election Commission*, 558 U.S. 310 (2010).

25 Susan D. Phillips and Steven Rathgeb Smith, "A Dawn of Convergence? Third Sector Policy Regimes in the 'Anglo-Saxon' Cluster," *Public Management Review* 16 (2014): 1141.
26 BRIDGE was seeded by the organizations already registered in the databases of the Foundation Center, GlobalGiving, GuideStar, and TechSoup Global, four organizations that hold data for a combined total of approximately 3 million NGOs, accessed October 25, 2016, http://bridge-registry.org.

Index

For Product Safety Concerns and Information please contact our EU
representative GPSR@taylorandfrancis.com
Taylor & Francis Verlag GmbH, Kaufingerstraße 24, 80331 München, Germany

www.ingramcontent.com/pod-product-compliance
Ingram Content Group UK Ltd.
Pitfield, Milton Keynes, MK11 3LW, UK
UKHW020937180425
457613UK00019B/445